Divine Complexity

Divine Complexity

The Rise of Creedal Christianity

PAUL R. HINLICKY

Fortress Press
Minneapolis

DIVINE COMPLEXITY
The Rise of Creedal Christianity

Additional resources, including brief chapter summaries, a glossary of key terms, questions for discussion, ideas for ongoing research, and a complete bibliography for this book are available at fortresspress.com/hinlicky.

Cover image: *Christ and the Twelve Apostles*, probably ca. 1400. Taddeo di Bartolo (1363–1422). Image © The Metropolitan Museum of Art / Art Resource, NY.
Cover design: Alisha Lofgren

Library of Congress Cataloging-in-Publication Data
Hinlicky, Paul R.
Divine complexity : the rise of creedal Christianity / Paul R. Hinlicky.
p.   cm.
Includes bibliographical references (p. 241) and index.
ISBN 978-0-8006-9669-6 (alk. paper)
1. Trinity—History of doctrines. 2. Bible. N.T.—Theology. I. Title.
BT111.3.H56 2011
231'.044—dc22   2010018980

The paper used in this publication meets the minimum requirements of American National Standard for Information Sciences — Permanence of Paper for Printed Library Materials, ANSI Z329.48-1984.
Manufactured in the U.S.A.

For Will

Thinker, writer, artist, teacher, our Adeodatus.

I, unless blessed Augustine would say otherwise, but I would say, that the Father is not the Father except from the Son or by filiation. Thus neither by Himself is He wise, but through the Son who is His wisdom by which He is wise. Neither by Himself is He good, but through the Holy Spirit who is His goodness. Thus it is that whenever He is called powerful, wise, good, always at the same time all three persons are named. The reason is because "father" is relative. And, as Ambrose puts these things: He is not able to be named or called Father, unless the Son is also co-named. Thus being wise and wisdom are relative. And He is not able to be named such, unless the Son also is co-named.

—Martin Luther

Contents

Introduction   ix

Chapter One
The Primacy of the Gospel   1
  Augustinian Critique of Epistemology   1
  The Primacy of the Gospel   7
  Natural Theology? Divine Simplicity?   16
  Kataphatic Theology   22

Chapter Two
From Resurrection Kerygma to Gospel Narrative   25
  The Resurrection of the Crucified as Hermeneutic   26
  The Chief Question: Resurrection as the Spirit's Narration   29
  Resurrection as Event in the Life of God   31
  Resurrection as Possibility in the Life of the World   35
  Resurrection as Reality in the Life of the World   41
  Resurrection's Retroactive Causality   48
  Bultmann's Objection   49
  The Gospel as Promissory Narrative   60

Chapter Three
The Scriptures' Emergence as the Church's Canon   69
  Jesus—New and Living Temple   70
  The Johannine Bridge   72
  Critique of Modern Johannine Criticism   76
  Käsemann's Dissent   81
  Hoskyns's Theological Interpretation of John   87
  The Johannine Theology of the Martyr   92
  Ignatius, Polycarp, and the Martyrs' Canon   96
  The Knowledge of God in the New Testament   106

Chapter Four
The Trinitarian Rule of Faith   109
   Paul as Theologian   110
   Paul's "Canon" of Faith (Galatians 6:16)   114
   Early Christian Dogma in the Pastoral Epistles   119
   Martyrological Ethos in the Pastoral Epistles   124
   Christian "Atheism" in Justin Martyr   128
   Justin against Gnosticism   133
   Irenaeus and the Theology of the Martyrs   137
   The First Dogmatics   140
   The Economy of God   145
   The Rule of Faith and the Trinity   152

Chapter Five
The Confrontation of Biblical and Philosophical Monotheism   159
   The Problem of Christianity and Platonism   160
   Overview of Trinitarian Doctrine and Trinitarian Errors 161
   Two Kinds of Monotheism: The Living God of Radical, or Exclusive,
      Monotheism   167
   Two Kinds of Monotheism: Divine Simplicity   173
   Eternal Generation   179
   Systematic Theology as Systematic Apologetics   184
   Arius as Consistent Platonist   193

Chapter Six
The Holy Trinity as the Eternal Life   201
   The Martyriological Background   202
   The Creed at Nicea 325   203
   Theology of Redemption   212
   Lord and Giver of Life   222
   The *Homoiousions* and the *Homoousions*   223
   The Failure of Biblicism   228
   The Trinitarian Theology of the Cappadocians   231
   Worshipped and Glorified, Together with the Father and the Son 233

Postscript
The "Impassible Passibility" of the Trinity   237

Notes   241
Index   276

Introduction

This work aims at instruction for today in the primary theology of Christianity. I take "primary theology" to be the gospel narrative given in canonical Scripture and parsed by the creeds of the ecumenical church and the Reformation confession of justification by faith. I take "today" to indicate the better understanding of these sources and norms than in the past made available by modern, historical-critical method, by the irenic ecumenical method of dialogue, and by the situation of post-Christendom in which Euro-Americans pursue Christian theology.

This book then is intended for spiritually motivated and intellectually serious seekers both within and without the churches. By these, I have in mind those who want to understand the cognitive claims of that faith in God which the gospel brings, as the church catholic has understood the matter and still seeks to understand it better, under the assumption that the development of doctrine and the task of critical dogmatics are unfinished. The starting point in this task, as Augustine put it, the *initium fidei*, is faith in God who comes in His Word. This "God" is the One in whom alone, according to the First Table of the Commandments, faith is to be invested, whose name is not to be taken in vain but spoken truthfully in accord with the divine self-donation of the gospel, whose purpose in speaking is to gain the doxological echo of the redeemed people of God. Theology is about God and exists in response to the prophetic and apostolic *Deus dixit* (God has spoken). As such, theology is an autonomous, nonspeculative discipline that is written "from faith for faith." Such theology advances, strictly speaking, one and only one proposition: *God the almighty Father is determined to redeem the creation through His Son, Jesus Christ, and bring it to fulfillment by His Spirit.* All other doctrines are but articulations or extrapolations of this one, fundamental claim about true deity.

While efforts in the church's primary theology are common enough, this book is unusual in its approach in that it seeks to utilize and indeed in part to reconcile several competing, if not today conflicting, disciplinary traditions within the domain of Christian thought: Patristic studies, Reformation theology, and liberal Protestant historical criticism. In this book, all three of these methods are at work—alongside as well a tacit dialogue with the philosophy

of religion! Such a cross-disciplinary approach, as it seems nowadays, will pre-
dictably displease purists in each of the foregoing camps; of necessity it qualifies the exclusive procedures of each method and relativizes the insights of
each by those of the other. Yet in the author's view such a synthetic approach
is urgently necessitated by the sudden and perilous polarization emerging
between these traditions of theology today after so much apparent ecumenical progress in the preceding century.

I have argued elsewhere that for Luther the Bible and the ecumenical
creeds together form a hermeneutical whole: it is not the Bible as such but
the canonical Bible rightly interpreted by the ecumenical creeds and the Reformation confession of justification that constitutes the written word of God,
the source and norm of doctrinal theology.[1] In another work, I sought to lay
out the *Wirkungsgeschichte* (the history of the interpretative effects) of this
Reformation theology to the present day via Leibniz rather than Kant,[2] since
the latter made Luther's emphatically *kataphatic* (revealed) theology impossible under the epistemic conditions of modernity. In the chapters that follow,
I wish to focus attention in the other direction, retrospectively, back to what
twentieth-century Protestant theologian T. F. Torrance so rightly called the
evangelical theology of the ancient, Greek-speaking *catholic* church.[3] Historians likewise have undertaken this task with great success, for example, J. N.
D. Kelly[4] and Jaroslav Pelikan,[5] and most recently the splendid and eminently
useful textbook of Tarmo Toom.[6] I will shamelessly draw on their expertise in
coming chapters. I am deeply inspired in what follows by a seminal analysis
made some years ago by systematic theologian Robert W. Jenson.[7] But for
various reasons, others have not found convincing the case for the primary
theology of the church as both evangelical and catholic—thus this new effort.

Pivotal to the new case being made are several equally unusual theses, which
I will simply list here in preliminary, dense formulation by way of preview. One
is a historical-critical account of the pivotal role played by the Gospel of John
as a theological interpretation of the Synoptic tradition in the development of
early Christian doctrinal theology. This is an account following British theologian Sir Edwyn Hoskyns and European scholar Udo Schnelle (but not Rudolf
Bultmann).[8] This location of John's theology in the development of Christian
doctrine, I argue, corroborates the insight of Reformation theology into the primal (historically speaking, the "apocalyptic") form of the Pauline gospel as God's
word in the resurrection of the Crucified One, signifying and effecting the justification of the godless (not the justification of the existentialist).[9]

Another unusual thesis is the theoretical account of the critique of epistemology and revision of metaphysics detected in the development of the
doctrine of the Trinity, following the pioneering study of Jenson previously
mentioned.[10] At stake in this is the status of the important (though ambiguous) doctrine of divine simplicity (the metaphysical doctrine that God's being

is uncompounded, and so indivisible, hence indestructible, and so to be thought as the pure act of being itself) with its correlate of divine impassibility. This doctrine derives from the negative theology of the Platonist tradition; recently Catholic theologian Lewis Ayres has impressively defended its role in the trinitarian development.[11] But I argue throughout this book that "simplicity" is and can be no more than a rule of reverent speech: so speak of the singular creator of all else that His ineffable singularity as cause of all causes (though not maker of all choices) is respected. But what the theological notion of simplicity is not and cannot provide is any positive account of God's being, that is, the more or less traditional notion that God is God as a timeless, spaceless, incommunicable, self-identical nature, especially when such divine essence is actually thought of as a "fourth" reality over against the Father and the Son in the Spirit. Against this I will argue *esse deum dare*, that is, that for God to be God is to give; moreover, this self-donation has a time and space of its own as the divine life of the Trinity, which makes a place and finds a time also for us. This ontology of charity is what I designate the *complexity* of divine life, in complement, not contradiction, of "simplicity"—rightly understood—that is, as qualifying the suffering of the man Christ as divine suffering, "impassible passibility."

Yet a third unusual thesis of this book is that the Reformation's parsing of the gospel as justification of the sinner by faith alone correlates with the articulate faith in the triune God, as Wilhelm Maurer once uncovered.[12] Indeed, without this trinitarian articulation of the One who is believed, I argue that Reformation theology collapses into existentialist anthropology and systematic apologetics of the sort that moral philosopher Alisdair MacIntyre once pilloried as giving unbelievers less and less in which to disbelieve.[13] In contrast, I find an ethical correlation between Trinitarianism and the ethos of the early Christian martyrs—in pointed contrast to the at times insightful, now fashionable but in the author's view profoundly confused thesis of German theologian Walter Bauer about coeval orthodoxy and heresy in early Christianity.[14] Simultaneously, and in mutually reinforcing ways, this book argues for all three of these theses in accounting for the rise and enduring normativity of creedal Christianity's trinitarian interpretation of the word "God."

Like medicine and law, which were theology's former colleagues in the higher university faculties, the technical language of theology derives terminology from Latin as well as Greek and Hebrew. This vocabulary can be intimidating for beginners, for whom the ideas of Christian theology, even paraphrased into their own native tongue, are already demanding enough. Add to this the need to fathom the twists and turns of an intellectual tradition approaching two thousand years in duration. Yet such is the inescapable element of drudgery in learning, which cannot be eliminated this side of the eschaton. As in any other discipline, it is necessary to absorb the technical jargon, which efficiently captures complex ideas that in turn contain, as it were, episodes in Christian intellectual history. Learning this vocabulary is the beginning of fluency in a specialized discourse. I have tried by immediate paraphrase or parenthetical comment to explain such technical terms on the first occasion of their use in this book, and I spend what more accomplished theologians might consider inordinate time and indeed homiletical effort unpacking ideas for new learners.

I am grateful to the students of the Evanjelicka bohoslovecka fakulta, univerzita Komenskeho in Bratislava, Slovakia, who listened to the first version of this book in the form of lectures on the history of doctrine during my six-year stay there in the 1990s. Father Michael Plekon was of invaluable assistance in those days in supplying me with shipments of books and articles that I needed for my research. I am likewise grateful to students at Roanoke College who have studied this material in various iterations in the past decade. Their enthusiasm and feedback have given me the energy to proceed with publication. I am grateful also to colleagues who have read various portions of this work and provided criticism in recent years, particularly Hans Zorn, David Delaney, Sarah Wilson, and especially Robert Jenson, who read the penultimate draft and provided valuable suggestions and encouragement. This book is dedicated to my son, Will, who has sacrificed some of his youth for God and for country.

Sources and Abbreviations

Generally citations from the church fathers are drawn from the Hendrickson Press 1995 reprint of *Ante-Nicene Fathers* (hereafter ANF), ed. Alexander Roberts, D.D., and James Donaldson, LL.D., and *Nicene and Post-Nicene Fathers* (hereafter NPNF), second series, ed. Philip Schaff, D.D., and Henry Wace, D.D. The first occurrence of a given writing will be footnoted. Thereafter, references will be given in the text in parentheses following the citation, supplying abbreviated title, chapter, and verse or other enumeration provided by the editors of ANF or NPNF, but without page numbers. Thus, for example, Athenagoras's "A Plea for the Christians [Apology]," chap. 24, ANF, vol. 2, p. 191, would be given as (Apol 24). On occasion, I have utilized more felicitous contemporary translations of the church fathers, as found especially in the theologically astute series The Message of the Fathers of the Church (Michael Glazier, 1987). In such cases, I credit the editor/translator on the first occasion of such a citation and thereafter the same abbreviated title with chapter. Citations from *Luther's Works—American Edition*, ed. Jaroslav Pelikan et. al. (St. Louis: Concordia; Philadelphia: Fortress Press) are given as LW followed by volume and page numbers, for example, LW 12:27. On occasions where the title of the Luther writing and/or its date are important to a proper assessment of the citation's weight, that is provided as well.

CHAPTER 1
The Primacy of the Gospel

This chapter considers the distinctive features of Christian theology as a discipline that starts in faith. It does so by moving from the critique of epistemology implied by the starting point of faith to the primacy of the gospel as a narrative through which God gives Himself in a promise to faith. Such gospel narrative constitutes the discourse of Christian theology. This chapter concludes by indicating what is meant by the corresponding trinitarian revision of metaphysics and the task of kataphatic theology as critical dogmatics.

Augustinian Critique of Epistemology

Epistemology is a discourse that wants first to ground knowledge by a theory of itself. It claims to establish a knowledge of knowledge before any content of knowledge can be entertained. The circularity is evident. But theology as a method or discipline turns entirely on the *theos*, or deity, it serves and seeks to understand. Christian theology is the cognitive discipline of the Spirit of Jesus and His Father. As such, it thinks to participate in God's own self-knowledge as imparted in Christ by the Spirit through the gospel. The term *theology* denotes *knowledge* of God. But if, as both prophets of Israel and critical philosophers in the tradition of Plato teach, only the eternal God knows God, Christian theology is possible only as a *sacred* discipline that "thinks after" God's saving self-impartation (*sola gratia*), as Christians believe, teach, and confess, through *Christ alone* (*solus Christus*). The "exclusive particle" (*solus,* "only," see the Apology of the Augsburg Confession, IV:73) makes theology the work of faith (*sola fide*) in Jesus Christ, where faith itself is understood not as human opinion but as divine self-impartation by the Spirit's repetition in believers of Jesus' own obedience of faith—not then an opinion about Jesus but Jesus' own belief for us in His Father, in us by His own Spirit.

As such an ecstatic form of human reason grasped by its content, faithful Christian theology critically tests the coherence of beliefs in the church (1) against God's self-donation, (2) with each another, and (3) in relation to other forms of human reason in the world. The knowledge of God ultimately consists in a *coherent and comprehensive system of belief* (still in process of discernment and formation) that awaits eschatological verification. In the interim, the God of the gospel is identified "from faith [that is, from the canonical prophets and apostles as handed on in the church catholic] for faith [that is, for worship, fellowship, and service in each new time and place] and so, in the process, critically distinguished from fantasies and superstitions, idols and demons, deviations (heresies) as also other possible eternities (that is, other religions or worldviews). "In earnest invocation of God it is necessary to consider what one wants to address, what God is, how he is known, where and how he has revealed himself, and both if and why he hears our pleas and cries . . . [lest one] fall into the error of addressing as God things which are not God."[1] Such a procedure has its content, before it ever reflects on formal modes of knowing, "this true God who revealed himself to his people with sure testimonies." Just so, its method consists merely in not letting its "thoughts waver and wander after other gods."[2]

"*Our* Father, who art in heaven." As the invocation of God in Christianity is communal, the theological identification of the God of the gospel under the foregoing terms thus constitutes the church's doctrinal unity, as this originated in the primitive triadic confession of the baptized and developed into the *regula fidei* (rule of faith). "Our Father" is ours through His own Son who invites us into His own relation with Him by their own Spirit. Christian theology, so understood, is both *evangelical and catholic*; that is, this theology springs from the contingent fact of the gospel's coming (so the need of initiation in baptism) but just so brings the knowledge of God that is held everywhere, at all times, by all (even if only tacitly or confusedly) in the church as the fellowship of the baptized in the name of the Father, the Son, and the Holy Spirit. Baptism too has its origin. The church's knowledge of God arises from the Easter narration of a paradox: the coming of Jesus as the Lord's anointed and His fateful end in ignominious defeat on the cross are, paradoxically, the Father's saving deed of merciful identification with those lost to him in the person of His Son. This paradox is not logical nonsense; it does not assert a contradiction. Rather the paradox resolves in that this Crucified One was raised from death and so vindicated and revealed the Son of God in power. At the far depth of the Son's coming into the world, then, is the *harrowing of hell* on account of that godforsaken death on the cross. Reckoning with so daunting a paradox at its very center, no system of Christian theology short of the eschaton achieves the perfect coherence of theology in glory. Theology on the earth and in time is and only can be the stumbling, struggling, sighing theology of the cross that cannot say all things at once but must honor instead the subversive rhetoric of the paradox in a dialectic of *sic et non*.

Theology consequently is and always will be a conflicted discipline that is in dispute about what it is and ought to do, since other constructions of the deity of God than Jesus' "our Father" contend for our prayers. The reason for this, as we have just elaborated, is that theology as a method or discipline turns entirely on the *theos*, or deity, it serves and seeks to understand. Within classical Christian theology, this conflict plays out preeminently in the question of whether the deity of God will be known by Jesus who was born of a woman, under the law, and crucified in the flesh under Pontius Pilate. In subsequent chapters, this book accordingly traces out the rise of creedal Christianity from its origins in the Easter kerygma to the full formulation of the doctrine of the Trinity at the Second Ecumenical Council at Constaninople in 381. As I shall tell it, however, this is almost entirely a story transpiring in the Greek-speaking Eastern half of the ancient Roman Empire. Western theology, denoting that which arose in the Latin-speaking half of the Empire, is dominated by the towering figure of Augustine, who already received this trinitarian faith from the East as an accomplished fact. This root dependency of Western theology creates several kinds of interpretive problems for a book like this, stemming out of Western traditions like Reformation theology and historical criticism. For a pertinent example, an influential thesis has been that unlike the Eastern approach to the doctrine of God, which begins with the three of the gospel narrative and discovers their oneness, Western theology since Augustine has begun with a metaphysical notion of oneness as divine simplicity and used it to minimize, even efface, the distinctiveness of the three.[3] Recent scholarship has rightly sought to qualify this broad characterization,[4] but the unsettling question then surfaces: How do we understand the unity of God who is Jesus, His Father, and their Spirit? What (unexamined) notions of divine nature do we bring with us to the task of Christian theology? How do we decide what is, and is not, fittingly said of the presumably unique entity "God"? Is the classical notion of divine simplicity—that divine being is not composite or compounded, thus incapable of coming apart and disintegrating—apt to this task, if central to the identity of the God in question is the creation of a world other than God, with the incarnation of the Son and the sending of the Spirit into it? Might not *complexity* rather better characterize the God of the gospel?

God's *oneness* in philosophical monotheism is not in any case, as I will show in what follows, the simple equivalent of the *radical or exclusive monotheism* of the biblical narrative, which tells of the unique being of the creator of all reality in the one history of salvation that, when heard with faith, requires exclusive allegiance and total conversion. The idea in philosophical monotheism is that divine nature is *simple*, in that it is not compounded out of anything else, and that this natural *simplicity* tells how it transcends everything else that exists materially in the form of compounds. Divine nature has no internal differentiations or relations that would threaten it, so to say, with instability or dissolution. Unlike mortals who have their contingent being in becoming, God is not a composite. Being "one," God cannot come apart, disintegrate, fall to pieces under duress. As divine being is the eternally self-identical act of thought thinking itself, it exists at one with itself and is therefore changeless, indestructible, eternal. This is what it means to be divine, to exist as the one worthy, so to say, of complete satisfaction with self, unaffected by any other, never then motivated to change or be changed. This notion of the divinity of God as pure, timeless, intellectual self-identity provides the standard of what is worthy or fitting to say about God. Negative theology aims both to protect the unknowable and ineffable divine essence from profanation and yet to ascend to it by the progressive transcending of all inadequate representations.

Augustine's position on such questions is disputable,[5] not least because there is a definite development in his thought from his early Platonism toward increasingly pronounced Paulinism. We can hardly even raise the question here without going far afield. In what follows it is rather a matter of bringing certain Augustinian presuppositions of the Western tradition to critical awareness. Happily, we can do that by following Augustine's doctrine of the *initium fidei*, the starting point of faith, as a critique of the epistemology that dominates secular Western thought since Descartes and even Protestant theology since Kant. I cite here the argument of a British theologian of a generation ago, Alan Richardson, who, focusing on what I am calling the critique of epistemology, called Augustine's *De civitate dei* "the outstanding example of a Christian apology directed toward the interpretation of the historical situation of a particular age." Augustine's endeavor "possesses an enduring interest for every generation of Christians because it shows how the biblical-prophetic insights can become the key-categories of a total philosophy of history."[6] Richardson sharply attacked the rationalistic "idea of an impartial abstract reason." He called this idea of reason "a mirage, a notable illustration of man's perennial temptation to exalt himself among the gods, knowing good and evil," as if "human reason is, in virtue of its own inherent perfection, a competent and impartial judge of truth and falsehood in all matters."[7]

> Modern philosophy since Descartes has largely recapitulated the course of ancient philosophy and has ended in the same skepticism and disillusion. The time has surely come for Christian philosophy to be frankly

Augustinian again and to call in Christian faith to liberate reason from the toils of rationalism and its corollary, skepticism. Rationalism loves to represent the issue between itself and Christian philosophy as one of reason versus "belief" or "mere opinion"; it does this by concealing its own faith principle. . . . [But] there is no key of universal understanding that is, or can be made, evident to all rational beings . . . it is only by the creatively imaginative act of boldly grasping a faith-principle as a key of understanding that a great and noble system of philosophy can be built. . . . Faith, then, is necessarily bound up with reason, and neither reason nor faith can be understood without the other. . . . Our knowledge of God in this life is essentially a rational knowing made possible by faith in the biblical revelation . . . mediated by the word, that is by the address of God as of one rational being to other rational beings. . . . No wordless knowledge of God or immediate apprehension of Him is claimed as a result of Christian faith. Faith is not a mystical but a rational activity. . . . Our knowledge of God is a mediated knowledge, and the One Mediator is Christ the Word.[8]

The critical statement in the foregoing excerpt is this: "There is no key of universal understanding that is, or can be made, evident to all rational beings." In other words, there is no such thing as One Universal Human Rationality, as Kantianism imagined its "tribunal of Reason." There is only, for example, Confucian rationality, or Marxist rationality, or Christian rationality, or Scientific rationality, or some other particular rationality, all of which are based on some original act of faith that is socially mediated to us by a particular tradition. "Reason cannot work until it first makes an act of faith, and it does not work correctly—that is, rationally—unless it makes the right act of faith, unless it has faith in the Truth itself."[9] As a result, the theologian today, Richardson writes, is "freed from the temptation of trying to come to terms with the reigning thought-system of the day and consequently of subordinating the distinctive faith principle of Christianity to that of an alien philosophy."[10] He rejects the claim of "rationalists or 'liberals,' who maintain that the human mind is capable of laying aside the prejudices of social conditioning and proceed by reason, whether deductively or inductively, to an impartial or objective verdict upon religious, philosophical and historical questions."[11]

Richardson tried to expose "the elaborate rationalizations which conceal the initial act of faith" upon which any worldview, including secularism, is based and which in turn blinds it to the coercive mechanisms it deploys.[12] The result of this Augustinian critique of epistemology is that competing "gospels" (fascism, Marxism, liberalism) are all placed on a level playing field as partisan acts of faith in the objectivity of value (except nihilism, which Richardson regarded as an illogical, that is, self-contradictory faith in the nonobjectivity of value). No such act of faith possesses as a given some evident foundation, for then it would cease to be an act of faith and become an act of comprehending the evidence before one's own eyes. What is reasonable for human creatures who seek to understand the meaning of life is rather to make such basic acts of faith. These reasonable acts of faith provide the actual "foundations" of (various kinds of) rationality. All reason is reasoning on the basis of such an act of "initial faith." The real and difficult question then is how these particular acts of faith are rationally to be warranted. Is the "revelation" that elicits faith a true revelation or a demonic deception? Is the salvation it offers intelligible as a real salvation? Believers themselves must rationally "test the spirits" and "give an account of their hope." But how?

Richardson's account of human knowledge as "founded" on risky though reasonable human acts of faith (and thus not "rationally" founded on simple, obvious, universally accessible truth) exposed the situation to which post-Enlightenment, Euro-American culture has come with the breakdown of rationalism: "The Marxist, the secular humanist, and the Christian all wear their own spectacles and therefore cannot see the truth that the others see. Each inhabits his own universe of discourse and cannot understand the others' language. Here for the Christian (as for the others) arises the supreme difficulty in the task of evangelization, that of making real contact with those for whom the very language one uses has no meaning because their thought-forms have been shaped by such widely differing assumptions."[13] The result of this analysis is to place contemporary Christianity back into the world of competing gospels, just like in early Christianity, no longer privileged but also no longer ghettoized in the gilded chancel of official establishment. *Such critique of epistemology today is the Augustinian move.* The situation of the church today resembles most the church's social-cultural location in the year 410 AD, when Rome had fallen at the hand of the Goths and "Christ and his church" were blamed. Our recent century has witnessed in Hitlerism, in Stalinism, and in the colonial, ecological, and atomic crimes of liberal capitalism the repeated failure of the modern dream of secular, enlightened culture. These twentieth-century secular crimes, which by an inexpressible magnitude eclipse whatever sins a misguided medieval Christianity once committed in inquisition and crusade, are crimes against humanity. They have their express roots in the repudiation of Christianity. Yet bizarrely the Christian faith is blamed for these evils. Today, a tough-minded apologetic must once again refute those "who hold Christ responsible for the evils they deservedly suffer for their wicked lives" (Augustine). Thus reads Alan Richardson's near-contemporary account of a renewed Augustinianism as a critique of epistemology.

In my preferred reading, it is not so much that Augustine, or Luther in his footsteps, utterly denied natural theology, as famously did Karl Barth who regarded it as a Trojan horse sneaking in the monster deity of the philosophers.[14]

Rather they executed a critique of epistemology in the name of faith that might correlate with the "natural theology" of skeptical (but not dogmatic) Platonism, while at the same time pressing the argument against skepticism as most significant of all.[15] Luther famously did so in his diatribe against Erasmus; but he had come to this Augustinian position much earlier: "It is certainly true that the law of nature is known to all men and that our reason does speak for the best things, but what best things? It speaks for the best things not according to God but according to us, that is, for things that are good in an evil way. For it seeks itself and its own in all things but not in God. This only faith does in love. Hence knowledge and virtue and whatever good things are desired, sought, and found by natural capacity are good in an evil way."[16] Likewise Luther, following Augustine, elaborated a corresponding revision of metaphysics in the name of faith's object, the triune God. Again, in Luther's early words, commenting on Romans 8:19: "The apostle philosophizes and thinks about things in a different way than the philosophers and metaphysicians do. For the philosophers so direct their gaze at the present state of things that they speculate only about what things are and what quality they have, but the apostle calls our attention away from a consideration of the present and from the essence and accidents of things and directs us to their future state . . . Look how we esteem the study of the essences and actions and inactions of things, and the things themselves reject and groan over their own essences and actions and inactions! We praise and glorify the knowledge of that very thing that is sad about itself and is displeased with itself . . . Wise men and theologians, infected by this same 'prudence of the flesh' . . . derive a happy science out of a sad creation, and from the sighings they laughingly gather their knowledge with marvelous display of power."[17]

In a compelling account of Luther's theology, Oswald Bayer accordingly writes, "The deepest conflict with Greek metaphysics and ontology must of necessity come at the point where the biblical texts are taken with utter seriousness. What is ontologically unthinkable is described in Hosea 11:7-11, which ancient metaphysics would reject as mythology: an 'overthrow,' a change within God himself—God is not the one who is identical with himself, who corresponds to himself: 'My heart has changed within me; my remorse grows powerfully. I will not execute my fierce anger. I will not again destroy Ephraim; for I am God, not a human being' (Hos 11:8-9)."[18] God surpasses God and so establishes His deity—that is the gospel's revision of metaphysics.

The Primacy of the Gospel

In the earliest years of the Reformation, just before the schism of the Western church became definitive with Luther's official condemnation as a heretic, the Wittenberg professor tried to answer a critical objection to his Bible-based critique of the sale of indulgences: By what right do you contradict customary teachings and practices of the church and presume to correct or purify them? Luther famously appealed to the Word of God and offered straightforward exegetical arguments from the Bible about the meaning of texts to justify reformatory teachings, namely, (1) that repentance, or turning to God, concerns the whole life of the believer, (2) that divine mercy cannot be bought or sold but only received in faith as a free gift, and (3) that therefore the true treasure of the church is the gospel of the grace and glory of God in the crucified and risen Christ, which should be openly exhibited, freely offered, and purely explained for the sake of the penitent.[19]

Luther quickly discovered, however, that opponents could challenge his interpretations of Scripture by construing texts differently, questioning his selection of texts, or pointing to contradictions in the Bible leading to endless disputation that could only be settled in turn by the teaching authority invested in the papacy.[20] Consequently, in the course of the controversy, the question was refined. The opponents came to ask: How can you appeal to *the* Word of God when they are so *many* words of God? To this more nuanced question, Luther replied: I am speaking of the word of God that first of all speaks to us Gentiles making us people of God, namely (citing Rom. 1:3), "the gospel concerning his Son."[21] The gospel provides epistemic access to the region of theology by claiming auditors with God's own self-imparting word and effecting, as the Spirit pleases, faith in them to receive this royal and merciful claim.

With this Luther undertook to follow Paul the Apostle in the Epistle to the Romans in asserting *real primacy* in theology (not, be it noted, for the Epistle to the Romans) for the *gospel concerning the Son*—this is the power of God, which effects the new situation in which Christian theology arises.[22] This proclamation of the divine deed both authors and authorizes the new life of the Christian community, which is precisely the holy community in the world that holds these gospel beliefs in turn as epistemically primary.[23] Epistemic primacy is an important notion recently introduced into theology by Bruce Marshall. It denies that any beliefs are primary that are able to be abandoned or even revisable when they conflict with other beliefs on which the continued existence of a community depends. Primary beliefs are rather those on which the community's very existence depends, that cannot be sacrificed without the community's disintegration. If we follow Luther, then (but also the Lutheran–Roman Catholic dialogue today, which has lifted up this precise terminology[24]), the gospel articulates such primary belief since it tells believers who and what they are in God's sight and provides as well God's justification for this judgment about them in the cross and resurrection of His Son. So it both authors and authorizes.

In this effective action the gospel reveals God as God who gives not merely all temporal gifts but God's very self in time and for eternity. The gospel is not then merely the first item to be consulted on a checklist, or the teaching that must always be honored before we go on to other things along other lines. Rather in its very enunciation, the gospel is abidingly the powerful word of God to make a new beginning in human affairs that is always effectively primary, especially in the cognitive work of theology as the work of critical dogmatics in the life of the church in its mission in the world. It is the access by which knowledge of God is imparted, such that any other approach to theology is speculation that reduces, on careful, critical examination, to alternative narratives. The gospel indeed gains theological primacy not least by framing the very question to which it will provide the answer and so refusing to be co-opted as an answer to some other set of questions deriving from some other narrative than the gospel's. It demands: What is our true need and plight that we should need *this* incarnation of God, *this* revelation of the justice of God, this Christ *crucified* for our sins and *raised from that godforsaken death* to make us right again with God (Gal 2:21)? Posing *this* question, the gospel will not then be hijacked by other projects, retooled as religious ideology dressing up preexisting human ideas about our problems and prospects. But God speaks a unilateral promise to those so questioned in the story of Christ that questions all our questions and answers (Phil 3:4-14) in order to speak an unsurpassable divine *yes!* both radical and transformative: "If anyone is in Christ, new creation!" (2 Cor 5:11).[25]

In making this reformatory theological appeal to the *primacy* of the gospel concerning Christ, however, Luther by no means intended to found a new church on a new basis. If so, he would have had to assume that the gospel had actually been silenced by recent papal error or that the gospel was in need of his own scholarly work to bring it to life and make it speak. To think in such ways would have undermined the very primacy of the gospel as the efficacious power of God in His word that Luther sought to lift up to new theological clarity. Luther in his best moments knew better.[26] His initial aim accordingly was to call the Latin-speaking church of the West (part of which would become the confessionalized Roman Catholic Church subsequent to the Western schism) back to her first love and to do so by no other means than lifting up afresh—with the notable help of the "blessed Augustine"—what had recently been obscured from view by certain medieval penitential practices (underpinned theologically by the modernist-naturalist theological philosophy of Scotus, Occam, and Biel).[27] That is why he could take up and exposit the traditional doctrinal standard of the West—the Apostles' Creed—in his catechisms and do so (it is surprising perhaps to learn of this) without ever even mentioning by name his allegedly indispensable doctrine of justification by faith alone.

Such a move was possible for Luther because what later became the confessional Lutheran doctrine of justification by faith alone, "the article by which the church stands and falls," is not primary theology but belongs to a second order of reflective theology. As such, it provided a rule about the true sharing of the gospel, in the way that grammar provides rules for proper speaking of a language (but is not the speaking itself).[28] This second-order doctrine of justification was, as Robert Jenson has urged, an instruction to preachers: Tell the story of Jesus in such a way that He with His blessings of peace with God is ours in the mere surrender of penitent faith to His merciful promise.[29] Just as effective English can be spoken by people knowing little theoretically of grammar, this gospel gift can be effectively spoken and its story be rightly told even when people do not explicitly know or understand justification by faith as a doctrinal rule (or even oppose what they mistakenly take this rule to be saying). Indeed, the gospel somehow has been spoken truly enough all along, for otherwise *ex hypothesi* there would be no church to reform. In light of just such clarifications today about the confessional Lutheran doctrine's regulative function, Lutherans and Catholics have converged in joint teaching on the (second-order) doctrine of justification.[30]

At the same time it is important to recall that the second-order, reflective doctrine of justification as a rule for correct gospel speaking arises from the primary theology of the gospel narrative that in turn it seeks to clarify. Here the "justice" in justification by faith is of a piece with the first-order language about the faith/faithfulness (or "righteousness" or "obedience," Rom 5:18) of Jesus Christ in the advent of God's reign, as portrayed in the gospel narrative and proclaimed by the Apostle. The gospel story sets before us this remarkable justice of the gracious reign of God advancing to us in Christ's life, death, and resurrection, which gives saving righteousness in exchange for lethal sin. On this primary level, the Reformation teaching about justification is a sample of the traditional New Testament and patristic rhetoric of the *admirabile commercium* (wonderful transaction) of the gospel narrative: "O marvel at the loving-kindness of the Word, that for our sakes he is dishonored, that we may be brought to honor" (Athanasius).[31] In Luther's idiom, this tradition became the celebrated "joyful exchange": "For it is sufficient that our sin displeases us, even though we do not get entirely rid of it. For Christ carries all sins, if only they are displeasing to us, and thus they are no longer ours but His, and His righteousness in turn is ours."[32] This narrative understanding of Christ giving what is His by assuming what is ours is the primary, constant, and indeed "catholic" element in Luther's understanding of the reformatory gospel.[33]

In primary theology, *justification designates this concrete, historical exchange of a remarkable justice that comes on the scene with the crucified and risen Christ, giving what is not deserved in place of what is.* This is a justice then that reveals its author as true God and creator in the very act of the redemption and in prospect of the creature's fulfillment. It is precisely *not* the primacy of the gospel, then, if such telling of Jesus' story is short-circuited or even replaced by the boring, if not (performatively speaking) *legalistic,* reiteration of abstract ideas (even true ones, like "God is love" or that we are saved by "grace alone")—even though this is how later Lutheranism, mutating into liberal Protestantism, began to think. Dietrich Bonhoeffer attacked this latter in the opening salvo of *The Cost of Discipleship*: "Cheap grace means grace as a doctrine, a principle, a system. It means the forgiveness of sins proclaimed as a general truth, the love of God taught as the Christian 'conception' of God. An intellectual assent to that idea is held to be itself sufficient to secure remission of sins. The church that upholds the correct doctrine of grace has, it is supposed, ipso facto a part in that grace. In such a church the world finds a cheap covering for its sins; no contrition is required, still less any real desire to be delivered from sin. Cheap grace therefore amounts to a denial of the living word of God, in fact, a denial of the incarnation of the word of God."[34] Bonhoeffer's polemic here is directed against the teaching of modern German theology stemming from Schleiermacher and Ritschl, for which the narrative of the Son of God's "journey into the far country" (Barth) had been reduced to the inspiring example of the human Jesus' filial faith in God's "fatherly goodness" (Harnack)[35]—one of those boring, abstract ideas now taking the place of Christian dogma.

A proper sense for the primacy of the gospel as narrative of God's self-involvement with human woe would never quite wholly be extinguished in later Protestantism. Yet it is safe to say that its eclipse was sealed already not by the later liberals but by the early confessionalists, with their polemical scheme of Protestant Scripture versus Catholic tradition, now in a savage irony put forward as epistemology, as the miracle of the Bible's self-validating inerrancy rather than as the gospel's critique of epistemology. It is mandatory today to overcome this polemical antithesis, which misleads in every direction, since in it Luther's crucial clarification about *which* word of God bears authority in the life of the church was obscured.[36] In its place, both sides of the Protestant-Catholic divide succumbed to a juridical mentality where legalistic proof-texting replaced dramatic interpretation of scriptural narrative (the latter is materially the content of critical-dogmatic theology as we are defining it). On the Protestant side, a miraculous, inerrant, and infallible book (which happens to contain the gospel alongside other things) telling about everything under the sun was set up as the primary authority over against the allegedly miraculous, inerrant, infallible teaching office of the Roman papacy. The question provoked by the gospel —What authorizes specific practices that gather the church by repentance and faith in the name of Jesus?—was displaced by the question, What authorizes the Protestant or Catholic confession in opposition to the other? In the process, the gospel was eclipsed as primary; it lost the kind of primacy in theology that Luther at his best wanted for it, that is, the power to frame the basic questions we ask in theology to probe the churches for fidelity to their author and authorization. The epistemological question of early modernity (the Cartesian quest for indubitability) instead became primary in Protestant theology in the form of whether the Bible was credible or verifiable as the supernatural basis for revealed knowledge of geography, geology, and other secular matters. Embracing Kant's critical epistemology, liberal theology arose to disown that hopeless position of Protestant Orthodoxy. In either case, with disastrous results for divided modern Christianity, the "gospel" then became a polemical slogan, a confessionalized epithet.

For other reasons as well, theology in Europe and North America today is profoundly conflicted. The issue is whether biblical canon with its creedal interpretation is to be taken merely as a historical marker forming a (disputable) *precedent* for contemporary speculative thought (so-called constructive theology) or instead is to be taken to demarcate (definite) *boundaries*, "the pure, clear fountain of Israel, which alone is the one true guiding principle, according to which all teachers and teaching are to be judged."[37] In the former approach, theology is a constructive discipline in harmony with the modern, Cartesian-Kantian "turn to the subject," which constructs reality up to and including images and conceptions of deity. In the latter approach, theology is an autonomous, nonspeculative, and communal tradition-discourse that reflects upon reality as revealed by God's self-expression through the gospel. Between these approaches there seems simply to be a choice inasmuch as there is no dogmatically neutral, narrative-free conception of theology as a discipline by which to adjudicate the alternatives these represent. Clearly siding in this contemporary conflict with Luther's definition of theology as "the new language of the Spirit," this book perhaps quixotically aspires to make a case rather than to demand a choice. In fact, every definition of Christian theology entails some account of classic Christian doctrine along the fault-line of canon with its creedal interpretation. An account of this origin and coming and course is internal to the practice of theology and constitutes the "prolegomena to dogmatics" needed in the present situation in the West. The present claim is that Christian theology arises as reflection *on* the contingent event of the coming of the gospel of God *from* the Scriptures *in* the church *for* the world.

Primary theology is narrowly the gospel's narrative of the Son's death and resurrection and broadly the biblical narrative, understood as promissory.[38] The gospel is a story to be told, which in the telling draws us in and refashions us by means of the transaction between Christ and the believer that comes about by the former's unilateral promise. As Luther wrote in his introduction to the New Testament: "Thus this gospel of God or New Testament is a good story and report, sounded forth into all the world by the apostles, telling of a true David who strove with sin, death, and the devil, and overcame them, and thereby rescued all those who were captive in sin, afflicted with death, and overpowered by the devil. Without any merit of their own he made them righteous, gave them life, and saved them, so that they were given peace and brought back to God. For this they sing, and thank and praise God, and are glad forever, if only they believe firmly and remain steadfast in faith."[39] Robert

Jenson comments: "The message of faith, the 'gospel,' is a narrative. . . . It is the story of Jesus told as that story from which the hearer may hear their destiny, hear what life is for. For the gospel is the story of Jesus told as the story of the last future, as a message of hope. It says: the story of life-out-of-death and love-out-of-hatred that is enacted in the events of this man's life will be the conclusion of your life also. Thus the gospel is a proclamation of a future hope with a narrative content."[40]

For purposes of pedagogy, we can descriptively sketch the canonical gospel as follows, with elaborations and warrants provided in the footnotes:[41]

The gospel is the Easter message[42] of the God of Israel,[43] whom Jesus[44] had addressed as Abba, Father.[45] This word from God concerns the same Jesus who appeared to Israel prophetically announcing the imminence of His Father's reign but was crucified as a messianic pretender, the would-be "king of the Jews"[46] on the outskirts of Jerusalem by the Roman imperial governor Pontius Pilate. He had proclaimed and inaugurated the reign of God by making fellowship in God's name with the outcast, sinful, and diseased.[47] Paradoxically,[48] in obedience to God, Jesus lived on behalf of and died in solidarity with these lost sheep of the house of Israel, as the one most truly forsaken by God.[49] As such He descended into hell.[50] By the resurrection[51] of the crucified, God effected and announced Jesus' victory of love on behalf of those for whom He lived and died and so exalted Him as coming Judge of the world, who sends His Spirit to anticipate this paradoxical judgment in repentance, forgiveness, and the imparting of new resurrection life to all who believe.[52] Thus penitents[53] from all nations, called out to faith by this good news[54] and designated children of God by baptism, are united in eucharistic worship[55] and empowered by the same Spirit[56] to form that earthly body that lives His crucified and risen life[57] to the glory of God the Father, now and forever.[58] In this way, the reign of God comes.[59] Consequently, the gospel has a history[60] in the world that is itself theologically relevant, that is, relevant to the knowledge of the God of the gospel.[61] This doctrine (doctrina evangelii is both given as this primary, promissory narrative and developed by means of rules (regula fidei) in the course of its earthly career, which are irreversible and cumulative decisions within the universal community of faith about the gospel's interpretation that have been required if the story is to continue to be told as God's merciful promise of inclusion to the lost and perishing.

Note first that the basic fact or datum of Christian theology is a narrative that makes a promise, "the gospel of God." This primary theology is "the medium in which God's own act of promising may intelligibly be said to occur. . . . Faith is present whenever the proclamation of the gospel is heard as God's first person, present indicative promise to us."[62] The term *gospel* has roots in Second Isaiah, Paul, and Mark. It denotes news of a history-making event that is not true by reference to "what already or antecedently is experientially present." "Consider not the former things, nor remember the things of old," says the Lord according to the second Isaiah. "Behold, I am doing a new thing." Gospel "is not of the same logical type as a symbol that articulates and lifts to the level of conscious referentiality some prelinguistic or formerly unconscious state of being."[63] Gospel is not a "revelation" of what is always and everywhere the case. But the gospel is revelatory of the divine agent who acts in this event to promise Himself to others for a common future, that is, the one who is who He is by speaking and acting in just this self-involving way: "I am yours and you are Mine." "The objectivity of God is to be understood as that of a promisor's active commitment to others in the present for a future. . . . Whether 'God' indeed does so act can only be proven in forthcoming events."[64]

Consequent to this logic of promise, all the doctrinal beliefs listed or implied in the preceding narrative summary are to be understood as articulations of God's self-involving gospel promise; they cohere as elements of the promissory narrative and cannot be understood apart from their place in it. Their truth as beliefs is not determined by any other frame of reference than the promised future of God that they convey, and this truth is not settled by anything other than its fulfillment (or its falsity settled by its non-fulfillment). Both faith *and disbelief* live in this tension.

Second, the gospel message decisively derives from the New Testament claim that Jesus who was crucified nevertheless lives and reigns. Something unprecedented and beyond the reach of all human power, wisdom, and goodness has happened that expresses an ultimate, unsurpassable judgment about Jesus. He who died godforsaken on the cross is nevertheless vindicated as God's own Son. Just so, however, He is now seen to have died then "according to the Scriptures," that is, in accordance with God's eternal plan to justify the ungodly. Thus this "good news" from all eternity had been preached ahead of time in the promises given to Abraham and his descendents, the people of Israel, and onward up to the proclamation made by this same Jesus in His own lifetime. Indeed, the gospel expresses the eternal decree and self-determination of the triune God.

Third, the narrative structure of this gospel event is trinitarian—not, of course, in the sense of the fully developed conceptual distinctions of the one essence and three persons that arrived at Constantinople in 381. But in the gospel we meet three distinct figures—Jesus, His Father, and their Spirit—and it is in following their narrative interaction that we come to understand these three as the one and indivisible God who creates, redeems, and fulfills the one world. The developed trinitarian doctrine just mentioned comes about later on in the course of the gospel's history, due to a crisis in interpretation on which the continued telling of the story turned (as we shall study in detail in this book's final chapter).

Fourth, human repentance-and-faith comes about by the Spirit as real participation in Jesus' very own, historically particular trust and obedience; that is, it is the obedience of faith in God's free favor, active in self-giving love of others, an ecstatic existence in the Spirit who anticipates the new creation. Faith decenters the old self of its previous incurvation and recenters it outside of itself in trust in God, love for the other, and hope for the world. As such, faith is not in any way the initiative or act of this old self-centered being, which rather in conversion dies spiritually by abandoning its old identity. Faith is never the old Adam's cognition, valuation, choice, decision, emotional discharge. Faith is new being in Christ, who is the New Adam; it is the Spirit's repetition in believers of Jesus' own faithfulness: trust in God, love for neighbors, hope for the earth. As such, the faith that comes from hearing the gospel is not an instantiation of a general human inclination to trust something greater than themselves, which is rather the idolatry of collective egoism. Faith rather consists in lifelong repentance or conversion, turning from sin and turning to God. Faith without repentance, not to mention the works of love and hope, is dead, fictitious, illusory, just as it cheapens grace blasphemously.

Fifth, this faith-participation in Jesus' life is oriented to the eschatological glorification of God. The gospel-promised fulfillment of life is the joyful praise of God in God through God. Worship is the final horizon of this way of life, just as the truth of the gospel turns on the fulfillment of the eschatological promise—the resurrection of the dead. In the interim, this future hope of glory is anticipated in the eucharistic worship of the church, by which the Lord's death is proclaimed until He comes again, as the gathered faithful offer their sacrifice of praise and thanksgiving in union with the Son.

In sum, in primary Christian theology as *doctrina evangelii* (doctrine of the gospel) we are not talking about a heap of unrelated ideas, historical facts, myths, worldviews, dogmas, and beliefs behind which we might discover a historical Jesus or an anthropological need. Rather the doctrine of the gospel brings *a coherent though continually revised apprehension of reality as sinful humanity and the redeeming God in Jesus Christ, generated by the very progress of this gospel through time and space.* As doctrine of the gospel, theology has considered many distinct beliefs—creation out of nothing, original sin, the Incarnation, and so on—as articulations of the one, primary promissory narrative. Strictly speaking, however, there is only the *one* cognitive proposition involved here, that is, in the *region* of theology, which is the area or field of possible eternities: God the almighty Father is determined to redeem the creation through His Son, Jesus Christ, and bring it to fulfillment in His Spirit. The gospel proposition is a genuinely *synthetic* statement—God's eternal self-determination is God's free choice; it could have been otherwise—that correspondingly must be verified eschatologically, or, in absence of that verification, falsified. In the interim, its cognitive power is tested by its interpretive power in the region of theology, that is, as opposed to other claimants of possible eternities. Correspondingly the multitude of human conceptions of the sovereign power that determines all things is not to be identified willy-nilly with this God of the gospel, nor *must* the Trinity's turn to include humanity in its own divine life through Jesus Christ be understood as any kind of necessary unfolding of divine being, however "fitting" it may appear to be in retrospect.

Primary Christian theology issues in critical dogmatics (that is, not the confessional apologetics of the divided church). This endeavor to state the coherence of Christian beliefs as identifying God who justifies the ungodly—and so also humanity as the justified sinner—opens up the possibility and reality of newness of life. *Fiducia*, or personal trust, as we heard, occurs when this gospel proposition is heard and believed as the Trinity's own promise *pro me*. Then the believer acquires the assured faith in every affliction that nothing can separate from the love of Christ, since the God of the gospel is known in faith as determined also to redeem *me* and to bring *me* to His kingdom. Just as clearly, however, the latter conviction of personal trust entails the church's knowledge of Christ in His love. Morse makes the point this way: "Revelation discloses both self-involvement and propositional content, that is, both a thou and a coming kingdom, both a 'someone' and a 'something.'"[65] Reinhardt Hütter has written, "The locutionary content and the illocutionary role of what is narrated (or stated) are inseparably connected, albeit in the quite specific logical sequence that makes the illocutionary character of what is narrated completely dependent on its object. . . . The gospel is a doctrine (*doctrina evangelii*) stating who Jesus Christ is and what he did and suffered . . . Properly speaking about who Jesus Christ is, what he said, did, and suffered necessarily also—qua object—issues a promise, a *promissio*, to those listening. The illocutionary quality, however, depends entirely on the locutionary content, namely, who Jesus is."[66] Why this is so, as Bonhoeffer contended[67]—why Christology precedes soteriology, why the mere "Jesus of history" is ambiguous and so becomes a helpless cipher at the mercy of salvation-sellers new and old[68]—is a fundamental question; it is a version of the perennial question about the role of natural theology in what we are calling the critical dogmatics of Christianity, where the primacy of the gospel as critique of epistemology holds sway. But if soteriology is permitted to govern Christology, then any given natural self-understanding, with its own account of human need or aspiration, is granted epistemic primacy. If Christology rather has the right and power to expose and construct the human need or aspiration that it meets, then epistemic primacy is accorded to God's Easter decision to recognize the crucified, dead, and buried Jesus as truly His own beloved Son. If God can in turn be coherently understood so to "decide," however, antecedent notions of divine simplicity come under scrutiny and a revision of metaphysics is under way.

Natural Theology? Divine Simplicity?

"Natural theology" is not natural, in the sense of arising spontaneously from experience, once freed from the imprisonment of human artifice in tradition or custom. It is a definite tradition of Western philosophy, originating in Plato's critique of the poets for their unseemly representations of the gods. Writing in reference to the seminal Platonic dialogue, *Euthyphro*, Drozdek states, "The divine should be purged of attributes unworthy of the gods, even of men . . . [and] include only lofty, spiritual characteristics that befit God. There will be thus one essence of divinity to which all the gods are subsumed . . . conceptually by being manifestations of one concept."[69] As such, natural theology has to be understood historically. The problem natural theology faces is one of social peace. Representations of the divine are notoriously at variance with one another, but social peace seems to depend on mutual toleration in matters of religion. Hence the crucial move of natural theology is *apophatic*: to transcend the "human, all-too-human" representations of the divine by appeal to an essence beyond image, beyond language, beyond thought, beyond being. In the Western, Latin tradition, Cicero's *On the Nature of the Gods* was a foundational text of critical reflection along these lines. Arguably, the great Kant found his agnostic and Pelagian philosophy of religion anticipated in it. Writing in the fateful times of the end of the Roman republic and the transition to dictatorship and imperialism, Cicero undertook natural or philosophical theology as a way out from the situation of polytheistic conflict in and among the religions, just as Kant too sought new foundation for culture after the post-Reformation wars of religion. Thus a brief consideration of this classic of natural theology well merits our attention here.

The dialogue between an Epicurean, a Stoic, and an Academic Skeptic at one point considers the argument that if the "the true gods are those whom we worship by tradition, then why not include Isis and Orsiris in their number? If we do this, why repudiate the gods of other races? Then we shall be making gods of oxen, horses, ibises, falcons, asps, crocodiles, fishes, dogs, wolves, cats, and all manner of beasts."[70] Following a survey of the cults known to the disputants, the conclusion is drawn: "All this and much more of the same kind may be gathered from the ancient legends of the Greeks, and you will see that such fables must be discredited, if religion itself is not to be brought into confusion and disrepute."[71] The theological way out is to resolve the diversity of concrete but misleading and contradictory images of divine being by the way of negation. This way to the knowledge of God excludes the imperfections of being in time; so the mind step by step arises to the notion of impersonal, ineffable transcendence. Therein, however, lies a difficulty: "Your argument was such that in trying to define the nature of the gods, you only succeeded in showing that they do not exist at all. You pointed out how difficult it is for us to think otherwise than through visual images. Then you said that as there could be nothing more excellent than God, the universe itself must be God, as there was nothing more excellent than the whole scheme of things. If only we could think of it as a conscious being. . . . But what do you mean by 'perfect?' If you mean 'beautiful,' I agree. If you mean 'fitted to our needs,' I agree again. But if you mean there is nothing wiser than the universe, then I do not agree at all."

The reason for dissent becomes clear. The cosmos, even as a totality, is a body or bodily system, but in it is "no immortal body, no individual atom that cannot be split and pulled apart. Every living thing is therefore in its nature vulnerable. There is none that can escape external influences. All must endure the rigor of necessity: and all must feel and suffer. But if every living thing must suffer, none can be immortal."[72] The procedure culminates in articulating the dilemma of the doctrine of *im*passibility: true God is the God beyond the gods, whose perfection consists in the so-called alpha-privatives (the Greek *alpha* being the prefix of negation, as in English un- or in-): *un*changing, *in*visible, *in*corporeal, *im*measurable, *in*finite, and so on. Yet such an *im*passible being is nothing living, not even something existing (since even the atoms can be split!), something then utterly inconceivable: "a being that feels neither pleasure nor pain cannot be alive at all."[73] So the damning result is reached: By the way of negation, you have "only succeeded in showing that the gods do not exist at all." What actually follows is that the "divine Providence" moving all things in the cosmos works rather like an algorithm, "either unaware of its own powers or . . . indifferent to human life. Or else it is unable to judge what is best."[74] Divine providence thus lacks both wisdom and values; as such it can provide no ethical direction to human seekers: "There can be no divine guidance of human affairs if the gods make no distinction between good and evil." It might seem that this line of argument "plays into the hands of the criminal." Thankfully, however, Cicero's natural theologian, just like his latter-day follower Kant, is able to resort to the autonomous conscience of humanity: "And so it would [play into the hands of the criminal], if virtue and vice were not deep matters of our own conscience, quite apart from any gift of reason from the gods. If conscience goes, then everything collapses around us."[75] At the end of natural theology, "conscience" comes on the stage as a veritable *deus ex machina*—the dethroning of the gods gives way to the deification of conscience. The irony of Ciceronian natural theology is that to save the gods from idolatrous representation, they must be denatured. Denatured, however, they can give humanity no direction. Not to worry, though—conscience may now reign in place of the gods.

An even greater irony, however, ought to be seen in the endeavor by Christian theologians to use such philosophical construction of *im*passible and *in*effable perfection—a veritably Nietzschean divinization of Unlife or Nonbeing—as a foundation for their talk about God as opposed, say, to revealed theology's own disclosure of divine nature in the perception of the dynamic harmony of power and wisdom in the divine *passion* of love. The division of labor had critical philosophy, or natural theology, telling us what the divine is (really, what it is *not*) and then revealed theology telling us Who this What, rather this Not, is and how it relates itself to us.

But if theology is the knowledge of the God of the gospel, the Trinity is not one topic alongside others but the very structure of theological knowledge.[76] Faith knows God as the Father with Jesus His Son in the free favor of their Spirit's love such that what may or may not be deemed "fitting" to the divine nature is something to be learned from the revelation, not imposed upon it from the outside. Christian faith knows God in the very same good pleasure that He now takes in those baptized into Jesus' death and resurrection, pouring love into their hearts by the Holy Spirit: first comes the gracious movement of *katabasis*, or condescension, of free and loving favor; just the same and inseparably, faith, hope, and love follow, knowing God in the newness of life returned in this same love, now following Jesus, carrying the cross in service of the needy to glorify the Father—the *anabasis*, or ascent, of the Christian life.

The descent and ascent of grace in this sequence mark the self-giving movements of the divine and triune life, actualized in time-space in the ministry, Easter vindication, and final triumph of Jesus Christ, the incarnate Son of God. Such participation is imparted to believers in repentance and faith. Trinity is not then revealed frosting superficially plastered on the cake of metaphysical construction of perfect being that provides the real, operative knowledge of divinity. Trinity is itself the divine life revealed in dazzling conjunctions of perfect power, wisdom, and love. Theology as cognition occurs within these movements: "In the word the Holy Spirit brings to human hearts God's love, which has been revealed in the cross and resurrection of Christ. The Holy Spirit brings us into community with God. But in Christ himself the church is already established. When Christ comes "into" us through the Holy Spirit, the church comes "into" us. The Holy Spirit, however, moves us by putting Christ into our hearts, creating faith and hope. But this faith in Christ generated by the Holy Spirit includes faith in the church-community in which Christ reigns; love, however, as the love of the heart of Christ in us, is given to us as a new heart, as will for good. Faith acknowledges God's rule and embraces it; love actualizes the Realm of God."[77] Bonhoeffer's back-and-forth in this passage between the act of the Son and the call of the Spirit locates the theological life of the church within the very movements of God's triune being as something implicating human believers in the here and now. To think "God" this way today entails disentangling the fateful but peculiar alliance of Christian theology with the cosmo-theological scheme of Greek metaphysical theology (thinking of God as the highest link or supreme cause *within* the cosmic great chain of being), and more insidiously by means of the Platonic "axiom of impassibility" (God is not what everything else is), otherwise known as the doctrine of divine simplicity (taken not as a rule for reverent speech but as an insight into the being of God).

This is a complex and still uncompleted task. For it is true, notwithstanding all that has been just argued, that Christian theology made and can continue to make common cause with *critical* Platonism's critique of myth and sacrificial cult. The fact that natural theology is soteriologically idle in the light of revelation, indeed positively misleading apart from the light of revelation, does not mean that natural theology is simply illusory, as for example Nietzsche thought. Rather it becomes useful in an unanticipated and surprising way in the light of revelation, which retools its own critique of myth into a corresponding critique of metaphysics. The highly controverted passage of Romans 1:19-20 adopted ideas from the best available philosophical theology: "For what can be known about God is plain to them, because God has shown it to them. Ever since the creation of the world his eternal power and divine nature, invisible though they are, have been understood and seen through the things he has made." But the context of this statement is Paul's apocalyptic discourse about the revelation from heaven of the wrath of God. What Paul accordingly sees is a pervasive human idolatry that in turn somehow presupposes among the idolaters a *sensus divinitatis*: "God in his invisibility, and in the [deity] that distinguishes him from cosmic being . . . is eternal, perpetual power."[78] So the early Luther, following Augustine's seminal interpretation of the sin of idolatry in using God for human purposes,[79] exposited the text: "All those who set up idols and worship them and call them 'gods' or even 'God,' believing that God is immortal, that is, eternal, powerful, and able to render help, clearly indicate that they have a knowledge of divinity in their hearts . . . calling upon him, worshipping and adoring him . . . It follows most surely that they had a knowledge or notion of divinity which undoubtedly came to them from God, as our text tells us. This was their error, that they did not worship this divinity untouched but changed and adjusted it to their desires and needs."[80]

It is important to discern here that Luther does not locate the error of natural theology in the mere fact of its sublime representation of the divine as transcendent causality but rather in the use of this idea to capture God for human purposes. It is the function of representation, crude and polytheistic or sublime and monotheistic, to turn God to the purposes of the worshipper; this is criticized as idolatrous, not the representation of God as cosmic cause as such.[81] The acknowledgment of the truth of God in thanksgiving would presumably be the act that turns the creature to the creator's purpose, ascribing to Him alone all power, wisdom, and love. Presumably there could be a true representation of the God whose eternal deity and power are to give gifts up to and including a share in His own divine life. But by an act of exchange, the truth of God as the One to be thanked, not used, is suppressed, rendering humanity guilty and subject to the wrath of God. Thus Paul, as Käsemann tells, "does not here explain, prove, defend, or seek a point of contact. He accuses, reduces Hellenistic motifs to a minimum, characterizes God's deity as a power that encounters us, concentrates it in lordship, and perceives human guilt, not in ignorance, but in revolt against the known Lord."[82] What Paul offers in Romans 1:19-20 then is not a Stoic natural theology but a theology of nature, that is, an interpretation of antecedent religiosity and its own best critical theology in the light of the gospel. "Since [Paul] based his proclamation on God's ever-present work, it was impossible for him to find this work only in himself and in his churches. Believing in the presence of God means to affirm it in every event. Paul's God was the creator to whom they all belong. Where the word of Jesus is, God's righteousness becomes evident because that is where faith arises; for where the word of Jesus is not, there is not the absence of God but wrath that becomes effective, because that is where all kinds of godlessness and injustice are found."[83]

One might of course respond that an analogical knowledge of God's being as eternal, omnipotent, and divine, seen and understood in relation to the cosmos as a whole like the cause of an effect within the world, should be possible on Paul's very logic. *Insofar as human beings know themselves as creatures*, that is, in accord with the teaching of Genesis 1:26 that humankind is made in the image and likeness of God, should they not understand themselves and all else as caused by God in the same way that they, intelligent agents in the world, refashion the little world around them according to their own causality? On the basis of this special relationship to God, human beings would be justified in drawing the causal analogy, since they would be able to reckon not only with divine power (the argument from effect to cause) but also with divine truthfulness, wisdom, and love. God, being good and wise and truthful, would not, like Descartes' demon, make a world that is a grand and cruel deception.

Yet for Paul this hypothetical world sounds like a long-forgotten dream. When called to mind, it makes sense of the universal practice of idolatry. But in fact, as Paul immediately goes on to write, human beings do not acknowledge themselves as the creatures of God by giving thanks and worshipping the Creator. Instead they actively exchange that worship for a peculiar form of self-glorification (Rom 1:21) and degradation, idolizing their own corrupt desires in the representations they construct of the God they know to be causer, never caused. The point is epistemic. Whatever the fallen creation under the power of sin knows of God will be used idolatrously, religion putting God to use for human purposes rather than human beings to service in God's reign.

Knowing oneself as the creature of God is no general or neutral presupposition of the gospel's revealed theology but rather what it accomplishes in and for us for our salvation. It is a recognition discovered though salvation in Christ, the new and true Adam, something to be learned in the act of living in Christ to the eschatological denouement. The knowledge of God the creator in Paul's theology is concretely the knowledge of faith told by the gospel, which comes from hearing (Rom 10:17) of the genuinely contingent event of the resurrection of the Crucified, by which action of His Spirit God has freely given Himself to be known in His Son (Rom 4:19-20). Creation, in other words, is not only or even chiefly the act of origin but comprehends eschatologically all of reality in Christ on the way to the consummation. Just so, Christ is the image and analogue of God. As this free divine self-giving comes to be understood as the *fitting*, though *not necessary*, expression of God's own divine life in space-time, it challenges and ultimately revises all hitherto prevailing human conceptions of the sovereign power holding sway. It is grace that finally determines what is "natural" in the very act of the "redemption of our bodies" (Rom 8:23) through union with Christ's death and resurrection. The perfection of nature is likewise eschatological (Rom 8:18-25), just as God is really asserted and believed to be the almighty Father who is determined to redeem the world through Jesus Christ and bring it to fulfillment in His Spirit. The ongoing revision of the world's antecedent natural theologies is Christian theology's most fundamental but still uncompleted task in the work of critical dogmatics.

Kataphatic Theology

The dogmatic theology of the classical Christian tradition is *kataphatic*. As such, it has within its own way an apophatic moment: "No one has ever seen God," we are told in John 1:18 (RSV). Yet the text immediately continues: "The only Son, who is in the bosom of the Father, he has made him known." Divine simplicity may be taken accordingly as a rule qualifying all Christian discourse about God as discourse regarding a singularity that lives in unapproachable light. Yet the point of the rule is not to disqualify but rather to qualify the coming forth from this unapproachable light of the light that shines in the darkness in the glory of Jesus Christ, in whom the grace and truth of God are manifest here and now in space and time. In Christianity, the apophatic moment is observed in service of the kataphatic, which tells of God in the act of His being in the necessarily complex ways noted in the Christian dogma of the Trinity, the personal union of the divine and human natures in Christ, and the justification of the ungodly by grace through faith active in love and sustained by the hope for the redemption of our bodies. We thus conclude this opening chapter by asking how the primary Christian theology of gospel narrative produces in the course of its history certain such truths—dogmas—that must be affirmed along with it if the story is to continue to be told truly.

The gospel narrative in the course of its history has indeed yielded doctrines: that "crucified Jesus is the Son of God"; that the one God is nevertheless three; that sinful human beings enter into Jesus' relationship with God by the grace of the Spirit, not by the merit of their own initiatives; that the gospel may be truly narrated in visual images or musical sequences or sacramental ceremonies just as it may be truly articulated in human words and theological concepts. What kind of logical or conceptual status do these characteristic

Christian theological ideas of the post–New Testament development possess? Are they propositional truths embedded in the story, to be extracted then like nuggets of gold from the coarse ore? Arranged in a systematic display as the hard kernels of essential truth liberated from all the husk of poetry? Following Lindbeck we will suggest in the end of the next chapter that for the most part such doctrines emerge as rules for speaking correctly the primary theology of promissory narrative, in that dogmas are *analytic* of the story. The developed doctrine of the Trinity, for example, of "three persons in one essence," emerges first as a practical rule for telling of the three distinct *personae* of the gospel narrative: Jesus, His Father, and their Spirit as one in the divine decision to create the world, redeem it, and bring it to fulfillment. And so the three are one in a free act, and so eternally one capable of a free act. The truth of the doctrine is not in the first place the formula—three persons in one essence—taken as a proposition that corresponds to an object, but rather the formula taken as indicating the right speaking of the word "God" in Christian discourse, where "speaking" is and must be as performative as ostensive.

Such a pragmatic reading of primitive Christian doctrinal beliefs has the strength of avoiding the abstraction of Christian truth into a system that takes on a life of its own on account of the conceptual framework that will be borrowed from elsewhere to organize the abstractions systematically. In this way, the doctrines become less and less related to the promissory narrative that they actually arose to serve. Such arid and speculative forms of theology have occurred time and again in Christian history, eclipsing the drama of biblical narrative telling of the three who are one in the decision to create, redeem, and fill the world. The pragmatic account also has the virtue of corresponding historically to the actual rise of creedal Christianity, which generally did not ask how the Bible could be true (what is the ontological import of its presumed propositions) but rather asked what is the truth of the Bible (what is the soteriological import of the story it tells). In the latter perspective, dogmas arise as acts of interpretive clarification that resolve real dilemmas about how rightly to read and tell the gospel conveyed in the Scriptures as truly good news. If Jesus is only creature like me and you, for example, He needs God as savior just like you and me and cannot be our savior (so Athanasius, as we shall see in detail in chapter 6). Therefore speak of Jesus the creature in such a way that He is indiscernibly one person in the world with God the eternal Son, who "for us and for our salvation came down from heaven and was made man." This is how the Nicene Creed's famous (or notorious) *homoousios* (of the same being as the Father) works, taken as a rule.

But of course, such rules are also formulations of tacit beliefs brought to us by the gospel. Thus, even after taking due note of the rise of dogmas in the interpretive praxis of the missionary church as rules for overcoming dilemmas and obstacles in the way of continuing to tell the gospel story, we shall have to ask whether or how such dogmas may be understood to be true to their divine object—God—as Dennis Bielfeldt has rightly insisted.[84] How could the apparent contradiction—this man is God—ever be understood to be true to divine reality, which is creator not creature? The question is neither idle nor avoidable. First, dogmatic rules acquire validity and can function to rule the performance of speech in Christianity just because they contain beliefs about reality that, like any beliefs, are in principle questionable and so must be warranted. We can no more make up our own rules than we can make up our own facts. Dogma does not license dogmatism. Theology is a critical discipline. Critical dogmatics explores such difficulties in belief. A more sophisticated theological pragmatism will not beg this question of ontological import, then, but will press beyond the rule theory's reticence to account for the claim to correspond to divine reality embedded in dogmatic rules of Christian belief. Second, certain (in principle questionable) beliefs elevated to the rank of dogmas and functioning as rules can do so because they are and must be held as true (as corresponding to divine reality). Just as a promise without its fulfillment would be null and void, so also an essential belief without its corresponding object would be null and void. As such, these beliefs, lifted up as rules and claiming to correspond to divine reality, come to share in the epistemic primacy of the gospel itself, promising us nothing less than God.

How are they justified then as beliefs? A belief is justified, according to pragmatism, not because we can see its immediate correspondence with its object but insofar as it coheres with other beliefs we hold true or at least does not fatally contradict them. Pragmatist philosophy, reflecting its idealistic and Protestant Christian roots, posited an eschaton of knowledge at the end of inquiry in which perfect consensus would emerge, reconciling all beliefs. Correspondence with reality was attributed to this final state of knowledge. Theology can reclaim the Christian insight embedded in this secularization of its own thought. Dogmas arise pragmatically, to keep the reading and telling of the gospel story going with its promise of salvation. They are tested along the way for coherence with all the other beliefs we hold true. But they will be reconciled with reality, purified and judged, only when the object to which they point—the living God in the coming of His Kingdom—reveals His reign in fullness and power. Such final correspondence with reality in the eschaton has import for ordering Christian beliefs along the way. All such rules or dogmas systematically cohere in *one fundamental proposition* in the region of theology (possible eternities): *God is determined to redeem the world through Christ and bring it to fulfillment in His Spirit*. This proposition is *caused* by the resurrection of the Crucified, when the sense of resurrection is rendered by the story it comes to tell of the Father, the Son, and the Holy Spirit in the gospel narrative, that one of the Trinity became incarnate and suffered for our redemption. That kataphatic claim to ultimate truth is at stake in the rise of creedal Christianity, to which we now turn.

CHAPTER 2
From Resurrection Kerygma to Gospel Narrative

"The entire New Testament is written from a post-Resurrection perspective. Faith knows no life and death of Jesus abstracted from his destiny."[1] Accordingly, in this chapter we consider how the message of the cross and resurrection of Jesus provides the hermeneutical basis of the narrative theology of primitive Christianity as it took form in the gospel genre. By the same token, we see that the proclamation of the Easter promise of God to be for us in "Christ and Him crucified" required narration. This took shape in resurrection stories, terse creedal formulations identifying Jesus by the events in His life story, filled in gradually with edifying episodes from Jesus' antecedent mission and ministry and linked together to compose the gospel genre.[2] Performatively, God's promise of inclusion in the kingdom is made to auditors and readers through this act of narration, since theologically God's promise to us first of all consists in what transpired between Jesus as our representative and His Father, the God of Israel. In this way, we see that there is a specific priority of Christology[3]—what Jesus means for God—over soteriology—what Jesus means for us. This priority of Christology serves to define our salvation as (1) defeat of the anti-divine powers oppressing creation, (2) reconciliation of the sinner with the holy God, and (3) fulfillment of the creation in God's eternal life. The relation of gospel narrative to what post-Kantian inquiry deemed "history"—*wie es eigentlich gewesen ist*—is (aside from the epistemological conceit contained in the latter) not a question of founding theology on the plausible reconstruction of Jesus' private consciousness but of self-critical testing in theology for fidelity to Jesus' public purpose, the reign of God and our inclusion for His mercy's sake.[4]

The Resurrection of the Crucified as Hermeneutic

The "origin and future of all creation is bound up with [Jesus'] life, death, and destiny," writes Christopher Morse; "the Resurrection is the primary reference point from which the apostolic testimony announces this conviction."[5] Morse notes accordingly that the New Testament contains "references to events that do not fall within the limits" of world history as the modern mind understands things. The presence of Christ as a "coming" (recall the many statements in the New Testament like "The Son of Man has come to seek and save the lost," or "I have come that they may have life abundantly") "is narrated as a movement from outside our ordinary boundaries of time and space as historians would define them, into them, and outside them again."[6] The debate about this admittedly extraordinary traffic is usually framed in modern times in terms of the "ugly ditch" between the empirical and the transcendental, time and eternity, or the finite and the infinite. This ditch between two spheres requires of interpreters a choice to proceed either "from below" in history or "from above" in mythology—though few would really choose the latter! As a result of importing this modern dualism into their approach, it becomes difficult for modern interpreters to think of the earthly name Jesus and the heavenly title Christ together as does the New Testament; doing so amounts to an act of sheer force of will, a "value judgment" (Ritschl). Within this framework of thought, the New Testament text is taken as *symbol* more or less adequately representing Jesus as He actually existed in the distant past or, perhaps, as the heavenly Christ as religiously experienced in the mysteries of the cult, or some confused jumble of these two. Or, in opposition to these alternatives, conservative modernists take Jesus Christ to be present as the putatively *miraculous text of the Bible*, the eternal in time, the infinite in the finite, at the disposal then of the church, the theologian, or the believer. Given such unhappy consequences of the dualistic modern framework, we might question whether we moderns have misread the intention of the New Testament narrative to tell of "a *coming* into the world and an *overcoming* of the world"[7] in Jesus Christ.

Rejecting the dualistic alternatives of immanence and transcendence in favor of apocalyptic *imminence*—the kingdom of God is *near* (Mark 1:15)—Christopher Morse worked out a solution along these lines by taking seriously the *destiny* of Christ as ascended Lord and coming Judge. "To sit at the right hand of 'the maker of heaven and earth,'" as the Apostles' Creed situates the exalted Lord Jesus Christ, "is not to be absent now from the affairs of this earth on sabbatical leave, as it were. . . . It is to be present in the sense that imminence may be said to be a form of presence that brings both incarnate immanence and resurrection transcendence to bear materially on current affairs."[8] Jesus Christ is *at hand* to help (not "in hand" to be used), present *in faith* though not to sight, as the resurrection and exaltation narrative tells of the life and death of this singular human being as the promised destiny of the world. Proclaimed this way by the jarring oxymoron "Christ crucified," gospel narrative functions as rhetorical paradox, so that Jesus Christ comes in the form of faith (or disbelief) in His (and our) promised future. Such capacity to be present as promised in spite of having truly died is of course not a merely human one, but indication of the power that characterizes true deity to give life to the dead.

Morse's approach here adopted and developed is thus in accord with sober New Testament scholarship that still remembers that theology is *about God,* as is also this particular collection of literature, the New Testament's Gospels, which deserve then *theological* interpretation. In a concise monograph that binds together in analysis doctrine, ethics, and relation to the wider world,[9] Arland Hultgren demonstrated—against the nontheological tendencies current in contemporary "Jesus research"—that at the root of the development of the "normative Christianity" reflected in the New Testament canon is the kerygma of the cross and resurrection of Jesus. This kerygma or proclamation worked neither as a fixed deposit of doctrine nor as inspired exhortation in the existential moment but as a *hermeneutic,* that is, gathering, sifting, embellishing, and ordering traditions about Jesus that in this way mediated a definite relationship to Him in the life of communities of faith created by the gospel of His resurrection.[10] In short, the resurrection announcement of the act of God narrated the crucified Jesus in a way that rendered Him present as saving Lord of His "new testament" congregation, indeed as coming Lord of all. But He remains that very One who once ate and drank with sinners and tax collectors with all else that is said about Him.

It is certainly true, as the circle of criticism stemming from Walter Bauer's insightful but profoundly flawed[11] *Orthodoxy and Heresy in Earliest Christianity*[12] maintains, that "the impact of Jesus upon later generations exceeds those circles that produced the documents that came to be canonized."[13] It is a matter of history that there have been and remain relations to Jesus other than the one demarcated by the emergent New Testament canon with its gospel narrative as just defined.[14] These are represented in apocryphal texts, especially Gnostic or Gnostic-like literature that flourished in the late first and second century,[15] continuing down even to the Holy Qur'an of Islam.[16] We can give Bauer his due in this connection: If the classical theory of heresy was one of morally perverse departure from a clear, full, and original deposit of doctrine, his "negative attack on the classical theory of heresy stands" even as his "positive reconstructions fall."[17] Orthodoxy and heresy, if we may use these terms loosely, were rather in contention from the beginning, just as their meanings were being defined along the way up to the present day. The real question then is which specific relation to Jesus "from the beginning" is it that becomes normative in the canonical New Testament? It "was the *creed* of Jesus' having been raised from the dead that was," Hultgren writes, citing Helmut Koester (an important scholar in Bauer's school) "'[the] central criterion of faith for the 'canonical writers' and the orthodox church.'"[18] This is to acknowledge, if not to concede, the fundamental point: there is no canonical access to Jesus other than by that narrative of His mission constructed retrospectively by the proclamation that He who was crucified as the Christ was nevertheless raised from death, divinely acknowledged as Son of God, and so present to help as saving Lord. This synthesis of primitive Christian convictions may be designated without anachronistic prejudice (as I shall use it in what follows) "early Catholicism," in the sense of the statement of Ignatius of Antioch, "Where there is Jesus Christ, there is the catholic church."

Why did it happen this way? Speaking as a historian and employing sociological insights from Clifford Geertz, Hultgren describes the emergence of a *generous orthodoxy*, a *"broad* stream" of early Catholicism that included the four familiar Gospels that are in some notable tension with each other yet "claimed that there were limits to diversity. . . . That stream did not consist simply of a collection of ideas guarded and perpetuated by a core of ecclesiastical leaders," as Bauer had polemically sketched second century bishop-theologians like Irenaeus of Lyons (the subject of chapter 4 below) as ecclesiastical tyrants. "Instead one can observe a succession of faith and life over time, a faith lived in working communities, capable of sustaining itself, while other expressions of Christian faith and life could not sustain themselves. . . . What emerged as orthodox was but the ecclesiastical validation of a broad stream of convictions and ways of living that had staying power." We can recall here the concept of "epistemic primacy" introduced in the previous chapter: Those beliefs have primacy on which the continued existence of a community depends. Such beliefs become "dogmas" when, to resolve a crisis of interpretation, the community defines its beliefs in a particular way in order that its founding story can continue to be told. The central conviction holding the broad stream within its banks and flowing forward from Nazareth and Jerusalem to form early Catholicism was that "Jesus—known to have been killed, but now considered living an exalted life—is confessed as the incomparable revealer of God and redeemer of humanity."[19] The creed of the resurrection of the Crucified was the hermeneutic by which the traditions about Jesus were remembered and ordered, because this creed possessed *epistemic primacy* in its demonstrated capacity to sustain the Christian community in recognizable continuity with Jesus as the Christ, the Son of God, in ways that Gnostic revisionism, indeed invention, did not.

Thus in this way the resurrection narrative of the crucified Jesus as the parable of God promising a future to all who repent and believe in Him, historically speaking, drove forward the formation of normative Christianity. In the following chapters we shall trace out these steps in the formation of canon with creed, that is, the grand Genesis-to-Revelation narrative of the origin and destiny of the world with plot synopsis and *drammatis personae* provided by the baptismal creed. These elements constitute the core components of primary Christian narrative theology. At the root of this development lie the resurrection narratives of the New Testament that portray the *bodily* resurrection of Jesus Christ, that is, that *link* the proclamation "He is not here. He is risen!" with Him whose life in mission of the kingdom of God brought Him to shameful death on the Roman gibbet.

The Chief Question: Resurrection as the Spirit's Narration

N. T. Wright has thoroughly scrutinized the *scandalous mistreatment* of the resurrection narratives in contemporary scholarship. The "dominant paradigm for understanding Jesus' resurrection . . . accepted in the worlds both of scholarship and of many mainline churches,"[20] Wright claims, does violence to the New Testament material and deviates as a result from the theological and hermeneutical intention of the cross and resurrection kerygma. Wright, it is important to note, is *not* arguing for the historicality of the resurrection event itself that in the nature of the case eludes scientific-historical method as do all acts of God that are perceived and understood only in faith, itself a divine effect. Rather he argues for the historicality of the Easter *reports* of the witnesses.[21] He is thus arguing, in other words, against a spiritualizing assumption inspired by modern, philosophical dualism (discussed at the beginning of this chapter), in the treatment of the resurrection narratives that denies in principle the narratability of resurrection. This modern assumption accords more with the theological and hermeneutical intentions of early docetism (from Greek *dokeo*, "to seem," which taught that Jesus only *seemed* to be a human body). Docetism denied the bodily resurrection—the very thing that the texts preserved as normative in the New Testament pointedly affirm. Like ancient docetism, this spiritualizing tendency of modern interpretation slights the Jewish context of belief in the resurrection of the body; it denies that Paul and other early Christians believed in bodily resurrection and rather conceived of resurrection as exaltation or ascension of the soul or spirit or personality to heaven; it maintains that the stories of the empty tomb and of seeing the risen Jesus developed only subsequently, or that whatever visions of the risen Jesus might have occurred were religious experience internal to the subject (that is, hallucinations); consequently it holds that whatever happened to the body of Jesus, it was neither resuscitated nor understood as "raised from the dead" "in the sense that the gospel stories, read at face value, seem to require."[22] "Why did early Christianity not only get under way at all, but tell this kind of story, without antecedent or obvious parallel?"[23] That is the question.

Wright is correct then to argue for the historical intention of the Easter narratives as testimony and report of the witnesses. Yet, as Wright would grant, in the nature of the case, the claim of the resurrection narratives is not mundane and simply historical. This is indicated by the fact that the historical claim of the reports—"The Lord is raised indeed!"—is tightly interwoven with extra-mundane motifs that purport to reveal God in His saving deed. The stories are regularly introduced with the announcement of peace that re-gathers the scattered and restores the guilty. Yet these motifs do so precisely by rendering the public *persona*[24] of Jesus through the gospel story of the reversal of His fate. The New Testament resurrection narratives cannot be taken without violence to this fundamental theological-christological intention as other than testimony to discovery of the vacated tomb and subsequent experience of Jesus as manifested alive in a *recognizable* form, that is, a *bodily* form. *Easter is a story to be told about what happened to Jesus' body-and-soul such that this body-and-soul can act anew as this same agent in the world*. That is the intention of the texts: to narrate the Risen One who had been crucified. But what can this mean?

What is "resurrection" that it can generate narrative? A narrative that in a brief course of time comes to tell not only of empty tomb and Easter appearance but thence the story of the antecedent coming of this Jesus in the flesh in fulfillment of Israel's expectation, yet only to end up forsaken on the cross by God and by man? A narrative that in turn can launch the inquiry of theology into the being of God for the creature, the sinner, the perishing? What is resurrection of the body?

In the previous chapter we introduced the thesis that the gospel, as the Easter word of God concerning His crucified Son, thus as the contingent genesis of theology in the church catholic, will entail a critique of the antecedent epistemology and revision of metaphysics. This happens by means of the resurrection narration of Jesus' story, which requires that our ordinary assumptions about knowing as also about the nature of reality suffer a reversal and new creation. This reversal is crucial. Otherwise, we shall be forced at length to think that the resurrection narratives are what need critique and revision by real knowledge of real nature. The divine judgment on Jesus is communicated to us in the gospel in order that we entrust ourselves to it, that is, to the promise of His reign as God's Son and our Lord and so of our justification before the Father on His account. Faith is not warm feelings in the heart about Jesus nor a decision of the will to follow Him nor an intellectual conviction about His authority, though faith includes all these elements. Faith in Jesus as the crucified and risen Son of God is primordially faith in the speech-act of God the Father on Easter morn and so in turn the speech-act of the risen Christ to disciples who had failed to follow, who had rather fled and denied: *Peace be with you!* In this witness of the Father to the Son and the Son to the Father on the earth, a public change of lordship transpires in history by the Spirit—the believer's coming to faith corresponds to God's reversal of Jesus' fate.

Thus *"the fact that dead people do not ordinarily rise is itself part of early Christian belief,* not an objection to it. The early Christians insisted that what had happened to Jesus was precisely something new; was, indeed, the start of a whole new mode of existence, a new creation. The fact that Jesus' resurrection was, and remains, without analogy is not an objection to the early Christian claim. It is part of the claim itself."[25] Not only is the finality of death in the prevalent understanding of reality embraced in Christian belief, then, but the corresponding perception in faith of the resurrection of Jesus as something new and without analogy is likewise embraced in Christian belief. The belief itself here—without analogy in history—means, as we shall see: "In fulfillment of his primal decision about his own being and identity, God becomes incarnate: not simply in a human nature or 'a human history,' but precisely by actualizing the particular history of Jesus Christ. . . . "Incarnation' can be ascribed only to Jesus Christ,"[26] that is, to the particular figure or public persona generated by the resurrection narrated. If this is the narrative, and this the theological claim it ultimately entails, all the more pressing our question: What is the unparalleled event, resurrection itself?

Resurrection as Event in the Life of God

Even though the Gospels are written "from faith for faith," when we meet Jesus in them we are not overwhelmed with proofs of His wisdom, goodness, and power that compel faith in Him as God's Son. The Jesus whom we meet in the Gospels is rather a disturbing figure. He invades the routine human world with a prophetic call for absolute change. The good things he does are profoundly disturbing acts of radical mercy that threaten to undermine all sense of law and order. It is not by accident that the Jesus of the Gospels collides with the Law—not merely "Jewish" law or "Roman" law but *the law of God* that judges and condemns as evil what is actually harmful to the creation. This conflict of the man of mercy with the law of God (note well, taken *not* as Torah's ethic, let alone "Jewish legalism," but rather *juridically* as a collision with God Himself acting to judge and reject what is sinful) creates an immense tension in the gospel story, when read theologically: Jesus, who calls us to follow Him in new obedience to God in an ethic of mercy, does not prove to be followable. He goes alone to an uncanny collision with God—yet, nonetheless, as we are clued in the baptism and transfiguration stories, at the same time as willed by God.

In fact, then, no one in the Gospel story succeeds in following Jesus all the way to the end, to the cross. All forsake him at the critical hour. Jesus' earthly life taken as his journey to the cross in putative obedience to God did not succeed in creating faith in Him but rather offense at His godforsaken end. He perished a messianic pretender, refuted; His God did not rescue Him nor send Elijah from heaven to deliver Him. He died accursed, to all eyes justly punished for the blasphemy of acting in God's name in ways subversive of God's judgment on sin, not least by making Himself out to be the Son of God with authority sovereignly to forgive. We have to acknowledge then that if we come to faith in this crucified Jesus as God's true Son, it will only be, as it was for the first Christians, on the basis of resurrection faith. That is to say, it is the divine act of the resurrection overcoming *this* fate of Jesus condemned and put to death for unlawful mercy with *another* fate that condemns that lawful condemnation that now makes possible for human beings to follow what previously had been *unfollowable*.

It is not difficult to demonstrate the foregoing claim. Think of Jesus' characteristic acts: table fellowship with sinners; healings and exorcisms often provocatively done on the day of Sabbath rest; the calling of disciples to complete devotion to His cause as if to God's—these acts led ultimately not to recognition but provoked opposition. Think also of Jesus' preaching and teaching: in striking parables He told the nearness of God's reign and so called to repentance and faith; He simplified drastically the law of Moses in the double love commandment, and with the same instinct for the essential expanded the commandment to include love of enemies. His proclamation of the loving care of the heavenly Father lavished unmerited mercy on all who penitently return to His waiting arms—but this teaching led not to joyful acceptance but to lethal rejection by all who are figured in the elder brother of Jesus' great parable, that is, those who could and did question the justice of lavish mercy. Who pays for this feast? By what right are gifts lavished on the one who squandered half the family's wealth? Jesus' acts and preaching thus had to raise the issue of His authority. The implication that He acted in the name of God as the Son of God (Mark 2:1-3:6 for the Synoptic tradition; John 5 and 8 for the Johannine tradition) and Lord of the Law constituted the blasphemy for which He was condemned to death by the Sanhedrin and crucified by the Romans as a messianic pretender. Jesus' public existence ended in disgrace, with the sign of mockery posted over His tortured and dying body: *King of the Jews*. Not only did His enemies taunt Him: His own betrayed Him, fled from Him, or denied Him. Jesus' earthly life did *not* create faith in Him as God's Son.

Indeed, this end of Jesus' earthly life at the cross rendered faith in Him *theologically* impossible, that is, according to the law of God as "the ancient doctrine of the Two Ways"[27] deriving from the curses and blessings of Deuteronomy 30, distinguishing and separating the accursed sinner from those blessed because they are just. Not just for Jews but also for the Jew Jesus and His Jewish disciples, and later also for the Jew Paul, the Torah is the revelation that constitutes the divine-human relation. In the mind of law-observant contemporaries, including Jesus Himself, Jesus' godforsaken death demonstrated in accordance with the Two Ways that God Himself had rejected Jesus and repudiated His acts, His teaching, and His claim. Jesus dies "accursed," as Paul, recalling his training as a Pharisee, rightly glosses (Gal 3:13).[28] An accursed Christ? That is the impossible paradox behind the jarring oxymoron "Christ crucified." The Gospels are surprisingly frank about this state of affairs. We can let an example from Luke stand for Mark, Matthew, and John in this connection. Upon Jesus' third passion prediction, Luke comments about the disciples, "But they understood nothing about all these things; in fact, what he said was hidden from them, and they did not grasp what was said" (Luke 18:34). This noncomprehension by the disciples during Jesus' earthly life of His prophecy of the death and resurrection corresponds to the words of the risen Christ to the two disciples on the road to Emmaus: "Then he said to them, 'Oh, how foolish you are, and how slow of heart to believe all that the prophets have declared! Was it not necessary that the Messiah should suffer these things and then enter into his glory?' Then beginning with Moses and all the prophets, he interpreted to them the things about himself in all the scriptures" (Luke 24:25-27). Accordingly, it is only the risen and present Jesus, crucified yet now becoming recognizable, who creates true faith and just so reveals to the very faith being created the divine necessity of Messiah's lonely way through sufferings and the cross. One could easily demonstrate the same pattern of thought in the other Gospels and Paul.

There are then at least three reasons why it is the resurrection of Jesus from the dead that establishes faith in Him as the Son of God. First, the identification of Jesus as a public figure in history is not complete until one sees how His message and action led fittingly to that shameful death on the cross. Literally, then, one cannot yet say that the so-called historical Jesus in His words or deeds is the Christ because *Jesus'* identity in history is not complete apart from His sufferings provoked by those words and deeds and His patiency (active suffering in faith, corresponding to agency, active love and hope springing from faith) in them. A striking illustration of this, we may here recall, is found in Mark 8, where midway through the gospel narrative Peter confesses that Jesus is the Christ. According to Mark, Jesus does not contradict Peter but immediately discloses to the disciples for the first time that He is going to David's city, not to seize the throne with the help of heavenly armies of angels, but instead to suffer and die. Peter takes offense at this and rebukes Jesus as if a devil had taken hold of Him. Jesus rebukes Peter with a counter-exorcism: "Get behind me, Satan!" Mark's point with this episode is that whatever we want to say christologically about Jesus cannot be true unless by the name Jesus we are *referring* to the One who, thinking not as human beings think but as God thinks, went on to Jerusalem and died on the cross. It is impossible prior to the actual performance of this obedience all the way to its ultimate conclusion to say who in history the man Jesus is. What if He had turned aside and so betrayed His own words and deeds? Would He then be the Christ? It is by owning His words and deeds in active suffering (patiency) for all He has said and done that He is the Son of God, the Christ, whom God His Father declared, as Luke's version of the temptation of Christ by Satan (Luke 4:1-13), reiterating in mockery at the crucifixion (Luke 23:35-43), makes especially clear.

Second, as already indicated, the theological scandal of the cross must be taken with full seriousness. Jesus' earthly life indeed put Him in jeopardy of blasphemy. The objection to Jesus' way of life is concisely expressed in Mark 2:7: "Why does this fellow speak in this way? It is blasphemy! Who can forgive sins but God alone?" That is indeed the question that Jesus' life and works raised, all the more so His death on the cross. In the context of the scriptural world in which both Jesus and His enemies lived, death on a cross could only mean that Jesus was forsaken and accursed by God. Paul the Apostle classically described this in Galatians 3:13: "Christ redeemed us from the curse of the law by becoming a curse for us—for it is written, 'Cursed is everyone who hangs on a tree.'" The cross, understood scripturally as God's publicly exhibited rejection of Jesus as Him who was made sin for us (2 Cor 5:21), *really* seals off any possibility of human faith in Jesus, unless the same God incorporates and moves beyond that rejection on Easter morn. According to the New Testament, Jesus really dies rejected by men *and by God.* As living Judaism has always maintained, it would be *against God* to believe in Jesus the crucified (were He not risen from the dead). *Faith in accursed Jesus' suffering the rejection of the very sin He had forgiven in God's name, in turn, is identical to the Easter faith that He is risen and so vindicated as God's Son for this very patiency of love.* That is the real—messianic—divide between living Judaism and faithful Christianity (which follows the gospel narrative) to the present day.[29]

Third, it follows from the foregoing that not only will faith in Jesus as the Son of God be determined by the resurrection, but the resurrection strictly defines what such divine Sonship could mean when it is predicated of the Crucified. Here we must think, as noted in passing above, of the Gospels' accounts of the testing of Christ's Sonship by Satan. Faith in Jesus as God's Son is not faith in Jesus' psychological processes (other than the fact that He, like us in every respect except sin, had them). It is not faith in Jesus' words or acts, taken in isolation from each other, nor above all taken in isolation from the destiny of death on the cross which those very words and deeds brought upon Him. In the light of Easter morn, Jesus' way to the cross signifies that Jesus is the One who loved God perfectly as His one true Son in the very particular and personal act of loving the ungodly, giving himself in their place, the righteous for the guilty, making His own the very sin that He has forgiven in His Father's name. The cross indicates that Jesus, out of love, so completely identified with sinners whom He had forgiven in God's name that He suffered separation from God in order to be rejected in their place. He is the One who forgave sinners, not by the wave of a magic wand that dissolved their guilt into thin air, but as the One who took upon Himself their burden of guilt and load of debt. He made Himself their ransom (Mark 10:45). Having brought God mercifully near to sinners and taken their hell, their separation, their rejection upon Himself personally, Jesus in faith left it to His Father to vindicate this love as His own. In this *ethically* radical *fulfillment* of the law by the self-giving love of the Son, the Father justly incorporates and henceforth moves beyond the lawful condemnation of the sinful to a new mercy. In this creative self-giving love, Jesus *is* the divine Son.

It follows from the foregoing that we can comprehend the resurrection of Jesus theologically when we say that in this event the God whom Jesus knew as His Father acknowledged the completed act of love for the unworthy in the crucified, dead, and buried Jesus *as His very own*.[30] The resurrection is *God's answer* to the question about who Jesus the crucified is, the One who was actually now dead, accursed "for our sins according to the scriptures" as already the earliest tradition has it (1 Cor 15:3). The foundation of Christian faith is not what we or the apostles think about Jesus, or even what Jesus thinks about Jesus, but what God His Father thinks about Jesus. The empty tomb is the sign of this divine decision, and the appearances of the risen and exalted Christ are revelations to us of it, namely, of a mysterious event that has transpired between Jesus and His Father by the Spirit, that is to say, within the very life of God.

Resurrection as Possibility in the Life of the World

Granted then that resurrection is to be understood first and foremost as a divine event, a mysterious occurrence within the life of God, the question remains what kind of event resurrection is in our space-time. Can it be regarded as a *causal* event in space and time that establishes Jesus as the Christ, God's Son, the world's atonement and reconciliation with God, as seems to be indicated in the ancient formula Paul employs in Romans 1:4? So Karl Barth (on his good days) contended: "The atonement is history. . . . To speak of it, we must tell it as history. To try to grasp it as supra-historical or non-historical truth is not to grasp it at all. It is indeed truth, but truth actualized in a history and revealed in this history as such—revealed, therefore, as history."[31] Or should resurrection be thought of as the noncausal disclosure of what antecedently is the case, as modern liberal theology prefers in various versions (in continuity with the Platonic doctrine of divine simplicity)? As Tillich put it, resurrection "expresses the eternal root of the New Being as it is historically present in the event Jesus the Christ,"[32] at length noting that the "New Being is not dependent on the special symbols in which it is expressed."[33] This difficult alternative has profoundly troubled theology. It is surely right, as we have just argued, to affirm with Jüngel that "Jesus' resurrection is not an 'intervention' of God into the world's structures, which then leaves behind a new fact within the world, but does not affect the being of God."[34] A mere intervention would be no more than a resuscitation, restoring Jesus to the status quo ante, not the vindication and exaltation to lordship by which God determines Himself in relation to us. Moreover, such a mere intervention would only provide an artificial comic ending to the otherwise tragic story of Jesus' end by means of a *deus ex machina*, rather than, as Jüngel rightly affirms, God's own costly self-definition: "In the resurrection of Jesus, the issue is not only one of divine action, but of the divine being itself."[35] Granted. But is it also a matter of divine action in the world? What kind of thing is that?

It is by no means an evasion here to invoke again the venerable notion of the *mysteries* of faith to invoke a proper reticence in this connection. As the causal act of God alone, resurrection is of a type that admits in principle of no natural, intra-mundane explanation, unlike many other actions in the world that God does in cooperation with created nature, where God's hand must be critically discerned in the providential weaving of events rather than in their merely natural mechanism. In the providential ordering of nature to the purposes of grace, God works by natural means; in this sense, even the wondrous works attributed to angels and demons in Scripture are natural events (since angels and demons are creatures too), even if beyond immediate human power or comprehension. By contrast, miracles in the strict sense are the mysteries reserved to God alone that serve strictly as demonstrations of the freedom of the creator God's love wisely to initiate new possibilities of grace beyond the orderly, lawful, natural processes that He Himself instituted and preserves. This kind of divine action is constitutive of nature and is designated *creatio ex nihilo* (creation out of nothing), as in Romans 4:17. In this regard, resurrection as new act of creation within the creation is akin to the origination of the world out of nothing that first constituted this natural order of space-time or, again as in Romans 4, the justification of the ungodly. Resurrection belongs then to the essentially mysterious deeds that God reserves to Himself alone and whose glory God shares with no other. Like the birth from the Virgin that initiates Jesus' coming into the world, the resurrection from death after His natural life's end is to be taken as such a singular deed of the almighty creator, not the creature, to be received with praise and thanksgiving, not comprehended by analysis. This reception acknowledges that the true God has possibilities beyond what we can know or even imagine.

Indeed, never, not in all eternity will we understand how God creates, be it in the origin of the world, in the conception of Jesus by the Virgin and His resurrection from the dead, or in making sinners newborn children of God. God is God and we are not, and the mysteries of Christian faith designate this border. Our natural science will never bridge this gap but rather meets its limit here. As an act that belongs exclusively to God's infinite scope of possibilities, we cannot ask scientifically how resurrection is possible nor deny that it is possible scientifically. If we could, God in His own singular deed would be treated as nature, subject to our scrutiny and ultimately our control. If we could so comprehend the resurrection, we would then be gods over God, just as in fact in our science we are gods in principle, though not in power over nature. But if we understood how God creates, we could at least in principle do the same, and there would then be no principled difference between God and us. That can never be. There is an ontological barrier here between the natures of creator and creature that can never be crossed, though creator and creature can in the concrete way of Jesus Christ graciously share or participate in each other's conditions and properties.

If these events are the divine events Christian faith believes them to be, they are not natural events at all, even though they take place in nature and are manifested as effects in nature. As they are divine events, God imparts and reveals Himself in them not least as the almighty Father, creator of heaven and earth, of all things visible and invisible, who spins the galaxies on His fingertips, who called the world into being out of nothing, yet who forgives sins, wipes the tears from our eyes, and imparts His own life to the dead, taking on human flesh and living a human life, by this means giving His Spirit that we become in Jesus the children of God and heirs of resurrection life. Such mysteries inform us. They have a cognitive function, as in Romans 4. They tell us what it means to believe in God, who has possibilities beyond what we know or even imagine. If we believe in God at all, we believe that with human beings some things are impossible, but with God all things are possible. Of course, not all things possible are fitting. Not all things possible are wise. Not all things possible are just. But with God all things are possible, and by raising Jesus from death and in this particular way establishing Him who befriended sinners as Christ and Lord, God wisely and justly finds the way to reach all in whose solidarity Jesus died, to grasp them and hold them fast in Jesus and so to bring them to Himself, delivering them by the same Spirit who raised Jesus from the dead from the lethal egocentricity in which they are captive. The mystery of resurrection unveils God's almighty power at work in this wise and good way.

The significance of the mysteries is to disclose to faith—in the very act of eliciting faith—the self-determination of God to be our God by grace. The signature of God is creation out of nothing,[36] and strictly speaking all the mysteries are of this nature: the origin of the universe, the conception of Jesus in the Virgin's womb, the justification of the ungodly, and the resurrection of the dead. These latter mysteries are acts of creation within creation and so function as deliverance to faith in the gracious God beyond all exhausted human and natural possibilities. As such, they create and sustain faith in His coming reign. Biblical faith depends causally on the time-space manifestation of these divine mysteries as effective signs, in the theological sense, of the self-demonstration of the creator's power, wisdom, and love coming from beyond immanent space and time.

By that very token, then, we are not dealing here with magic tricks or occult powers that human beings can dream up or perhaps discover and put to work but with God powerfully seeking, finding, and winning human beings to Himself, just as the resurrection gospel is the power of God to save those who believe. Just so, it is the great joy and a special human dignity that believers do come to understand *why* (though not *how*) God does what He does, that in Christ we know and have the mind of God in the sense of fathoming His purposes with us. It is the glory of human beings to understand *why* God does what He does, in faith understanding that these mysterious acts of divine power are fitting, just, good, and wise. God is all-powerful, Christian faith understands, to give gifts that seek from us one thing only: praise, thanksgiving, new hearts full of adoration in new lives of joyful service. For in Jesus Christ, born of the Virgin to die godforsaken on the cross in our place, yet risen from the dead and revealed as God's own Son, God over and above all temporal gifts has given us His very own self, that is to say, a share in His own eternal life, the life of the Trinity. Why the birth from a virgin? Why Jesus? Why death on a cross and then resurrection from that ignominious end? God aims to liberate our human nature from the needy, greedy egocentricity into which it has fallen and is held captive and to re-create it in the image of the self-giving Jesus, the New Adam. Even though showing this kind of love in our needy, greedy world brought Jesus to the cross, Jesus sealed His divine Sonship by giving Himself there in our place, the innocent for the guilty, the author of life for the dead. By this self-donation, all the sin of the world was buried with Him and left forever in the oblivion of the tomb when God powerfully raised Him from death to His exalted new life. That is why God does things in this way, so that by the same Holy Spirit who once caused Jesus to be conceived in the Virgin's womb and then again caused Him to rise from the grave, we too may be born anew, rising from spiritual death to live new lives to God. That is why God does what He reveals Himself doing in Jesus Christ by the Spirit.

So a causal claim *is* involved, even though it is nothing so meager as an ad hoc intervention. What we have just seen in the foregoing analysis is that the initial formulation of the problem as choice between resurrection as God's causality and resurrection as noncausal disclosure of what antecedently availed has to be reformulated when we speak concretely of God in the trinitarian way. As God's judgment about the dead and accursed Jesus, the resurrection is *the Father's* speech-act recognizing anew in the Crucified One His own beloved Son on whom He breathed His Spirit. Divine causality in the world is parsed the trinitarian relations, not simply by the classical philosophical binary of divine action opposed to creaturely passivity. There is rather obedience and humility in the life of God, a patiency and mutual forbearing that is integral to divine power when power is also at the same time an exercise of divine wisdom and divine love. "What marks out God above all false gods is that they are not capable and ready for this. In their otherworldliness and supernaturalness and otherness, and so on, the gods are a reflection of human pride which does not bend, which does not stoop to that which is beneath it. God is not proud. In His high majesty He is humble. It is in this high humanity that He speaks and acts as the God who reconciles the world to Himself."[37]

Trinitarian or not, however, this great biblical miracle of the resurrection, taken as a causal claim on which the validity of the proclamation of Jesus as the Son of God depends, is greeted with incredulity by the modern mind—not least because a *false* appeal to miracles as if to evidence that should persuade the neutral observer provokes justified incredulity. Cheesy apologetics in the form of "evidence that demands a verdict" confirms nothing but the suspicions of the closed mind of unbelief. But it is on theological grounds that theology has to reject the tacit assumption that the primary function of biblical miracles is to convince supposedly neutral observers with physical evidence. Jesus consistently rejects requests for a sign to validate His ministry. This reserve about miracles as proof to skeptics is also true of the resurrection. The Risen One appears only to chosen witnesses. Strictly speaking, we in turn can only believe the testimony of these witnesses to the Risen One.

On the other hand, the apodictically closed mind of contemporary disbelief in the God who gives life to the dead is no doubt grounded to some extent in a scientific dogmatism that a priori excludes the very concept of divine action in history because in spiritual pride it will not allow to God possibilities other than the human mind can imagine—as we have seen, one aspect of the very thing that miracles taken as mysteries demonstrate for faith. This mind closed to the almighty power of God is actually in a stance of metaphysical naturalism, which is its own kind of dogmatism.[38] Biblical faith has little choice but to contradict metaphysical naturalism, just as it contradicts theological voluntarism, on both scientific and theological grounds: with the God of the gospel all things are possible (Mark 10:27; 14:36). He is God who gives life to the dead and calls into being things that are not (Rom 4:17-22), summoning "an exodus from the sphere of the calculable into horizons opened up by the word, namely, the horizons of a future under the saving will of God. . . . Faith arises over the graves of natural possibilities."[39] To believe at all in God the almighty Father, creator of heaven and earth, of all things visible and invisible, is to believe that God has possibilities infinitely beyond the finite set thus far actualized in the time-space of this world.

On philosophical grounds it has to be pointed out that naturalism is no more demonstrable than any other basic stance of "initial faith" (Richardson) that takes in view all of reality and is itself a kind of theology, namely, of fate, fortune, and luck, in today's lingo, random quantum fluctuation. Christian theology can further insist that contemporary cosmology is *not* tantamount to such metaphysical naturalism but rather newly poses the question about the creator of the creation. "Why does the universe go to all the bother of existing?" physicist Stephen Hawking asks. "Is the unified theory so compelling that it brings about it own existence? Or does it need a creator, and if so, does He have any other effect on the universe? And who created Him?"[40]

What causal function, then, have the biblical mysteries, which certainly do disclose in true light what had already been the case though hidden (crucified Jesus is the Son of God), but only by causing as an effect that true light to shine in the darkness (God raised Him from death)? Faith understands itself to be faith by means of the mysteries disclosing this free creator God's decision and act, not faith in faith, that is, fideism, let alone in miracles separated from this theological function that would be sheer superstition. At issue in acknowledging the mysteries is strictly the conception of God as God to whom all things are possible; what is involved in claiming by faith the time-space reality of God's sole causality in these mysteries as divinely caused effects is that faith too is itself caused in this very act of apprehending the mystery as God's own. Faith is not a human power but the work of the third of the gospel three, the Holy Spirit, who calls believers into union with Jesus, into His own relation to His Father, into His obedience of faith, into the mystery of the resurrection of the dead.

Pannenberg faults Barth for failing against his own best intentions to transcend the circle evident in the foregoing account and thus remaining trapped in human consciousness and its religious experience: If I can appeal only to faith, itself a miracle, as the basis for the miracle of Easter, then I beg the question of whether faith is actually caused by something external to the self. But I do not see that this is a real problem, unless one aspires theologically to the universal science of God as the unity of all experience, as Pannenberg in fact does. Then there is an objectivity to miracles that really is independent of the stances of faith or disbelief. But if theology adopts the kind of pragmatist perspectivalism that I have urged,[41] disbelief in miracles is also a kind of divine judgment and effect—precisely *not* the self-securing skepticism the disbeliever imagines. "As you believe, so you have" (Luther). But this entails a Holy Spirit who blows where He wills, indeed who can, as needs of the kingdom require, just as readily harden Pharaoh's wicked heart as melt the heart of stone in Saul of Tarsus. In any case, it is important theologically to emphasize the correlation between change in reality and change in the one who understands the changed reality. Faith is not a subjective opinion or value judgment of humans but is also a mysterious divine effect: the changed perspective caused in apprehending reality changed by the resurrection of the Crucified and the proclamation of this news in space and time.

Resurrection as Reality in the Life of the World

In any case, all this so far does not amount to an argument for the factuality of the Easter miracle or its actual causality in space-time, only its possibility. For this latter there are further problems, not concerning the objectivity of miracles, as per Pannenberg, but concerning the *fittingness* of miracles, that is, the wisdom and goodness of actualizing such possibilities. Does forcing a "happy ending" by a miracle do an injustice to unhappy suffering that preceded? Is it wise to jeopardize the regularity of nature by an event without analogy? How could we ever understand a miracle as something truly good and truly wise, as *fitting*, not merely or solely as *powerful?* To recognize a deed as God's creative act alone, we would have recognize it not only as powerful but also as good and wise. Otherwise it is just a strange, unexplained event, like a UFO.

In this light, the real problem we have today with resurrection faith is not the dogmatism of the atheists or the seemingly slight historical evidence of the biblical testimony but the *unintelligibility* of the concept of resurrection itself, especially among Christians. One of the chief motives for the popularity of the idea of a noncausal resurrection as disclosure of who Jesus really was all along is the contemporary sense of the unintelligibility of resurrection as a causal event. The problem here is not whether resurrection is abstractly possible, as previously discussed, or whether the causal resurrection of Jesus is historically probable, for which Wright argues, but what the notion could possibly mean. Is it the revival of a corpse, like that of Lazarus in John 10? But Lazarus died again. Is it a symbol of the immortality of the soul or the appearance of a ghost? Biblical accounts resolutely reject such a proto-docetic interpretation (for example, Luke 24:39). Is it, then, the metamorphosis of Jesus' corpse into a new kind of being—the "spiritual body" of which Paul speaks in 1 Corinthians 15? But what is that? What kind of existence has the risen Christ, who passes through locked doors yet eats fish and has Thomas trace His wounds only then to vanish away? Who appears to Peter and Paul and many others but never to the general public, and whose appearances cease after some time in favor of his eucharistic promise of presence as the One crucified for us in His own body and blood? How can such a being be the same person as Jesus of Nazareth? How do these two fit together? Why would such identity matter? This is the really difficult question of intelligibility that, I will now argue, provides the acid test for the recognition of the Easter mystery as an act of exclusive divine causality in history. Indeed, much of modern liberal theology is motivated by insisting upon this difficult but crucial question, though for theological purposes other than my own.

The Nestorian tendency of contemporary liberal theology (that is, to separate the historical Jesus and the risen one, or Jesus and the Christ, or the son of Mary and the Son of God) thinks of the resurrection as a disclosure myth created to express the conviction of the disciples that Jesus, as they already knew Him, could not really have died and disappeared. "The belief in the Resurrection is an early Christian form of expression, a form of expression conditioned by its environment, for the authority Jesus had attained over these people. Today we shall not be able to regard this form of expression as binding on us. But the authority of Jesus that this form of expression wishes to convey can very well be binding on us."[42] Thus "resurrection" expressed their conviction of faith that Jesus' authority as previously experienced continues for them despite His apparent defeat on the cross. The resurrection does not create faith, according to this reconstruction; the resurrection expresses faith that has been previously created by their ordinary human and historical experience of the man Jesus, now "overcoming," as Bultmann often said, "the scandal of the cross." This critical insight is necessary to us today, so it is argued, because otherwise naive resurrection faith mythologizes Jesus of Nazareth, making Him inaccessible to us as a real, historical, vulnerable, and fallible person like us, a creature of His own day and age but One who, if only we can recover authentic experience of Him, can still inspire us to follow Him. The naïve resurrection myth, taken literally, transforms Jesus into a divine being to whom we cannot relate. So one must critically deconstruct the mythical form of faith in the Risen One and try to rediscover the historical Jesus, who is and always was the real inspiration of faith that follows Him in deeds, not dogmas.[43]

It is important, as previously noted, to allow that these critical questions of liberal theology are provoked by the biblical testimony of the resurrection narratives, which on examination inspire such incredulity. What is this event that no one ever saw, that transforms the crucified Jesus into the omnipresent heavenly Lord? How can an empty tomb establish faith in a resurrection, since, even assuming such was the case on the third day, it can be explained in a multitude of ways? Indeed, for many in liberal theology, the hypothesis has suggested itself that the idea of resurrection originated as an *inference* (Marxsen) from the chance event of the loss of Jesus' body (crudely: "The dogs got it"—Crossan). The traumatic loss of the body then induced hallucinations of seeing Jesus alive among the female devotees, beginning with Mary Magdalene (Schillebeeckx). The concept of resurrection was available and seized upon to explain these happenings. So many modern critics have suggested on the basis of close, critical reading of the resurrection narratives. Resurrection is not the foundation of faith but an inference drawn by faith—and not a benign one at that.

The power of such critical questions is immense, as anyone who knows the history of the last two hundred years of Protestant theology can attest. If we take the biblical testimony in isolated pieces and try to make it answer questions posed from other frames of reference, the foregoing analysis becomes inevitable. As disturbing as this line of questioning is, however, we should not at all resist it. For it requires us to ask the truly important question of what kind of conceptual frame would be needed for the notion of *resurrection-generating narrative* to become intelligible, such that all the previously mentioned elements—Jesus' teaching and works, destiny on the cross, vindication by God, reign as Lord, sending of the Spirit, creation of faith and mission—all these cohere in a single though complex event: the beginning of the reign of God in the *body* of Jesus.[44] As Wolfhart Pannenberg so acutely argued against the basic premise in liberal theology in his *Jesus: God and Man*:

> There is no reason for the assumption that Jesus' claim to authority taken by itself justified faith in him. On the contrary, the pre-Easter Jesus' claim to authority stands from the beginning in relationship to the question of the future verification of his message through the occurrence of the future judgment. . . . Thus has been shown the proleptic structure of Jesus' claim to authority. . . . This means, however, that Jesus' claim to authority cannot by itself be made the basis of a Christology, as though this involved only the "decision" in relation to him. Such Christology— and the preaching based upon it—would remain an empty assertion. Rather, everything depends upon the connection between Jesus' claim and its confirmation by God.[45]

This connection turns on the fate of Jesus' body (and soul), in that He who freely (or blasphemously) forgave sins then bore those sins in His body on the tree. No human act of faith overcomes the abyss of the cross, on which Jesus died godforsaken, His body buried. Only God can overcome the judgment of the cross with a new possibility, for in its depth that judgment on sin that Jesus endured as His own in bodily (and spiritual) death is God's own judgment—just as the sin Jesus bore was real sin, even if it was not His own doing that incurred guilt but ours. If the resurrection is taken as a disclosure myth created by the disciples, Paul wrote to the Corinthians, faith is futile and we are still dead in our sins and his own apostolic preaching is found to be *false*, misrepresenting God by commending faith in an authority that was never justified and in a vindication of its claim that never occurred (1 Cor 15:12-19). Resurrection as noncausal disclosure event then is a false faith, either a faith in Jesus' way of life that is in fact ultimately hopeless or a faith against God who rejected Jesus. In either case, we would be wrong to recommend a false faith. If the resurrection is the believer's expression in mythical form of his or her own overcoming of the scandal of the cross, the historical Jesus proves to be an *especially* illusory basis of faith.

So much for the solution of liberal theology: "The Jesus of Nazareth who came forward publicly as the Messiah, who preached the ethic of the Kingdom of God, who founded the Kingdom of Heaven on earth, and died to give His work its final consecration, never had any existence. He is a figure designed by rationalism, endowed with life by liberalism, and clothed by modern theology in an historical garb."[46] Albert Schweitzer was right to reduce the argument of liberalism to absurdity: in the grip of fanatical messianic pretensions, Jesus' imperious "forcing of eschatology into history is also its destruction; its assertion and abandonment at the same time."[47] In other words, Jesus was wrong and resurrection as so-called disclosure event perpetuates His error. The so-called historical Jesus proves even more elusive than the risen Jesus who had been crucified.

Nevertheless, the question remains of the intelligibility of the concept of resurrection as an event in space and time. Liberal theology's attempt to found faith on a "historical Jesus" is no solution to the very real problem of the intelligibility of predicating resurrection of Jesus. What is resurrection? How does it purport to establish true faith in Jesus from Nazareth who was crucified as the Christ, the Son of God? We have argued that resurrection amounts theologically to an assertion of exclusive divine causality, also in our perception of the crucified Jesus as alive and present through the gospel to be for us who He was. The word *resurrection* is itself a metaphor for a *singularity*, a unique, unprecedented event of new creation within creation. The metaphor is built upon the ordinary experience of arising from sleep. As one arises in the morning from bed, so Jesus rose from the grave where His corpse had been laid. If we ask the New Testament, however, to depict for us that singularity of the body-and-soul rising, we are greeted with complete silence. No one in the New Testament witnesses the act of the resurrection itself; people are informed of the event as "resurrection" by angelic messengers and then confronted with its reputed consequences. What transformation occurred is not depicted, described, or explained. This indicates, as already mentioned, that the event of the resurrection is something that transpires divinely, that is, between Jesus and God, and so must remain veiled in mystery, even though it happens in the world. What the witnesses in the New Testament encounter are, strictly speaking, only consequences of the unseen event itself. These considerations lead us into the heart of the problem for understanding.

Hans Conzelmann, a sophisticated adherent of the Bultmann school, wrote that the resurrection "is regarded by the church as an event in space and time (cf. the list of witnesses in 1 Cor 15:3) . . . [Yet for us today] history cannot establish the facticity of the resurrection. It can only establish that men testified that they had seen Jesus alive after his death." So far, so good. But Conzelmann then continued: "With this the assertion that the resurrection is not a historical event must be adhered to quite clearly. The assertion implies that theology can postulate no historical facts (*Tatsachen*) and does not need to do so, since it lives by proclamation . . . The object of faith appears only to faith itself. Revelation is not 'facts laid out before a person'; it emerges— today—in the word."[48] In other words, even though the unreflective early church thought of resurrection as an event capable of narrative attestation, and actually thus told the story of empty tomb and Jesus' Easter appearances as events in history, they did so as witnesses of faith in a word that is itself not historical. For us today and on critical examination this nonhistorical "Word alone" must suffice.

Thus we have to note a fundamental ambiguity in the way the Reformation slogan about the sole efficacy of the divine word has come to be used. It referred to the externality and newness of the message of the resurrection of the Crucified as the Word that God alone can and does speak, sovereignly effecting in the ungodly the resurrection to faith. This is the *verbum externum* in the Reformation sense. But the slogan as such has come to be pitted against human speech and language, the natural means and physical instruments that the divine Word employs to speak of the resurrection of the Crucified, as if to exclude the office of the keys, the ordained ministry, the sacraments, and the conversation and consolation of believers as the means by which the Spirit speaks the Word. This latter usage is a post-Kantian development, which I shall hence indicate by setting the slogan in scare quotes thus, "Word alone." Conzelmann is right, then, insofar as faith is the creature of God's word, which is the divine speech-act that demands what it gives and gives what it demands. The announcement of the resurrection of Jesus by the Word resurrects the auditor to faith (or seals the door of the tomb over unbelief). But leaving the matter this way is misleading. Strictly speaking, the Gospels tell us that the disciples had no clear idea or expectation of resurrection as a possibility for the crucified Jesus on the third day (Mark 9:10) but that it came to them as news from God "on the third day"; that is, it was the angelic messenger who provided the clear sense and application of the singularity, "resurrection," to the crucified Jesus, in this way acting by the Word alone. Precisely as such the Word alone *narrates*: "See the place where they laid. . . . He is going ahead of you to Galilee. There you will see him, just as He told you" (Mark 16:6-7). Thus it is misleading to conclude that the "relationship of faith to the historical Jesus can only be a specific punctiliar one. The single historical fixed point is in fact the naked 'that' of the existence (*Dagewesenheitsein* [literally, the being of having existed]) of Jesus (in agreement with Bultmann)."[49] The "historical objectivizing" that Conzelmann consequently denies in the resurrection narratives is exactly what the resurrection narratives do go on to provide. The relation of faith in Christ to Jesus who was crucified is something theologically more than the punctiliar presupposition of Jesus' mere existence, *das Dass* (the That) of His coming. There is bodily continuity, howsoever transformed this body is. To understand resurrection itself, then, we have to understand how it generated narratives about this body (and soul).

These are of two distinct types: memories of the discovery "on the third day" of the empty tomb and the various appearances of the risen Lord who

identifies Himself as Jesus of Nazareth in the period of time up to and including the experience of the Pharisee Saul of Tarsus on the road to Damascus. We
need not here delve into the complex history of these traditions, which biblical
scholars have done in detail. For our purposes it suffices to point out that these
two distinct traditions have complementary theological tendencies. The tradition about the discovery of the empty tomb on the third day emphasizes the
personal, indeed bodily, continuity between the crucified, dead, and buried Jesus
and the risen Lord. Whatever the risen Lord is, He has taken the place (thus in
space and time) of the dead body that was entombed. On the other hand, the
traditions about the appearances of the risen Lord to a variety of persons (1 Cor
15:3-8) stress the unprecedented transformation that has occurred. Jesus has
become the exalted, glorified Lord who appears at will from heavenly exaltation
manifesting divine power and authority. Jesus' presence in time and space is no
longer bound by the limitations of time and space; He sits at God's right hand,
that is, participates in God's omnipresent and almighty power. He is the exalted
Lord over all, the glorious figure who appears in Revelation 1:12. This does not
preclude His appearing in time and space as the One who He was and remains
but rather enables it: the Coming One who is at hand to help as promised.

The cosmological frame of reference that makes sense of this resurrected
existence derives from the prophetic and apocalyptic traditions of Israel,
which prophesy the establishment of the kingdom of God as the resolution
to the painful riddle of human history. The expectation of the resurrection of
the dead is a product of the prophetic faith and experience of martyrdom. It
was never based on any kind of devaluation or degradation of historical life.
Quite the contrary, it rather gave ultimate significance to what one does in the
body: one's eternal destiny depends on whether one bows down to the idol or
not. That is how filled with significance this bodily life is! Resurrection faith
is the faith of the martyrs of Yahweh who will not bow down to idols and do
obeisance to them. It is their faith that, although tyrants and satanic usurpers
can destroy their bodies in the present epoch, the Lord Yahweh will shortly
reveal His reign by raising His saints from death and exalting them over their
enemies. Indeed, in this very act the Lord Yahweh will reveal His deity to the
hostile nations, overthrow oppression, and show that He is the true God who
has power over death and establishes righteousness. Thus the resurrection of
the dead is the beginning of the reign of God. This vindication of the martyr
(the obedient witness to God in the time of trial) and his exaltation to rule
(as the coming judge of the living and the dead) is the original framework of
meaning behind the proclamation of the resurrection of the martyred Jesus.

Resurrection, for the earliest Christians, is thus closely related to the idea
of Jesus' exaltation as Lord, reversing the preceding story of humiliation (as
in Phil 2). Jesus who suffered as herald of the reign of God has now become
the agent of the reign of God, the Lord to whom the Lord has committed

his cause (as Paul thinks in 1 Cor 15:24-28). The idea is not at all that Jesus returns to life as before but that Jesus' personal identity is completely constituted by His filial obedience in the span from birth to death. It is in and as this body that Jesus is *as such* vivified with God's own eternal life, vindicated against the world that rejected him, and appointed the Lord over all as the One whom all will *see* at last in final judgment. So Peter preaches in an early sermon in Acts, "Therefore let the entire house of Israel know with certainty that God has made him both Lord and Messiah, this Jesus whom you crucified" (2:36). Resurrection faith is faith that Jesus has *been made* the Lord, so that in Him in whom the reign of God began on earth the kingdom comes at last in fullness and power. Consequently, there is no inferential leap to be made from the empty tomb and the visions of the glorified Jesus to the notion of a resurrection and divine Sonship "in a metaphysical sense."[50] On the contrary, the vision of the glorified Jesus is precisely what resurrection meant in its original frame of reference, the *novum* (the new and distinct thing) being rather its exclusive application to Jesus. Jesus' resurrection and the predication of His divine Sonship give equivalent expression to the in-breaking reign of God, as is visible in the traditional formula Paul appears to cite in Romans 1:3-4 (which does not presuppose the preexistent Son becoming incarnate, as Paul does in Phil 2). Here Käsemann rightly notes: "The gospel can present as its object the way of the earthly Jesus to his exaltation and enthronement, as Mark did in his own manner with his concept of the messianic secret. The path is thus prepared here for the writing of the gospels." Resurrection evokes gospel narrative.

In that case, the misunderstanding of the earliest Christians was almost the precise opposite of what liberal theology imagines. The earliest Christians inferred from their experience of the glorified Jesus that the general resurrection had begun, that Jesus as man had pioneered the way before them. They believed that the cosmic finale was about to unfold. Jesus was only momentarily held in heaven. At any moment, He would return on clouds of great glory to conquer God's enemies, gather the saints, and return the dominion of the earth to Yahweh, His Father. With the gradual realization that the imminent end of history had not begun, Christians began all the more to realize the implications of the uniqueness of Jesus' vindication. Jesus is *the only One* who has been raised from death's grip. We must still die and decay in the grave. But as He who once suffered and died on the cross and is now exalted as Lord, *this One is singular, unique.* He alone has been raised from the dead because He is the One who suffered and died for all. Thus in its *exclusive* predication of the crucified Jesus, resurrection increasingly underscores this *single* human being's identity as *without analogy*, that is, as the incarnation of God in a human life. That is what in fact quickly came about in primitive Christianity as a result of the *exclusive* predication of "resurrection" to the crucified Jesus: the telling of His story in the light became the story of incarnation of the Word.

Resurrection's Retroactive Causality

Pannenberg unpacked this difficult notion of a retroactive insight that is nevertheless theologically valid: while God from eternity may be understood to have intended to become incarnate as Jesus, crucified and risen, "the truth of such an assertion is dependent upon the temporal actuality of the thing. . . . What is true in God's eternity is decided with retroactive validity only from the perspective of what occurs temporally with the import of the ultimate. Thus, Jesus' unity with God—and thus the truth of the Incarnation—is also decided only retroactively from the perspective of Jesus' resurrection for the whole of Jesus' human existence. . . . Apart from Jesus' resurrection, it would not be true that from the very beginning of his earthly way God was one with this man. That is true from all eternity *because* of Jesus' resurrection."[51] The future causes its past. *Because* Jesus is risen, He *was* the *hidden* Son—whether Jesus knew it or not! It is His Father's judgment that causes Jesus to be the Son whom He is, was and always will be. Even if Jesus did already know this (as, per a historical judgment, I think He did), nevertheless His true death in obedience to the Father still threatened loss of self, loss of identity also as the Son. As Pannenberg stresses, "One could speak differently only by depriving the event of its contingency, of its element of newness."[52]

But resurrection generates this dramatic narrative of Jesus' way from the testing in the wilderness by Satan to the agony in the garden, not in the sense of disclosing Jesus' developing self-consciousness but rather in the sense of the public ordeal of His obedience in contest with Satan's testing. Here Jesus' very Sonship is at stake. Quoting an early Christian hymn, Paul says in Philippians 2:8-9, "He humbled himself and became obedient to the point of death—even death on a cross. *Therefore* God also highly exalted him and gave him the name that is above every name." Of course, this hymn is speaking "mythically" not of the human Jesus' Easter exaltation to divine Sonship but of the preexistent heavenly Son's descent, who became incarnate and obedient; yet that "mythical" speech is justified retroactively, as we have just seen, because from eternity "God is the ultimate subject of the human action and passion which comes to pass in [Jesus' history], because that history 'is there' only in virtue of God's immediate presence."[53] The son of Mary and the Son of God prove to be one and the same persona. Jesus *is* the Son of God.

Therefore early Christians increasingly concluded—under the promised guidance of the Spirit to lead to all truth, we should say—that Jesus had always been this unique person. He was from His conception in Mary's virgin womb the incarnate Son of God, though His glory and deity were hidden in the days of His flesh. The discovery of the empty tomb fixed Easter faith in the exalted Christ strictly on Jesus of Nazareth, that body (and soul) that was crucified, dead, and buried under Pontius Pilate. In time this identification of Jesus as the

Christ, the Son of God, led to the realization that what had happened in Jesus' life and death was from the beginning of His earthly existence, indeed from before the creation of the world, the intended and now actualized incarnation of the eternal Son of God. That is to say that the person of Jesus disclosed in His gospel work is indiscernible from the Lord God's own eternal and personal self-expression, the Logos, the eternal Word. Resurrection issues at length in the confession of Jesus, bearing in His body the marks of nail and spear, "My Lord and my God!" (John 20:28).

Who He is and what He has done for all must now be told to all—"The kingdom will not come until the gospel is preached to all nations" (Mark 13:10). On the basis of this deeper insight into His Person, early Christians also began to realize that the risen Lord was summoning them to a mission to the nations in analogy to Jesus' mission to the lost sheep of the house of Israel during His earthly days. *Pentecost* is the name of this realization: the sending of the Spirit, the creation of the missionary church, and the mandate to proclaim Jesus to the nations. The author of Luke-Acts is the biblical theologian (whose writings constitute one-fourth of the New Testament) of this further development. This proclamation established a fellowship of love in Jesus' name that individuals entered through a ritual act of death and resurrection, signifying a complete transfer of allegiance (baptism). Believers were in the same way to be sustained in this new identity by a meal (Eucharist) that recalled Jesus' table fellowship with sinners and sacrificial death for them and at the same time anticipated the eternal feast of the messianic banquet. By new life in Christ the risen Lord, believers were summoned, enabled, and expected to break with the systematic violence of their civil and domestic environments and live as witnesses, even at the cost of martyrdom, of the messianic kingdom. Resurrection faith issues in such *practices* of reconciliation that constitute, as in Acts, the further history of the risen Lord Jesus in His people on earth. In all these ways resurrection issues in "historically objectivizing" narrative. The real *das Dass* is not the mere fact of Jesus' existence as the occasion of a nonhistorical "Word alone." It is the resurrection event of exclusive divine causality in reversing Jesus' fate and human perception of the same. The real theological task arising from this is not to demythologize the New Testament but rather to trace the effects of this cause in generating the gospel narrative and beyond in order to continue telling the story.

Bultmann's Objection

In a lengthy letter to Karl Barth written in November of 1952, Rudolf Bultmann acknowledged in response to a query of Barth's: "Yes, I purport to say that Christ (insofar as he is relevant to us) is the kerygma, because he is Christ only as Christ for me, and as such he meets me only in the kerygma. If he were not present in the event (of the kerygma and faith) he would be a mythical figure. And for this reason I regard christology and soteriology as a unity. Certainly Christ as God's act precedes my faith. The kerygma is *address* (*verbum externum*, external Word, *Ker. u. Myth.*, II, 204). But it does not follow from this that christology must precede soteriology in theological explication. Naturally it is easy to argue against me from the statements of the N[ew] T[estament], but only because the christological statements of the N[ew] T[estament] are clothed in the language of mythology which I want to strip off. Hence such arguments do not affect me at the basic level."[54] Any number of perplexing questions arise in understanding Bultmann's objections against resurrection narrative. For it is not only unclear how Christ as event for me remains external to me apart from relations of His own to the Father and the Spirit. It is also unclear how the One who exists only as Word for me is not also a "mythical figure" in the worst sense, that is, an ideological mystification of what may be critically exposed as merely human address in the church that pretends to speak in His name, but with neither historical nor theological justification. The "Word alone," it might seem, is assertion alone.

It might appear that the fulcrum of Bultmann's objection turns on the notion *presence*: to be relevant to us, to be "Christ for me" as event, Christ is equated with the kerygma, the contemporary announcement of God's saving act. Bultmann conceives any alternative to such kerygmatic presence as construction of a self-standing "mythical figure," and indeed several pages later criticizes a statement of Barth's in this way: "The statement that the first disciples beheld the 'glory' of the incarnate Word in a resurrection from the dead in time and space, that they saw this with their eyes, heard it with their ears, and touched it with their hands, I regard as sheer mythology nor does it seem to me to catch the real meaning of 1 John 1:1."[55] Clearly, however, since Barth too is concerned with the *Christus praesens* whom those first disciples attested by their antidocetic accent on touching and beholding, it cannot be presence as such, but the rendering of presence *as body* which is at issue between Barth and Bultmann. In Bultmann's view, Christ is rendered present when human consciousness is affected by contemporary proclamation in the same way as happened in Jesus' preaching[56] or in the early preaching of Jesus as the Risen One.[57] Christ is present in the reiteration of a Word-event effecting the same state of conciousness, albeit translated into contemporary thought forms with the help of the existentialist analysis; and this existential content can be known by historical exegesis informed by the best available anthropological theory that lifts up the underlying possibilities for existence from beneath the mythical garb it wears. The knowledge of what happened existentially to primitive believers in Christ can thus be mediated by the Word announcing what God has done, opening up, as Bultmann came to see it, the possibility of unsecured freedom of radical faith. Thus Christ as this existential possibility is rendered present by the "one bridge of the Word alone"—in an expression of Bultmann's disciple Gerhard Ebeling—"all other bridges have been broken up"[58] by refusal of the "mythical figure."

To press home this objection to resurrection narrated as a "mythical figure" in favor of narrative-free kerygma: in his famous essay on "demythologizing," Bultmann assembled a hodgepodge of verses, primarily from the apostle Paul, and presented them, consciously or not, as a parody of the second article of the Creed. This supposedly represents the "New Testament world-view" in which the "mythical figure" of Christ appears: "'In the fullness of time' God sent forth his Son, a pre-existent divine Being, who appears on earth as a man. He dies the death of a sinner on the cross and makes atonement for the sins of men. His resurrection marks the beginning of the cosmic catastrophe. Death, the consequence of Adam's sin, is abolished, and the daemonic forces are deprived of their power. The risen Christ is exalted to the right hand of God in heaven and made 'Lord' and 'King.' He will come again on the clouds of heaven to complete the work of redemption, and the resurrection and judgment of men will follow."[59] Bultmann now asked whether Christian preaching can "expect modern man *to accept this mythical view of the world as true*" and replied that it would be both "senseless and impossible" to do so, because "there is nothing specifically Christian in the mythical view of the world" and because no one "can adopt a view of the world by his own volition—it is already determined for him by his place in history."[60] This latter is indeed true, as is the general point that "modern man" thankfully no longer believes in ghosts. One might, however, pass right over the astonishing claim embedded in the passage. According to Bultmann, *there is nothing specifically Christian about the church's primary theology*—what Hans Frei a generation later called the "biblical narrative"[61] now "eclipsed" by the anthropological interpretation of the Bible Bultmann championed by means of existential analysis of the human condition.

In fact, as is well recognized today, Bultmann's notion of demythologization trades on equivocation. He uses the concept of myth in at least three logically distinct senses to designate (1) a prescientific animist worldview, (2) objectifying of the ineffable, and (3) analogous language for God. Depending upon the sense, Bultmann can say that myth is respectively (1) impossible in modern culture, (2) misleading representation, and (3) inevitable in the doxological life of the worshipping community as a kind of poetry.

The question, then, is whether the caricature of creedal faith Bultmann erected is really to be understood as either a prescientific "worldview" or "objectifying representation." These two are not the same, and objection to one is not the same as objection to the other. The mistake of sending someone with bipolar disorder to an exorcist is not the same mistake, along Kantian lines, of confusing the divine Word with its historically contingent vehicle. Only a pathological literalist would think that fidelity to Jesus as the Word made flesh equally entailed subscription to the popular demonological ideas of New Testament times. In fact, the only way "literally" to be faithful to Jesus would be to fly back in a science-fiction time machine and follow Him there where once He trod. Ever thereafter, and so from the very beginning, following Jesus is a matter of grasping the letter about Him as the Spirit intends, who also first led Jesus on His way to the cross. In this light, the supposed "error" of confusing the eternal and the temporal by objectifying representation may represent precisely those Spiritless epistemological and metaphysical views which, we are arguing, are rather critiqued and revised by the gospel narrative.

In that case, Bultmann is arguably wrong on both counts. The gospel narrative, we will argue, in fact functions to de-divinize the world, not animize it. It is not the gospel narrative that needs to be demythologized but the gospel narrative that demythologizes the powers and principalities. Moreover, in this prophetic critique of a cosmos that pretends to be eternal and immutable, the resurrection narrative's objective representation of the crucified and risen *body (and soul)* of Jesus does not stuff the divine into a box at human disposal, as the objection holds. The gospel narrative renders Christ present in His own divine agency and act of presenting, committing, promising Himself concretely and historically as the One who bore away sin in His body on the tree in order to bestow righteousness by sending His own Spirit to draw hearers and readers into His story to form His earthly body. In Bultmann's theology, however, Christ's real presence, for example, as in Luther's "joyful exchange," actually dissolves into sheer assertion ("Word alone" indeed), an empty event of kerygmatic declamation that may or may not touch individuals existentially but does not and cannot form them socially as church at work on the earth, making history. In identifying the eternally divine Word with its historically contingent vehicle—Jesus is *homoousios* with God; the man Jesus and the eternal Logos are one and the same *persona*—the resurrection narrative by contrast makes history of its own. So it provides for those whom it calls a new place-and-time in the world (the church and its practices of reconciliation), not merely a new "self-understanding" for individual decision within a world still dominated by forces other than the coming reign of God.

In his superb study of Bultmann, James F. Kay has unraveled the complicated background of Bultmann's repudiation of narrative identification of Christ in the collapse of the nineteenth-century quest of the so-called historical Jesus, as that was imagined along the lines of the Kantian doctrine of *Persönlichkeit*. Thinking of "personality" as moral character that resists natural inclinations stemming from the lower, animal, bodily condition, in order to perform moral duty, the nineteenth-century thinker thought of an "austere autonomy, independent of the mechanisms of nature, which marks beings as moral and spiritual, and thus as truly human. . . . the bearer of moral consciousness, standing upright, over against nature."[62] Seeking to re-found "faith" understood this way on the new recovery of Jesus' "personality," liberalism had been foundering by the time Bultmann's academic career took off. After World War I a civilization allegedly formed by the historical influence of Jesus' God-consciousness collapsed. At the same time, historical-critical advances in understanding the literary genre of the New Testament materials found no interest in Jesus' "personality" at any level of the traditions about Jesus. Bultmann the exegete had pioneered the form-critical investigation of the Synoptic tradition, which resolved the material into discrete units of tradition orally transmitted until at last assembled and preserved for us in the form of the gospel genre, which knit these units together on a plotline elicited by the needs and devised by the authors of a later generation. Bultmann did not regard the narrative plot of the gospel as inherited from the Jesus tradition. "The Christ who is preached is not the historic Jesus, but the Christ of the faith and the cult. . . . The [units of oral] tradition had to be presented as an unity from the point of view that in it he who spoke and was spoken of was he who had lived on earth as the Son of God, had suffered, died, risen and been exalted to heavenly glory."[63] Bultmann followed the scholar Richard Reitzenstein in identifying a Gnostic redeemer myth current in surrounding Hellenism as that which supplied early Christians with a plotline on which to hang the episodes from the Jesus tradition. Thus Bultmann "holds that the Gospels derive their essential story-line from this soteriological myth . . . The Palestinian forms are now embedded in a unified editorial framework, 'the epiphany of the heavenly Son of God.'"[64]

In these ways "critical research and the cultural crisis conspired to make the incomparable personality of Jesus as inauthentic a dogma as the Christ myth [of classic doctrine] it had supposedly replaced."[65] The result for Bultmann was that the variable is the New Testament's time-bound mythological depiction of the person, whether classically of Christ descending once upon a time from heaven and thence returning, or liberalism's reconstruction of Jesus' developing moral consciousness; the constant is the soteriological need to be existentially addressed by God in the contemporary moment. There "has never been a Jesus Christ who is soteriologically present apart from the proclamation."[66] Christ *is* neither the historical Jesus nor the narrated figure of the Gospels, but *exists soteriologically as* the contemporary event of being addressed and summoned to authentic existence before God. This is the dominant insight and claim of Bultman's theology, as indicated at the outset of this section in his 1952 letter to Barth.

Bultmann's theory about the Gnostic Redeemer myth is widely discredited today, but the riddle of the gospel plotline remains. With this reservation in mind, we can now sketch out how Kay successfully defends Bultmann against common but less worthy criticisms, the most important of which for our purposes is Hans Frei's. Frei has been a significant voice in calling attention to the loss of biblical narrative under the impact, not of historical method per se, but rather of the systematic apologetics of mediation theology. This strategy regards biblical narrative, in its strange fusions of historical report and mythic imagination, as unintelligible for modern people and thus in need of translation into contemporary thought forms. But such "translation" destroys the story, which consequently no longer functions as the canonical Bible had previously to present to theological understanding the characters of God and Christ in their dramatic roles in a history of salvation. Frei argues, like Karl Barth, that this amounts to a reduction of theology to anthropology and effects irreplaceable loss.

In qualification of Frei's argument, Kay writes:

> A story, even a "realistic narrative," does not necessarily function as a "performative utterance" by a "self-involving" agent. Admittedly a narrative can render character identities, as good storytellers know, and, arguably, a "realistic narrative" may do this better than a "myth." Indeed, a narrative can depict the identities of putative subjects and agents; but a narrative as narrative, unlike a promise as a promise, does not render self-involving agency, which is what the *Christus praesens* entails. Short of this kind of "self-involving" presence, a narratively rendered presence of Jesus Christ can only be, at best, the presence of information, of an "entity," or of a literary character. . . . Help comes only when, in faith, I find myself addressed by Jesus Christ with his word of promise.[67]

Kay therefore faults Frei for only describing objectively the character Jesus Christ and offering "no account of how faith finds itself addressed by Jesus Christ." This leads Kay to a scathing assessment of Frei's alleged relapse into the classic liberal attempt (which Bultmann had abandoned) to construct the "personality" of Jesus as an object of emulation in the name of "history-like narrative," even though the result is without real foundation either in the gospel genre or history. Frei's so-called gospel narrative "refers to no work of literature whatsoever but only to a literary-critical construct imposed on the synoptic gospels by Frei's imagination. What he presents us with is a postmodern 'harmony of the Gospels,' which, like its older liberal siblings, still picks and chooses from the three Synoptic accounts whatever it needs to construct, in Frei's words, 'Jesus' inner life,' albeit 'within the story.'"[68]

Might the same criticism, however, be directed back to Bultmann's sheer Word-event? Can there be speech of Christ without a recognizable person of Christ who so speaks and gives reasons to be heard? Kay himself concludes: "Identifying the One who enacts his own presence in the proclamation of the kerygma is precisely what realistic narrative can give us, even if it cannot account for that enactment as such."[69] This is correct according to our argument: it is resurrection as causal that accounts for the self-enacting presence of Christ. With this more appreciative note of Frei's concern, Kay seems tacitly to concede that it is questionable whether Bultmann's kerygmatic event can coherently be thought of as rendering the *same* self-involving agent *in absence of any narrative identifiers, even self-identifiers*. Whose voice do we hear in existential address? What difference does the possibility of different, or fraudulent, voices make to promises of presence and accompaniment? Kay maintains with Bultmann that "even when Paul stretches out his punctiliar kerygma into a linear narrative, its succinct spareness still lies far from the kind of literary realism Frei finds essential for depicting the identity of Jesus Christ. . . . Paul's indifference, or even opposition, to 'fleshing out' Christ's identity does not prevent him . . . from proclaiming Christ's presence."[70] This is an argument from silence with all the perils that involves. In any case, Paul thought the world was about to end and the question of narratability, beyond its "succinct sparseness," does not yet become urgent for him. For the church that continues to exist in time, the question is not idle but becomes ever more urgent. The mere assertion of presence does not make it so (thus, we must tell about God's causality in the story of Easter morn, as He raised Jesus from real death, as Paul does "succinctly" but pointedly), nor does it explain how this presence is identifiably Christ's and not another's (thus, we must tell about that body broken and blood poured out for us, as Paul does, however "sparsely").

The question of narratability is not theologically idle but lies at the very origin of the gospel genre: "False messiahs and false prophets will appear and produce signs and omens, to lead astray, if possible, the elect. But be alert; I have already told you everything" (Mark 13:22-23). Who is this latter "I" who demands His people to test the spirits, if not the One identified in Mark's story, even as He is speaking contemporaneously to Mark's readers and hearers by virtue of His resurrection and exaltation? Did not Mark need to tell the story of "the beginning of the gospel" (Mark 1:1) just because the relatively "unfleshed out" Pauline kerygma had become vulnerable to co-optation by "false messiahs and false prophets"? "Beware that no one leads you astray. Many will come in my name and say, 'I am he!' and they will lead many astray" (Mark 13:5-6).

Kay's sharp critique of Frei is focused on the latter's book *The Identity of Jesus Christ: On the Hermeneutical Basis of Dogmatic Theology*. With the help of literary critical devices, this book tried to interpret Mark's Gospel as effecting the progressive supercession of Jesus' intentional action by God's self-manifestation so that as Jesus grows increasingly passive in His passion, He becomes increasingly transparent to the condescension of God. Kay's critique of this is on target insofar as the hermeneutical basis of theology, as we have seen, lies in the kerygma of cross and resurrection understood as God's Word and so in reading Mark's narrative about Jesus, not as biography, but as parable of God's reign breaking into the strong man's house. Nor is it true to the specificity of Mark's Gospel, since the confrontation between the Father and the Son at the cross is not transparently, as in a novel, a story of God's condescension. It becomes so, like the parables of Jesus in Mark 4, when and where it pleases the Spirit of God. It is in this latter mode of apocalyptic that Mark writes, as we shall see below. In spite of these criticisms, however, Frei has struck upon something that is decisive. The resurrection narrates *something* of the Crucified One—perhaps not as Frei himself tried to formulate it, but *something*. What?

To this, Kay rejoins on Bultmann's behalf, "The issue is not whether Paul's gospel presupposes a saving narrative centered on Jesus Christ, but whether this narrative is 'mythical' or 'realistically storied' in genre."[71] If we turn to Frei's *Eclipse of Biblical Narrative*, we find this distinction of Kay's confirmed: "The chief issue that haunts the debate over myth in the Bible is not merely the applicability of the category to its various narrative portions, nor whether these portions of the Bible are unique in meaning, therefore, subject only to a completely special hermeneutics; the heart of the matter is the question whether ancient narratives of doubtful ostensive value but realistic or history-like form, exemplifying a close relation between narrative form and meaning, no matter where they are found can be unlocked by the identical interpretive device—that of myth, and more broadly, any category separating the meaning from the depictive shape." Frei's "history-like narrative" in contrast to myth renders its meaning by the storyline, not by translation of its into symbols and plot into another, putatively more basic general scheme of anthropological understanding. Theologically, history-like narrative is parable, not allegory. Thus Frei's point against Bultmann would be that "every narrative of the sort in which the story and meaning are closely related may have its own special hermeneutics,"[72] that is, that this specific biblical narrative cannot be rightly interpreted either by reconstructing what really happened or by resolving the text into general theories of the underlying key to myth and religion. For there "interpretation [becomes] a matter of fitting the biblical story into another world with another story rather than incorporating the world into the biblical story."[73] What resurrection narrates then would be the incorporation of the memories about Jesus into the coming of the reign of God.

Likewise in *Eclipse* Frei drew attention to the same problematic, idealistic construction of consciousness as "personality" that Kay criticizes. He contrasts this to the narrative "dynamics" of "descriptive shape—for which the characters, their social context, the circumstances or incidents, and the theme or themes are all interdependent" in rendering a persona, a public face that others can identify by recognizing its characteristic disposition and action.[74] Such a persona is precisely not a "mythical figure" that would be a symbol of something or someone else. On the other hand, Frei gave no little consideration to criticism of "personality" in his discussion of Schleiermacher, focused upon the latter's astonishing theory of a *Scheintod*, that is, that Jesus had not really died but revived in the cool of the tomb.[75] What is remarkable about this, Frei observes, is that "it never occurred to [Schleiermacher] that there is something unfitting, indeed ludicrous, about rendering the story of Jesus in a way that makes such a thundering anticlimax possible. But the fact, of course, is that it becomes possible, indeed perfectly fitting, if the crucial continuity of the story . . . lies in the inner being of Jesus—his consciousness as manifest in a connected pattern."[76] Whatever else resurrection tells in the Gospels, it tells of something that happens *to* Jesus as to a really *dead* person, dead also in relation to the One he knew as Abba-Father God. Resurrection in the Gospels must be understood as "simply the affirmation that the whole of Jesus' self-manifestation is in fact the self-manifestation of God, a disclosure that cannot be seen until the end of the story and thence covers all of it in retrospect"[77]—an argument on the resurrection's retrospective causality that parallels Pannenberg's.

Thus, in Frei's perspective it was Bultmann who never completely overcame the nineteenth-century view, classically argued by Feuerbach, that religious "myth" is the objectified projection of human aspiration. Myth is therefore illusory qua objectivizing history. In Bultmann's own words: "The real purpose of myth is not to present an objective picture of the world as it is, but to express man's understanding of himself in the world in which he lives."[78] While this may or may not be true of "myth," for Frei it is precisely not true of "history-like narrative," which puts "man" into the social dynamics of history where self-understanding is constantly at play with others and always in jeopardy. Bultmann's operative assumption is that human self-understanding can be abstracted as a structure of possibilities for decision from time-bound and erroneous understanding of the surrounding world like a kernel from a husk. So unveiled, the possibilities opened up in faith in this basic decision structure can serve disclosively as occasion and model for our own existential decisions. Yet the supposition that in this way one reiterates the same content is highly problematic, since it has already been supposed that self-understanding can be isolated from an objective picture of the world as it is. How could Paul's Damascus road "decision" (in Paul's view it was not his own decision at all!) to abandon his former Pharisaic righteousness be justified, one wants to ask, when that decision in fact consisted in leaving his people and heritage and then running around the Mediterranean world in the delusion that he was saving Gentiles from the impending wrath of God? There is an awful lot of husk to be stripped away here. Is there really any kernel to be found? It is as if existential authenticity in a risky decision of faith is all that matters, no matter how deluded—"decisionism" supplants faith which knows in whom it believes and why. This is a problem that Bultmann, and theology in his train, has never really solved and in principle cannot solve.

There is a final twist. It is the assumption that language about God is a way of elevating the speaker, which is why Bultmann allows mythological language in the third sense mentioned above to remain in the cult, though not in the pulpit or in theology. Take for example the primitive Christian exclamation "Jesus is Lord!" If this exclamation is pace Bultmann the echo among us of God's Easter word concerning His Son, "God's self-identification with the Crucified One frees us from having to find God by projection of our own perfections."[79] Here the exclamation of praise, attributing glory to God in Christ, is not a mechanism for getting close to God but of acknowledging the God who in Jesus has drawn near to us. But if we continue to assume the former, namely, that praise is a way of elevating the self to union with the divine, then "Jesus is Lord" becomes highly problematic. Even deliteralized and reduced to the basic anthropological assertion involved as the believer's "overcoming of the scandal of the cross" (Bultmann), how can the confession of Jesus avoid fixation on the historical vehicle? But then it risks exposure as a triumphalistic and ideological assertion that "our Jesus" is better than "your Moses" or "your Muhammad." The problem is made even worse, of course, by the rivalry between such contenders for whom doxological attribution corresponds to the reality of God. One theologian in Bultmann's school went so far in thinking out the logic of this self-elevating account of doxology that she introduced the neologism "Christofascism," that is, that belief in Jesus as the Christ betrays *fascism*, that is, a claim to superiority that legitimates violence against others.[80] Rosemary Reuther came similarly to a notion of Christology as "the left-hand of anti-Semitism."[81]

In principle such critique, like the classic Feuerbachian exposé of the idolatry that commonly passes for faith, could be welcomed by Christian theology.[82] George Lindbeck showed how with an enormously fruitful thought experiment. Is the statement *Christus est dominus* (Christ is Lord) theologically valid, Lindbeck asked, when exclaimed by the crusader as he hoists his sword to cleave the head of the infidel?[83] In Lindbeck's account, self-elevating theories of doxology are titled "expressive-symbolic" and correspondence theories of doxology are called "propositional" in contrast to his own rule-theory, that is, that doctrines as doctrines are second-order rules for properly applying or using first-order discourse (which, in the present argument, is gospel narrative as the church's primary theology). An advantage to his approach, Lindbeck argues, is that "heresy" is impossible for a "Gentile"[84] and "damnation" is senseless to those outside the religion's language game.[85] Religious systems, with their varying language games, are "incommensurable."[86] Different religions have different warrants, to which theologians must do justice.[87] For all these reasons, an advantage of his proposal, Lindbeck argues, is that it does not entail the inevitable inferiorization of other religions as false or incomplete objectifications of some supposedly common, core religious experience that makes them rivals in claiming true correspondence. Judaism and Islam are not, by mere virtue of not being Christianity, inferior, let alone idolatrous. Lindbeck's approach can rather approve of religious others as genuine others, from a Christian perspective, as objective anticipations of other values included in the kingdom, even as such recognition fosters critical exchange.[88] Lindbeck's theory of doctrine evokes a critical, rather than vulgar pluralism. Opposition to the liberal expressive-symbolic model thus has less to do with excluding non-Christians than preserving the *solus Christus*,[89] that is, the One who harrows hell,[90] whose word of liberation cannot be restricted. Preserving the *solus Christus* matters precisely in the life of the church, whose constant temptation to faithlessness is to remake Jesus into the symbol of its own contemporary self-consciousness.

On the other hand, Lindbeck acknowledges a place for correspondence in his model, when a lived religion "as a whole" corresponds to the being and will of God.[91] This view of the place of correspondence to God has the merit of protesting Christian triumphalism, since it bears witness to the being of Christians qua individuals as *simul iustus et peccator*,[92] no matter the truth of their doctrine or the profundity of their feelings. It underscores that they are elected to faith for service.[93] *Christus est dominus*—is it true when the crusader cries it out in a war whoop? Lindbeck's attention to rules for usage denies that it is so in this case. Any possible ontological correspondence depends on a usage that is "intersystemically coherent." In other words, *Christus est dominus* acquires propositional validity as part of a performance in language, which performance itself helps to create the very correspondence—a point Lindbeck particularly credits to Luther and Paul.[94] Doctrine as rule theory gives attention to the *usus*, to what we are doing with the language of belief so that in being performed rightly it corresponds adequately. Lindbeck's little parable rightly suggests that the Christ who is invoked in the crusader's way is not the Crucified, who calls disciples to bear the cross with Him, in the power of His Spirit not the sword, to the glory of God's coming reign, not the empire's lust for domination. In the crusader's usage, the statement "Christ is Lord" is false to the narrative content it bears.

But in that case Christ *must be identifiable* and not simply a function of (the crusader's!) soteriological need; resurrection must therefore objectivize itself in narrative not only to be real in the world but to resist and withstand abuse. The danger of abuse is then to be met with a trinitarian dialectic of Word and Spirit (the incarnate Word understood according to the Spirit's intention, the Spirit's intention discovered from the Spirit's scriptural words telling about the Word incarnate)[95] rather than Bultmann's elusive doctrine of punctiliar revelation by the "Word alone." As Robert Jenson puts the point: "If a historical event is eschatological, this, for Bultmann . . . must reduce its historical reality to a sheer moment without temporal extension, and so to something that cannot essentially be *narrated*. Thus the ruling maxim of Bultmann's famous program of 'demythologizing' is that no stories can be properly told about eternity; in his definition, a 'myth' is any sequential narrative pretending to be about deity, and 'demythologizing' means identifying the impact of such a narrative in a fashion as to obviate its claim *as* narrative."[96] Jenson's implied line of argument against Bultmann here, as we shall see in coming chapters, is the one that led the early church with inner necessity to the doctrine of the Trinity.

For the present, however, we note that Lindbeck's criticism of false practice in naming Jesus as Lord naturally presupposes a Christology truly uttered, namely, one that for our salvation contradicts the egocentric notion that speech about God is a way of elevating—unconverted—selves. That can radically be overcome only by a positive program of true speech about God as rendered in the gospel as resurrection narrative. True speech about God will contain genuine surprises. "That God as God is able and willing and ready to condescend, to humble himself in this way, is the mystery of the 'deity of Christ'—although frequently it is not recognized in this concreteness. This deity is not the deity of a divine being furnished with all kinds of supreme attributes."[97] Such true christological speech according to critical dogmatics comes from outside the self, even as it comes to include the human self. Yet this coming, if it is true to the gospel narrative, comes only by way of the self's ecstatic refashioning through spiritual death and resurrection, and then only as bound together in the company of all other unworthies made worthy by this grace in the costly confession of the church of the martyrs. Here the affirmation "Jesus is Lord!" tells of the God who has endured hell in order to empty it and reign over its prisoners now set free. This telling of the world's story extends from resurrection narrative back and forward, just as it entails understanding the gospel as promissory narrative.

The Gospel as Promissory Narrative[98]

"Help comes only when, in faith, I find myself addressed by Jesus Christ with his word of promise." So Kay rightly lifted up the proper and valid concern in Bultmann's theology, going back to Luther's doctrine of *fiducia* as the conviction that what is said about Christ applies *pro me*, for me. There are two issues here. How does this promissory *address* of Christ, which certainly is embedded in the gospel narratives, come to address a contemporary person? We have tacitly answered: by right of the causal resurrection, which renders Christ present as living agent when the gospel about Him is rightly proclaimed. Right proclamation, resorting to Lindbeck's rule theory of doctrine, would be telling about Jesus in such a way that He suffices completely and unconditionally for any auditor's acceptance by the holy God for life and service in the Reign. We will have more to say about this promissory address momentarily. For the present, the topic is a second issue concerning promissory narrative. *By what right* is the kerygmatic promise of the forgiveness of sins, life, and salvation proclaimed in *Jesus'* name, or conversely, how does this name entail such salvation? The question here recalls, not accidentally, the challenge posed to Jesus by the scribes and Pharisees in the early chapters of the Gospel of Mark,[99] the first literary instance of the gospel genre, extending resurrection narrative back to "the beginning of the gospel" (Mark 1:1).

The evangelist has assembled in chapter 2 a collection of controversy stories culminating in the first literary foreshadowing of Jesus' bitter fate (2:1—3:6). Jesus' announcement of God's impending reign in the opening action of the Gospel of Mark acts to heal the sick, expose the demons and put them to flight, and forgive sins. This action provokes resistance—shrieking demonic protest against Jesus' breaking into their house and robbing their possessions (3:27). But resistance is also found among the representatives of the divine law: Where is the justice in letting sins go? What authorizes this friendship with the unde-serving? What authorizes sharing table with disgraced collaborators and public sinners, that is, enemies of God identified and judged by God's own law (*not* by "Jewish legalism")? What authorizes celebrating rather than fasting in sad times still far from the dawn of redemption? What authorizes working on the day God commanded for rest? The issue is always the same. With what *justice*, or *justifica-tion*, by what *right* does Jesus speak and act in the name of God, especially when His works and words are in manifest tension with sanctioned custom, if not in contradiction *to other clear words of God*?

There is without doubt in Mark criticism of the tradition of the elders for corrupting the commandment of God (7:1-23), but it would be a dangerous descent into the kind of demeaning anti-Judaism of nineteenth-century scholar-ship to make this opposition to supposed Jewish legalism the heart and soul of the controversy Jesus provokes.[100] One must rather see how opponents stand for the clear Word of God in opposition to the dangerous innovation Jesus seems to bring—and so let God be the judge in the dispute by the resolution of this story. So again: With what *justice*, or *justification*, by what *right* does Jesus speak and act in the name of God, especially when His works and words are in manifest tension with sanctioned custom, if not in contradiction *to other clear words of God*? The answer to this challenge in the Gospel of Mark is that in Jesus' lifework of full obedience of love to His Father, He is the Son fulfilling the true intention of God's law (10:21) and therewith enacting a new redemptive initiative to free those cap-tive in the Rebel's prison-house and gain them for the Father's coming reign. This is expressly stated in so many words (10:45; 14:24), even as the narrative depicts this persona under way, fulfilling His calling under the imperative of the Spirit (1:12). Jesus fulfills His baptismal calling as the beloved Son (1:11) by refusing diabolic means (1:13) and instead living and finally dying in solidarity with sinners and the diseased (2:17), culminating in the awesome but revelatory paradox of the beloved Son's godforsaken death on the cross as their representative (15:34). The right by which Jesus heals, liberates, forgives in God's name is established in human eyes only after Jesus is seen to have drunk fully the bitter cup of obedi-ence to His heavenly Father (14:36). Not only do prior human attempts to say "who Jesus is" fail (8:27-33); they must positively be foiled, because Jesus' identity in His redemptive mission cannot be understood in terms of preexisting ideas and categories with the usual kinds of self-elevating, egocentric questions behind them that people ask about God, the world, and themselves. "Truly this was Son of God"—so the *executioner* proclaims in Mark's climactic moment, upon "seeing how Jesus died" (15:39).

This highly improbable piece of historiography serves as *revelation, apoca-lypse, parable, paradox*. Who—mind you, it is the *executioner* who finally tells the truth of Jesus' identity!—*who* could put those *two* thoughts together of divine Son and godforsaken death *except* as divine *revelation*? The paradox here is not meant as logical nonsense, but to render the divine apocalypse, dramatically assailing our normal categories of judgment, evoking the divine questioning of the questions people normally pose about God ("Wait, let us see whether Elijah will come to take him down from the cross," Mark 15:36) so that human minds, like the Son's tomb, will be opened up for the new thing God is doing in the godforsaken death of the beloved Son, namely, harrowing hell, provided only that we see ourselves now as those there imprisoned.

This is a revelation, however, for which readers of Mark's Gospel have been well prepared by the course of the story. The climactic address of Jesus to His Abba-Father in the Garden of Gethsemane (14:32-42), in which Jesus surrenders Himself to drink the cup, shows them the resolve of the obedient Son of God. His earthly story as a whole leading up to this moment of final self-surrender is therefore called "the beginning of the gospel" (1:1) as it enacts that obedience. The point of this is *not* psychological. It is not a revelation of Jesus' self-consciousness, messianic or otherwise. Jesus must think of Himself as God thinks (8:34) and profess God's word concerning Him at the cost of His own life and reputation (14:62), at the cost of His own self-consciousness. Moreover, the gospel of this persona, Jesus Christ the Son of God (1:1), has continued on its course, making history by forming the ecclesiastical context that readers form around Mark's text. "Marcan eschatology is such as to imply a continuation with the Church of the same kind of history as characterized Jesus' history, i.e., a struggle between Spirit and Satan, until the final outcome of that struggle is reached and the goal of history is attained."[101] From the beginning then the story of Jesus has broken out of the dead past on account of the causal resurrection to render this persona present to speak the *same* word of promise now (years later) to the nations ("And the gospel must first be preached to all the nations," 13:10). Such believers are called by the gospel narrative to come to see Jesus as God sees Him (9:3) and believe Him as God's Word (9:7) and so also to think about Him as God thinks (8:33)—in just these ways breaking ranks with the kingdom of Satan.

With Mark the Evangelist, writing, as I think, *before* the destruction of the temple, the temple still held christological significance and so the current siege of Jerusalem by Roman armies may have been the occasion of the narrative he draws (13:2, 14).[102] Gospel narrative in any case interprets history prophetically. Jesus has come not to be served like a king on the throne in Jerusalem but to serve as a priest; He goes to Jerusalem to lay down His own life as the royal Son of God to be the ransom for many (10:45). From the very beginning, His assertion of authority to forgive sins, to heal on the Sabbath, to show mercy without regard to human status or deserving has brought Jesus into the conflict that will terminate with His crucifixion (3:6). This conflict leads Jesus into the temple in Jerusalem (11:11). The story of the Cursing of the Fig Tree (11:12-14, 20-26) brackets the Cleansing of the Temple (11:15-19). The Cursing signifies divine indictment of the worship in Jerusalem. The temple has failed to bear fruit in service to the redemptive purpose of God directed to all peoples. Jesus says this explicitly in justification of His action in the temple courts: "Is it not written, 'My house shall be called a house of prayer for all the nations'? But you have made it a den of robbers" (11:17). From Mark 11:27 to 12:44, the teaching of Jesus, which seals the lethal conflict (12:12; 14:1), unfolds within the temple precincts even as this climactic section of teaching culminates in Jesus' solemn prophecy of the destruction of the temple in 13:2. The passion narrative immediately follows in which false witnesses bring the charge in Mark 14:58, "We heard him say, 'I will destroy this temple that is made with hands, and in three days I will build another, not made with hands.'" At the very moment of Jesus' death on the cross, immediately preceding the confession of the centurion, the sign of divine rejection of the temple and its (not *Israel's!*) supercession is given: "And the curtain of the temple was torn in two, from top to bottom" (15:38).

As the blood of the new covenant is shed once and for all, the temple cult is finished. "In this death, therefore, Jesus Son of God supersedes the temple and its cult as the 'place' where God henceforth grants, to all humankind, the remission of sins. Additionally, Jesus also becomes the 'builder' (14:58; 15:29) of the new community that is God's eschatological people (10:29-30; 14:22-24; 16:7)."[103] The legal barrier between the holy God and sinful humanity that John's preaching had announced at the beginning of the beginning of the gospel (1:4-5) has been broken down in the ransom death of the Son of God. The apocalypse of the crucified Son of God henceforth opens up and gives form to a new place of worship in the world wherever the good news of Jesus' vicarious life and death for others is sounded and heard, remembered, and partaken in the meal of the new covenant. One unnamed woman had prefigured this (14:3-9). She anointed *the body* of Jesus beforehand for burial, in this way professing, declaring, indicating, teaching, narrating in action Jesus as *the crucified Messiah*. This act of loving devotion toward Jesus was no waste. Far from turning attention away from care of the poor, as maliciously impugned by those who want to use Jesus for their own politics and purposes, her devotion represents the worship of the new humanity. In it she already gives thanks for the very love that does not despise the poor but goes on to care for them always. It is therefore the model ever after to be held in honor among believers: "Truly I tell you, wherever the good news is proclaimed in the whole world, what she has done will be told in remembrance of her" (14:9). Her story becomes part of His story. An exchange of narratives transpires within the gospel narrative of exchange. The promise is pronounced like no bolt of lightning in the night sky but initiates and sustains a new *life together* that can be told.

So the anointed, broken, balmed, and buried *body* of Jesus becomes the new, spiritual temple, not held in a tomb but as it goes before them to Galilee (16:7). Risen, Jesus ever acquires earthly form, in other words, in His people, and His people in turn are "Christ existing as community" (Bonhoeffer). The eucharistic community of the New Testament (14:22-25) is no mere association of individuals, but forms a living organism, the divinely wrought community in faith, hope, and love to which any individual is joined in order that he or she may believe, love, and hope. Christian faith participates in this *koinonia* of Christ; it has no individual existence apart from it. Such life together is the immediate ethical implication of the christological confession of the Crucified; it is the practice of reconciliation that accords with doctrinal profession of the crucified Christ. For the recipient in faith of Christ's sacrificial love is implicated immediately in Christ's love for the other. The church, figured in the nameless woman, which loves Jesus for the love received from him, and loves the other with the same love of Jesus, is the church that knows the living Word of God precisely and not otherwise than as this story of Jesus on the way to the cross. To hold the doctrine of Jesus the crucified Messiah is not, of course, a precondition of His love, but it is analytic of it; it is the grammar that makes sense of this particular story, as that promissory narrative in turn creates and sustains the Christian community.

In every respect, we return to the proposition with which we began this chapter: Easter is the presupposition of the gospel genre. The gospel genre *is* this event of recognition of the Son by the Father also *in us*, the very Son who had recognized His Father in the surrender of Gethsemane *for us*. That is why the denouement in Mark can be intimated at the very center of the narrative, while the story ends so awkwardly in 16:8, where we might expect much more. In Mark, what God the heavenly Father *does* at Easter is anticipated literarily by what God the heavenly Father already *says* (to Peter, James and John) in the Transfiguration: "This is my beloved Son. Listen to him!" (9:7, repeating to them what the heavenly Voice had said to Jesus in 1:11). Human listening in faith actually then occurs. The story continues. As they listen to Jesus, they begin to lose their lives and find them new (8:34—9:1). Simon the denier becomes Peter the rock, and the ambitious Sons of Thunder servants of all; and even though they lose mother, brother, sister, and father, they find a hundredfold more mothers, brothers, sisters, and fathers in the community of the covenant in Jesus' blood (10:28-31). As they listen to God by listening to Jesus, they are re-identified by Jesus as His brothers and sisters, the children of God, the eschatological family, and become so to one another (3:31-35). Listening to the gospel draws in and involves believers in these divine-and-human transactions, so that they come to identify themselves in Christ just as God identifies Himself with Jesus. In these identity transactions, history is being made, the church is formed and ever re-formed along the gospel's mission way—as the Spirit through the Word authors and authorizes these new relationships and practices of reconciliation in the course of a real history pioneered by the gospel through time and space. In all these ways, Mark is properly historicizing the eschatological, since the sense of the resurrection of Jesus, rightly understood, is His unrestricted agency as the very one He was.

This latter conclusion is fitting, looking both backward and forward. As Willi Marxsen rightly noted in the conclusion of his seminal study of Mark as an author, *already* in the traditions about Jesus which Mark took up and integrated into his Gospel, this historicizing of the eschatological was under way (though not with a biographical intention). Rather synthesizing Pauline and Synoptic traditions, Mark "proves to be the consolidator"[104] of the antidocetic impulse at work in both traditions to historicize rather than mythologize the eschatological figure of the crucified but risen Jesus. In this he saves Paul from Gnosticism[105] and paves the path to Luke-Acts that in the end "won out"[106] on the way to early Catholicism.

Many today regard these Marcan moves to be historically understandable but questionable for Bultmannian reasons. They are historically understandable because Mark is writing to churches that are being overrun with miracle workers, messianic pretenders, false prophets trying to read the signs of the times, all claiming to speak in the name of the risen Lord (Mark 13). They are saying that they have the mind of Christ, that they speak in the voice of His Spirit. They preach an attractive but false message of escape from the tribulations all around them that permits evasion of confessing the name of Jesus as God's Son and disdains as unspiritual the willingness to suffer as a martyr for that confession. This false preaching raises anew and acutely the christological question as a burning contemporary concern: Who really is Jesus Christ? Which spirit is His Spirit? Which story of deliverance really is *Jesus'* story? What difference does the *name* of Jesus make, that it cannot be substituted (that "no other name under heaven is given by which we must be saved," Acts 4:12) with another name? What does the name of Jesus name?

Names are references, words that work *ostensibly* by pointing to something and picking it out. Apart from this work of pointing, a name can become a clanging gong, a magical incantation, as if chanting "Jesus, Jesus" in itself effected His promised liberation (Matt 7:21). But the *truth* of the *name* of Jesus is His personal identity. What is that? Mark answers: the persona of Jesus is that figure *revealed by* God in His gospel and as such awaited *from heaven* by the suffering church. As apocalypse, Mark's Gospel will in telling its story perform enlightenment and blinding, promising and threatening (Mark 4:12); as parable, it will reveal and conceal. For Mark it lies with the sovereign Spirit to open or close the gospel narrative to human faith. But given the existence of church and faith at all, the truthful use of the name of Jesus in this interim is that which accords with the *revelation* of Jesus' personal intention (His coming in obedience as the Son of Man to give His life a ransom for many), His destiny (what happens to Him in the cross and resurrection), and not least His cosmic victory (the return of the Son of Man in glory to save). The revelation is rendered in unfolding the *definite plot* (the divine "necessity" that backs the thrice-repeated passion prediction, Mark 8:31; 9:31-32; 10:32-34), and it is this which gives *narrative definition* to the name of Jesus as this public identity. "Word alone," as sheer kerygmatic event, cannot do this. It cannot form the church in its engagement with the world, withstand abuse, and act to reform it when it goes astray. The kerygmatic event does not suffice for the speaking of the gospel through *continuing* time in face of radical challenges. Perhaps it might have sufficed, if Christ had returned in clouds of glory as the first generation of believers expected (Mark 9:1; 13:26-27). But what shall we make of the fact theologically that this expectation was, for our good, *falsified* (since we would not be here to debate it and so the good of our existence would never have transpired)? Rather, so far as the delay of the parousia, so called, equates with the exclusive predication of resurrection to Jesus, the resurrection kerygma *requires* narration of His new beginnings with new peoples until the gospel is preached to all nations, provided only that they accord with the "beginning of the gospel."

If Jesus is identified this way by narrative, we return now to the issue of His promissory address. How does Jesus rightly identified present Himself to be heard? Is it by miraculous new inspiration? Some have spoken of a rival "divine man" theology in Mark said to be presented in the first half of the Gospel—much like Bultmann's mythic redeemer figure—which Mark took up dialectically as the position of his opponents, in order then to refute it in the second half of the Gospel.[107] But neither Mark nor his opponents had objections to miracles. Mark's opponents performed them (or claimed to perform them) "to lead astray, if possible, even the elect" (13:22b). But Mark's Jesus also works wonders ("Who then is this that even wind and sea obey him?" 4:41). The problem is not the widespread belief in miracles, nor particularly the fact that under the inspiration of the Spirit early Christian prophets of the post-Easter church spoke "in the name of the Lord" and in this way put words in Jesus' mouth.[108] Mark himself is willing to contemporize Jesus in this way and does so dramatically in making Jesus speak directly to his community's dire situation in the Gospel's thirteenth chapter (13:37). As we have argued, belief in the contemporaneity of Jesus as the unrestricted, active, communicative agent of salvation in the community was the proper implication of faith in His resurrection. The risen Christ is the living subject, not merely the object of faith. Consequently all true preaching was for them prophecy in "the name of the Lord" to and for the community of faith.

It is only within this context of *kerygmatic address* that the problem is properly perceived. It is this: Within the circle of resurrection faith there have arisen *false* prophets speaking in the name of the Lord Jesus who have detached and, indeed, must detach their message of salvation from the persona of the man who was crucified *sub Pontio Pilato*. They are *remythologizing* Jesus in the sense that they are *de-personalizing* Him, that is, robbing Him of His own *public* face as the Forsaken and Crucified One vindicated mysteriously by God but still hidden from the world. They use His name *magically*, that is, as an incantation, without regard then to the narrative rendition of His earthly coming as the Son of Man who serves, earthly fate as the Crucified, and cosmic destiny as apocalyptic Son of Man who saves. We can see this concretely in the words that Mark's Jesus addresses to the urgent situation of war and persecution (Mark 13:5-8) in which Mark's suffering community looked for the coming of the Lord Jesus in clouds of heaven to rescue them: "And if anyone says to you at that time, 'Look! Here is the Messiah!' or 'Look! There he is!'—do not believe it. False prophets and false Messiahs will appear and produce signs and omens" (13:21-22a). For Mark, faith knows its object; it must be able to distinguish true and false prophets, the true from false Messiahs. The demonstration of wonder-working power or charismatic oratory does not suffice for this task. The problem runs far deeper. The false prophets too have a "gospel," a contemporaneous message of liberation; in working wonders and sounding authoritative it even resembles Jesus' own beginnings. But decisively the false prophets are now promising escape from the tribulations surrounding the community. This message of liberation *as escape*, tested against Mark's story of Jesus' way to the cross, is what the gospel judges theologically false and spiritually ruinous. The address of Jesus calls instead to endurance as to salvation itself (13:13).

For the same reason, the Holy Spirit in Mark is no source of independent revelations, but the same One who leads disciples, as He had led Jesus, into conflict with Satan and his unclean spirits (1:8, 12, 23-27) and so gives courage and words of witness to suffering disciples in the time of trial (13:11). Against the deep-seated human prejudice to which the false prophet's message of escape appeals, the counterintuitive truth that God's salvation comes not in escape from sufferings, but through bearing the cross, had to be articulated and expressly taught: "You will be hated by all because of my name. But the one who endures to the end will be saved" (13:13). "But be alert; I have already told you everything" (13:23). The name that is hated is the subject who speaks. The "I" who speaks through the prophet, now through the evangelist, belongs to the persona of Him who once told the truth in His own time of trial (14:62) and suffered for it. In this way, the gospel narrative requires express teaching about the "name" of Jesus, if the "I" of Jesus is to be understood truly, rightly recognized and followed faithfully in continuing history. In a world of contending stories that promise liberation, the name of Jesus figures that singular path once taken from the glory of the miracles in Galilee through the ignominy of the Roman stake outside Jerusalem to the life of the resurrection, by which He now lives in His earthly community assembled again in Galilee (14:28; 16:7). The Spirit, if it is *His* Spirit, therefore implicates all true users of His name in the same destiny, freeing them in the process from their own willful and persistent incomprehension (8:33). The name of Jesus is not magical incantation, but a real object in the Spirit of theological knowledge, just as the persona of Jesus displays the leadership and intentionality of the Spirit (1:12). The act of Jesus in establishing the new covenant reveals the Spirit's aim. The call of the Spirit reveals Jesus as the agent of God's new community. This dialectic comes to synthesis in the church's confession of faith, "Crucified Jesus is the Son of God," taken as revelation, as a word beyond all human possibilities, as a Word from above. The Word of Jesus cannot be separated from the Word about Jesus. Here Mark leaves us, with the address of Jesus so concretely focused on the crisis in which he and his church are suffering that one must—for very Marcan reasons—wonder what Jesus will say after that crisis has passed.

Gospel narrative thus renders the public figure of Jesus as a parable *of God* in the sense of *paradox*, not *simile*; that is, it tells this Man, ultimately the Crucified One, *to be* the Son of God (not *like* a Son to God): "The parable is a metaphor that presents an imagined action to the hearer in such a way sufficiently arresting to require him to rethink the whole in a new way"[109]—namely, to think of this crucified man as the Son of God (Mark 15:39). The clarification of the difference we have taken in the chapter for framing our thinking about the God-world difference by apocalyptic as opposed to philosophical dualism is important because of a long tradition in liberal theology of reading Mark as providing, despite legendary accretions, the historical framework for Jesus' inner, psychological development of "God-consciousness." Here the resurrection of Jesus is regarded as the noncausal disclosure of who Jesus secretly had been all along, rather than as the divine vindication, apart from which Jesus would have died godforsaken and remained godforsaken (15:34). Such rethinking of the whole represents the transition from what Luther called the old language of philosophy (with its natural theology) to the new theological language of the Spirit (with its doctrine of God as Trinity).[110] Along these lines, the first Gospel to appear, indeed the pioneer of the gospel genre, should be read as *parable*, that is, "really an extended metaphor in the sense that it is a narrative with at least a rudimentary plot" that renders the One who died on Golgotha alive and at the door as the unique Man from God who is the Man for others.

If we abandon as futile the quest of liberal theology for a historical Jesus and read Mark as parable of God not biography of Jesus, we will discover real congruity (though not identity) between the preaching of Jesus and the early church's preaching about Jesus. For the memory of Jesus' proclamation was taken up and incorporated into the gospel narrative. But this congruity will be discovered only on account of taking the resurrection as a causal divine event. "Jesus concentrated on parabolic speech because he himself was a parabolic event of the Kingdom of God."[111] The implication then is that the saving presence of the risen Jesus by the promissory narrative preaching about Jesus that developed in the gospel genre is congruous with the historical preaching of Jesus. Hence, by "gospel narrative" we shall mean such memory and representation of the crucified Jesus of Nazareth as parable of the kingdom of God from the perspective of His proclaimed resurrection that renders Him present to save.[112]

CHAPTER 3

The Scriptures' Emergence as the Church's Canon

The formation of the New Testament as rule of faith, coupled with the Hebrew Scriptures as its "Old" Testament, constitutes the first dogmatic decision of normative Christianity. This dogmatic decision corresponds with the historical fact that the various primitive Christian communities that arose from apostolic narrations of the Easter kerygma recognized each other in the course of the later first and second centuries. The catalyst of this mutual recognition was a common theological decision against docetism (teaching that Christ only appeared to be a particular human body) in Christology, corresponding to dualism in the doctrine of God (teaching two gods, one good God of light and spirit and another evil God of matter and darkness). Ethically, this decision against docetism and dualism correlates with the stance of the early Christian martyrs, who bear witness in their bodies of allegiance to the reign of God under duress of persecution. Faith and ethos coincided with the Reign's promised vindication of its witnesses in the gospel of the resurrection of the Crucified. The emergent biblical canon thus reflects a multifaceted convergence of various streams into the broad stream of a generous orthodoxy in "early Catholicism." "Where Jesus Christ is, there is the catholic church" (Ignatius of Antioch). Jesus Christ, whose crucified and risen body becomes the new and living temple of the Spirit of God on the earth: Where the canonical Scriptures are received, read, and interpreted, and so passed on. The canon consisted in the Genesis-to-Revelation story of the creation, redemption, and fulfillment of the one world by the one God in the persona Jesus Christ, who in turn speaks to the church from these Scriptures by the promised advocacy of the Holy Spirit. The Gospel we call John, with its prehistory and reception, played the critical role in this development.[1]

Jesus—New and Living Temple

The church father Athanasius of Alexandria (c. 296–373), who played the leading role in the formation of Nicene orthodoxy, spoke of Jesus as the new and living Temple. He writes in the *Letter to Adelphius* that we "acknowledge this Logos [Greek: Word; John 1:1-18] to be God, even after it has come into being in flesh." Against Gnostics who denied the abiding human reality of the Logos's flesh, as well as against Arians who deny the full divine identity of the Logos who became flesh, Christians worship "the Creator of the universe as though in a created temple . . . the Lord who is in the flesh as in a temple." Why is that so? The Logos became flesh that he "might free everything through the creature, present the universe to the Father and give peace to all things." In the creature, in the flesh in which the Logos dwells as in a temple, the Word of God works the creation's reconciliation and fulfillment. Whoever "despises the temple, therefore, despises the Lord who is in the temple, while the one who separates the Logos from the body, rejects the grace given to us through the Logos." Christians are both to "acknowledge the divinity the Logos shares with the Father and worship his presence in the flesh."[2] The divine Word is thus inseparable from its historically contingent vehicle. Jesus Christ is *homoousios* (Greek: of the same being) with the Father; this public persona in the world is "the Logos become flesh" (John 1:14). Athanasius learned to think this way from the Gospel of John.

The "incarnation" is John's theological concept for the true *worship* of the true God, which is an event that occurs first of all within the life of God, namely, the Son's self-offering to the Father in the power of the Spirit. The worship of the church comes to participate in this divine event, which precedes the church and comes to incorporate its worship through the gospel. In this way, it accomplishes the inclusion of the nations that the temple of Jerusalem should have achieved but did not, as we shall shortly see. The evangelist uses a verb in John 1:14 that says literally that the Logos "tabernacled" among us, evoking memories of early Israel's pristine worship in the desert wanderings.[3] Indeed, John relocates the story of the Cleansing of the Temple from its place in the Synoptic Gospels to the beginning of Jesus' activity (2:13-22), making of this episode a heading over all that follows. Thereby the entire ensuing conflict leading up to Jesus' death and resurrection is defined theologically in 2:21: Jesus "was speaking of the temple of his body" that would be destroyed and then rebuilt in three days. To the Samaritan woman at Jacob's Well, the Johannine Jesus declares, "You worship what you do not know; we worship what we know, for salvation is from the Jews. But the hour is coming, and is now here, when the true worshipers will worship the Father in spirit and truth, for the Father seeks such as these to worship him" (4:22-23). The evangelist organizes his narrative of Jesus' activity around the scheme of three visits to Jerusalem and the temple during the major Jewish festivals; by this device he repeatedly contrasts the old from the new worship Jesus brings. It is a special emphasis of the Johannine passion narrative to make survival of the temple cult the pretext of the conspiracy to put Jesus to death—for the alleged blasphemy of Jesus in making Himself the Temple of God (11:48). Indeed, the very first occurrence of the term "the Jews" (which might better be translated the "Judeans," those first-century Jews politically, economically, and religiously attached to the temple in Jerusalem) in 1:19 ("This is the testimony given by John when the Jews sent priests and Levites from Jerusalem to ask him, 'Who are you?'") likewise indicates that what is at issue between Jesus and "the Jews" in the Fourth Gospel is the supercession, not of the Jewish people, but of the temple in Jerusalem by the new community in Jesus whom the Father gathers in the Spirit for true worship. Immediately following this exchange in 1:19, not by accident, comes the true witness from Israel, John the Baptist (notorious, like the Essenes, for his scathing critique of the temple establishment in Jerusalem). He introduces Jesus to the Gospel's readers: "Behold the Lamb of God who takes away the sin of the world" (1:29). Jesus is the One who will fulfill Israel's hope for atonement and communion with God, superceding the temple in Jerusalem.

In these ways, the evangelist indicates that Jesus' crucified and risen body, that is, the eucharistic assembly of believers that feeds on the "Bread from heaven" (John 6), is to become the new Temple where the Father is worshipped in Spirit and in truth. God's plan to redeem the nations will be realized in Jesus' community. At the midpoint of the Gospel, Jesus knows that "the hour" for which He has come into the world has arrived when some Greeks in Jerusalem ask Philip whether they can see Him (12:21-23). By dying, Jesus declares in response to their inquiry, He will bear much fruit (12:24), the very fruit of the nations won for the worship of God that the Jerusalem temple has failed to produce. Lifted up from the earth on the cross, Jesus will at the same time be lifted up by the glory of God to the life of the resurrection, lifted up to reign over the nations by sending the Spirit to carry His words into the world, forming the church as a worshipping assembly from all nations. Spreading the message of life in His name, Jesus will draw all people to Himself (12:32). The so-called High Priestly prayer of consecration at the end of the Farewell Discourse concludes with the same thought: believers come to dwell in Jesus, as in Jesus the Logos dwells in the flesh, as henceforth the incarnate Logos dwells in the Father (17:20-23). Climactically, at the end of the Gospel, Thomas falls down before the risen Lord Jesus who bears the imprints of nail and spear acclaiming, "My Lord and my God!" providing in conclusion the very image of the rightly worshipping and rightly believing community (as opposed to the heterodox docetist community claiming the authority of the apostle Thomas that denies that the crucified and risen body of Jesus is Lord and God).[4] Just as

Athanasius saw, this community worships "the Lord who is in the flesh as in a temple." For the Gospel of John, the persona of "the Word made flesh" accomplishes the reconciliation and communion of God with humanity to which the temple in Jerusalem had been appointed but failed to achieve.

The Johannine Bridge

The Gospel of John has played a central, even decisive role in the history of Christian doctrine by interpreting the synoptic account of the "beginning of the gospel," seen in the analysis of Mark in the previous chapter, as the incarnation of the divine Word.[5] Peter Stuhlmacher has rightly commented: "Over against the first three gospels, the Gospel of John represents a new phase of tradition. It assumes (especially) the Petrine tradition . . . as familiar, continues it critically, and supplements it in the perspective of faith. . . . The early Church considered the Gospel of John as the true, spiritual Gospel, whose witness of truth encompasses and culminates that of the other three gospels."[6] The British New Testament theologian James D. G. Dunn likewise notes, "John has served as a bridge between the beginnings of Christianity in Jesus, and the orthodox faith that achieved definition at Nicea and that has provided the dogmatic basis of Christianity ever since."[7]

Yet many in modern times have thought that John represents a dubious *hellenization* of the gospel.[8] Indeed, a subtle shift seems to occur with John 1:1-14 away from the language of the Son and His heavenly Father inherited from the early traditions about Jesus to that of God and His coeternal Word; this shift has bedeviled and misled those who fail to read John as theological commentary on the Synoptic traditions. For John emphatically, indeed massively, retains and develops the analogy of Jesus' relation to God as that of a son to a father, just as he leaves all reference to "the Word" behind after the prologue. After we hear John speak of this eternal Logos, who became flesh, we are to "come and see" (1:46) what this language means in the story that follows. It is not at all obvious then that John would import here some drastically different kind of relation, say, that of Mind to the Thought of itself that it generates like a copy (and then a Thought of the Thought, and then again Thoughts of the Thought of the Thought and so on in a great chain of really existent, graduated conceptual forms emanating from the One to the many, as in Neoplatonic thought). That would indeed be a kind of "hellenization." For we would then allow an abstract and impersonal metaphor from mental life to override the father-son analogy—a figure of social life—language that descends from Jesus' own proclamation and history. Then a psychological trinity, so to say, would absorb the figures of Jesus the Son and His Abba-Father and their Spirit-Advocate, effacing their society and rendering the dramatic and decisive history that transpires between them in the gospel narrative into so many shadows dancing on a wall.

It would be quite wrong to think that in some such way the Johannine theology of the incarnate Word represents a turn away from the simple Galilean
gospel of Jesus to Greek metaphysics. The crucial statement in 1:14 continues,
interpreting its own meaning, "and we beheld his glory, the glory *as of a father's
only son*, full of grace and truth" (emphasis added). The claim here is for the
visibility of the object of faith in a specific way, *not* the alleged imposition of
Greek metaphysics; and this claim to visibility, to seeing the glory of God in
the man Jesus, represents the real problem for understanding the Fourth Gospel. In terms from the previous chapter, the narratablity of the resurrection is
being further extended by John into a depiction for faith of the visibility of
the Incarnation.

Who is this "we" speaking in 1:14? This "we" denotes first of all certain disciples of Jesus of Nazareth, including one especially beloved by Him (though
he remains nameless, cf. 19:35, and may be a symbolic figure), whom by tradition we name "John." His testimony to Jesus is authoritative for the distinctive early Christian community among whom this text evolved. This "we" also
includes the evangelist who both identifies with and distinguishes himself from
the Beloved Disciple (21:24). And this "we" also includes the first readers to
whom the Gospel was addressed. It includes in fact all those who do not see as
the first disciples uniquely saw but nevertheless believe in Jesus "through their
word" (17:20), and thus likewise in very truth apprehend Jesus' "glory." For if
they perceive *this glory*, they have *seen* all that *matters* about Jesus of Nazareth
as the divine Logos made flesh. "The Fourth Gospel was written in order that
the Christians of a later generation might be confronted by the authority of
this earlier witness and in order that, created by it, they also might be invested
with apostolic authority" (Hoskyns).[9] As pertains to the theological content of
the formula "Word made flesh," we should likewise not presume to know in
advance from the intriguing hints in the Prologue what it might mean to have
such authority (namely, to likewise become "beloved" disciples, "to become the
children of God," 1:12), or what it means to be an apostle, that is, to be sent to
do God's will (20:21). We should rather be prepared by the Prologue to "come
and see!" (1:39, 46), as once did Andrew and Peter and Philip and Nathanael.

If recent scholarship is right in relocating John in Jewish traditions,[10] what
we would find, if we looked back behind John's *Logos*, is the mighty active
Dabar YHWH, "the Word of the Lord" in Hebrew Scriptures, where this same
Word of the Lord was already a known, though assuredly elusive, figure in
the traditions of Israel.[11] The Logos who becomes incarnate as this man, as
the Prologue indicates by echoing the opening verses of Genesis, is the eternal persona, the *hypostasized, that is, personified (ho logos)* self-communication
of the self-communicating God, who as such is the light and life of all creation. In that case, the Logos is not the immaterial spook often caricatured, a
mythological entity emanating from an alien, utterly transcendent deity who

descends to occupy the shell of the human figure for a time in the gross realm of rude matter, only then to discard the shell of flesh and return to its true being in light. John's Logos, having "become flesh," remains this flesh forever (John 6:53; 20:27), just as the saving function of His incarnation, as we have heard, is to procure in His crucified and risen body the worship of the nations on the earth. Raymond Brown was right in this regard to claim that the Johannine "Prologue is a description of the history of salvation in hymnic form"[12] and that its theology of the Incarnation "would not have been compatible to gnostic or docetic strains of thought. . . . Instead of supplying the liberation from the material world that the Greek mind yearned for, the Word of God was now inextricably bound to human history."[13] This affirmation anticipates, as we shall see, the Nicene *homoousios* (the same essence).

The assumption of the flesh by the Logos is the turning point in the scriptural drama of the redemption of the world. "The flesh of Jesus is the new localization of God's presence on earth. . . . Jesus is the replacement of the ancient Tabernacle. . . . In dwelling among men, the Word anticipates the divine presence that according to Revelation (21:3) will be visible to men in the last days."[14] Paul LaMarche similarly interprets the Prologue in terms of a conception of the progression of the history of salvation: "God through his Logos conceived, prepared, and effected the salvation both of the Gentile world (1:1-9) and of Israel (1:10-11). Right from the beginning, despite certain rebuffs (1:10-11), he planned to unite them into a single community of the children of God (1:12-13)."[15] John's Logos then *is* God's eternal decision to create, redeem, and fulfill the world through Jesus Christ, the plan that is implemented in the history of salvation (and later laid out in the Genesis-to-Revelation canon). In this light there is then nothing logically "paradoxical" as such about the "becoming flesh" of this Word of the God of Israel to bring about the creation's redemption and fulfillment, however much its appearance as *Jesus* offends in that He subverts accustomed ways of thought. As Craig L. Koester has so rightly concluded, "The Fourth Gospel present a particular message with a universal scope. . . . The Gospel writer cannot say, 'Jesus is the way for me but not for you.' To say that would be to say that 'the love of God is for me but not for you.'"[16] The offense of particularity resides not in the becoming flesh (for Israel's God is capable of time and history), but in the particular flesh assumed and for the particular purpose undertaken. The son of Mary's flesh was at length crucified, in order that by this hidden and ignominious form God would be glorified in taking away the sin of the world. Therefore "to make the message less particular would mean making the love of God less radical, since the evangelist understands that the divine love is definitively conveyed through the crucified and risen Messiah."[17] In this light, the Incarnation as such is simply the concrete realization of the divine will to create and redeem and fulfill the world by God's own participation in its processes. Such participation is the glory of the scriptural God, not His humili-ation. In turn, the "Gospel as a whole is nothing other than the narrative of the history of Logos, who was in the beginning with God."[18] The Johannine Logos attains this purpose and reaches this goal in "becoming" flesh and "taberna-cling" among us, just as human creatures attain their divinely prepared destiny in "beholding His glory."

In light of such Jewish background, incarnation of the Word "must be understood as the unique interpretation *of God*,"[19] that is, incarnate not as Caesar but as *Jesus*, not as Herod but as *Jesus*, not as Moses or Torah but as *Jesus*, who is the Son of the heavenly Father, not of these others. For the same reason, illumination *in us* by the Spirit is necessary precisely because revela-tion *of God*—of the Father who sends His Son, of the Son who shows His Father's heart (1:18)—has here a genuinely novel content that we could not have known apart from it. "Behold the Lamb of God who takes away the sin of the world" (1:29)—*this* sin-bearing is how *Jesus* is full of "grace and truth." This is the "glory" of His love for His friends, the glory made visible, the glory to be seen in this *particular* man and none other.

As noted, the special position of John as hermeneutical keystone of the New Testament canon that provides as such the bridge from the apostolic gen-eration to the great Christological and trinitarian dogmas of the early catholic church has been massively disputed in the modern period. The objection, by now familiar, runs: How can the visibly glorious Jesus of John's Gospel be *one and the same persona* as the godforsaken Jesus of Mark? How can Paul's mes-sage of the justification of the ungodly be reconciled with John's message of eternal life for insiders? The man Jesus who appears in the Fourth Gospel is already the risen, ascended, and glorified Lord who speaks to His own by His Spirit and Word today and every day, not Jesus of Nazareth who came into Galilee proclaiming the nearness of God's reign (Mark 1:14). Indeed, in John we hear the voice sounding out of the only Son who enjoyed divine glory with the Father before the foundations of the world. The personal subject, the *Ego* of the man Jesus of Nazareth, is not any human personality of the man of Nazareth, but the only-begotten God, the Son of the Father who regularly pronounces the divine *I am*. While there are striking depictions of Jesus' physi-cal pathos and emotional feeling in John, the human mind of the man Jesus appears strictly and exclusively in John under this determination from above to be the Son of the Father, who goes "in an entirely sovereign manner" (J. L. Martyn) to the paradoxical exaltation of the cross. We meet in John one, con-crete, indivisible persona: the weeping Jesus (11:33-35), the Christ, the Son of God "who has overcome the world" (16:33). This apparent "contradiction in terms" is *The Problem* of the Gospel according to John.

It is crucially important not to cut the Gordian knot here. It is certainly *not* some "historical Jesus" who speaks in John, though everything that is said is said by Jesus of Nazareth. Neither is it some "historical Jesus" who speaks in the Synoptics or in Paul or in Q or whatever. The strangeness of John's Jesus should not be approached by means of this heavily freighted distinction between a so-called Jesus of History and the Christ of Faith, for there is no Jesus whatsoever who is not remembered in faith (or disbelief, which is another kind of faith). Nor is it a question of the difference in historical and dogmatic approaches to biblical exegesis, as if theology could simply invent history, as if history—the history of *Jesus* of Nazareth—were not a theological riddle from start to finish. The second-century church's struggle to receive John into the canon is sufficient testimony to the early recognition of the oddity of the Fourth Gospel, just as the eventual placement of John in the canon is a key to understanding the true dogmatic unity of the New Testament. The historical criticism of the Gospel of John also has a history, one that needs to be known and criticized, if traffic on the Johannine bridge is to be restored. That would in fact be a two-way traffic. Not only does the Gospel make intelligible to us the historical movement that led with inner necessity to the early dogmas, but this Gospel also becomes our (that is, Gentile) access to the world of the Bible, providing us with the theological categories in which the biblical canon coheres. As such, it provides rules for the right, evangelical, and catholic use of the Bible to render the persona Jesus Christ as God's promise to be for us in the specific form of union with the Son, in the power of the Spirit, to the glory of the Father—the temporal and eternal doxology of the New Temple people of God.

Our thesis in this chapter is that historically the Johannine corpus was formed by the experience of martyrdom for the name of Jesus and that this theology of the martyrs as such opposes christological docetism and theological dualism. To see this we must in some detail review the main features of the modern critical discussion of John and then study the Gospel's earliest reception.

Critique of Modern Johannine Criticism

The starting point of any contemporary discussion of the theology of the Gospel of John still belongs with Rudolf Bultmann. We have already noted the striking feature of John: his bold reworking of existing materials. Bultmann's interpretation seized upon this critical insight. His interpretation of John discovered a precedent in the biblical canon itself for his program of demythologizing by showing how the Fourth Gospel had already executed a sovereign reinterpretation of the apocalyptic mythology of primitive Christianity about the coming of a new, supernatural world. The evangelist has come to understand that a new world does not come, but a new relation to God comes to the individual believer by a decision of faith in the Word of Christ that "overcomes the world." "John indicates that the Church's word must sound forth ever the same yet in ever new form. How it may do so, the Gospel of John itself illustrates by the way in which it both adopts and sovereignly transforms the tradition."[20] How, according to Bultmann, has this come about?

Bultmann brought into focus his fundamental claim for the revisionist "Eschatology of the Gospel of John" (1928)[21] with a study of the concept of *krisis* (judgment, division). The term *eschatology* (doctrine of the last things) is still justified, for the work of Jesus is "'to give life' and 'to judge.' These last (in the sense of ultimate) works of God do not refer, however, to the 'last judgement' or to the 'parousia' as to a visible cosmic finale that will happen to the world sooner or later." Rather, with the contemporary event of preaching the crisis of life and death is already precipitated for the individual whose personal existence is a matter of ultimate interest but at the same time an unresolved enigma. Faith likewise is "defined eschatologically." Faith is the possibility of decision bestowed by the encounter with the Word of Jesus "in time . . . [in] the uniqueness and contingency of the revelation." Referring to texts like John 5:24-5; 3:18; 8:51; 11:25, Bultmann concluded, "Life is already here, the unbeliever is already judged." This is emphatically not to be understood as "spiritualization or mysticism," Bultmann writes, because "the event which as a fact in time transforms the world (because it judges) is the sending of Jesus"; so also, by extension, the witness of preaching that reiterates it. "The judgment is an event occurring in the world and in world history; it is not a process in the soul." Close studies of Johannine terminology demonstrate this revisionist eschatology. "'The world' is primarily mankind." The intent of the Johannine Prologue, which asserts that the world was created by God through his Word, is to "*qualify* the world as 'created.'" As a result knowledge of God is not anything about God, as in classical dogmatics, but simply the human "acknowledgement" of createdness—self-knowledge as a finite creature. It follows that "just because [the world] is creation, the possibility has been given to it of misunderstanding itself, of setting itself against God." Creation asserts its autonomy over against the Creator and in this decision again and again becomes the fallen world. Bultmann conceives the event of revelation in turn as the direct challenge to this world's self-misunderstanding as autonomous, as self-created. In the event of this challenge by revelation to autonomous human self-understanding, two possibilities become actual for the hearer. One can "cling firmly to oneself," "deliberately appropriate" one's fallenness, and therewith condemn oneself. Or in a "new sense" one can proceed "out of the world—really outside it, no longer to belong to it."

With these choices precipitated by the "coming of the Revealer," a *crisis* occurs, meaning a fork in the road, a judgment that divides. "This is the *crisis* of the world, that is, the challenge to the human self-misunderstanding as independent of God." As already noted, the choice between autonomy and theonomy already tacitly attends creation as the fundamental spiritual possibilities. The Revealer, by the fact of His coming and calling human beings to decision for God, really only makes these latent possibilities articulate and so actual and decisive. "The two possibilities are distinguished in the way in which the Word is heard. The crisis is brought about in the nature of the reaction to the revelation." Because of the latency of the two possibilities, Bultmann can maintain that "the *crisis* is consummated *in the present,* that is, at the definite time when the response is made to the sending of the Son." Yet "it is this eschatological *now* only when it is strictly bound to the 'Word become flesh.'" Why is a choice thought to be latent in creation made only now in response to the contingent advent of the Word of Christ and then bound to it? Because "the Word that speaks to me and is heard is simply the Word that proclaims that fact," that is, that the Word has come, is present, in this sense is "incarnate," forcing the issue. This preaching *is* the eschatological event that forces the latent choice of creation to the surface and so "divides all history into two halves, into two aeons."

Thus Bultmann's picture of the Christian message according to John is sharply, indeed exclusively focused on the call of God to faith, the proclamation of the Word of God calling to trust and away from security, of which Jesus Christ is the agent. The content of the Revelation is nothing but the fact that Jesus Christ comes as the Revealer of God with this call to faith, thus the mere "that" (*das Dass*) of His mission, the fact of His coming and call. The evangelist regards the sources and witnesses that he employs going back to Jesus Himself as theologically *nothing but* the contingent vehicle of the "eschatological" call of God to a radical break from the fallen world of human autonomy. Against this summons to radical faith, however, human beings try to secure themselves even, if not especially, with religious myths and dogmatisms that objectify faith into knowledge along with the security and power that come from knowledge. Whoever has knowledge trusts the evidence of their own senses or the power of their own insight. In this subtle way, radical faith is compromised by theology itself and the authentic Word of Christ calling the individual to existential decision is made absurd and offensive by presenting an outmoded cosmology as if it were a revealed worldview. Special knowledge of a mythical figure appearing somewhere in the world replaces trust in the call of the Beyond in the event of preaching. But John's Christ "is not to be understood as a figure of this world, but his appearing in the world is to be conceived as an *embassage from without, an arrival from elsewhere.*"[22]

This is a curious antinomy, typical of Bultmann's thought. Does the coming from without preclude becoming a figure in this world? One should think, *prima facie,* that the dwelling among us of a figure beheld in glory makes the Johannine Jesus very much in, thought not of, this world.

Historically speaking, the Gospel of John, according to Bultmann, daringly employed heterodox Gnostic-docetic ideas to break free from the grip of the apocalyptic myth about a future cosmic event in which the earlier traditions

about Jesus were ensconced. "In short, then, the figure of Jesus in John is portrayed in the forms offered by the Gnostic Redeemer Myth"—not to supplant
one myth for another, one objectifying discourse with another, but to overcome myth by myth. The evangelist dares to do this: "The believer may not
base his faith on the authority of others, but he must himself find the object
of faith; he must perceive, through the proclaimed word, the word of the
Revealer himself. Thus we are faced with the strange paradox that the proclamation, without which no man can be brought to Jesus, is itself insignificant,
in that the hearer who enjoys the knowledge of faith is freed from its tutelage,
is free, that is, to criticize the proclamation that brought him to faith. This is
why it is impossible ever to give a definite dogmatic statement of the proclamation."[23] Something like the first chapter of this book on what the gospel is
then is ruled out as impossible.

Bultmann's *attack on the very possibility of dogma* has become a widely dif-
fused truism since his time, both in Reformation theology where contemporary Lutherans have preferred it the nightmare of Karl Barth's neo-orthodox
renewal of critical dogmatics and also in liberal Protestant biblical studies (even
where Bultmann is otherwise no longer followed). In the Fourth Evangelist's
precedent-setting freedom over against the previous Christian tradition and in
his concern to retrieve the authentic core of that tradition as contemporaneous existential address, Bultmann established as virtual alternatives the Word
taken as report and the Word taken as address: "Man is not asked to believe
in a set of dogmas on the authority of a preacher without credentials; what is
demanded of man is a faith that experiences Jesus' words as they affect man
himself."[24] To be certain, Bultmann acknowledged the "strange paradox" to
which this distinction leads, that "the proclamation, without which no man
can be brought to Jesus, is itself insignificant." Indeed, as we shall see, the
problem runs far deeper. Jesus Himself becomes no more than a cipher for
any choice among the existential possibilities latent in the human condition.

What is curious about Bultmann's interpretation as a whole is that he so
confidently knows what cannot be known about God, that is, his apophaticism.
Bultmann's interpretation of the statement in 1:18, "No one has ever seen God,"
reveals the master presupposition of his theological exegesis. "God ceases to be
God, if he is thought of as an object." Though Bultmann thinks that both he and
the Fourth Evangelist stand here on the purest soil "of a radical form [of] the
oriental and OT idea of the sovereignty and absoluteness of God," the claim is
historically vacuous.[25] In fact, it is the Platonic tradition of negative, natural theology with its own program of demythologizing going back to Plato's torutred
relation to Homer that reaches its modern denouement here.[26] "What the world
calls a mystery is not a true mystery at all. In its foolish mythology it turns its
mysterious, transcendent origin into something belonging to this world. It imagines that it has criteria by which it can determine whether and where God's

mystery has become visible."[27] It is important to grasp just how far reaching Bultmann's Platonism extends.[28] The "Word made flesh" in order to be beheld by humans in faith does not mean, according to this, exactly what it says: that He dwelt among us. The critical enterprise of dogmatic theology of testing by this very criteria (formulated against docetism, as we shall see) to discern the incarnate Word from impostors is ruled out of bounds.

It is in fact such notions of God's ineffability—that God cannot in principle be represented in the categories of worldly language without fatal contradiction—that stand behind the supposedly "paradoxical" nature of revelation in time and space, which accordingly has *no content* other than the bare announcement of Jesus as the Revealer who "by his coming does not become a phenomenon of this world, but . . . remains a stranger who takes his leave again." Accordingly, "the revelation is much more a denial and a questioning of the world; the acceptance of its gift therefore demands that man abandon all human desires and imaginations, all human striving for possession and mastery."[29] Correspondingly, the revelation comes without any worldly accreditation: "It would no longer be God's Word if it demanded other authorities recognized by men to confirm its authenticity."[30] Yet it rings true to faith, because it finds a point of contact with human existence in the latent sense of the creature's own, aforementioned questionableness: "whether man, when confronted by the event of the revelation, will remain true to his genuine prior knowledge of the revelation [that is, his own sense of his questionableness as a creature], whereby he sees it as an otherworldly event that passes judgment on him and his world; or whether he will make his own illusory ideas the criterion by which to judge the revelation."[31]

Bultmann's impressive and influential *Commentary on John* restored the classical status of John as a theological key over against nineteenth-century liberalism's post-Straussian dismissal of the Gospel as so much flight from history to Greek metaphysics; yet Bultmann rehabilitation came at the tall cost of his program of existential interpretation and demythologizing and his historical thesis about a Gnostic source. The persona of Jesus evaporated into the punctiliar event of the eschatological Word calling for the individual's decision for God and against the world. The whole of salvation history—that is to say, the canonical Scriptures running from Genesis to Revelation—was critically reduced to this razor-thin edge cutting vertically into the world from above as the two-sided sword of the Word in the event of the preaching of the cross. The cross "makes it ultimately plain what the *one* offense is: it is that a mere man, whose life ends in death, solemnly lays the claim that he is the Revealer of God!"[32] The old church's employment of the Gospel of John as bridge from the earliest proclamation of the resurrection of the Crucified through gospel narrative to the classical christological and trinitarian dogmas has been based on a literalist misunderstanding of the Gospel, akin to Nicodemus's bumbling reaction to Jesus in John 3:4.

Käsemann's Dissent

Bultmann's *Commentary* opened up a double-sided development that has determined Johannine scholarship for the past fifty years. Historically, Bultmann's proposal that John used some Gnostic literary document led to a source-critical quest for the history of the traditions behind the Gospel. This quest, however, led more and more away from the Gnostic sources that Bultmann posited. It eventually led to the realization of the thoroughly Jewish milieu of the Gospel. Theologically, however, something somewhat different occurred. Here as elsewhere Ernst Käsemann defined the rebellion against his teacher's existentialist reduction of primitive Christian theology's cosmic and ethical claims. In the case of John, however, Käsemann denied that the Fourth Evangelist had escaped apocalyptic literalism without himself succumbing to Gnostic mythology. On the contrary, Käsemann finally came to the view that the Gospel of John as the Trojan horse of Gnosticism in the church for its depiction of Jesus as "a God striding upon the earth," obliterating the humanity of the man from Nazareth. The effect of Käsemann's attack was to return theologically to the mistrust of John in favor of a new (the so-called second) quest of the so-called historical Jesus. Thus post-Bultmann historical and theological tendencies diverged. Not a few of the numerous reconstructions of the history of Johannine community that ensued were motivated by the desire to resolve the historical and theological perplexities arising from the Bultmann-Käsemann debate. Typically one imagined an original "Signs Gospel" that proclaimed Jesus as a Gnostic, wonder-working "divine man" over against which the evangelist executed a theologically correct redaction. But in all this, some of Bultmann's most basic construals of the Fourth Gospel's theology and historical setting went unchallenged. Let us review the matter more precisely.

The key critical supposition underlying Bultmann's historical criticism of John, and also of Käsemann's even in his sharp dissent from Bultmann, is that something like the so-called Gnostic Redeemer Myth of a preexistent ascending and descending divine being stands behind the Johannine notion of the Logos. The argument between Käsemann and Bultmann about the interpretation of the Incarnation in 1:14 was based on this common assumption. Bultmann believed that the Fourth Evangelist had not himself become ensnared. For the evangelist simultaneously "demythologized" the Gnostic Redeemer Myth by means of his christological paradox. All the mythological speech about the preexistent Logos is referred to the man, nothing but the man Jesus, who neither offers a defense of His claim nor explains any content to it but bears witness from the cross to the call of God. According to Bultmann, "the *offense* of the gospel is brought out as strongly as possible" by 1:14; he glosses the verse this way: "It is in his sheer humanity that he is the Revealer." This is the "paradox that runs through the whole gospel," that otherworldly glory is to be seen in the flesh, only as flesh, "in a peculiar *hiddenness*"[33]—that is to say, not seen at all but thought. Bultmann then did not think of faith as something *created* by the perception of Jesus' glory; rather he spoke of faith as the human decision about its own self-understanding that *overcomes* the scandal or offense of the Logos's fleshly incognito to recognize in the mortal Jesus the ineffable call of God to live without security. In this way, too, the Gnostic personification of the Redeemer figure is also jettisoned.

Bultmann sensed the difficulty with his bold interpretation of John 1:14 when he wrote that John "frees himself from this mythology, but at the same time retains its terminology"; he resolves this tension with the thesis of intentional paradox. The Johannine Jesus' "doctrine is the *that* of his mission, that fact that he is the Revealer,"[34] since Jesus has no such credentials and others have no criteria by which to assess His claim. The paradoxical revelation of God is nothing but Jesus from Nazareth and His Word: "His very proclamation consists in the scandalous claim that his origins are in heaven."[35] Exegetically the problem with this bold claim is that in John the signs and discourses interpreting them are positively valued as creative of faith in Jesus as the Son of God bringing life in His name. "We have seen his glory" (1:14). The flesh of Jesus is not a veil that faith penetrates to reach a thought or a concept, treating the flesh as a stumbling block that must be overcome; it is rather the vehicle of glory, "the place where the Word of God is recognized" and faith is born. So Bultmann's rebellious disciple incisively argued against his teacher's "strange mixture of truth and falsehood" in exegesis of the Gospel.

Käsemann's correction of Bultmann, that "the 'flesh' [of 1:14] for the Evangelist" is not in paradoxical contradiction with otherworldliness of the Logos, but is rather "the possibility for the Logos, as the Creator and Revealer, to have communication with men," has far-reaching implications. It places the Gospel's christological paradox in a different setting and gives it a different sense: it "does not in any way imply that the becoming flesh as such is the stumbling block," but rather provides the means by which the Creator "enters the world of createdness and in so doing exposes himself to the judgment of the creature." Bultmann's reading accordingly runs the risk of "interpreting the incarnation of the Logos in the sense of the 'kenosis' [Greek: emptying] doctrine . . . [when in fact] according to the Fourth Evangelist (and for that matter, according to the Synoptics) he who has become flesh does not cease to exist as a heavenly being." The "kenosis" doctrine, a nineteenth-century doctrine developed to teach that in the Incarnation the divine Son gave up all divine prerogatives, may or may not be a solution to theological problems created by the modern historical criticism of the Bible. But as exegesis of the Gospel of John it is fanciful.[36]

So Käsemann responded to Bultmann's line of interpretation in a 1957 essay where he denied that any such "demythologizing" of the Logos as the Gnostic heavenly being that has emptied itself into the mere humanity of the crucified Jesus is evident in the Gospel. On the contrary, "it is characteristic of the whole Gospel . . . that the humanity of Christ recedes totally into the background,"[37] swallowed up by the portrait of "Jesus as the God who walked on earth."[38] The seeds of the all-out attack on the Gospel as "naive docetism" in the *Testament of Jesus* (1968)[39] are thus already evident in this earlier article. Käsemann was most concerned to forbid any illicit harmonizing that would mute the radical distinctiveness of the Fourth Gospel. In this connection, he scored a real point against Bultmann's modernizing, kenotic-christological interpretation of the Gospel's supposed paradox of revelation in hiddenness, which has more to do with post-Kantian fideism than Johannine theology. With this, however, Bultmann's thin line of defense against the historical-critical judgment on John as himself a Gnostic collapsed. John had not taken over Gnostic mythology merely in order to demythologize apocalyptic. He took it over and was taken over by it—and brought it into the church—so Käsemann would eventually conclude.

In 1957 Käsemann could still manage fine pages on the theology of John. Against Bultmann's chief idea that the christological paradox lies in the "peculiar hiddenness" of the flesh, Käsemann insisted on the visibility of the glory of Jesus in John, and formulates its function acutely: "To the world, however, the scandal . . . [is] not the becoming man as such but its function, that is, that by means of it God moves in to the attack. The world survives by keeping God at a distance even while making him a manageable and predictable object of its speculations. . . . Through Jesus this safe distance is annihilated."[40] In *Testament of Jesus*, however, Käsemann vented his full and considerable fury against the Gospel that he now clearly regarded as virtually Gnostic. The world in John is persistently depicted in hostile terms and salvation is imagined as the removal of elect individuals from it. All that matters is the preaching of the Word, the present experience of world-transcendence, the call to faith. Cultivation of a sectarian brotherhood of true believers replaces the apocalyptic hope for the redemption of the creation. The Johannine Jesus is an inhuman impostor; the cry of dereliction from the cross is unimaginable from the lips of the Johannine demigod whose death is nothing but the first stage of his ascent to his true, heavenly home. And so on.

In an important rejoinder to Käsemann's polemical tract, G. Bornkamm, aside from correcting any number of the foregoing exaggerations, wondered what the widespread assumption means, that "John *presupposes* Gnosticism."[41] Allowing that assumption to stand, Bornkamm nevertheless construed its significance rather differently than Käsemann: "The fact that John speaks from within the same conceptual world is important for grasping his significant differences from gnosticism."[42] Bornkamm highlighted the Gospel's refusal to disqualify the world in the sense of a metaphysical dualism and above all the Gospel's faith in God the Creator that is operative "not just [in] the decisions men make for themselves . . . but the decisions which God makes in their regard." The Johannine *theology*, that is, its understanding of the loving act *of God* for humanity is," Bornkamm concluded, "most decidedly an anti-gnostic understanding of faith."[43]

These exchanges among Bultmann and two of his most significant students revealed not only a fundamental lack of historical clarity about the bewildering variety of Gnostic and/or docetist motifs, but also a lack of theological clarity. What exactly is objectionable about Gnosticism? and from what point of view? What is docetism? Bornkamm held that the Gospel of John asserts "with unprecedented, unremitting and perhaps exasperating one-sidedness . . . that purely *as* world, the world is impure and that the only road to salvation is a union with God and Jesus disclosed in the word and seized on by faith."[44] Is that Gnosticism—or is it Christianity? One also has to wonder historically whether the underlying hypothesis of a Gnostic source has fundamentally confused the discussion. One has to wonder whether multiform, heterodox, apocalyptically stamped Judaism (such as we know of from the Qumran texts), before the year 70 when the siege of Jerusalem concluded and the temple was destroyed, provides the whole store of motifs needed to locate Johannine traditions historically, including the rise of Gnosticism among apocalyptically disillusioned Jews. In that conceptual world, early Gnosticism and a non-Gnostic Gospel of John could readily be conceived to arise as contemporaneous responses to the same phenomenon: the collapse of the apocalyptic faith of the Zealots, and the consequent theological consolidations of Jewish and Christian communities under the duress of the religious and political disaster of the failed revolt.

This criticism brings to light a second serious objection to Bultmann's essential contrast of the evangelist's theology of the "now" of salvation over against "the Jewish hope—and consequently to all imaginary visions of a future salvation."[45] Against this, one must rather see how John's Christology sustains the apocalyptic theology of the God who is realizing and revealing His plan to give life to the world, even in face of the shattering experience for the little flock of Jesus of the world's rejection of grace and preference for darkness. Bultmann's exegetical insight into the Fourth Gospel's theology of *crisis* then rather belongs, according to Nils Alstrup Dahl, to a "christocentric and forensic conception of history." Against Bultmann, however, that conception means that there is a comprehensive view of reality in John as a history of conflict with the *civitas terrena*; the figure of Jesus and His Word cannot be abstracted from this construction of history without fundamental distortion: "The sin of the world is its self-assertion against the Word in which it was created, the Word who was in the beginning with God and who became flesh and dwelt among us. The conflict between light and darkness, between Christ and the world, is the one essential theme of history."[46] In the figure of the Logos, John takes up the prophetic witness of the Scriptures; he depicts a "cosmic lawsuit," in which "Christ is the representative of God," leading up to the climactic proceedings before Pilate. As such, "the ministry of Jesus in Israel, his voluntary death as 'king of the Jews,' and his glorification by God are, thus, the historical and juridical basis for the life of the church and for the witness which it brings to all men." The Holy Spirit is precisely described as Paraclete, Advocate, *prosecuting attorney* (John 16:8-11, "And when he comes, he will prove the world wrong about sin and righteousness and judgment"). Led by this Spirit, the disciples will be enabled "to play their role in the lawsuit of history" as true martyr-witnesses. "The Christocentricity of the Fourth Gospel does not exclude a sense of historical continuity, going backward from the church Universal to the first disciples and eyewitnesses of Jesus in Israel and farther back to those who believed and bore witness to him before his incarnation. In this sense, John is aware of a 'history of salvation' and sees the church as the 'true Israel' to which the 'children of God scattered abroad' have been added. The church has also a historical task in the present, through its existence and through its preaching to bear testimony to Christ in a world which is still hostile to him, even if it has already been legally defeated."[47]

Dahl's biblical-canonical correction of Bultmann's one-sidedly existential interpretation of John's theology of crisis suggests in turn that Jesus' notorious conflict with "the Jews" (which term Bultmann construed as a symbol of the hostile world of human autonomy) bears in fact a more concrete meaning, as suggested above. Certainly the conflict with Pharisaic Judaism from the period after the fall of Jerusalem and the destruction of the temple in 70, during which Christian Jews were expelled from the synagogues, overlays John's terminology. The term "the Jews" therefore may not be taken straightforwardly as "historical" without absurdity (Jesus is "a Jew"!). Moreover, for all the hostile rhetoric against "the Jews" in John, there is in this Gospel no simple supercession, as is often thought, of the Jewish people; what is superseded is rather of the cult of the temple in Jerusalem, as we have seen.[48] More profoundly, John's theology of the Incarnation as "tabernacling" is incomprehensible and historically groundless apart from its specific rootage in Israel's knowledge of the living God as experienced in worship and represented in the theology of the temple. Therefore Dahl correctly pointed to John's notion of the "true Israelites, of whom Nathanael is the type." "The Jews," that is, the theologians of the temple in Jerusalem, do not belong to this true Israel. Rather believers from Israel as also from the Greeks will be found to constitute the new, true Temple whose High Priest prays on the eve of His perfect self-sacrifice, "I ask not only on behalf of these, but also on behalf of those who will believe in me through their word, that they may all be one. As you, Father, are in me and I am in you, may they also be in us, so that the world may believe that you have sent me" (17:20-21). To be precise then, in John's theology Jesus and His believers do not replace Judaism (which as a religion, so-called normative or rabbinic

Judaism, also comes into existence also as a response to the destruction of the temple[49]). Rather it is the temple in Jerusalem as the place where the God of Israel's gift of life is actualized on earth that is replaced.

In light of these criticisms of the modern criticism of the Fourth Gospel, we can conclude this section with the perceptive remark of Dunn that any justification of John's traditional role in the theological reading of the Bible today would turn on the question of whether John's Gospel allows itself to be understood as a bridge: "If the Johannine distinctives *are* derived from the earlier Christian tradition, they have to be explained as a *development* of that tradition."[50] The historical-critical and theological question is whether John merits this traditional, canonical role. Methodologically, there must be a justification "by at least some reference to the meaning intended by the fourth evangelist."[51] Dunn scathingly comments that that will require something other than the source-critical "pursuit of the phantom of the pre-Christian Gnostic Redeemer Myth."[52] The one safe control against sophisticated speculation in the name of source criticism is the first real task of exegesis, which is to uncover the historical-literal sense of the received text: "Only by uncovering its historical context can we hope to hear it as the first readers were intended to hear it, the allusions and nuances as well as the explicit teaching."[53]

With these points Dunn is reviving the forgotten approach to John taken in the commentary of Edwyn Hoskyns, an English contemporary of Bultmann's, who had insisted that we respect "the man who wrote the Fourth Gospel [as] master of his material" and that we who would understand him must "take up [our] position where the original readers stood."[54] A true historical and critical interpretation does not speculate about what lies behind the text in order to deconstruct it (by means of a speculative reconstruction of supposedly "what really happened"), but rather labors to sit before the text to read and understand it as would its first audience. In the particular case of the biblical writings—preeminently the Gospel of John—such a historical-critical listening must at the same time be theological exegesis. This literature is *about God.* The insight that John is a *theologian* working in narrative fashion on the traditions he has received and of which we know something from other books preserved in the New Testament thus becomes crucially important. Although John recalls many of the notions and titles expressive of what Jesus meant to various peoples—"Rabbi," "Teacher," "King of Israel," "the Prophet," "Savior of the World," "Man from Heaven," but also "Son of Joseph and Mary," "Samaritan and son of the Devil," "the Man," "King of the Jews"—John is primarily concerned to know: Who is this Jesus of Nazareth, indeed with all these controversial and bewildering historical relations—*for God?* Indeed, that is properly the question of Christology: Who is Jesus *for God?* And *who then is God* because of this relation to Jesus? These questions and their answers constitute the real dogmatic unity of the New Testament, when John is understood both historically and theologically as the bridge.

Hoskyns's Theological Interpretation of John

We can begin anew studying the Gospel of John in the knowledge that "the Church clearly intends the book to be read in close connection with the earlier gospels, and not as an isolated, independent work."[55] So urged Sir Edwyn Hoskyns, the Cambridge biblical scholar best remembered perhaps as the translator into English of Barth's *Epistle to the Romans*. But Hoskyns was the author of an unjustly forgotten, tragically unfinished commentary on the Gospel of John. He made this canonical insight into the hermeneutical function of the Fourth Gospel the axis on which his lucid, learned, and moving interpretation of the Gospel turned—interestingly in the same period that Rudolf Bultmann was composing his influential commentary that would dominate the future of scholarship and direct research and reflection in an opposite way, as just discussed. Hoskyns did not claim that John had editions of the Synoptic Gospels in front of him as he wrote, for "his relation to them is not one of an editor."[56] He recognized that Johannine parallels to the Synoptic materials contain far too many unmotivated deviations from the Synoptic accounts to posit literary dependence or redactional activity in the strict sense. This opinion has gained ground among biblical scholars. "John knows and reflects the Synoptic narratives, but they are hardly his sources in the usual sense" (de Solages).[57] But Hoskyns already posed the key question. "The important question is not whether the Fourth Gospel depends upon oral tradition, or upon written documents, but whether it is or is not a work existing in its own right and whether it is or is not to be interpreted independently and by itself."[58] Bultmann affirmed the Fourth's Gospel's autonomy; Käsemann insisted on it with almost fanatical zeal and with equally one-sided results. Hoskyns's counter-thesis, which denies that the Fourth Gospel "exist[s] in its own right" and "is adequate for its own interpretation," has gone unheeded until recently.[59]

For his own part, Hoskyns followed in the way of earlier British scholars, particularly Scott Holland for whom "the existence of the synoptic gospels had evoked the Fourth Gospel."[60] The enigma of the figure of Jesus, an enigma that had been created by the Synoptic Gospels' conservative method of assembling in a narrative framework small units of tradition to render the paradoxical persona of the eschatological in history, cried out for explanation. "The Fourth Gospel is a work of interpretation; but the interpretation was not made up of allegory or of mysticism or of philosophical speculation." Rather Holland imagined a "veritable eyewitness who, after long years of 'brooding meditation,' had been enabled to see that what he remembered made sense of the synoptic gospels and provided them with a proper theological and historical background."[61] In more sophisticated fashion than Holland but in essential continuity with him, Hoskyns went on to ask whether "some strict relationship, if not between the Fourth Gospel and the synoptic gospels, at least between it and the tradition that has been preserved in it," might be discovered.

He first took note of the striking and unaccountable absence of so much Synoptic material in John. Where, he asked, are the "important single epi-sodes—the Baptism and Transfiguration of Jesus, His Temptation, and the Agony in the Garden of Gethsemane?" "Where are the crisp, sharp aphoristic utterances, such as, 'Wheresoever the carcass is, there will the vultures be gath-ered'?" "Where are the parables?" "Where is the all-controlling, ever-recurring theme of the *Kingdom of God* . . . [whose] place is occupied by the *ego* of Jesus, the Son of God[?]" And "where is the insistent, precise call to repentance, urgent because it is uttered in the midst of this acute eschatological tension?" "Where are the short compressed narratives of the healing of the poor sick and distressed men and women . . . the pictures of Jesus standing in the midst of the poor and the outcast, moving towards publicans and sinners and drawing to Himself the tiny children—irresistibly?"[62]

Hoskyns then turned attention to an even "more surprising and embarrass-ing" gap between John and the Synoptics: "In the perspective of the Fourth Gospel, the scene of the ministry is altogether different: "Judaean, nay more, it is a Jerusalem topography. Moreover, Jesus speaks and acts not merely in Jerusalem, but in the Temple; not merely in the Temple, but in the Temple on the occasion of a series of Jewish feasts." From this Hoskyns deduced the evan-gelist's critical intent to underscore that "Judaism—Jewish faith and unbelief, Jewish worship, Jerusalem, the Old Testament Scriptures—was the veritable background of the teaching of Jesus and His actions, however much He may have said and done in Galilee," as represented in the Synoptics. Finally, all such differences pale before the difference in literary form. The Fourth Gospel, quite unlike the Synoptics, is "a literary unity, not an arrangement of incidents. The reader is required to move with the movement of the book . . . [noting] the self-contained allusiveness. The book moves on spirally. Incidents and dis-courses are everywhere interlocked . . . [so] that the reader shall be—shall we say?—overwhelmed by the singleness of the theme that is Jesus of Nazareth, son of man—Son of God."

The knowledge of such differences raises the historical problem of the Fourth Gospel to "an almost intolerably acute form: What has the author done? And why? What relation is there between his work and the earlier tradition?" This acute question, we recall, also formed Bultmann's point of departure, who took it as precedent and basis for his program of demythologizing the New Testament. Hoskyns considers both the radical thesis of H. Windisch, that John wrote to supersede the Synoptics, and the conservative thesis of much earlier British scholarship, that the Gospel is a "primary historical document" that derives from the unique witness of the Beloved Disciple. But he rejects both these views because "each in its own way denies the tension of history, which is the major theme of the Gospel." By this reference to the "tension of history," Hoskyns means to pose the historical question of what the Gospel could have meant to its primary audience. "Does the author of the Fourth Gospel presume his readers to be familiar with the current oral tradition of the primitive church?" If so, the horizon against which John's acknowledged (21:25) *selection* of material for inclusion in his writing would become visible and help us to understand "how the original readers of the gospel should be expected to be able to fill in these gaps in the narrative and to catch its allusions."

Indeed, close reading of the Gospel shows that the evangelist presumes knowledge among his readers of many other miracles that Jesus did and of parables that He told. The witness of John the Baptist in the Gospel's first chapter "is almost unintelligible unless the reader knows already that his work, and very particularly his imprisonment, formed the starting point of the ministry of Jesus." Knowledge of "an extended ministry of Jesus in Galilee" is assumed, as is Jesus' origin in Nazareth, His activity in Capernaum, and the Galilean background of His leading disciples. It is assumed that the apocalyptic language of "the Hour, the Last Day, Judgment, the Son of man, and the imminent return of Jesus" will be intelligible without explanation. The Passion "seems to assume its readers' knowledge of a trial before Caiaphas and even of Simon of Cyrene." Hoskyns then adds to this general knowledge of the tradition about Jesus evidences in John of knowledge "in particular of the tradition in its Marcan form." Particularly impressive are verbatim parallels in the stories of the Feeding of the Five Thousand and the Walking on the Sea, the Cleansing of the Temple, the Entry into Jerusalem, the Anointing of Jesus by the Woman, and episodes in the Passion narrative. Notable too are the places where "the framework of the Johannine narrative" follows Mark, particularly the sequence in John 6–8 of the Feeding, the Flight, the Walking on the Sea, and the Confession of Peter, as well as in the Passion. Hoskyns concluded that the original readers of John's Gospel "knew a great deal, and what they knew, they knew, roughly at least, in the form of what lies before us in the Marcan Gospel." (Further considerations could point to some intriguing affinities in theology and perspective with Luke's Passion and Resurrection stories.[63])

However much he might be inspired by traditions unique to his own community, the author of the Fourth Gospel is then no isolated or self-isolated figure. He is operating within the mainstream of early Christian traditions. In that case, however, it is all the more "clear that the author of the Fourth Gospel is not content to leave this knowledge in the form in which it was already possessed by his readers." Bultmann, we recall, thought that it was the need to de-literalize the received apocalyptic worldview that motivated John. But for Hoskyns John wrote "to disclose the underlying meaning of the tradition" about Jesus. He was compelled to do so because "the presentation of the life of Jesus in fragmentary episodes must have been a grave danger at the turn of the first century, for the scattered Christian communities had no generally accepted creed that would keep the evangelical episodes in a strict theological context. . . . There was as yet no Saint Ignatius to struggle for the meaning of the tradition." This allusion to Ignatius of Antioch is, as we shall shortly see, a telling indication of the bridge built by the Fourth Gospel. It follows in any event that John the Evangelist is best understood, according to Hoskyns, as John the Theologian[64]—a theologian of the very type that Bultmann proscribed, a theologian who seeks to know God in the "Word made flesh" as Someone to be beheld, glorified, and just so critically distinguished from impostors.

In this later connection, Hoskyns held (similarly to Bultmann, but probably inspired by Barth) that the chimera of the so-called historical Jesus in the minds of contemporary liberal Protestants represents a particular obstacle to proper understanding of the Fourth Gospel. For, he argued, "the meaning of the history of Jesus precedes and conditions its occurrence. This is what the author of the Fourth Gospel has seen."[65] Logically, Hoskyns's meaning in this dense formulation is the same as Pannenberg's notion of the resurrection's retroactive causality, discussed in chapter 2. Since Jesus is risen, since only Jesus is risen, Jesus is and always had been from the foundations of the universe the Son of God who would become incarnate in the fullness of time. This (divine) meaning of Jesus as Son of God precedes the historical occurrence of Jesus of Nazareth's coming and destiny. In turn, that claim implies that in its inmost *historical* particularity, this enigmatic Gospel unlocks itself only to *theological* exegesis. "If the gospel [of John] be relegated, dogmatically, to the past, it must remain, for all our historical imagination, a foreign, strange work, at times attractive, but also at times repellant."[66] Looking for a "historical Jesus" in John at the basis of some odd and marginal stream of tradition, then, is in fact an evasion of the theological problem that in *historical* fact lies at the center of this particular body of literature, expressly in John, implicitly in the Synoptic traditions, which John intended theologically to interpret. Dunn says concretely: "Only when we have a clear grasp of what is Johannine can we hope to distinguish what is pre-Johannine in any systematic way."[67]

In theology as critical dogmatics, historical knowledge of Jesus of Nazareth is a matter of theology's own self-critical testing of the one term of the confession of faith that this Jesus is the Christ, the Son of God. But such questions about the truthfulness of Johannine theology to Jesus, born of Mary and crucified under Pontius Pilate, can hardly be posed before successful exegesis of the received text of Scripture brings to light the several meanings of that judgment of faith regarding Jesus, such as its first readers would have understood it.[68]

In reproach of mere historicism in biblical studies in favor of theological exegesis, we can surely detect the stimulation Hoskyns derived from the early Barth. Hoskyns joined the early Barth in withering satire of historical-critical biblicism. These words, written more than fifty years ago, could have been written yesterday as they capture the recurring academic folly of the "quest for the historical Jesus":

In the midst of this rich, varied gallery [the Gospels], the reader can wander about. He is magnificently free. He can pause and admire, where he will. He can select an incident, visualize it, meditate upon it, and then preach about it, allegorize it, interpret it, symbolize it, apply it to his own circumstances, use it to pillory his enemies or to encourage himself and his friends; he can, in fact, construe it according to his own will and satisfaction, and finally, he can interpret it so as to escape from the teaching of St Paul, say, in the Epistle to the Romans, or so as to thrust the Fourth Gospel well onto the periphery of the Christian Religion. And in doing all this he can pride himself that he is acting in obedience to the highest authority, that of the authentic teaching of Jesus of Nazareth, and that he is a true disciple of the "Jesus of History" because he has heard Him speak and seen Him act.[69]

Barth had famously written in defense of his "pneumatic" exegesis in the preface to the second edition of his *Romans,* in words that Hoskyns himself had translated into English: "The critical historian needs to be more critical,"[70] that is, to engage the Criticism of us, would-be critics, which the content or subject matter of the biblical writings make in their witness to that God "who is in heaven, [while] man is on the earth."

Hoskyns nevertheless did not embrace the dialectical Platonism of the early Barth.[71] The early Barth could not understand the flesh of Jesus as more than the crater left by the bombshell of revelation—the negative imprint in time of the elusive divine and eternal event. But Hoskyns would not so drastically cut the Gordian knot of the "problem of history," since the gospel narrative not only constructs a picture of Jesus as the Christ from the perspective of resurrection faith but in so doing ineradicably *refers to* Jesus of Nazareth *as to this same person.* Jesus *passus sub Pontio Pilato* is a datable, locatable event in space and time. By the same token, this particular piece of history—Jesus of Nazareth—requires us to judge it too, precisely if we are to understand it in its own true historical distinctiveness. Without such historical-critical judgment of Jesus of Nazareth, predication of the title of Christ to Him amounts to docetism, the name "Jesus" becoming an apparition, without a content of its own, a malleable cipher. In continuity with his Anglican tradition's simultaneous commitments to reformation and patristic theology, Hoskyns accordingly made his *Grundtext* the Johannine *kai ho logos sarx egeneto*; here the one conviction and the one question of Christian theology is focused. "The Evangelist, writing after the destruction of the Temple, [does not] bemoan its loss. . . . The presence of God has not been withdrawn, for Jesus has taken the place of the Temple. . . . In the perspective of the Gospel, the abiding of the Word of God in flesh merges in the abiding of the Son of God in all those who believe in him."[72] Or again, "The visible, historical Jesus is the place in history where it is demanded that men should believe, and where they can so easily disbelieve, but where, if they disbelieve, the concrete history is found to be altogether meaningless, and where, if they believe, the fragmentary story of His life is woven into one whole."[73] The meaning precedes the occurrence, but the occurrence qua historical event raises the question acutely of its meaning. C. H. Dodd put Hoskyns's observation of Johannine perspectivalism in plainer words: "In the first place, there is [in John] a form of vision, simple physical vision, which may exist without faith. Many of the contemporaries of Jesus saw Him in this sense, without any saving effects. But when simple vision is accompanied by faith, it leads to vision in a deeper sense. . . . Faith then is a form of vision. When Christ was on earth, to have faith was to 'see His glory.'"[74]

The Johannine Theology of the Martyr

If we take our point of departure from the Farewell Discourses of John 13–17 as the express statement of John's theology, the Gospel as a whole, according to Hoskyns, is about "*the apostolic foundation of the Church* . . . [which] conditions the movement and 'lay-out' of the gospel; its horizon narrowing until Jesus, after the final rejection by the Jewish authorities and by the crowds, is depicted alone with His disciples, entrusting to them His authoritative mission to the world in the power of the Holy Spirit of Truth."[75] This reading would then put John in parallel to the development of Luke-Acts and the role played by the post-Easter sending of the Holy Spirit from the risen Lord on Pentecost. In *this* light, the fragmentary story of Jesus is woven together into the "whole" of the continuing story of His community in the world by the Word that remembers Him and the Spirit who so, and only so, leads to all truth. This ensuing history of salvation, however, is not to be thought of as a visible parade of mighty acts that marches, as the crowds assumed, from "victory unto victory." In the moment we try to take over Jesus and make Him our king—He flees (6:15). But John, understood to intend a theological interpretation akin to Luke in the opening chapter of Acts, nevertheless tells a history that is visible and in which God acts to overcome the world in the paradoxical *stance of the martyrs. John's Jesus reigns from the cross, victorious in apparent defeat.*

The ethical key to this paradoxical conception of the history of redemption, proceeding in time and space from "crisis unto crisis," lies in the *figure of the martyr*. The continuity of the history of salvation is perceived only but truly in the uncanny light of the cross (15:18). If we lose sight of this *martyrological* context in which John's depiction of the glorious passion of Jesus is drawn, however, we almost inevitably misunderstand Jesus' passionless passion, so to say, and fall into Käsemann's error of characterizing the Gospel as "naive docetism."

Concretely, Hoskyns detected at this point the impressive material affinity between the Fourth Gospel and Ignatius of Antioch (c. 110), the bishop-martyr whose seven letters on the way to the Coliseum in Rome have preserved a true treasure for us. Historically Ignatius is in near proximity to the Fourth Gospel, and Hoskyns could describe Ignatius's understanding of martyrdom in a very Johannine way: "that [Ignatius] has been summoned to become a place where the especial character of the Church can be apprehended, is what gives him his authority. . . . [He] sees his impending martyrdom as a dogmatic, theological, Christian event, as a visible occurrence, almost transparent with eternal significance; and which is therefore a parable of the faith of the Church."[76] Note well, it is not because Ignatius is a "bishop" that he possesses "authority," but it is because he is a martyr that he claims authority in his letters to instruct the churches. In this endeavor, Ignatius, who *defines* antidocetism *theologically* in early Christianity, thus drew upon the Fourth Gospel as a theological inspiration, if not as a certain ally.

But what is antidocetism, or for that matter, docetism? Here we may call upon Raymond Brown's helpful clarification that docetism should not be understood as an implausible depiction of the psychology of Jesus (as Käsemann tended to think following the liberal Protestant tradition). Nor does docetism stand for the sheer denial that the Logos had a human body or soul. Rather the docetism that the First Epistle of John attacked theologically is most likely the belief that "the human existence of Jesus, while real, was not salvifically significant . . . [but] only a stage in the career of the divine Word and not an intrinsic component in redemption."[77] With this important clarification about what docetism is, antidocetism then indicates by contrast a theology in which the human dwelling with us of the incarnate Word is decisive for salvation itself. What matters about Jesus of Nazareth, for John as for Ignatius, is the continuing saving significance of His human life, His signs and discourses, no less than His suffering and death—thus also in turn the significance of the suffering and death of those who follow Jesus in martyrdom. If Jesus only "seemed" to die, Ignatius cried out, then I only "seem" to wear these chains, I will only "seem" to be devoured by the beasts! The theological sense of antidocetism is that incarnation is not the instrument of a revelation that is conceivable apart from it. Incarnation itself bears the content of the revelation. God does not merely use a human vehicle to speak a Word that is essentially detachable from it, but God speaks His own Word in assuming flesh and making it forever His own in all its historical particularity and apparent contingency. The particular humanity assumed by the divine Word then *is* (not "is like") the content of the message. Can we say more about this?

Edwyn Hoskyns wondered whether the First Epistle, with its emphatic antidocetic affirmation of Jesus "who has come in the flesh," could shed light "upon the original readers of the Gospel as well." Hoskyns remained quite tentative about the precise relation between the Epistle and the Gospel. But he posed precisely the right question: What did the readers of the Epistle (which never directly quotes the Gospel) know about Jesus? "What was it that was open to such facile and invidious misunderstanding"[78] as to affirm that Jesus' particular life made no difference to the saving message He preached, as if to separate His putative message from His own personal destiny? This "facile and invidious misinterpretation" would indeed have to abandon the gospel as report in order to hear the gospel as address of Jesus. Had the First Epistle's readers an edition of the Gospel of John, Hoskyns wondered, which "was open" to docetic misunderstanding, as Raymond Brown suggested, even itself "naively docetic"?

More recently, Raymond Brown ventured that "all our evidence points to the fact that a wide acceptance of the Fourth Gospel came earlier among heterodox rather than among orthodox Christians."[79] This claim, we shall shortly see, is overstated in regard to a time when the boundaries of orthodoxy and heresy are still in flux. Brown's own hypothesis is that the First Epistle of John was written to save the Gospel from a (plausibly) docetic interpretation of it. Yet this hypothesis is in some tension with Brown's own quite positive assessment of the relation of the Gospel to the assuredly antidocetic Ignatius.[80] Brown was, however, correct to suppose that if taken in isolation, that is, apart from the martyriological ethos and its hermeneutical relationship to the Synoptic tradition as theological commentary on it, the Gospel *could* be read as a spiritualizing *alternative* to the Synoptic tradition, along the lines of the *Gospel of Thomas* and later gnostic gospels. In this case, the passionless passion of the Johannine Christ could indicate some kind of ontological immunity to bodily persecution and anguish of soul. But that is simply to restate the real problem, which is how the Gospel's first readers would have understood John's Gospel.

Hoskyns therefore wondered if these first readers of John had no previously written whole, only disconnected and theologically disorganized traditions about Jesus. Were these traditions as such vulnerable to being cast into a new framework, say, very much like the Gnostic Redeemer Myth, which would plausibly but drastically alter the sense that these episodes about Jesus had? In that case, Hoskyns was led to ask, Was the First Epistle written prior to the Gospel, and the Gospel then in turn composed as a response to docetist teaching that the First Epistle first identified and combated? Hoskyns found that "in one important passage the same particular situation that underlies the Epistle appears also in the Gospel"[81]: the eucharistic teaching of John 6. At this "remarkable turn in the narrative," we witness a "defection of disciples" (paralleling 1 John 2:19) that is "quite clearly narrated" to turn upon the "stern, uncompromising reference to the flesh of Jesus"—in other words, the "identical cause" of the schism referred to in the Epistle.[82] Hoskyns drew no certain conclusions, but in recent times, Udo Schnelle has utilized the same insight to argue that "if the Gospel presupposes this very conflict and engages it theologically, the letter would have the chronological priority."[83] Schnelle discovers the same connection in John 6:53, "Very truly, I tell you, unless you eat the flesh of the Son of Man and drink his blood, you have no life in you." It is essential to grasp the connection of this provocative statement with the controversy about docetism. Its "surprising sharpness" and "emphasis on the Eucharist as the indispensable condition for salvation gives the impression that the Evangelist is deliberately placing an antidocetic accent on his words at this point. It is only the Eucharist, so devalued by the Docetists, that mediates the saving gift of eternal life." [84]

Thus both Schnelle and Hoskyns see antidocetic theology in John 6 and regard it as a key for the overall understanding of the Johannine literature. In this case, it would not be too much to say that already in Ignatius's campaign against docetism, the Fourth Gospel is acquiring the privileged theological position that would be so important for the future, as we shall shortly examine. Moreover, Ignatius's apparent use of John would show that antidocetic Christology is *the material decision at the fonts of Christian theology.* Christ is to be thought of as One who saves by His coming in the flesh and in no other way than as the particular instance of human flesh that Jesus of Nazareth was and is. Henceforth "God" as well is to be thought of as God *the Father,* who in the person of His own Son's *flesh and blood* suffered death at the hands of His own rebellious creation and just so, that is, *as this Spirit-led man,* overcame with omnipotent love the world that opposed God. That is *in nuce* the theological sense of antidocetism; it has *next to nothing* to do with imagining or wanting a realistic psyche in Jesus!

The public persona of Jesus in John, to the contrary, is the witness/martyr. The aura of sovereignty that attends Jesus' earthly way and shines forth from the signs He does in the Fourth Gospel brings him to His death, where nevertheless He fittingly performs His supreme witness to God and true life. The climactic miracle of the raising of Lazarus triggers the plot to put Him to death, and in the same way all the previous signs elicit and precipitate again and again *crisis* and in no way overcome it or resolve it. Likewise Jesus' discourses drive disciples away, cause schisms, harden hearts, and finally elicit the capital charge of blasphemy. By visible signs and audible discourses the faith or disbelief that Jesus provokes is forced into the open. The incarnate Word's entire existence in the Gospel of John is directed therefore to the crisis culminating in the cross. A mere prophet deflects attention from her own person and personal history, just as the Baptist in fact does in this Gospel. "He must increase, but I must decrease" (3:30). But Jesus by contrast inexorably draws attention to Himself, to His public persona, which is the Ego of the eternal Son of God bearing witness against the world and for God the Father. The first half of the Gospel directs His earthly course to the "hour" for which He had come, to His being "lifted up" on the cross. Thus the predications of glory, "Bread of Life," "Light of the World," "Good Shepherd," and the rest, belong to this Jesus who loved His own to the end and wore for them the crown of thorns. The Bread of Life is the flesh and blood of the Crucified, the Light of the World must for an eternal moment be extinguished, the Good Shepherd lay down life for the sheep. "Behold the man!" says the contemptuous Pontius Pilate—*the Man* who reveals God as His own Father in this Gospel, so that all who believe Him also become with Him—strange salvation!—fellow martyrs of truth in the world of dark corruption and mendacity. What children of God! "I have said these things to you to keep you from stumbling. They will put you out of the synagogues. Indeed, an hour is coming when those who kill you will think that by doing so they are offering worship to God. And they will do this because they have not known the Father or me" (16:1-3).

How could they know? What is the *source* and *norm* of theology? It is the gospel, we are arguing, concerning the Son, taken as God's Easter judgment on this crucified man. But this Word takes on flesh and tells its story by incorporating witnesses/martyrs into it as vehicles of its continuation into space and time. This is how the Scriptures emerge as the church's first dogmatic decision against the docetist alternative, and it is as such that they provide the source and norm of Christian theology. We may see this development in the previously mentioned Ignatius and his associates.

Ignatius, Polycarp, and the Martyrs' Canon

The seven preserved letters of Ignatius[85] take up the Johannine theology of the martyr in the emerging situation of persecution, no longer by the synagogue expelling believers in Jesus in consolidation of normative Judaism following the temple's destruction, but now by the Roman state. The letters never expressly tell us why the author has been arrested and condemned to death in the Roman Coliseum. What we have is a collection of letters, written in Asia Minor on the way to Rome, dated around A.D. 112. There are five letters to churches in Asia Minor whose bishops have come to greet the prisoner-author on his way, another letter forwarded on to the church in Rome, and a final one sent back to Polycarp, bishop of Smyrna. Associated with the collection of these letters of Ignatius is a very significant epistle of Polycarp to the Philippians, written within weeks of these events as an addendum to the collection and publication of Ignatius's letters.

We learn from these letters that Ignatius had been the bishop of the church in Antioch, a notable early Christian center. Continually imploring prayers on behalf of the troubled community he has left behind, he alludes to an intimidating persecution there as he counts himself "the last [or least] of the faithful there" (*Eph.* 21). He is now "bound [in chains, on route] from Syria on account of the common name and hope," Jesus Christ (*Eph.* 1). This allusion to the public confession of the name of Jesus is as close as Ignatius comes to telling the reason for his condemnation. What to us cries out for greater elaboration seems self-evident to him and to his readers: the spiritual authority of the crucified but risen Lord Jesus, which made him a bishop now makes of him a martyr. This is how Ignatius understands the Johannine *crisis*: not as private decision for authentic existence but as public division of authorities in the world. Indeed, it is as though nothing could be more self-evident in Ignatius's letters.

The letters disclose an interesting tension within Ignatius: Jesus, his hope, will not fail Ignatius, but he, Ignatius, can fail his hope. What is of urgent concern to Ignatius in all his letters is that he not fail to endure in the approaching trial. With the help of the intercessory prayers that he solicits, Ignatius hopes that he will "attain"—the same word Ignatius uses for gaining God and eternal life—"to the battle with wild beasts" in Rome (*Eph.* 1:2). In engaging in this battle, Ignatius gains God's eternal life, just as Christ, enduring the cross, had been lifted up to glory. Such engagement comes along with the name of Jesus Christ and the crisis of authority it works in the world. The paradigmatic engagements of the "birth, the passion and the resurrection," he writes, are those of "Jesus Christ, our hope." Thus Ignatius urgently and repeatedly calls upon readers to hold fast to these historic engagements of this historical person, as to the very hope they bear of sharing in the eternal life of God (*Magn.* 11:1). Jesus unites these two, historical engagement and eternal life. He "is one physician, who is both flesh and spirit, born and unborn, God in man, true life in death, both from Mary and from God, first subject to suffering and then beyond it, Jesus Christ our Lord" (*Eph.* 7:2). Antidocetism is then but the negative pole of this positive christological model of worldly engagement. But docetism evades the crisis of public authority provoked by the name of Jesus as Ignatius discerns that by the narratives told about Him.

Bultmann acknowledged the existential import of Ignatius's christological paradoxes, asserting the unity of the way of the cross with the hope of glory. Bultmann wrote that "Christ's passion, death and resurrection are understood as events which continually condition Christian existence"[86] and that "faith as orthodoxy is not to be separated from faith as an attitude of life, the will to share in suffering with Christ."[87] Indeed, having *such* hope of eternal life which comes from the lordship of Jesus leads to battle with contra-divine powers. Confessing this Lord implicates the confessor in His fate. In fact, the anticipated battle with "wild beasts" has already begun—Ignatius writes ahead to the congregation in Rome in a metaphor about the ill treatment of the police guard that escorts him (*Rom.* 5). But he rejoices for that, since it prepares him "to become more completely a disciple," "to die for Jesus Christ," to become "an imitator of the passion of my God" (*Rom.* 6). Especially in the letter to the Romans, Ignatius seems to welcome—perhaps even to *exult* in—the prospect of violent death.

He uses shocking and graphic images: "Come fire and cross and grapplings with wild beasts, wrenching of bones, hacking of limbs, crushings of my whole body!" (*Rom.* 6). Were this not disturbing enough to modern sensibilities,[88] Ignatius pleads with the Roman Christians not to interfere with his impending fate or try to rescue him from it. He wants for himself this "opportunity to attain to God." "If you are silent and leave me alone, I am a word of God," he explains (*Rom.* 2). Such *witness* of the Word of God on the earth defines the place of the *martyr* in the gospel's *continuing* history in the world.[89]

In fact, that is what happened in the course of the second century in the emergence of the biblical canon, not only for the original churches to which Ignatius wrote. Ignatius did become a "word of God." His witness was received and served to unify scattered apostolic churches in face of powerful Gnosticizing forces, as William R. Farmer has demonstrated in an insightful monograph. In this situation of being "threatened by a seemingly uncontrolled plethora of theological and exegetical speculation that sapped the strength of the Church in its resistance against the wiles of the 'evil one,'" Farmer argues "the New Testament canon is a martyr's canon which can be traced through Origen, Hippolytus, and Irenaeus to a particular traditional idealization of Christian martyrdom exemplified by Polycarp and Ignatius and reflecting the martyrdoms of Peter and Paul in Rome. In this tradition the letters of Paul have always been united with books that witness to and emphasize the reality of the death as well as the resurrection of Jesus Christ [that is, the canonical Gospels]."[90] Thus the collection, distribution, and continuing influence of Ignatius's letters through the second century, together with Polycarp's addendum (followed a generation later by the *Martyrdom of Polycarp*), were catalytic in the synthesis of Petrine, Pauline, and Johannine traditions, and their integration as the "New Testament" to form a canonical whole with Israel's scriptures, telling the Genesis-to-Revelation story of one God who creates, redeems, and fulfills one world through Jesus Christ, crucified and risen and coming in glory. This canonical development was simultaneous and coextensive with the church's discovery of her christological confession as the bond of catholicity in the ethos of the martyrs, persecuted for the name of Jesus, but steeled by the Spirit for their own passionless passions in imitation of the Lord's.[91]

At this point we may entertain an objection. To some today (following, say, Nietzsche's seminal critique of Christianity),[92] Farmer's thesis might of itself suffice to show that the wells of the New Testament were poisoned from the start by world-denying malice. It will seem to such people that we have in Ignatius an illuminating instance of fanatical early Christian hatred of the world, together with all the other evils works of "early catholicism": episcopacy, sacramentalism, dogmatism and heresy-hunting, realized eschatology, high Christology, and so forth. There can be no doubt these elements actually appear in Ignatius and form an inalienable whole that completely determines the sense of authority in early catholic Christianity. That is *true*. When we take up the Bible, we hold in our hands this early catholic church; when we read it, and believe it, we identify ourselves as the spiritual heirs of these martyrs. Yet contrary to the objection we are now entertaining, for Ignatius the church in her witness and martyrdom plays a critical role in the gospel's ongoing history. By the defenseless testimony of the martyrs, the church is overcoming the violence of the world and showing forth the merciful reign of the Lord Jesus in sovereign contempt of the death threats of the demonical powers holding sway in the *civitas terrena*. The rhetoric of violence embedded in Ignatius's texts reflects the systemic violence of Ignatius's world, of that "ancient kingdom" of the evil one, as he named it, with which the suffering and oppressed eucharistic communities coexist on the earth until their separation in a final *crisis*, the day of the Lord's coming. His pleas to the Roman Christians, therefore, can hardly be taken as some kind of perverse wish for pain. The offending passages are rhetorically dramatic expositions of Ignatius's theology of martyrdom. They summon readers to the same courage of faith and involvement of love, howsoever differently the Lord leads each of His own to follow Him. There is no trace of *real* fanaticism in Ignatius, which would try to manipulate readers to follow him into an act of willful self-destruction.

In reality, no one seeks martyrdom, not even Ignatius. A generation later, the Christians of Smyrna who recorded *The Martyrdom of Polycarp* stated it as rule: "We praise not those who deliver themselves up, since the Gospel does not so teach us" (*Polycarp* 14). Martyrdom is thrust upon one. In that case, the trial of faith is to receive the torture, not as the demonic usurpation over one's destiny that it pretends to be, but rather as the holy and uncanny calling of the God who spared not His own Son; therefore it is to be received in the obedience of Gethsemane and willed in accordance with the Holy Will by which the kingdom comes in Jesus Christ, crucified yet risen. Ignatius calls on his readers to imitate himself, but follow Jesus; to emulate himself, but serve the Lord. His own calling to martyrdom illustrates with supreme clarity the faith and love required of all who feast in the Eucharist on the crucified but risen Lord. Like Paul before him, Ignatius sees his life, his conduct, his fate, his persona in the body located here on the earth as his one true—not yet finished—sermon. Preaching for him is not "Word alone" but Word incarnate in life, as power, eliciting discipleship, sustaining martyrdom. Such preaching points away from the self and its decisions to the reign of the crucified but risen Lord Jesus in the believer's self, for whose name one has no true choice but to suffer. Ignatius points to himself, yet not to himself, but rather to Christ who reigns in him. Christ's lordship is only visible in his pathetic obedience, but it really is visible there—why else, he asks, does he wear the prisoner's chains?

The bishop of Antioch had named the name of the Crucified as Lord in a world in which this act was and was perceived as the subversion of its

dominant values; this cruciform content, not the mere fact of His coming, provoked crisis, not in existential self-understanding, but of authority in the public world, where the individual is persona, public face, witness, indeed *either* a
Word of God *or* a minion of the evil one. By the time the letters are composed,
in any case, Ignatius's worldly fate has long since been settled; no reprieve is
possible. Delays, negotiations, bribes, attempted ransoms by the Christians in
Rome would be futile and only distract from his resolve. From the hour that he
had publicly confessed the name of Jesus as Lord before the imperial authorities in Antioch, his earthly life was forfeit. Resolve to make of his cruel fate a
public testimony to the victory in him of the Lord Jesus motivates the letters,
their theology, their collection and influence in the second-century church.
Taking into account the brutal and brutalizing constraints of Ignatius's world,
Schoedel writes with complete justice that Ignatius's theology of "martyrdom
proves to be not a denial of this world but a final affirmation of the significance of what is done in the flesh."[93] By the same token, Ignatius's embrace of
martyrdom is not heroic. Psychologically, it is transparent that in the chilling
rhetorical anticipations of violent death, Ignatius is steeling himself for the
ordeal. He dreads the thought that he will lose his nerve, fall to pieces, and
give his oppressors the victory of seeing him cower, begging mercy, as though
their violence should speak the final word over his persona.[94] He implores the
reader's prayers that he may instead become God's victorious word of life in
the face of imperial terrorism. Ignatius's life, up to and including the sheer
negativity of this evil death, has become for him the open-ended drama of salvation, a history being written in the light of his communion in the body and
blood of Christ. His life is at the same time determined and yet unconcluded,
in tension therefore and under threat of loss until the final hour.

What provokes this tension-laden engagement with the world and sustains Ignatius in it, Schoedel explains, is the Christology: "One pole of Ignatius' christology—the emphasis on the reality of the incarnation—sanctions
the godly use of the things of this world. Everything is pure to the pure (Tit
1:15). Another pole of Ignatius' christology—the emphasis on the reality of
the passion—lends reality to Ignatius' own suffering (Tr 10, Sm 4:2) and provides a model for Christian forbearance in a hostile world (Eph 10:3). Such
world affirmation and world denial are not contradictory. Both are rooted in
Ignatius' emphasis on the inescapable obligations that faith and love—and the
incarnation—entail."[95] The futility of human works and an engaged life was being
proclaimed in an "age of anxiety" by a widespread "gnosticizing tendency" (E. R.
Dodds).[96] These second-century fathers thus faced a radical undervaluation of
the human body and life on the earth; loss of the sense of community and the
moral values of commitment; despair of the historical process as something
embattled yet meaningfully directed under divine providence. They faced
apathy among Christians themselves, a weariness with doing good probably

generated by disappointment of apocalyptic hopes.[97] Their cultural world was dominated by widespread despair of the human being as God's image in the work of creation, as Irenaeus would conceive and articulate it at the end of the second century—that is, as the creature made for history, for achieving a partnership with the Creator, as we shall see in the next chapter. On the basis of the Incarnation, therefore, Ignatius and his followers came to the defense of human dignity and the integrity of creation and the significance of deeds done and sufferings endured in the body; they labored against the spirit of the age to teach that precisely the engaged, active, inevitably conflicted and sorrow-laden life of Christ's suffering way of loving service and courageous witness in the world nevertheless "attains" to God. Such a life attains to God because the way had been opened up once for all by the incarnate life of the crucified but risen Lord Jesus, the "author and pioneer of our faith," as the Epistle to the Hebrews proclaimed Him in the same martyriological sense.

Faith and love are for Ignatius the beginning and end of the whole Christian life, conceived of as a meaningful progression in history, a pilgrimage on the earth whose goal is participation in God's own eternal life (*Eph.* 14). To Ignatius, it is axiomatic that faith is expressed in love. Faith without love would be an abortion of the Christian's new life. Christ's love is active, not only within the new unity of the eucharistic community, where the victory of Christ over death establishes itself on earth. But this love also spills over into the renewal of the secular institution of marriage and domestic relations (*Pol.* 4-5). Despite ethical rigor, there is nothing legalistic about Ignatius.[98] The possibility of the profoundest commitment of martyrdom is the working out of salvation itself in a personal history, since salvation is liberation not only from the guilt of sin but also from its dominating power. Short of the ultimate engagement, there is the new life together in the church. In Ignatius's ecclesiology, it is the Lord Jesus who lives and reigns for His people. His people in turn are those who live for Him, and in Him for one another, and all together for the kingdom of God. As surely as Jesus is Lord, He and His people live a new, interdependent life already now, upon the earth. "Where Jesus Christ is, there is the whole church." Therefore, the martyr-bishop's impassioned last will and testament sounds: "Observe one Eucharist! For there is one flesh of our Lord Jesus Christ and one cup unto union in His blood; there is one altar, as there is one bishop" (*Phld.* 4); "Do nothing without the bishop! Keep your flesh as a temple of God! Cherish union, shun division! Be imitators of Jesus Christ, as He Himself also was of the Father!" (*Phld.* 7).

All Ignatius's urgent summons to unity as church and church as unity are not only negatively directed against Gnostic dissent and fragmentation. They are positively motivated by the soteriology of human reconciliation through communion in Christ already now, on the earth, as the church is gathered from the nations. The church is that form of worship on the earth that ascribes all glory and honor to the Lamb who was slain, that "sings in unison with one voice through Jesus Christ to the Father" (*Eph.* 4). The call to worship is the call to salvation itself: "Meet together more frequently for Eucharist to the glory of God! For when you assemble frequently, the powers of Satan are cast down and his evil works are undone by the concord of your faith. There is nothing better than peace, in which all warfare of things in heaven and on earth is abolished" (*Eph.* 13). "A great cosmic conflict is presupposed in which Satan's powers are destroyed by the prayers of worshippers. Thus the theme of prayer in Ignatius again illustrates the high significance he attributes to his own martyrdom in bringing to expression the underlying unity of all the churches."[99] By the same token, the peace of Christ is not equanimity or inner tranquility. It is Christ's victory peace, the peace of Easter morn that Christ has won for guilty and perishing humanity, peace that extends over the earth just so far as the new community comes together in it and abides in it; just so, the darkness of this world is therewith pushed back. As Paul Wesche paraphrases Ignatius's thought: "Believers *become ekklesia*, they *become* the elect only as they *become* one body with Jesus Christ, the *Ekklesia*, through the partaking of that Eucharist that is in fact his life-giving body and blood."[100] This *pax Christi* is the church of the martyrs of Jesus, the inaugurated reign of God, the eucharistic ecstasy of faith and love, the confession of the Name that will be above all other names, the hope that leads to engagement with the world, the life that fulfills creation's purpose and becomes forever God's.

By means of Ignatius's witness as a martyr, scattered, persecuted communities, threatened by the attractive but false gospel of docetist escapism, came to discover each other and enter in a new relationship, creating a new reality, a communion of communions.[101] This discovery of the whole church wherever the crucified and risen Jesus Christ is present is a *new event* in the history of the gospel taking place in the second century. Now the oppressed and scattered churches recognize in each other the same crucified but risen Lord Jesus, in spite of diverse apostolic foundations, histories, semantics, and even theologies. In this context, the martyrs make perceptible a hitherto elusive unity: persecution clarifies everything. Now the authentic figure of the Crucified, with His martyr-apostles Peter and Paul, and churches that are likewise suffering today for adherence to this common Name and Hope, come together simultaneously to protect themselves from the explosion of speculative, escapist, Gnosticizing literature and to engage the literature of these hitherto isolated communities in a new, creative interaction: the emergence of the Scriptures as the canonical story of the Genesis-to-Revelation Bible.

The theological interaction between Petrine, Pauline, and Johannine communities is at the center of this canonical development over against the disintegrative forces of Gnosticism. By the time of Ignatius, the apostolic explosion of early Christianity has given way to the new experience of Pauline, Johannine,

and Petrine congregations discovering one another. What we observe in Ignatius is theological thought that is integrating for the first time Synoptic, Johannine, and Pauline sources into a new, proto-canonical synthesis. The figurative
allusions (*Phld.* 5) to the Gospels ("the Gospel as the flesh of Jesus") and the
Epistles ("the apostles as the presbytery of the church") are connected with
Ignatius's pointed recognition in this letter of "the prophets" (of the Hebrew
Scriptures, which Ignatius now considers "Old" in relation to the "New" Testament, that is, the eucharistic meal of Jesus). A similar interpretation is possible
of the following passage in which Ignatius reports a statement he made against
Judaizers who appealed to the authority of the written text of the (Hebrew)
Scriptures: "My charter," Ignatius writes, "is Jesus Christ, the inviolable charter
is his cross and his death and his Resurrection, and faith through him" (*Phld.* 8).
Jesus Christ is, Ignatius explains, "the door of the Father, through which Abraham and Isaac and Jacob enter in, and the prophets and the apostles and the
whole church; all these things combine in the unity of God. But the Gospel has
a certain preeminence in the advent of the Savior, even our Lord Jesus Christ
and his passion and resurrection" (*Phld.* 9). The point is not to denigrate the
Hebrew Scriptures but rather to claim and integrate them into the emerging
gospel narrative that, as we argued in chapter 1, bears epistemic primacy for
the correspondingly emergent early catholic church. The passage suggests that
for Ignatius it is the written Gospels that have this hermeneutical preeminence
within a larger, proto-canonical whole. That whole now includes in one great
harmony the voices of Israel's prophets and the martyr-apostles, preeminently
Peter and Paul. All of these together speak in various ways the one Word of God,
Jesus Christ; the Crucified and Risen One is in turn the key to their coherence
within the emergent canon. Here the gospel as promissory narrative has the
primacy; from this center the unity of Scripture is discerned.[102]

Certainly such an understanding is implied in Polycarp's *Letter to the Philippians*, the "Afterword" appended to the collection and publication of Ignatius's
letters. This text reads like a catalogue of the emerging New Testament canon.
Farmer notes, "According to Bishop J. B. Lightfoot's edition of the *Apostolic
Fathers*, there are a total of forty-six New Testament allusions in the text of
Polycarp's letter," that is, to the three Synoptics, Acts, Romans, 1 and 2 Corinthians, Galatians, Ephesians, Philippians, 2 Thessalonians, 1 and 2 Timothy, 1 Peter,
and 1 John.[103] Marshaling citations from the great majority of witnesses that
later became the New Testament, Polycarp weaves together a unified account
of the martyrs of the catholic church and their role in actualizing the righteousness of God on earth. At one point Polycarp suggests that these Christian
writings that he is citing are already regarded as "sacred writings" (*Phld.* 11).
Polycarp's letter integrates the Ignatian theology of martyrdom with the love
ethic of the Sermon on the Mount from Matthew; it then sets this ethos into
a more Pauline framework in the spirit of the doctrine of justification. The

theme of the letter is God's saving righteousness, which includes the ethical righteousness active in the church of the martyrs. This proto-canonical synthesis comes together as a whole against the same docetists whom Ignatius so passionately criticized for denying the reality of Christ's humanity and divine sufferings (*Phld.* 9). When these aspects of the content of Polycarp's letter are connected with the letter's function as an afterword to the publication of Ignatius's letters, the picture is complete: our New Testament, indeed our Bible of the Old and New Testaments, is emerging here to create a dynamic unity of hitherto varying traditions of the crucified but risen Lord Jesus, even as communities hitherto isolated are now recognizing one another as expressions of the same universal assembly of those called out of the *civitas terrena* and onto the *civitas Dei*.

But what is the principle of coherence? In what precise sense is this literature found to be in agreement? Farmer's thesis of a "martyrs' canon" answers the question on the historical level. It linked those "Gospels" that realistically depicted the passion of Christ with those apostles, preeminently Peter and Paul, who realistically represented Christ with their own apostolic sufferings as martyrs. On the theological level, this suggests that the principle of coherence in the formation of the canon was the saving significance of the death and resurrection of Jesus of Nazareth for those who suffer for his name—the very creed of the resurrection of the Crucified that we argued in the previous chapters generated gospel narratives in the first place. In that case the gospel is the *norma normans* (the "norming norm") in Christian theology, and the Scriptures with creed are the *norma normata* (the "normed norm"). That is to recognize critically that the Bible as we have inherited it is a big book in which one easily gets lost; as such the Bible is vulnerable to all sorts of theological abuse (as, for example, with Ignatius's "Judaizers," who treat something else than the gospel narrative as epistemically primary), particularly when there is widespread ignorance of its actual historical genesis in the theology of the martyrs. What is authoritative for Christian theology is the resurrection of the Crucified Martyr of God. For this is the Father's own knowledge of the Son Incarnate. The Logos dwelling with us and for us is the Word of God in the primary and proper sense. He is the key to reading Scripture rightly and using it properly as the written Word of God.

Here too Ignatius and Polycarp may be seen to be taking up the legacy of John. It is certain that Polycarp drew on the antidocetic First Epistle of John when he wrote in his Epistle to the Philippians: "For everyone 'who does not confess that Jesus Christ has come in the flesh is antichrist' [1 John 4:2-3]; and whoever does not acknowledge the testimony of the cross 'is of the devil'" [1 John 3:8]; whoever "twists the sayings of the Lord to suit his own sinful desires and claims that there is neither resurrection nor judgment—well, that person is the first born of Satan. . . . Let us return to the Word delivered to us from the beginning [1 John 1:1]." Scholars have usually conceded to Ignatius a similar relation to the First Epistle on account of the bishop's antidocetic polemic. Somewhat surprisingly, however, direct citations of the First Epistle such as Polycarp's are not to be found in Ignatius's letters. What we see instead may be only a few striking allusions: "No one professing faith sins, nor does anyone possessing love hate" (*Eph.* 14:2) echoes themes in I John; likewise the statement to the Smyrnaeans against those "who blaspheme my Lord by not confessing that he was clothed in flesh" picks up the thought of the First Epistle about those who deny that Jesus Christ "has come in the flesh." Yet one searches in vain in Ignatius for the virtually verbatim citations of the First Epistle we find in Polycarp's letter. More frequent in Ignatius are apparent references to the Fourth Gospel, though in the allusive manner of paraphrase (but perhaps the bishop in chains dictates to a secretary from memory). Yet these allusions, if that is what they are, arguably are of great theological import for the martyr-bishop. Ignatius often speaks of his martyrdom as a means of "glorifying Jesus Christ," a usage unique to John (the Synoptics and Paul speak of glorifying the Father usually through good works, not Jesus through martyrdom); Ignatius uses the Johannine adjective "true" and the Johannine noun "life" together to speak of the content of salvation, "our true Life" (*Eph.* 11:1; *Trall.* 9:2; *Smyrn.* 4:1). He can speak of Jesus as the "door" to the Father (*Phld.* 9:1; John 10:9), of the Spirit like the wind who "comes and goes" as he will (*Phld.* 7:1; John 3:8), and of the "children of light," who "follow like sheep where the shepherd is" (*Phld.* 2:1; John 10:4-5). Even more impressive are those allusions to theological ideas that are specifically Johannine yet manifestly play important roles in Ignatius's own thinking. Chiefly these are the references to the sacramental teaching of John 6, "the bread of God" (*Eph.* 5:2) that is the "flesh of Jesus," and "drinking his blood" (*Rom.* 7:2-3). We also find interpretive allusions to the Fourth Gospel's doctrine of the Incarnation, of "the Word spoken from silence" (*Magn.* 8:20), "Jesus Christ, who before the ages was with the Father" (*Magn.* 6:1), "who did nothing apart from the Father, being united with him" (*Magn.* 7:1), who "came forth from one Father and remained with the One and returned to the One" (*Magn.* 7:2), "God in man, true life in death" (*Eph.* 7:2). The existence of this significant mass of doctrine specifically drawn, as it appears, from the Fourth Gospel demonstrates at least that it would be arbitrary to concede to Ignatius knowledge of the Epistle but not of the Gospel. In reality, it seems likely that he draws on both the Gospel and the Epistle for his theology of martyrdom.

So far in this argument no interpretation of Ignatius's reception of Johannine theology and ethos has been ventured on the basis of what is surely one of the most striking features of his letters: the sharp polemic against the docetists, who are saying that Christ only "seemed" to suffer. The point has been that it is the positive conviction of the Lord Jesus that inspires the bishop-martyr, provokes the enmity of the world with its persecution, unites the church in the Eucharist, and requires local eucharistic communities to recognize each other in the persons of their pastors-bishops. All this is what draws together their literature and generates thereby the proto-canonical perception of the church as a whole. Here and now the new experience of catholicity anticipates in a still dark and violent time the future reconciliation of eternal life in God; it is at the same time witness to God's conflict with the demonic powers of violence. In this context of Ignatius's positive evangelical and catholic convictions, the nature and necessity of the sharp repudiation of the docetist teaching as "heresy" becomes obvious. The deviations of these revisionists lose hold of true salvation in Christ, according to the bishop-martyr's theology: the "consequences of such teaching are the loss of the 'Passion' and 'Resurrection,' the 'Kingdom of God' and 'immortality,' paralleled with the gain of 'death' and 'unquenchable fire.'"[104] Ignatius, in chains on the way to a cruel death, is hardly in the political position of a monarch to expel theological deviants, as imagined in Bauer's fervent anti-Catholicism.[105] The only authority Ignatius actually has resides in the Word and his theological arguments for it, by which he conceives of salvation as unification in love: "Ignatius's overall attempt appears to be to preserve unity, rather than to exclude impurity."[106] Udo Schnelle states, "If the opponents [of Ignatius] deny the resurrection, then the Eucharist is also emptied of meaning and the grace of Christ is reduced (Smy 6:2) so that it is only logical for the opponents to absent themselves from the eucharistic celebration (see Smy 7:1; further 6:2)."[107] Absence from the Eucharist, as we have seen, is absence from salvation itself for Ignatius, since he conceives of salvation socially and corporally. The refusal of Christ's human reality as crucified, as risen, as present in his glorified body and blood at the Eucharist is "heresy" therefore in a wholly analytic sense: refusing this Meal simply is to deviate from the access to salvation that God has provided, hence from the unity in love that salvation is. This judgment prevails not because docetism represents some theological interpretation different than Ignatius's own pet theory. It is "heresy" because it cannot and does not conform to the reality of salvation itself. Heresy attacks what is axiomatic, constitutive, unconditionally necessary, epistemically primary in the saving proclamation of Jesus as Lord for the gathering of believers as church. It is "heresy" because it deviates into some other doctrine of salvation than the reign of God, some other way to salvation than by Jesus' cross and resurrection. It *is* some other knowledge of God than found in the emergent Scriptures.

The Knowledge of God in the New Testament

A prophet calls to decision, like Moses or John the Baptist. But Jesus in His Person and personal history *is* the Decision—*of God*, who "so loved the world that he gave his only Son." As this theological "meaning precedes and conditions the history," Jesus appears from the very beginning of John's Gospel as the

Decision of God for the world that rejects and hates God. The will of Jesus is manifest in His resolute willing of the will of His Father, as in John's remake of the Synoptic Agony in the Garden: "Now my soul is troubled. And what should I say—'Father, save me from this hour'? No, it is for this reason that I have come to this hour" (12:27). As such, for John, the relevant thing to say about this man *as man* is that He lives and reigns as the victor who has "overcome the world" by willing the will of God. That involves no speculation on Jesus' inner life but only observation of the firm purpose of the singular persona of the gospel's man in mission. Jesus' "personality" has no independent existence; it subsists in the persona of the Father's only Son sent from heaven. As such, the man *is* the body and soul of the incarnate Word, the eternal Son of the heavenly Father. From this perspective, modern attempts to set the theology of the Word against the theology of the Incarnation, or to set the gospel as address against the gospel as report, are regressive and lead to nothing but mind-numbing paradox, baffling assertion of logical nonsense, muddled declamation of what is nothing but a contradiction in terms. The solution to the very real difficulties for understanding created by the rhetorically paradoxical predications of divine glory to the man Jesus are rather to be sought in Trinitarianism.

Gregory of Nyssa for instance derived from his Johannine studies razor-sharp rules that correlate the knowledge of God as the Father with knowledge of God the Son. Paradoxically glorified on the cross, Jesus here becomes the new Temple of all peoples. As faith arises at the Spirit's call, it is swept into Jesus's Sonship, wed to Him who glorified His Father by the loving sacrifice of His all. This ecstatic existence of Spirit-wrought faith in Jesus is the supreme confidence of love, namely, that love offered will be returned and more than returned; that in giving, being is replenished, not diminished or exhausted. *Esse deum dare*: to be God is to give. Thus "without the Son," Gregory of Nyssa observed, "the Father has neither existence nor name."[108] But whoever "does not believe in God the Father is not a Christian, even though in his creed he asserts an Almighty God."[109] The God of the gospel is Father of His own Son such that apart from this Son He is not true God at all. Knowledge *of God* (the Son) is *God's own* (the Father's) and is bestowed *by God* (the Spirit) and so makes of believers participants in the divine life in the sense of sharing in these mutual recognitions of the Father and the Son in the Spirit. The knowledge of God is therefore most properly and profoundly *doxological*, as befits existence in the new Temple of the Spirit, the Word made flesh. Doxology of loving praise is the end of this world and the attained goal of the knowledge of God: "I made your name known to them, and I will make it known, so that the love with which you have loved me may be in them, and I in them" (17:26). This is the worship of God for which the world was created, the beautiful harmony of creator and creature, the symphony of God who blesses and blessed humanity that sings praises, the rhapsody of faith that against the world loves the world because it sees God's glory in the man of whom Pilate said, "Behold." What disciples know in knowing God as Father is not their decision for God but God's decision for them and for all; what Christians acquire in knowing God by His own flesh who is this man Jesus is nothing so narcissistic as a new self-understanding but rather "their Lord and their God." "In christology," Otto Weber has rightly insisted, "the issue is not a change of our consciousness, but the transformation of the realm of lordship and thus of the very structure of life"[110]—of course, also then illumination, a change in self-understanding; indeed the new birth from above (John 3:1).

Following this order of theological knowledge certainly creates the acute question of continuity. This is the problem of intelligibility to which we have repeatedly alluded to this point. How is it that Jesus who died on the cross and Jesus who lives and reigns are one and the same Jesus, as John's Gospel so resolutely and offensively maintains? How is it that the *ekklesia* and Israel are one and the same people of God? How is that Saul the Pharisee and Paul the Apostle are one and the same human being? What is the continuity in the discontinuity? Who or what is the being in this becoming? We see in these questions the original form of the basic problem of primary Christian theology that we have been studying. How is Jesus the Christ, both the Crucified One and the Risen One, both the son of Mary and the Son of God, one, concrete, indivisible person? That is the fundamental problem of identity through per-sisting time, and thus of the capacity of critical dogmatics to identify God as God in space and time (pace Kant, pace Bultmann). It is the root problem of all Christian theology that proceeds from faith in the gospel by receiving as Lord and God *the Jesus who speaks from the canonical Scriptures.*

CHAPTER 4

The Trinitarian Rule of Faith

"In earnest invocation of God it is necessary to consider what one wants to address, what God is, how he is known, where and how he has revealed himself, and both if and why he hears our pleas and cries. And our thoughts must not waver as the thoughts of the heathen." So we heard from Melanchthon at the beginning of this book;[1] it is in answer to such questions, arising from the gospel's mission to the nations, that the trinitarian baptismal creed[2] emerged in the early catholic church. It arose from the same source of gospel narrative as did canonical Scripture: God's Word in the resurrection of the Crucified. Side by side with the biblical canon, it came to serve as its synopsis and *dramatis personae*.

In the eucharistic assembly[3] the Jesus who speaks to the baptized from the Scriptures is the Son of the God of Israel whom He knew as Abba-Father; correspondingly this assembly that hears Jesus speaking from the Scriptures is the new creation of the Spirit of the Father and the Son. The Creed forms the kataphatic rule for speaking rightly in and about this event on the earth of the assembling of the believers to hear God's Word and return thanksgiving. As entrance into this community of faith is by baptism into the name of the Father, the Son, and the Holy Spirit (Matt 28:19, that is, after the narrative pattern of Jesus' own baptism as in Matt 3:13-17), just so God is to be invoked and hence identified according to the trinity of persons. So already Paul consistently thinks: "For in [Christ] every one of God's promises is a 'Yes.' For this reason it is through *him* that we say the 'Amen,' to the glory of *God*. But it is *God* who establishes us with you in *Christ* and has anointed us, by putting his seal on us and giving us his Spirit in our hearts as a first installment" (1 Cor 1:20-22). The basis of the emergent trinitarian creed as second-order rule, be it then well noted, is the first-order truth of the primary theology of gospel narrative, namely: *"God* has sent the *Spirit* of his Son into our hearts, crying, *'Abba! Father!'"* (Gal 4:6).

This verse, if anything, makes an ontological declaration about the reality of the assembly, no matter how it otherwise looks to the unbelieving world. "With the gospel one has to accept oneself as completely new and as changed by Christ."[4] Accordingly, the primitive rule of faith, embedded in such creed-like trinitarian fragments as Paul employs, may be formulated: *One God, the almighty Father, creates, redeems, and fulfills one world though the missions of His Son and Spirit.* By baptism, the chosen assembly of believing hearts is *the place on the earth* where human persons participate in these missions by grace and faith (rather than by coercion and rote) and so acquire epistemic access to this very truth. As a rule then for speaking rightly of God and the church, the Scriptures are to be read as the *canonical* anti-dualist, antidocetist, Genesis-to-Revelation narrative positively setting forth Christ and His Spirit in mission from the Father for the sake of the world. Critically by this rule, the *ecclesia* discerns the One so acknowledged, loved, and trusted as true God in distinction from all other candidates for and claimants of divine authority. Negatively, then, the trinitarian rule of faith requires testing of the spirits, "Christian atheism," that is, knowing disbelief in the idols and demons that otherwise hold humanity captive and seek to invade and subvert the *ecclesia* by deviant teaching. The martyriological history of witness[5] stretching from Pauline origins may also be traced through Ignatius, Polycarp, and Justin Martyr on to Irenaeus at the end of the second century. It tells the story of the emergence of the trinitarian regula fidei from baptismal catechesis to dogmatic theology.

Paul as Theologian

Modern scholarship has emphasized to the point of caricature that the historical Paul is an apostle, not a theologian, regarding even his doctrine of justification as little more than a polemical device inspired by church-political considerations.[6] Over against this reduction of revealed theology to power relations as parsed by other schemes than canon and creed, it is proper to stress the coherence of Paul's theology and the principled behavior it required of its apostolic author.[7] One can do this without turning the earthen vessel into the treasure it contains. Certainly, the insight that Paul is an apostle (not a professor of academic theology) helps, if it gives the picture that it ought: of Saul-turned-Paul driven by christological passion to incessant action that he might reach the nations with the good news of Christ's imminent appearance in glory to finish off the old creation and inaugurate in fullness the new age.

In this context, however, the Apostle thinks. He does *think*—profoundly, radically, and in eminent fashion *theologically*. His theology is the apostolic paradigm. Victor Paul Furnish rightly argues that there is a way both to correct the domesticated Paul of ecclesiastical tradition and the mere iconoclasm of modern academic historical criticism and to reconcile the proper concerns of each. It lies in exegesis of Paul's letters that is at once historical and theological. But that means taking note of a hermeneutical consideration that academic historical criticism often overlooks—not to mention the ignoring of critical history by ecclesiastical domesticators!

Furnish reminds us of the historical fact, which is itself part of the historicality of the Pauline letter collection preserved in the New Testament canon, that "the responsibility for which of his letters have been handed down, and in what form, rests with one specific 'community of interpretation,' the church."[8] We have Paul to read at all thanks to the church (which admittedly more often put him on a pedestal than strove to understand him). All the same, the church, taken as a community of interpretation from faith for faith (as does Paul himself, 1 Cor 15:1-3), is our access to Paul, just as the church as creature of this gospel as handed on in the church is what Paul himself cares about (Gal 6:15). Putting Paul in its scriptural canon, the early catholic church had within it and preserved for the future a permanent source of reform, provided that genuine interpretation, not "confiscation" for other agendas, of Paul occurs. Such interpretation occurs, however imperfectly, when we discipline ourselves to understand the Pauline text as would its first auditors/readers, which is the proper method of history that wants to interpret texts rather than reduce the ideas texts bear to ideological justifications of alleged relations of power—that is, on the basis of some other set of texts! In this particular literature, that entails an equal commitment, Furnish concludes, "to a theological task . . . since encountering Paul requires engaging his thought, and since his thinking, as we have access to it, is mainly about his gospel—which means, about God (thus Rom 1:1; 15:16; 2 Cor 11:7; 1 Thess 2:2, 8, 9); there is no understanding him where his theological statements are not taken seriously."[9]

That is a strong statement: *no* understanding when Paul is not understood *theologically*. Furnish acknowledges the difficulty, but regards reflection on the "truth of the gospel" (Gal 2:14) as key. "Paul is the first Christian theologian of record, in that he sought to explicate the truth of the gospel, and to think through the implications of the Christian understanding of God that is intrinsic to its claims."[10] Of course, one would hardly want to separate Paul's reflection on the gospel's claims about God from the claim of God that he experienced in the gospel. In any case, we can set Furnish's strong claim directly against Jonathan Z. Smith's counterargument, including his insightful analysis of a blind alley that leads many interpreters astray: "the old Reformation myth, imagining a 'pristine' early Christianity centered in Paul and subjected to later processes of 'corruption.'"[11] Smith is right in showing how this Protestant progressivist "myth" has led, not to theology as critical dogmatics, but to an "enterprise undertaken in bad faith. The interests have rarely been cognitive, but rather almost always apologetic."[12] Granted. But Smith's solution (very popular today) of supplanting theology, which he takes as a noncognitive apologetics, with a religious studies approach is possessed of its own animus. This is an animus against Paul's alleged subjection, in Smith's own words, of "the Christ traditions, from a perspective of alienation and *ressentiment*, to a thoroughly utopian understanding . . . insinuating radical dualism at all levels of the system."[13] One may well suppose that such a reading will be the result of de-theologizing Paul!

Peter Stuhlmacher rightly argues that we can give a good account of Paul's theology (in Furnish's sense of claims about God intrinsic to the gospel) by focusing on the change of Paul's perspective on Jesus that accompanied the transformation of Saul the Pharisee, persecutor of the law-deviant Jewish Christians, into Paul, the apostle to the lawless Gentiles. "As a persecutor of the Christian faith, Paul had seen in Christ Jesus the lawless messianic pretender justly executed on the cross."[14] But now that disgraced pretender is seen in new light, as vindicated by God through His resurrection from the dead and exalted as Lord over all. The revelation to him of the crucified Jesus as the glorified Son of God turned Saul-now-Paul's world upside down. It made the persecutor, who wanted to separate holy Judaism from the unclean nations by the fence of strict adherence to and observation of the law, into the apostle to the Gentiles and champion of the freedom for which Christ had set free. Saul, turned into Paul, was now bound by the mercy he had received to extend the same divine and saving justice that rectified him to those very unclean peoples whom formerly he despised. The "truth of the gospel" from which Peter deviated in his practice at Antioch when out of fear he drew back from table fellowship with Gentiles, then, is a truth that involves the claim of God to be creating something new in the assembly itself, as harbinger, to be sure, of the redemption of the entire cosmos.

It is in this connection with his fundamental "truth of the gospel" that we must take note how Paul's gospel entails a definite "canon"—a "rule" of faith, which instructs believers how they are to walk together as new creation in the midst of the old, under threat of persecution from without and subversion from within. "As for those who will follow *this rule* [Greek *kanon*]—peace be upon them, and mercy, and upon the Israel of God. From now on, let no one make trouble for me; for I carry the marks of Jesus branded on my body" (Gal 6:16-17, emphasis added). This rule of Paul is dramatically pronounced at the end of the letter to the Galatians and correlated with the scars he bears for confessing Jesus. It holds sway in a realm of promised peace and mercy, the spiritual Israel embracing both Jew and Gentile, those "called out" from the nations for the coming Reign. Paul, who knows the lash of persecutors, pronounces the rule, not to evade persecution, but to fend off "those who want to make a good showing in the flesh," who "try to compel you to be circumcised," but "only that they may not be persecuted for the cross of Christ" (Gal 6:12). The ethos of the martyr, the doctrine of "the" faith (Gal 3:23) bringing about in the *ecclesia* enactment of cosmic reconciliaton (Gal 3:26-28) correlate. This belief and this ethic are the doubled-sided expression of the new creation's relation to the world, which "has been crucified to me and I to the world" by "the cross of our Lord Jesus Christ" (Gal 6:14). Clearly, Paul's doctrine is not doctrine for doctrine's sake, but doctrine for life. But it *is* doctrine, "canon," *regula fidei.*

What is this theological rule, this canon of gospel faith? "For neither circumcision nor uncircumcision is anything; but a new creation is everything!" (Gal 6:15). Luther comments: "This is the only true rule by which we should walk, namely, the new creation. . . . By it we live in faith in Christ and are made a new creation, that is, truly righteous and holy through the Holy Spirit, not through sham and pretence. Upon those who walk by this rule there comes peace (that is, the favor of God, the forgiveness of sins, and serenity of conscience) and mercy (that is, help in affliction and forgiveness for the remnants of sin still in the flesh)."[15] Luther's commentary here was directed against the medieval regard for monastic rules as proper interpretation of Paul's word "canon"; it thus reflects his age's focus on the individual's salvation in a way that does not quite bring out Paul's concern for the Galatians' life together as the *ecclesia.* Nevertheless, we can note here that "justification by faith alone" is, following Luther, a proper name for Paul's canon if, as in the cited text, we are talking of a true righteousness through the Holy Spirit, not a legal fiction, righteousness as both forgiveness of guilt and new power over hitherto dominating sin. Or to make the same point from another angle: justification by faith properly names Paul's canon, not as a punctilinear declaration solely to the individual conscience that leaves the world as it is, but as parsing the narrative of the great and joyful exchange between Christ and His people that concretely forms in this world the new creation, albeit yet "in affliction and [in need of] forgiveness for the remnants of sin still in the flesh."

What is under consideration for the present is the origin and development of the rule of faith from Jesus-scarred Paul's mention of this "canon" of faith in Galatians 6:16 and its relation to the "standard of teaching" (Rom 6:17), or the "tradition" (1 Cor 11:23) of the gospel (1 Cor 15:1-3; Gal 1:6-9) through the "sound teaching" (2 Tim 1:13) commended by the so-called Pastoral Epistles on to the second century. In this chapter we trace the course of the "rule of faith" in the theology of the martyrs from Pauline tradition through the towering second-century figures of Justin Martyr and Irenaeus of Lyon. As mentioned, in order radically to expose the moral perversity of the Bauer thesis, it is crucial to see in this development that *appeal to the standard of doctrine correlates with the ethos of the martyrs*. In the martyr-bishop Ignatius we have already seen the emphatic, antidocetist appeal to primitive forms of the baptismal creed: "Be deaf, therefore, whenever anyone speaks to you apart from Jesus Christ, who was of the family of David, who was the son of Mary; who really was born, who both ate and drank, who really was persecuted under Pontius Pilate, who really was crucified and died while those in heaven and earth and under the earth looked on; who, moreover, really was raised from the dead when his Father raised him up, who—his Father, that is—in the same way will likewise also raise us up in Christ Jesus who believe in him, apart from whom we have no true life" (*Trall.* 9). Saving union with Christ depends on doctrinally identifying this "real" Christ to faith in order ethically to participate in the crucified and risen reality that He is. This theo-logic of doctrinal fidelity is clearly Pauline: "Now if we are children, then we are heirs—heirs of God and co-heirs with Christ, if indeed we share in his sufferings in order that we may also share in his glory" (Rom 8:17). Ethos and dogma correspond in hope for the cosmic redemption of our bodies (Rom 8:23). Christian doctrine is such doctrine for life.

Paul's "Canon" of Faith (Galatians 6:16)

What is the new creation, the Israel of God, to which Paul's canon appeals? For Paul, the risen Lord really has an earthly body,[16] namely, His people on this earth called to faith by the gospel and bound together by their communion in His body and blood, which *union* is the *new covenant*. At the center of his theology of redemption through the cross of Jesus, Paul speaks in Romans 7:4 of Jesus' crucified body as the means through which believers belong to Him: "In the same way, my friends, you have died to the law through the body of Christ, so that you may belong to another, to him who has been raised from the dead in order that we may bear fruit for God." That bond of the new covenant of mutual belonging and service in the reign of God is constantly re-created, according to 1 Corinthians 10:16, at the Eucharist: "The cup of blessing that we bless, is it not a sharing in the blood of Christ? The bread that we break, is it not a sharing in the body of Christ?" Therefore Paul can always ground the behavior of believers in their membership in the body of the Lord, as in 1 Corinthians 12:27: "Now you are the body of Christ and individually members of it." Because Jesus is the body that bore the sin of the world, believers become His body, God's righteousness in the world (2 Cor 5:21).

It is the existence of this body of Jesus the Son that requires Paul, as it had also Mark, to speak of the God of the gospel in the trinitarian manner. As a body, Christians together worship the Father in the power of the Spirit because of their union by faith with the Son. "Because you are children," Paul writes in Galatians 4:6, "God has sent the Spirit of his Son into our hearts, crying, 'Abba! Father!' Paul expresses the same thought more fully to the Romans in 8:15: "You have received a spirit of adoption. When we cry, 'Abba! Father!' it is that very Spirit bearing witness with our spirit that we are children of God, and if children, then heirs, heirs of God and joint heirs with Christ—if, in fact, we suffer with him so that we may also be glorified with him." At the most primal level of the early Christian community's worship, the trinitarian pattern appears in Paul with the picture of the body of believers in Christ being drawn into His own relation with the Father by the Spirit. The *ecclesia* understood as communal being in Christ, beloved of the Father and loving Him by the Spirit, is not then some extrinsic by-product, an association of like-minded religionists, but rather *part of the gospel* (B. Marshall). It is fundamentally misleading therefore ever to think of Paul as an existentialist with an individualistic message of personal authenticity in the fashion that Martin Heidegger and his theological camp-followers have thought.[17]

Paul especially developed his ecclesiological thinking in response to the factious situation in Corinth where individuals thought it was their right to set themselves above or apart from others less spiritual than themselves on the basis of putative knowledge (Greek: *gnosis*). The Corinthian "enthusiasts," as scholarship calls Paul's opponents, stand in the same theological trajectory as the false messiahs in Mark 13, the docetists whom John opposed, and the Gnostics of the second century, as Conzelmann affirmed in his commentary on 1 Corinthians: "There are also isolated traces of the beginnings of the formation of what later presented itself as 'Gnosticism,' that is, Gnosticism *in statu nascendi* [in the state of being born]. The Corinthians could be described as proto-Gnostics."[18] In the name of being closer to Christ or God, in Paul's view, they separated themselves from brothers and sisters for whom Christ died. Seeking for themselves a superior wisdom, holiness, or spirituality, they actually opposed the wisdom of God that chooses the foolish in the world. Thus they subverted the true holiness and spirituality of the community as given in Christ Jesus, who died for the ungodly.[19] For in the wisdom of God, Christ's love holds together as a new humanity those who are despised in the world (1 Cor 1:26-31). Where Christ's love made known in the cross is in power, there is the new community of the *Holy* Spirit of God the Creator, *Spiritus Creator*. Against the elitist, individualistic tendency of the Corinthian proto-Gnostics, in 1 Corinthians 3:16-17 the Apostle makes the emphatic identification of *all* the believers in Christ as an *organism*: "Do you [*all, that is, plural*] not know that you [*all*] are God's temple and that God's Spirit dwells among you [*all*]? If anyone destroys God's temple, God will destroy that person. For God's temple is holy, and you [*all, that is, collectively*] are that temple."[20] The Corinthian factionalism tears apart what God is knitting together in Christ by the Spirit, the new community defined by baptism into Christ and eucharistic feeding on Christ: "For in the one Spirit we were all baptized into one body—Jews or Greeks, slaves or free—and we were all made to drink of one Spirit" (1 Cor 12:13). Paul asks rhetorically in 1 Cor 6:19-20, "Do you not know that the body of you [*all*] is the temple of the Holy Spirit among you, which you have from God, and that none of you are your own? For you all were bought with a price; therefore glorify God in the body of you [*all*]!"[21]

In Paul's thinking about the *ecclesia* as the body of Christ, it is as though all of human life on the earth has now become a field of contest between opposing worships, with the *ecclesia* marking the now advancing, now retreating front line of the "invasion of God" (J. L. Martyn), who seeks to win the praise of the nations (Rom 15:7-12). Just as the prophets of the old covenant contended for the true worship of God, so also the Apostle of the new covenant sees the true worship of God in the new life together of the Christians as earthly body of the risen Lord. Paul accordingly draws a doctrinal boundary in 1 Corinthians 8:10 and 9:13 against participation in pagan worship practices. In 2 Corinthians 6:16 this boundary is made unmistakably clear: "What agreement has the temple of God with idols? For we are the temple of the living God; as God said, 'I will live in them and walk among them, and I will be their God, and they shall be my people.'" Paul is writing these words long before the destruction of the temple in Jerusalem; that event is not on the historical horizon in the early 50s as he writes to the churches in Corinth. Nonetheless, here again we see, as we have seen across the spectrum of early Christianity, how the symbols, rituals, and theology of the worship of God in the temple in Jerusalem are being taken over and reassigned to the living *koinonia* of Christ. The deutero-Pauline author of Ephesians 2:21-22 sums up the Apostle's legacy when he declares that in the community of Christ "the whole structure is joined together and grows into a holy temple in the Lord; in whom you also are built together spiritually into a dwelling place for God."

Peter Stuhlmacher has argued that Paul inherited this new application of the scriptural theology of the temple to the community of Christians from the earliest Christian congregations in Jerusalem and Antioch (more precisely, from the scattered circle of Greek-speaking Jews around the martyred Stephen who were driven from Jerusalem for their criticism of the temple cult (as may be seen in Acts 6:13-14; 7:47-53; 8:1; 11:19-26). He calls attention to a foundational text in Pauline theology, Romans 3:24-25, concerning the "redemption that is in Christ Jesus, whom God put forward as a sacrifice of atonement by his blood," as a dogmatic affirmation that Paul would have inherited from the Stephen circle. Stuhlmacher argues that the Stephen circle "took upon themselves the risk of speaking of Jesus' public installation as the *kapporet* (*hilasterion*, 'mercy seat'), that is, as the place of God's revelation and of the atonement established once and for all by God, an installation that surpasses and renders obsolete all cultic atonement, making Jesus an antitype to the most significant Jewish atonement rite, the celebration of the Day of Atonement in accord with Leviticus 16."[22] Inheriting this tradition, Paul the Apostle reasoned, according to Stuhlmacher, that "the justification of the ungodly is thus made possible in that God, by putting forward Jesus to be himself a sin offering, creates that atonement by virtue of which sinners can be acquitted of the sins that both burden and rule them." It is the biblical idea of "sacrifice and atonement that enables Paul to think theologically about justification through Christ"[23] and the basis, as we have surveyed, of his thinking about his congregations in Christ as the new Temple of the Holy Spirit.

The argument has weight. Indeed, it is hard to imagine the christological significance of Jesus for His first believers without reference to the temple and its sacrificial cult, which still remained the visible sign of God's ancient promises to His people. How else could the first Jewish believers think about the meaning of the resurrection of the crucified Jesus? In His inclusive, representative public persona, Jesus formed the Temple of God; in His sacrificial work on the cross, Jesus became the once-for-all atonement of God. Since the Holocaust of Europe's Jews at the hands of resurgent paganism,[24] and the confessed liability in part for this wickedness of traditional Christian anti-Judaism,[25] it is very important for us today carefully to note that normative Judaism *as a religion*, like normative Christianity *as a religion*, both emerged in response to the destruction of the temple and its cult in 70.[26] For *both* religions, the sacrificial cult was ended by God Himself in this devastating historical judgment and so superceded by new forms of community; *both* religions have had to deal with this massive discontinuity in salvation history. Judaism, under the leadership of the scribes and Pharisees we know from the pages of the New Testament, transited into the new office of rabbi of the synagogue. The communities in diaspora replaced the role of the destroyed temple in Jerusalem. The rabbis also drew upon the old theology about the temple to create the new ideal of realizing atonement, praise, and instruction in the life of obedience to the Torah. Therefore, in speaking of the *supercession* of the temple by Christ's new covenant, we are *not* speaking of the supercession of God's ancient chosen race, the Jews. Even before the destruction of the temple, Paul the Apostle very clearly *denied* this implication in Romans 9–11, where he emphatically affirmed that God's election of the Gentiles in Christ does not imply or entail that He has rejected His people, the Jews. Studying a text like Romans 9–11, we see the need very carefully to attend to both the continuity and discontinuity of the history of salvation, appreciating Paul's and early Christianity's tortured but also complex relation to the many forms of pre-normative Judaism. And we need to draw the same moral for ourselves, as Paul went on to teach in Romans 12–15: Any Gentile who denigrates the religion of the Scriptures saws off the branch onto which he or she has been grafted. The terms that give the basic meaning to Jesus' death on the cross and vindication, not to mention Jesus' own ministry and mission, are drawn from Israel, and we cannot have Jesus without them.[27]

If the church is part of the gospel, then so also is Israel with her Scriptures into whom those called out from the nations in the church are grafted. In the Epistle to the Romans, Paul once again (as he had in Gal 4) looked back upon the faith of father Abraham. He argued that his exemplary faith in God, who justifies the ungodly, giving life to the dead and children to the barren, is what justified him (Gen 15) before he ever submitted to circumcision (Gen 17), the latter rite then "a seal of the righteousness that he had by faith while he was still uncircumcised" (Rom 4:11). Consequently, Abraham's faith is the prototype of the Christian who believes in the God "who raised Jesus our Lord from the dead, who was handed over to death for our transgressions and was raised for our justification" (Rom 4:24-25). For Paul the Jewish Christian, this promise of God to Abraham at the beginning of His ways with Israel is constitutive; the law of God given through Moses comes later as an interim measure "on account of transgressions" (Gal 3:19); its interim purpose was to be our "taskmaster until the faith would be revealed" (Gal 3:23). The true Israel is the Israel of promise, including both Jews and Gentiles who believe as father Abraham had believed.

Paul's "principal question" in ecclesiology then was "how Jews and Christians, Israel and Gentile church, should live together within God's plan of salvation. Not against one another, nor side by side, but with one another . . . fellow citizens, joint heirs, co-recipients of salvation, mutual witnesses, companions in the household of God, partners in combat, brothers and sisters, and so on."[28] The Israel who understands herself according to the Law and the covenant on Mount Sinai, in Paul's view, misunderstands herself and her true status before God; it is thus "on account of the veil of Moses" (2 Cor 3:15) that Israel does not and cannot believe in the crucified Christ who fulfilled the law on behalf of the weak and godless (Rom 5), in this way superceding its judgment of condemnation. But this veiling is God's own doing (Rom 11). Thus living Judaism that does not believe in Jesus nevertheless remains constituted by this original promise ("The gifts and calling of God are irrevocable," Rom 11:28-29); human faithlessness does not cancel out God's faithfulness. The Gentiles who have now been "called out" by the gospel to form the *ecclesia* are likewise constituted by this same promise, which has turned to them in the gospel. Consequently, both Israel and *ecclesia* for the meantime must live with this curious disagreement in agreement. Yet in the last days these two callings will converge again, "for God has imprisoned all in disobedience so that he may be merciful to all" (Rom 11:32).

Such is their new existence as the elect of Christ (side by side with the Jewish people): the Temple of the Holy Spirit, the body of Christ, new being in Christ. This new creation of Galatians 6:14 is thus analytic to the doctrinal "rule" of *faith* in *Jesus* as *sufficient* for membership. Ontologically, self-entrusting faith in the God who raised Jesus from death *is* the new creation in the midst of one old and dying, and as such it suffices for membership in the people of God, that is, the true Israel of the "circumcision of the heart" (Rom 2:29) by which "the world is crucified to me and I to the world" (Gal 6:14b).

For the sake of this "canon," if David Trobisch[29] is correct, Paul himself published the first collection of his writings (Romans, 1 and 2 Corinthians, and Galatians in that order, thus emphatically concluding with Gal 6:14) to make public his theological case for this doctrinal rule with which the collection of letters dramatically ends. The occasion was Paul's impending visit to Jerusalem, where he would deliver the offering he had collected for the Jewish poor from his Gentile converts and in the process face his opponents (the "Judaizers" of Galatians, the "super-apostles" of 2 Corinthians). Trobisch points out that in Paul's own lifetime, the conflict between him and these representatives of some of the Jerusalem "pillars" was in all probability not resolved. "It is this conflict . . . that pushed Paul to publish four of his letters. And it is this conflict that later editors had in mind when they prepared a collection of Christian writings for publication, a collection that came to be known as the New Testament. Besides the fourteen letters of Paul we find letters of the Jerusalem authorities James, John and Peter. . . . The picture conveyed by the writings of the New Testament to their readers is one of unity. The conflict between Paul and Jerusalem was resolved"[30] in this way—or forgotten.

Trobisch's argument is intended historically, not theologically, and is convincing so far as it goes. Certainly the New Testament as we have it is the synthesis that the post-apostolic generation made of the literature of parties that in their own time were at odds about the "truth of the gospel" (Gal 2:14). But the salient point at present is that Trobisch's reconstruction yields a view of Paul *as a deliberate doctrinal theologian* whose purpose in publishing his writing was, among others, "dogmatic." After his death (probably in Rome under Nero, perhaps simultaneously with his erstwhile opponent Peter, as tradition suggests, for example, *1 Clem.* 5), Paul's disciples expanded and developed this dogmatic legacy. If we were to be comprehensive in examining this development of doctrine, we would have to trace it through important writings like the epistles to the Colossians and Ephesians.[31] But for present purposes we can attend to decisive stepping stones along the way toward the emergence of critical dogmatic theology, that is, the trinitarian rule of faith. Thus we turn next to the post-apostolic Paulinist of the so-called Pastoral Epistles,[32] putatively written by Paul from prison to his young assistants Timothy and Titus.

Early Christian Dogma in the Pastoral Epistles

The Pastoral Epistles lift up the example and doctrine of Paul the Apostle. Paul had died a violent death at the hands of Roman justice, meeting the same fate as his Lord. But this cruel fact was compounded by an even crueler fact: Paul suffered in his imprisonment and death the immensely greater humiliation of abandonment by erstwhile Christian comrades in Rome. "At my first defense no one came to my support, but all deserted me" (2 Tim 4:16). The Pastoral Epistles' acknowledgment of this embarrassing fact is a key to their interpretation.

The very Paul lionized in the Acts of the Apostles as a hero who had evangelized the nations, founded churches, preached to kings, and silenced foes, the one who composed those powerful if difficult (2 Tim 3:15-17!) letters that defined the doctrine of grace in the first fires of battle—this Paul apparently perished abandoned and in disgrace. This denouement of his apostolic career may have called into question the validity and/or the sense of his legacy in the second Christian generation, at a time when an attractive but false and schismatic "knowledge" (*gnosis*; 1 Tim 6:20; Tit 3:9-11) was spreading through the communities of the martyred apostle. Indeed, it may already have happened during Paul's lifetime; in Corinth enthusiasm "may have emerged spontaneously as a result of Paul's own activity";[33] that is, a plausible but false reading of Pauline texts as Gnosis (2 Pet 3:15-16) may have developed. But Paul is no longer alive to correct the interpretation of what he had said or written. Thus "the time is coming," indeed for the Pastoral Epistles already is, "when people will not put up with sound doctrine, but having itching ears, they will accumulate for themselves teachers to suit their own desires, and will turn away from listening to the truth and wander away to myths" (2 Tim 4:3-4).

This is the situation of doctrinal chaos to which the Pastoral Epistles are addressed after Paul's death. Over against such false teachers, the memory of this martyred apostle is now held up as the model. He is the model of one transformed by the grace of Jesus Christ: "Though I was formerly a blasphemer, a persecutor, and a man of violence: . . . I received mercy, so that in me, as the foremost, Jesus Christ might display the utmost patience, making me an example to those who would come to believe in him for eternal life" (1 Tim 1:15-16). He is also held up as a missionary "teacher of the Gentiles in faith and truth" (2:7), as an exemplary pastor who "endures everything for the sake of the elect, so that they may also obtain the salvation that is in Christ Jesus, with eternal glory" (2 Tim 2:10). But above all he is lifted up as the exemplary witness/martyr: "As for me, I am already being poured out as a libation, and the time of my departure has come. I have fought the good fight, I have finished the race, I have kept the faith" (4:6).

One task of the Pastoral Epistles, then, is to overcome lingering suspicions and the sting of disgrace that surrounded Paul's memory. They do this by showing that Paul's cruel fate actually confirmed the authenticity of his apostleship to "Christ Jesus, who in his testimony before Pontius Pilate made the good confession" (1 Tim 6:13), also all alone, deserted by His people. So also had Paul stood alone at his own trial ("But the Lord stood by me and gave me strength, so that through me the message might be fully proclaimed and all the Gentiles might hear it," 2 Tim 4:17). The content of the confession is the one God's universal will to salvation through Jesus Christ ("God our Savior . . . desires everyone to be saved and to come to the knowledge of the truth," 1 Tim 2:3-4). This gnosis is the true "mystery," revealed and proclaimed in "the gospel" and defined and preserved in "sound doctrine." The Pastoral Epistles' exhortation, ostensibly addressed to Timothy, in fact speaks to all who will hear this set of three open letters read in the churches: "Do not be ashamed, then, of the testimony about our Lord or of me his prisoner, but join with me in suffering for the gospel, relying on the power of God" (2 Tim 1:8). The summons to "fight the good fight of the faith; take hold of the eternal life, to which you were called and for which you made the good confession in the presence of many witnesses" (1 Tim 6:12) has potential martyrs in the churches in view, who are thus urged to lay hold by faith the promised victory of the "crown of righteousness" already now in the midst of persecution. They can do so by imitating Paul's example.

This hope of eternal life in the early Christian theology of the martyrs, as we saw in Ignatius, is utterly theocentric, in the sense that this salvation is understood not as God's intervention on behalf of human purposes, but as God's action to win human beings over to divine purposes to enjoy divine community: "The Lord will rescue me from every evil attack and save me for his heavenly kingdom. To him be the glory forever and ever. Amen" (2 Tim 4:18). According to the Pastoral Epistles, these are Paul's last words. The onslaught of suffering caused by persecution, even the acute humiliation of betrayal or denial or abandonment at the hands of fellow believers, does not provoke doubts about God's justice but rather stiffens resolve faithfully to endure, "to fight the good fight." Theologically, however, the Pastoral Epistles' case for the restoration of Paul's reputation works if, and only if, this theocentricism remains in force. Like the historical Apostle himself, here too "if for this life only we have hoped in Christ, we are of all men most to be pitied" (1 Cor 15:19; Rom 8:18). We will return shortly to this fundamental matter of Pauline "otherworldliness" (Smith's world-denying "utopianism").

In the interim, the summons to the battle of faith is rooted in the primitive Christian understanding of the baptismal identification of Christ and the believer (Titus 3:4-5), in which the accent falls on Christ's gracious initiative and final triumph even on behalf of failing disciples: "The saying is sure: If we have died with him, we will also live with him; if we endure, we will also reign with him; if we deny him, he will also deny us; if we are faithless, he remains faithful, for he cannot deny himself" (2 Tim 2:11-13). In this appeal to the new life that baptism confers, the Pastoral Epistles rightly draw on the historical Paul's paradoxical knowledge of God's power made manifest in human weakness and need. Precisely as a believer, indeed as an apostle of Jesus Christ, the historical Paul had discovered that utter reliance on all-sufficing divine grace (2 Cor 12:9) is never a state to be transcended. This state of reliance on God is salvation itself, for in it God's almighty power, wisdom, and goodness are manifested. The Pastoral Epistles also know this paradox of power in weakness: "Remember Jesus Christ, raised from the dead, a descendant of David—that is my gospel, for which I suffer hardship, even to the point of being chained like a criminal. But the word of God is not chained" (2 Tim 2:8). The "good soldier of Jesus Christ" is the one who suffers with Him and just so reveals His power over the systemic violence of the present world order.

Arguments about authority in the church are thus ultimately resolved into the question of true Christology. That this christological resolution occurs in a new day with new results over against the historical Paul is evident upon close examination of the Pastoral Epistles. But in this christological approach to discerning the proper form of the community's faith and life, the Pastoral Epistles show themselves true heirs of Paul. The Pastoral Epistles know Christ both as the ransom for sin ("For there is one God; there is also one mediator between God and humankind, Christ Jesus, himself human, who gave himself a ransom for all," 1 Tim 2:5; Mark 10:45) and as the victor over it ("who abolished death and brought life and immortality to light through the gospel," 1 Tim 1:10). The "gospel" concerns Christ Jesus as savior of those alienated from God's purposes: "The saying is sure and worthy of full acceptance, that Christ Jesus came into the world to save sinners, of whom I am the foremost" (1 Tim 1:15). Salvation consists consequently both in Christ's sacrifice for them that obtains forgiveness and in Christ's life in them that leads to a joyful new obedience in conformity with God's purposes.

True Christology does not permit these two aspects of salvation to be played off against each other. True Christology keeps these two aspects of salvation together by the trinitarian linkages: believers as beloved with Jesus by virtue of God's free favor and believers as united with Jesus to live new lives to God by virtue of God's donation of the Spirit.

To learn obedience to God's purposes, readers are directed with Timothy to the Spirit-breathed Scriptures, that is, those "sacred writings that are able to instruct you for salvation through faith in Christ Jesus . . . useful for teaching, for reproof, for correction, and for training in righteousness (2 Tim 3:15-16). This recommendation of the Scriptures *of Israel* is vividly contrasted to "unprofitable and worthless" myth-mongering and idle controversy of theological speculation (3:9). It is not that the Pastoral Epistles are against *gnosis*, properly understood. Genuine "knowledge" in the church is knowledge of the "gospel," as instructed by the "scriptures" concerning the "mystery of the faith" (1 Tim 3:9; 4:1, 6; 5:8; 6:10; 2 Tim 3:8, following Col 1:26; 4:3). This points to a key early Christian theological concept, *oikonomia tou theou* (1 Tim 1:4), the saving plan of God as the cognitive content of genuine Christian gnosis—just as formulated in chapter 1 of this book: *God the almighty Father is determined to redeem the creation through His Son, Jesus Christ, and bring it to fulfillment by*

His Spirit. All other doctrines are but articulations or extrapolations of this one, fundamental truth claim. This is knowledge of God in God's providential rule, knowledge of the reign of God, which for Trinitarianism is God Himself, His being in action. This gnosis of faith empowers believers to cooperate with God by understanding their corresponding roles in church and in society. Thus in the "know," they are neither ashamed of suffering for the gospel nor distracted by heterodox doctrine, but are rather fully and actively engaged in realizing God's will both in their actions and in their sufferings. Orthodoxy and orthopraxis thus coinhere. Morality is not an autonomous sphere, a theological *adiaphoron* (matter of indifference). The Pastoral Epistles cannot imagine faith apart from life. It is in this sense that the Pastoral Epistles repeatedly exhort, like Ignatius: "Hold to the standard of sound teaching that you have heard from me, in the faith *and love* that are in Christ Jesus!" (2 Tim 1:13, emphasis added). And it is in this sense that the Pastoral Epistles go on thickly to describe the virtues that attend various offices in the church.

If modern critics object here to "bourgeois moralism" in the Pastoral Epistles, what they really have in mind with their ahistorical, anachronistic reproach is the apparent quietism and conformism that the Pastoral Epistles commend vis-à-vis the given social structures of the day: "First of all, then, I urge that supplications, prayers, intercessions, and thanksgivings be made for everyone, for kings and all who are in high positions, so that we may lead a quiet and peaceable life in all godliness and dignity" (1 Tim 2:1-2). Or critics have in mind the notorious counsel silencing women in the church (2:11) or demanding slaves to respect their masters (6:1). Such a criticism, however, is quite confused, if the point somehow is that the Pastoral Epistles have distorted Paul in this. In fact, the historical Paul shared the same apparent quietism and conformism (recall only Rom 13!).

To be sure, there is a theological difference between the historical Paul and the Pastoral Epistles. Seen from the christological angle, the essential thrust of the historical Paul's doctrine of justification (which is about the justice, that is, faithfulness or obedience, of Christ coming from God on behalf of the ungodly for the establishment of His reign) is correctly articulated in the Pastoral Epistles' vigorous and explicit refusal of works-righteousness. Yet the Pastoral Epistles' adoption of the emperor cult's rhetoric of epiphany and salvation has modulated the eschatological tension in the historical Paul's view. For the historical Paul, the notion of salvation is generally reserved for the future apocalyptic hope of "the redemption of our bodies" when the Creator visibly comes to defeat the usurping powers of sin and death. Salvation remains essentially cosmic in scope and situated in the future. Consequently, justification by faith, that is, in the personal act of entrusting oneself to this promised future, points to an essentially future salvation of God that becomes paradoxically present already now to faith (as in Rom 5:1). In comparison, for the Pastoral Epistles, faith in the sense of self-surrendering trust to the promised future Lord has become objectively "the faith" and subjectively "piety" (*eusebia*). The historical Paul's justification by faith in God's promised future becomes early Catholicism's justification by the grace of the predestining God, "who saved us and called us with a holy calling, not according to our works but according to his own purpose and grace. This grace was given to us in Christ Jesus before the ages began, but it has now been revealed" (2 Tim 1:9-10). This grace in turn is productive of the new life of *eusebia*, piety, which the Pastoral Epistles so emphatically recommend as the key to their catalogues of virtue.

It would amount to a distortion if we interpreted the historical Paul's theology in these categories of the Pastoral Epistles. Yet the Pastoral Epistles represent something much different than a tragic *mis*appropriation of Paul in the urgent situation after his death, in which his disciples had to foreclose the possibilities of Gnostic interpretation of "the faith" in Pauline texts. The Pastoral Epistles actually represent the only possible venue for theological appropriation of Paul for all following generations, that is, whenever appropriators become historically aware of their own actual standing (howsoever alienated) in "the household of God, which is the church of the living God, the pillar and bulwark of the truth," the steward of the "mystery of our piety" (that is, *eusebia*, translation altered), which is Christ incarnate and risen, exalted and proclaimed (1 Tim 3:16). *There is no escaping this hermeneutical circle. There is no other place in the world in which to appropriate Paul than in and through the early catholic church.*

Martyrological Ethos in the Pastoral Epistles

There is another, even deeper continuity in ethos that encompasses not only the historical Paul and the Pastoral Epistles, but stretches from the prophets of Israel through the second-century line of Ignatius, Polycarp (Polycarp's *Letter to the Philippians* probably contains the first direct attestation of the Pastoral Epistles of which we are aware[34]), Justin, and Irenaeus and beyond. This continuity in ethos may be designated "the theology of the martyrs" of the one God, who prefer death to obeisance before the worldly usurpers of the divine kingship. In spite of all alleged quietism and conformism, the earliest Christian confession, "(Crucified) Jesus is the (Risen) Lord," bore disturbing political overtones both in its native Jewish and in the wider Hellenistic environments. Jesus himself had been denounced and executed as a messianic pretender, "King of the Jews." We know from chapters 5 and 9 of the Gospel of John how among Jews belief in this crucified Jesus as the Christ led eventually to expulsion from the synagogue, persecution, and, according to John 16:2, even martyrdom. The book of Acts explains the stoning of the deacon Stephen in Jerusalem because profession of Jesus as the Christ entailed sharp criticism of the temple and its worship. Eusebius tells us that James the son of Zebedee was killed in Jerusalem in the

40s, and James the brother of the Lord in the 60s. As late as the 130s, according to the lost work of Hegesippus, "Barkohba, the leader of the [second] Jewish revolt [during the reign of Adrian], commanded the Christians alone to be led to severe and dreadful tortures, unless they would deny and blaspheme Christ Jesus."[35] The defeat of the Jewish revolts with the loss of the temple in Jerusalem and corresponding loss of political power ended Jewish persecution of early Christians. It also led to the definitive separation of Judaism and Christianity as rival religions. But it did not lead to the end of the persecution of the early Christians. Tradition held that the apostles Peter and Paul—despite their historical conflict—suffered martyrdom together in Rome, presumably for refusing to burn a little stick of incense to honor the Roman emperor Nero, confessing instead Jesus as Lord. The fullest early picture we have of Gentile persecution comes from the *Martyrdom of Polycarp*[36] dated around 160.

The eighty-six-year-old bishop, who as a young man had met Ignatius of Antioch in chains on his way to Rome, was hunted down, arrested, and brought before the crowd in the theater in Smyrna. He was attacked by the pagan mob as an "atheist," that is, "the teacher of Asia, the father of the Christians, the destroyer of our gods, who teaches many not to sacrifice or worship." The accusation is telling. Years before, the aforementioned Ignatius has written that the Eucharist is the one true worship of God because it "is the flesh of our Savior Jesus Christ, which suffered for our sins and which the Father by his goodness raised up" (*Smyrn.* 6:2). The world, in other words, is full of "eucharists," that is, thanksgivings, sacrifices, worships, attempts to ingratiate or expiate the gods.[37] In the Eucharist, as the very early, anonymous writing called the *Didache* shows, the Christians offered a sacrifice of praise and thanks through Christ for the peace God had made known (*Did.* 9–10). It was a sacrifice of self, which required reconciliation with God and one another (*Did.* 14) in contrast to bloody rites of expiation on all sides. The new and "bloodless" sacrifice in the Christian community, not of irrational beasts, but of themselves in, with, and through Christ in the power of the Spirit for service to the Father's dawning reign, differs from all these others, which do not know about the grace of God in Christ. "The general charge of atheism or impiety (non-participation in the state cult) touched upon the Eucharist, for the Christians abstained from the common sacrifices of the civic community, offering their own peculiar sacrifice and excluding others from participation in it. This inevitably led to charges that the Christians were undermining the state by declining to participate in the propitiatory sacrifices required by the polytheistic state cult."[38]

As previously argued, Ignatius's antidocetist specification of that "Eucharist alone which is the true body and blood of Christ" does not indicate in the first place some private idea, a theory, or an interpretation of something else. The force of the assertion is exactly the opposite. One cannot have a "theory" of the Eucharist; it is axiomatic. It is the thing itself. It interprets all the rest, especially the nature of the Christian fellowship. So Ignatius: "Mark those who hold strange doctrines concerning the grace of Jesus Christ which came to us, how that they are contrary to the mind of God. They have no care for love, none for the widow, none for the orphan, none for the afflicted, none for the prisoner, nor the hungry or thirsty. They abstain from the Eucharist and prayer, because they do not allow that the Eucharist is the flesh of our Savior Jesus Christ, which flesh suffered for our sins, and which the Father in his goodness raised up"(*Smyrn.* 6). The Eucharist *is* the gospel in community forming and sustaining power, the meal of the "new testament" after which the book is named. Any religious gathering that offers anything less than or something other than this is not the gospel, of which the church is part. Any gathering other than this is not the catholic church.[39] Polycarp the bishop had so presided at the Eucharist in Smyrna since his youth, when he first witnessed this teaching of Ignatius.

Feeling pity for the aged man, the magistrate pleaded with him, "What harm is there in saying, Caesar is Lord, and offering incense and thereby saving yourself? Swear the oath, and I will release you. Revile Christ." Polycarp replied, "For eighty six years I have been his servant, and he has done me no wrong. How can I blaspheme my King who saved me?"[40] To no avail, Polycarp reiterated to the magistrate the apostolic teaching (Rom 13; 1 Pet 2:17) that Christians are obedient subjects of the political authorities so far as their jurisdiction extends. But political jurisdiction does not extend to the relationship with God. The concrete limit of political authority is the confession of the crucified Jesus, not Caesar in imperial majesty, as the incarnate Son of God, and with this the practical refusal of the civic sacrifices in favor of the early catholic Eucharist. By this withdrawal and noncooperation, Christians formed a new assembly of humanity that gathered weekly on the day of the new creation, Sunday, the day of Jesus' resurrection. There in the ecstasy of the Spirit they rendered an exclusive worship to the Father in union with the Son of God who had sacrificed Himself for all. Polycarp implicates himself in this service and so refuses the magistrate's plea.

The Pastoral Epistles belong in this martyriological trajectory extending from the historical Paul to Ignatius and then Polycarp. In them the church realized that apostolic stewardship of the gospel required that Paul personally be conformed to the message he proclaimed, that he himself be saved by the Savior whom he preached: "For this gospel I was appointed a herald and an apostle and a teacher, and for this reason I suffer as I do. But I am not ashamed, for I know the one in whom I have put my trust" (2 Tim 1:12). Such knowledge of the true God as savior of His own is the genuine *gnosis* of God's plan of salvation, which accounts for the martyr's hope: "From now on there is reserved for me the crown of righteousness, which the Lord, the righteous judge, will give me on that day, and not only to me but also to all who have longed for his appearing" (4:8). Thus the manifest conflict with early forms of Gnosticism, alongside the prosaic, pedantic concern with church order and conventional behavior, ought not to obscure the one, really massive feature that stamps this literature as a whole: *the mortal conflict with the emperor cult into which Pauline Christianity reluctantly and perhaps unwillingly was drawn.* That cult acclaimed, "Hail Caesar, savior!" How could it tolerate the same ascription of glory to the Crucified One? In adopting and adapting the imperial cult's acclamation "Savior," the Pastoral Epistles made visible the inevitable collision between conflicting messiahships, as it were: the universal or catholic church of Jesus or the empire of the Romans. If it came to this, nothing but a choice could be made.

The command to Timothy to "share in suffering like a good solider of Christ Jesus" (2 Tim 2:3) only spells out the cost of the *exclusive monotheism* of biblical faith: "In the presence of God, who gives life to all things, and of Christ Jesus, who in his testimony before Pontius Pilate made the good confession, I charge you to keep the commandment without spot or blame until the manifestation of our Lord Jesus Christ, which he will bring about at the right time—he who is the blessed and only Sovereign, the King of kings and Lord of lords. It is he alone who has immortality and dwells in unapproachable light, whom no one has ever seen or can see; to him be honor and eternal dominion. Amen" (1 Tim 6:13-16). This profession of *exclusive monotheism*, now intruding into the heart of the world's darkness by the profession of salvation *only* through the *one* mediator between the *one* God and humanity, Himself human, the crucified Savior, Jesus, inevitably provoked a political conflict on the earth regarding *whose* is the kingdom, the power, and the glory, forever and ever. We fundamentally misread the Pastoral Epistles, along with the orthodox stance of the martyrs' theology, if we do not perceive the *massive provocation of the Pauline gospel*, which it wants to conserve and pass on.

The moral perversity of the Bauer thesis lies in willful incomprehension of this: painting the victims of imperial tyranny as ecclesiastical bullies when they were in fact battling with nothing but Word and Spirit against revisionism that sapped the courage of faith to resist seduction or stand up to intimidation under the *pax Romana*. Just so, the present account of the Pastoral Epistles provokes the question of whether the fashionable reading of Paul since the middle of the twentieth century as a liberating guru of existentialist justification has not made of him merely a Gnostic of a higher order rather than the biblical prophet of the justice of God revealed in Christ. But the Pastoral Epistles by contrast read Paul in continuity with the Jewish, scriptural tradition (as 2 Tim 1:3 alludes, "I am grateful to God, whom I worship with a clear conscience, as my ancestors did") of exclusive monotheism. If we grasp that "sincere faith" is not the tortured angst of isolated and agonized modern individualists wondering whether there is a Nanny in the sky, but is rather formation in a community of faith ("a faith that lived first in your grandmother Lois and your mother Eunice and now, I am sure, lives in you," 2 Tim 1:5) that is radically *atheistic* in relation to the civil theology, we can draw at least several pertinent conclusions.

First, the justice of God that overtakes in Jesus Christ assaults human greed—and can only "save"—not by satisfying greed, but by extirpating it. "If we have food and clothing, we will be content with these. But those who want to be rich fall into temptation and are trapped by many senseless and harmful desires that plunge people into ruin and destruction. For the love of money is a root of all kinds of evil, and in their eagerness to be rich some have wandered away from the faith and pierced themselves with many pains" (1 Tim 6:10). Second, preaching this way will surely send preachers back to their ordinations: "For this reason I remind you to rekindle the gift of God that is within you through the laying on of my hands; for God did not give us a spirit of cowardice, but rather a spirit of power and of love and of self-discipline" (2 Tim 1:6-7). Recalling their ordinations, preachers who preach Christ from the Pastoral Epistles will themselves hear anew the charge: "In the presence of God and of Christ Jesus, who is to judge the living and the dead, and in view of his appearing and his kingdom, I solemnly urge you: proclaim the message; be persistent whether the time is favorable or unfavorable; convince, rebuke, and encourage, with the utmost patience in teaching. As for you, always be sober, endure suffering, do the work of an evangelist, carry out your ministry fully" (2 Tim 4:1). In this they will discover anew "that the word of God is not chained"—even if its preachers, sometimes are.

Christian "Atheism" in Justin Martyr

Between the time of Ignatius, Polycarp, and the Pastoral Epistles at the beginning of the second century and Irenaeus at its end, we find Justin Martyr (c. 100–165), so named because he also sealed his teaching "in chains." "In the end he was denounced to the authorities by an angry rival, the Cynic Crescens. Tried before the prefect of the city, Q. Junius Rusticus, he refused to sacrifice to the gods and went unflinchingly to his death in 165."[41] A Samaritan Greek by birth, Justin tells us that while he was still a student of Platonism, a dialogue with an old man, presumably a Christian, shook his previous confidence in the Platonic doctrine of the soul's immortality: "For God alone is unbegotten and incorruptible, and therefore He is God, but all other things after Him are created and corruptible. For this reason souls both die and are punished" (*Dial.* 5).[42] Justin tells us that he was then converted to the Christian faith by his encounter with *the Scriptures of Israel*, which Justin read as *prophecy*. Studying them, he came to the conviction that their promises were being fulfilled in Christ as the promised Messiah and His church as the divinely promised society of a renewed humanity. The Scriptures, Justin says, "remain and anyone who has turned to them has received enormous help on questions of the source and goal of existence" (*Dial.* 7). From these Scriptures, Justin learned that "Christ has come in his power from the Almighty Father . . . calling all men to friendship, benediction, repentance and community. . . . Men from every land, whether slaves or free ... will one day be united with [Christ] in the land, to inherit the imperishable blessings for all eternity" (*Dial.* 139). W. H. C. Frend has emphasized the importance of this relation to the Hebrew Bible for the understanding of Justin: the "argument for prophecy was the cornerstone of Justin's defense of Christianity,"[43] that is, for a Christianity that itself "is grounded in the prophetic word of the Old Testament that formed part of an integrated structure of truth though which Christ, identified with the divine reason, guides and illumines mankind."[44]

The characteristic realism of Justin's eschatological expectation for the renewal of this material world in the passage cited is striking and confirms his close relation to the Hebrew Scriptures as the true basis for his lifelong opposition to Gnosticism. As Frend rightly concluded: "He was able to demonstrate to his opponents how necessary was the Old Testament to understand the Christian message, and how Creation, the Law, and the Prophecy described in it led up to the Incarnation and the church. . . . Through him and through Irenaeus' refinements this achievement proved to be a permanent legacy for the church."[45] We are entitled thus to take this autobiographical report by Justin on the nature of his conversion to Christianity via the prophetic Scriptures also as pivotal for the much-debated question of whether in Justin Platonism overtakes the Bible. Charles Nahm's conclusion from his survey of the extend scholarly debate is judicious; we can speak, he writes, at most of a "partial assimilation, whereby certain Platonic categories of thought were adopted as adjuncts or theological tools that in no way influenced the purity of Christian teachings or dogmatic contents."[46] More specifically, Platonism provided a vocabulary and conceptuality for "belief in the existence of the invisible realities";[47] for example, Justin utilized "such words as uncreated, ineffable, incomprehensible, and immutable to describe the divine attributes. These words were part of the Middle Platonic vocabulary." But the use of these terms was "for the adequate explanation of the biblical revelation."[48] In addition, Nahm mentions "that it was the spreading of Gnosticism among the second-century Christians which had caused alarm among the Apologists, so that they had recourse to Greek philosophies to combat it."[49] Platonism was, as we shall see, a tactical ally in the battle against Gnostic pessimism and dualism, an important historical fact the ignorance of which has led astray many an interpreter who take Gnosticism as but "extreme Hellenism," that is, Platonism.

Justin could freely adopt logical and conceptual tools from his philosophical training because of his scriptural belief in the new creation as the redemption of the earth: in principle, whatever is good upon it belongs to the new humanity and shares in the promised renewal. Christians have the Logos made flesh, Jesus; but this is the very Logos with which all others are at least partially acquainted by virtue of being "logical," that is, "rational" beings made in God's image. "I admit that I boast and fight with all my strength to be found a Christian, not because Plato's teachings are different from Christ's, but because they are not similar in every way, which is also true of the others, such as the Stoics, poets and historians. For each one spoke well in accordance with his share of the seed of divine reason . . . Whatever people have said well belongs to us Christians" (*2 Apol.* 15[50]). Taking up this widespread contemporary idea about the "seed of divine reason" distributed in greater or lesser degree among all rational beings, Justin thought to make Christ's divinity intelligible. The terminology was current in Stoicism for the idea of cosmic reason disseminated throughout the universe. But Justin transforms the notion; for Justin himself the "epithet 'spermatikos' does not mean 'disseminated' but refers to the logos in a special activity, that is, sowing his seed in religious and moral illumination . . . the logos *is* for [Justin] an active and divine potential, the sowing logos who sows in men, even before the coming of Christ in the flesh, a part of himself. . . . The idea of the logos-Christ sowing seeds in men was in essence his own."[51] The preexistent Logos, in other words, is actively and universally imparting and so revealing Himself; consequently, in time, all will be prepared to recognize Him when he comes in the flesh. He is not, then, the impersonal principle of rationality inherent in things, as with the Stoics. L. W. Barnard smartly comments: "It may well be that in the contemporary encounter with the non-Christian faiths Justin's insight will become relevant again."[52]

In keeping with the exclusive monotheism Justin learned from the prophetic Scriptures, Justin deflected with a trinitarian confession the hostile charge of atheism made against the Christians for their refusal to participate in the imperial cult: "We certainly confess that we are godless with reference to beings like these who are commonly thought of as gods, but not with references to the most true God, the Father of righteousness and temperance and the other virtues, who is untouched by evil. Him, and the Son who came after him . . . and the army of the other good angels who follow him. . .and the prophetic Spirit we worship and adore" (*1 Apol.* 6[53]). Justin's defense against the charge of atheism shows how that freighted term is ambiguous. The sense of "atheism" depends entirely on the candidate for deity under consideration. Saying Yes to the Trinity meant saying No to much else. The trinitarian rule of faith current in Justin's community in Rome visibly stands out in the cited passage. It works to identity the God of the gospel whom Christians believe in distinction from gods disbelieved. Christopher Morse has written: "From its origins Christian theology exemplifies the fact that a No is contained in the confessional Yes of faith. The Apostles' Creed as it gradually emerged from a baptismal confession used in Rome in the latter part of the second century refutes false teaching in each of its tenets. . . . The concern for a rule or a canon of faith during this same period to distinguish true from false testimony involved, in the language of the title of Irenaeus' major work, the struggle *Against Heresies*."[54] The No to the heresies within the community and the No to the false gods outside it are one and the same Yes to the Trinity and to the Trinity alone as God.

If we look closely at this typical passage from Justin, however, we notice an oddity that has to qualify Nahm's otherwise judicious assessment that "certain Platonic categories of thought were adopted as adjuncts or theological tools that in no way influenced the purity of Christian teachings or dogmatic contents." In the passage cited, the Father is not identified in the first place as Father of the Son, Jesus, but as the Father of virtues. With this formulation may Justin be thinking of the "Father of the universe" who, as it happens, also "has a Son, who being the Word and First-Begotten of God is also divine" (*1 Apol.* 63)? If so, the Son is associated with other (!) good angels and the prophetic Spirit, all of whom would come after God the Father as mediating beings of lesser, descending rank. With his idea of the Logos *spermatikos* actively imparting virtue universally, a retrospective, "orthodox" interpretation of Justin is possible. The Father of virtues is so just because of this activity of His own Logos. In any case, the carelessness and imprecision is startling in hindsight: in this passage Justin includes the angels among those whom Christians worship! How close Justin can come to pagan mythology is evident in another remark, that the Logos as "the first offspring of God" introduces "nothing new beyond those whom you call sons of Zeus" (*1 Apol.* 21). The Logos is called the "first power after God" (*1 Apol.* 32), as if a second god. Justin can also state that the Logos is indistinguishable from the Spirit: "The Spirit and the Power from God cannot rightly be thought of as anything else than the Word, who is also the First-born of God" (*1 Apol.* 33). Seen from the perspective of later trinitarian controversies and clarification, such muddles are highly problematic.

Justin seems oblivious, for the most part, to the problems that this language creates. The church's trinitarian rule of faith, the scriptural salvation history, and the concepts of contemporary philosophy are combining in his mind in an original and not yet fully synthesized way. Grillmeier's judgment about the appropriation of the philosophical Logos doctrine in Justin and other apologists is perhaps better balanced than Nahm's. On one hand, the philosophical doctrine of the Logos represented to Christians and non-Christians alike the "creative Word" at work in the cosmos, the "basis of knowledge and truth," the "embodiment of the moral law," the "psychological" basis of human thought, and the "revelation" of salvation. The Christian appropriation of this concept "show[s] that the Fathers were concerned with the totality of God, the world and history." The God of Jesus Christ is the God of all people, whose Word is somehow universally active and thus experienced, perceived, and even speculated in other discourses. Acknowledging this, Christian theology affirms the world as God's creation and freely appropriates whatever is good and true and beautiful for the cause of the gospel, as we heard Justin expressly say above. On the other hand, in the order of theological knowledge, such appropriation must be far more critical than Justin realized. "In calling the Logos the servant, the apostle, the angel of the absolutely transcendent Father, Justin gives him a diminished transcendence."[55] Citing H. Chadwick, Barnard points to the same difficulty: "that Justin's one major dependence on Greek philosophy, in a matter of real substance, was his belief that the God who appeared to the patriarchs in the Old Testament theopanies must be the logos-Son, as the Father was far removed, in His transcendence, from this world and in any case could not abandon His universal care for the cosmos to become circumscribed in one small corner of the earth."[56] From the perspective of later developments, such criticism is valid. But it is far from the whole of the story, and indeed it would leave a profoundly false impression of Justin to stop our discussion of him with it.

As previously mentioned, the significant thing for the development of early Christian doctrine is that Justin "incorporated [the philosophical Logos] into a theology of history and completely transformed [it]"[57] by giving it a biblical content. "Justin's Logos is Jesus Christ understood in the light of the same Old Testament 'Word of God' and Greek philosophy."[58] Recalling Justin's love of the Old Testament, his understanding of salvation as the redemption of the body, and his readiness for martyrdom, Grillmeier's summary of Justin's theology of salvation history merits an extended citation:

> The incarnation is the last link in a chain of events, during which the Logos had earlier already appeared on earth in other circumstances to reveal the will of the Father (Dialogue 75,4). The Logos maintains this function of being mediator of revelation until the end of the world. It comes to an end in the "second *parousia*"—a phrase which Justin coined (Apol. 1, 52, 3; Dialogue 14, 8; and often). Through the uninterrupted work of revelation of the Logos, the history of mankind becomes a carefully planned construction with beginning, purpose and end. Now in this way Christ also becomes the "Nomos" of the human race (after Ps. 1:2 and Isa. 2:3f; Apol. 1, 40, 5ff; 39, 1; Dialogue 11–25). By him order is brought into a world in which everything has been in confusion. The advent of this Logos-Nomos in the flesh also breaks the influences which the demons had exerted in history through the *nomoi* of the peoples. Herein lies the significance of the expansion of Christianity.[59]

The incarnate Logos and the mission in His name to the nations is breaking up the power of the warring demons of polytheistic culture. The gospel is reconciling peoples in the kingdom of Christ. The scriptural prophecy that nations shall "beat their swords into plowshares" is being fulfilled. As Justin writes: "For a band of twelve men went forth from Jerusalem, and they were common men, not trained in speaking, but by the power of God they testified to every race of mankind that they were sent by Christ to teach to all the Word of God; and [now] we who once killed each other not only do not make war on each other, but in order not to lie or deceive our inquisitors we gladly die for the confession of Christ" (*1 Apol.* 39).

From this perspective, we can see what an error it would be to forget for a moment that Justin Martyr was in fact a *martyr*. He says that he writes to the Roman Emperor "on behalf of men of every nation who are unjustly hated and reviled," himself included (*1 Apol.* 1). He tells the emperor that Christians are hated because they speak "of a kingdom with God, as is clear from our confessing Christ when you bring us to trial, though we know that death is the penalty for this confession" (*1 Apol.* 1). He even threatens the emperor with God's eternal punishment! Justin's *Apologies* were thus less academic treatises than learned confessions articulating the faith before the hostile court of pagan opinion (*1 Apol.* 55). Justin's intention is far more to be a witness, a confessor, a martyr than an academic philosopher or an apologetic theologian: "Now it is evident that there is no one who terrifies and enslaves us who all over the world believe in Christ. For it is open to all to see that though we are beheaded, crucified, thrown to the lions, cast in prison and into the fire, and made to suffer every other kind of torture we do not abandon our confession. But the more we suffer these penalties, the more others become believers and worship God through the name of Jesus" (*Dial.* 110, 5). Insofar as ancient philosophy was a spiritual question for true freedom or self-mastery (*autarxia, apatheia*), we could say in a nonacademic, existential way that Justin found the philosopher's quest fulfilled in the courage of the martyrs. In this existential sense there is a true synthesis in Justin of theology and philosophy. But, as we shall see, the ideal of *apatheia*, like the corresponding theological notion of divine simplicity, proved to be ambiguous. It could mean supreme indifference, freedom from others, but it could also mean freedom from self, selflessness, and thus freedom for others, freedom for love. The martyrs gave *apatheia* the latter meaning, following Jesus' "passionless passion" as it had been modeled for them in the Gospels of Luke and John.

Justin against Gnosticism

The only heresy that Justin ever mentions in his writings is Gnosticism. This is a significant clue to his theology and its use of Platonic concepts like *impassibility/apatheia*. Platonism was embraced by Christians as an ally against Gnosticism. For contemporary people, who do not share the universal ancient feeling for the misery of bodily existence and hence of religion as a means of coping,[60] this move to Platonism as an antidote to Gnosticism is difficult to understand. But it is a fact of history that Platonism was understood as an optimistic, world-affirming philosophy wholly at odds with Gnosticism, which was abhorred by Platonists and early catholic Christians like Justin alike as a world-negating and fatalistic belief.[61] From the modern perspective, we look back and see in Platonism and Gnosticism two very similar pictures of reality. In their dualistic tendency, Platonism and Gnosticism seemed so much alike that modern scholars, from Von Harnack to Frend, have often been misled to think of the Gnostic threat to Christianity as one of "acute Hellenism."[62] But this is a fundamental mistake. *The chief root of Gnosticism lies in disillusioned, apocalyptic Judaism.*

Kurt Randolph explains the significance of the discovery of the Nag Hammadi library for the historical reconstruction of Gnostic origins in just this way: "The writings confirm the independence of Gnostic from Christian writers, and so corroborate the thesis of the non-Christian origin of Gnostic teaching. At the same time, a strong connection with Jewish traditions, especially apocalyptic and extrabiblical, is visible. Thus the view . . . that Gnosis germinated on the margins of early Judaism can no longer be so easily dismissed."[63] Jaroslav Pelikan articulated this pivotal correction of scholarship in Harnack's tradition in his account of the development of Christian doctrine, which we are here appropriating: "Much of the origin of Christian Gnosticism lies in Jewish sectarianism and in the eclipse of the apocalyptic vision within Judaism. The earliest Christian Gnostics, therefore, stood on the borders between heretical Judaism and heretical Christianity."[64] This origin in disillusioned apocalyptic Judaism would mean that Gnosticism arose as a loss of scriptural faith in historical providence and cosmic redemption. It arose as hope disappointed in scriptural eschatology, as a turn away from the expectation of God's coming reign—quite in contrast to Justin's conversion to Christianity by reading Israel's Scriptures as prophecy and seeing in the gospel mission of the church to the nations their fulfillment.

As long ago as Hans Jonas's anthropological analysis of Gnostic mythology,[65] similar in method to Bultmann's interpretation of the New Testament, it has been evident that Gnosticism gives expression to the cry of the alienated individual who experiences this world as a shipwreck. Such an individual cries for knowledge of who she is, where she has come from, and where she is going. Gnostics, we might say, were the existentialists of the early Christian centuries. This stance is in precise antithesis, as just mentioned, to Justin Martyr's discovery of the meaning of the world's existence in the Old Testament prophecy, now being fulfilled by Christ through the advance of the church. Justin was persuaded to faith by the scriptural doctrine of salvation as redemption of the creation. A doctrine of salvation as escape from the creation could not have been more opposed to all he held essential. His willingness eventually to suffer the executioner's sword is the ultimate act of affirmation of the significance of what is done in the body. It is the faith that the body is the very object of God's redemption.

To make this clear, let us, painting with a broad brush for heuristic purposes, compare the attitudes toward the world in Platonism and Gnosticism. Plato in his youth had been the arch-critic of Homer and the poets. He was the first great demythologizer. In the *Symposium* and in the *Timaeus*, however, an older Plato resorted anew to myth to tell the story of the cosmos.[66] For Platonism ever afterward, the rational order (but not the irrational matter) of this world is understood as an expression of a superabundant spiritual or rational eros, which flows out from the One in a descending scale or gradation of rational forms and then returns from these many forms to unification again in God; so divine reason is pictured, coursing through the realm of becoming, forming rude chaotic matter so far as it allows into a cosmos, an ordered system of manifold forms. The system of the world is thus pictured as an organic whole, internally ordered into the realms of being and becoming, ideal form impressing itself upon and forming chaotic matter in the great chain of being. The realms of being and becoming are thus linked step by step by the outflow of superabundance and thence desire of the separated for erotic reunion in return. Eros runs like electricity back and forth through every link. The rational soul comes from God, is akin to God, and desires to go back to God—what Platonism means by the doctrine of its immortality. Knowing this, the wise person, the philosopher, can consciously affirm intellectual life, life qua rational soul. A teacher like Socrates is midwife of the rational soul who can awaken it to its true good. This true good is a philosophical life, a quest for rational freedom, self-rule, impassibility in face of the vicissitudes of bodily existence with its unruly passions. Thus it is the examined life that is worth living, even here below. In the parable of the cave in *The Republic*, the philosopher, although glimpsing the supernal light above, returns to the prison below to remain in solidarity with comrades and lead them also to light. In this way, this life is affirmed. The optimism is actually breathtaking.

For Gnosticism, on the other hand, the existence of this world and humanity in it is utterly a tragedy, a total fall from God. "Each in its own way, the Gnostic systems all included a diagnosis of the cosmological descent of the spirit into matter and sin."[67] The hierarchy of being that unfolds below the level of the Divine Fullness (the *Pleroma*) is in no way a positive expression of God's superabundant eros, but a horrid, progressively darker forgetfulness of God. Turning away from the divine center, little sparks of divine light are pictured as slipping free and falling, becoming thicker, denser, and darker on the way, sinking into materiality until they are overwhelmed by it. Vast hordes of angels, principalities, and powers are arranged by rank of their respective degree of forgetfulness of God; they stand like jealous watchdogs against any who seek to ascend again and unite themselves with the divine Light. All of reality is thus tragically trapped in greater and greater degrees of material embodiment and spiritual forgetfulness. "Frequently, this rejection of creation was associated with a revulsion at the processes of human generation and birth. . . . [Some] ascribed the origin of marriage and generation to Satan."[68] The creator of this visible world of the body is neither the transcendent God nor His Logos. The creator of this world is a cruel and petty lesser angel, frequently identified by name as *Yahweh*. He governs this world by terrible laws and cruel judgments, a god of wrath not love; He is the jealous, exclusive Jewish god. This deity is not the true God of the Gnostic, but rather the tyrant who holds her captive here, as in a prison, in oblivion concerning her own true being. Therefore Gnostic man does not know who he truly is. The spark of divinity within him is totally obscure to the physical and psychological levels of consciousness in which he lives. Not knowing, he experiences life in the body as nothing but pain and sorrow. Not even reason can save him. Only the appearance of a Revealer from heaven, a Mediator sent from God, can awaken man to consciousness of his forgotten divinity and call him to his true home above. He is the "Logos who has come from the *Pleroma* . . . the Savior, since that is the name of the work which he must do for the redemption of those who have not known the Father . . . liberation from matter and reunion with the light-world."[69]

Christian Gnostics identified this Revealer with Jesus, who had come down from heaven to call them back to self-knowledge as spiritual daughters of God. Depictions varied, but in general the Revealer was said to have descended on Jesus at His baptism and departed just before the crucifixion.[70] "One of the characteristics of Gnostic doctrine was its denial that the Savior was possessed of a material, fleshly body."[71] Indeed, according to one myth, the Revealer stood by invisibly at the cross, laughing in contempt at those who were killing Jesus physically (AH I:24). This is the perfect image of salvation according to the Gnostics. The Revealer had come, as an example and a path-blazer, to teach true disciples the secret knowledge of how to leave this world, this body, this mass of suffering behind; how then to liberate oneself from attachment to matter and ascend, as the spark of divine light one actually is, through the ranks of hostile angels and demons to reunification with the fullness of divine being. Such is the secret *gnosis* imparted in Gnosticism. "Redemption seems to have been equated with revelation; hence the emphasis on knowledge."[72] In Gnosticism, then, we have a revisionist understanding of the Christian faith that took over Jesus in order to vilify Yahweh; likewise, it rejected the Old Testament Scriptures with the prophetic understanding of salvation as a ministry of reconciliation in prospect of the resurrection of the body, the "kingdom with God" coming on this earth. It regarded this physical world as essentially evil, and it denied that Jesus' existence in the flesh had any saving significance. It abolished conventional codes of moral responsibility with a fatalistic myth of origins, and thus also rendered irrelevant the Christian idea of grace as forgiveness of sin. The awakened spirit rejects this life and lives in contempt of its petty rationality, morality, and organized religion.

According to Justin, Marcion of Pontus was teaching "that there is another God, greater than the Fashioner [of this world. . . . Marcion] has made many of every race of men to blaspheme and to deny God the Maker of the universe, professing that there is another who is greater and has done greater things than he" (*1 Apol.* 26). From what we have learned of Justin's conviction about the gospel as Christ's movement for peace and freedom on this earth, we can see what a terrible danger Marcion's teaching represented. Marcion attacked God the Father, the body, the planet Earth as God's creation, the saving significance and reality of the Logos's earthly life and death on the cross, the church, the sacraments, the Christian mission to the nations, and the witness of the martyrs with their lives. All of this no longer matters; as flesh it is excluded from the field of salvation. Marcion's kind of gospel could not but seem to Justin (and Polycarp before him and Irenaeus after him) as veritably a demonic assault on the heart of salvation in Christ. Modern scholarship does not think that Marcion was a Gnostic strictly speaking because the mytholgy of the divine spark seems to be missing in what can be reconstructed of his teaching. Nevertheless, Justin correctly associated Marcion with Gnosticism insofar as the latter's revisionist Christianity shared with the Gnostics significant soteriological and cosmological characteristics. Put positively, it was an escapist theology of liberation from the body that Justin disbelieved in the act of believing the God of the gospel, who gives life to the dead. If, in this context, Justin took a little help from the Platonists to affirm the true, if limited, role of human reason in theology, and the universal relation of God the Father to the cosmos by His ever-active Logos, he can be forgiven. He erred on the side of optimism in his interpretation of the rule of faith, but he did not err in its usage. He used the rule of faith to disbelieve both the triumphal gods of the empire and the contempt of this good earth by otherworldly pretenders to deity.

Irenaeus and the Theology of the Martyrs

Irenaeus (c. 130–200) studied in Rome, perhaps with Justin Martyr, whose writings he certainly knew. Originating in Greek-speaking Asia Minor, he went to work as a missionary pastor in Lyons, learning the barbarian language of the Celts. He first appears in history at Rome as a refugee from the persecution in Gaul that took place in 177. The surviving church elected him bishop in place of their fallen leader, and he then returned to Lyons for the rest of his life. *Against Heresies* is dated at 189.[73] He tells us in this book that as a child he knew Polycarp personally, who, he writes, "not only was taught by Apostles, and associated with many who had seen Christ, but was installed by apostles for Asia . . . and departed this life in a ripe old age by a glorious and magnificent martyrdom" (AH III:3:4). Irenaeus tells the anecdote that once, when Polycarp visited Rome, he encountered Marcion, Justin's semi-Gnostic adversary. Marcion asked Polycarp whether he acknowledged him as a fellow Christian. According to Irenaeus, Polycarp replied, "I know you—the first born of Satan!" Irenaeus thus stands at the end of the antidocetist and martyrological line that we have traced in this chapter from apostolic times through the second century.

The reception of Irenaeus by Protestant theology has been characterized by ambivalence. Yet John Lawson concurred with the judgment of Emil Brunner "that, though Irenaeus has more title than any other to be regarded as the founder of ecclesiastical theology [dogmatics], nevertheless in him the New Testament witness, Johannine and Pauline, the specifically New Testament and the whole-Biblical, are united as in hardly any other until Luther. . . . He often used the terms of Greek thought to express his conception of God, but the conception expressed was fundamentally Biblical."[74] This interpretative strategy will also be adopted here. Admittedly, ever since Erasmus of Rotterdam in 1526 translated and published the hitherto little-known *Against Heresies* as part of his campaign against Luther, the reception of Irenaeus in Protestant theology has been confused by Erasmus's polemical (and anachronistic) commendation of Irenaeus as an alternative to Luther. In Irenaeus Protestant polemicists find endorsements of Pelagian freedom, Roman primacy, episcopal succession, harmonization of the so-called fourfold gospel suppressing the primitive church's theological diversity, dogmatism in the intolerant spirit of heresy-hunting, and every other incipient evil of Roman Catholicism. Walter Bauer belongs in this Protestant-polemical tradition. The anachronistic projection backward onto Irenaeus the "heresy hunter" of every conceivable Protestant grievance actually misses the rather more massive fact of imperial persecution[75] that stamps Irenaeus, who writes theology to strengthen those who confess the Crucified as Lord; accordingly, such Protestant polemic minimizes the importance of the dogmatic rejection of docetist Christology and dualistic theology. Even more sympathetic contemporary Protestant interpreters still tend to think that the main problem raised by Irenaeus is one of "religious authority,"[76] that is, episcopal succession, and so fail to grasp that the motive force in Irenaeus' contention even in this connection is for the *public* tradition of the gospel of the resurrection of the Crucified as opposed to Gnostic claims of secret tradition. Thus in the present reading, we may entirely leave aside as marginal the question of Irenaeus's relation to the church in Rome.

Rather we locate Irenaeus in the tradition stemming from the gospel narrative through Ignatius, Polycarp, Justin, and those who had fallen in Lyons, developing theology *for* the "martyrs who bear witness and despise death, following the readiness of the Spirit rather than the weakness of the flesh," and so *against* the Gnostics, who by contrast "pour contempt upon the martyrs, and vituperate those who are slain on account of the confession of the Lord, and who suffer all things predicted by the Lord." In this way, says Irenaeus, the martyrs witness God's redeeming love for enemies, as did Christ their Lord "upon the cross: loving the human race to such a degree, that He even prayed for those putting Him to death." Empowered with Christ's Spirit, true disciples "take up the cross and follow" Jesus (AH III,18). Martyrdom is the sign of the true church. "The Church does in every place, because of that love which she cherishes towards God, send forward, throughout all time, a multitude of martyrs to the Father; while all others not only have nothing of this kind to point to among themselves,

THE TRINITARIAN RULE OF FAITH

but even maintain that such witness-bearing is not at all necessary, for that their system of doctrines is the true witness" (AH IV,32). The correlation of doctrine of faith and the ethos of the martyrs is explicit in this statement and indeed presupposed everywhere in Irenaeus.

Accordingly, the notion of the Spirit's powerful work in Christian witness is a major and integral theme in Irenaeus. One can reconstruct the picture Irenaeus has in his mind of the courage of those who died in Lyons, like Justin Martyr, Polycarp, and Ignatius (see AH V,28,4) before them. They did not curse Christ, swear by the genius of Caesar, or sacrifice to the gods. Why? "The flesh whose weakness has been so absorbed [by the Spirit] manifests the power of the Spirit. In absorbing its weakness, the Spirit receives the flesh as its own inheritance. A living human person is formed of these two: he lives by sharing in the Spirit; he is human by the substance of the flesh. . . . We cannot be saved without the Spirit of God" (AH V,9,2-3) But lest the Spirit become a pretext for leaving the flesh behind, the theology of the martyrs also required, so to speak, a christological "reality principle" in the Word Incarnate, as delivered by the Scriptures publically through the tradition of the church, against speculative and spiritualizing impulses. "Since men are real, they must have a real existence, not passing away into things which are not, but advancing [to a new stage] among things that are. Neither the substance nor the essence of the created order vanishes away, for he is true and faithful who established it, but the pattern of this world passes away. . . . But when this pattern has passed away, and man is made new, and flourishes in incorruption, so that he can no longer grow old, then there will be new heavens and a new earth. In this new order man will always remain new, in converse with God" (AH V, 36, 1). Thus, like Justin before him, Irenaeus also has a realistic eschatology drawn from the Old Testament.

Thinking out the God who *is* the coming of His reign on the earth pressed Irenaeus to write in effect the first dogmatic theology of early Christianity, that is, not yet a "system" as we see in Origen's *On First Principles*, but rather in the sense of systematic thinking through of the creedal plotline of the biblical narrative.

Richard A. Norris Jr. exposited this in an incisive article. He took up Irenaeus's complaint about the arbitrary treatment of the text of Scripture among his opponents. Irenaeus asked whether you could cut up a series of lines from Homer and then rearrange them to tell a story Homer never wrote (AH I, 8, 1). Why would this treatment not count as a claim to interpret Homer, even though the words are the same? Because when the order is changed, the sense changes. What is changed, Norris says, is the "plot, a coherent story-structure of some sort that involves and identifies a particular set of characters." That is the problem with Gnostic revisionist exegesis: it does not in fact represent or reproduce the plot of the Scripture. Indeed, it is a different plot altogether, and "involves, at least in part, a different set of characters."[77] Norris points out that it was this insight of Irenaeus that provoked him to think through the canonical Genesis-to-Revelation narrative in a new way: "Irenaeus is bound to identify the real 'plot' of the Scriptures. . . . It is to be found, he says, in the 'rule of truth . . . which one receives by way of baptism,"[78] namely, the trinitarian *dramatis personae* of God, God's Word and God's Spirit and the story of their actions to create, redeem, and fulfill the one world. This leads Irenaeus to the "wholesome circularity" of the theological dialectic of Word and Spirit, letter and sense: the "'rule' must somehow be derived out of the materials whose interpretation it governs, even as those materials are understood through the 'rule.' . . . The thought must be a distillation of the logic of the speech, even as the speech is interpreted and disposed according to the logic of the thought."[79] Yet the circle involved in such proper interpretation of scriptural narrative in light of the baptismal creed is not vicious: it is bounded in the two ways of apophatic and kataphatic theology. First, there is no going beyond God; God is the beyond "that no human creature has measured or explored." Second, God as such can only be known by self-revelation; all else is worthless speculation. Theology "can only start with what is *clear*—the witness concerning God that is out in the open,"[80] that is, the publicly transmitted gospel from the apostles down to today. The plain text of Scripture in the light of the creed is the place in the world to learn about God: "One cannot get 'beyond' it because one cannot get beyond the God who is responsible for the story—and hence the world—whose 'plot' it specifies."[81] Bounded this way, the task of critical dogmatic theology is to exposit the plot to make known the one God, *the almighty Father determined to redeem the creation through His Son, Jesus Christ, and bring it to fulfillment by His Spirit.*

The First Dogmatics

Gnosticism, as we have seen, had no problem with divine suffering. In the beginning God, so to say, had fallen to pieces. God lost part of God's own being in that shower of sparks of light that had fallen away from the divine fullness and were now trapped in human bodies. God ached to gain back God's own lost being and so sent the Revealer to heal this wound in God's own fullness. Thus informed, Gnostics had no trouble with divine passibility after a fashion. Their problem was with human suffering. Gnostics denied that the Redeemer suffered physically, since the Revealer rather redeems the divine spark from its material captivity—thus the strong docetist tendency in Christology. Early Christians, as we have seen in Justin, somewhat uncritically took over from philosophical monotheism the counterdoctrine that God cannot suffer, that God is impassible in His utter transcendence. As a result, however, Gnosticism may have become even more religiously attractive, according to Pelikan, in that its variegated myths of the divine emanations "spoke more meaningfully about man's alienation from the world, from his own true being, and from God" than did the

Platonic doctrine of remote divine impassibility toward which orthodox Christians gravitated.[82] It was virtually an axiom: God is "impassible,"[83] incapable of suffering. This axiom was of course in no little tension with the primal theology of the gospel narrative, the Incarnation and cross, and that tension led to highly paradoxical statements such as we heard in Ignatius, for example, that in Christ the "impassible became passible."[84] For the orthodox Christians somehow had to affirm a double-sided truth that in Christ *God* had suffered *as human* in order to tell of incarnation and cross as God's own free decision to suffer and yet in this way to act for the redemption of His creation. When Christians focused on the humanity of Christ, they were led to antidocetic Christology; when they focused on the deity of Christ, they were led toward the "impassibility axiom" of standard Platonism. The running question thus resurfaces: How can these two be one and the same persona?

A theologically adequate response to Gnosticism's challenge would have had to go beyond the repetition of biblical clichés and the mere appeal to authority to answer this question. The Gnostics had a false but attractive answer to the question of why the world is the way it is that spoke to existential anguish and physical suffering. Christian theology would have to ask and answer this question better than the Gnostics. It not only would have to demonstrate not only the unity of God's work in creation and redemption, but also would have to ask and answer the question of theodicy, Why? It would not suffice to assert and demonstrate that God said such and such in the prophets or in the Bible. In the first place, the Bible did not yet formally exist as a canon; Marcion was able radically to challenge the tacit proto-canon of the martyrs that we saw attested in Polycarp's *Letter to the Philippians*. Marcion in fact openly repudiated the Old Testament Scripture, and according to Irenaeus, "he mutilated the Gospel according to Luke, discarding all that is written about the birth of the Lord, and also discarding . . . [everything indicating] that the Lord confessed His Father as the Maker of the universe. . . . In like manner, he mutilated the Letters of Paul" (AH I, 28, 2). Marcion had published such a drastically reduced "Bible," but opponents found themselves in the embarrassing situation of possessing no formal alternative. Nor, in the second place, had they any clear idea of how rightly to interpret what they tacitly agreed upon. Theology would have systematically to put the question to the tacit canonical narrative of its plotline: Yes, God said thus and so, but why did God say just this? Pre-eminently, why did God become human to appear as this particular persona, the *crucified* Christ? How is that *good news*? With this reflective step, dogmatic theology was born, which links the dogmas, that is, the teachings of the Scriptures, to the mind and purpose of God and tests both within and outside the community of faith for coherence along these lines.

The Gnostics "adduce an untold multitude of spurious and apocryphal writings" (AH I:20), on the grounds that Jesus "spoke privately in mystery to his disciples and apostles and commissioned them to hand down privately these things to those who are worthy" (AH I,25,5). The Gnostics "disregard the order and the connection of the Scriptures. . . . They transfer passages and rearrange them; and, making one thing out of another, they deceive many" (AH I,8,1). In fact, as Norris showed us, Irenaeus saw how the Gnostics have "entirely fabricated their own system" and then "gather together sayings and names from scattered places" to serve as proof-texts. In this procedure they transfer the text's "natural meaning to an unnatural one" (AH I,9,3). They draw passages out of context to prove that "our Lord announced another Father beside the creator of the universe [such as] the words of the prophet Isaiah: 'But Israel does not know me, and the people do not understand me'" (AH I,19,1). "Ignorance of the Scriptures and of the dispensation of God has brought all these [heresies] upon [the Gnostics]. So," Irenaeus announces at the outset, "in the course of this work, I shall touch upon the *cause* of the difference of the covenants on the one hand, and on the other hand, of their unity and harmony" (AH III, 12, emphasis added).[85]

Irenaeus of Lyons undertook this critical task when he published the first great work in Christian dogmatics, the five volumes commonly called *Against Heresies*, but which he actually titled *Exposé and Overthrow of the "Knowledge"* [that is, Gnosis] *Falsely So-Called*. As previously noted, Irenaeus wrote "as a pastor and teacher of the Church, and addressed himself to other pastors to assist them in protecting their flocks from teachings that seriously perverted the gospel or replaced it by a jumble of speculations and encouraged either laxity of conduct or serious misbehavior."[86] The preface of the book contains a veritable program for theology as critical dogmatics. Humanity's true relation to God is at stake. "Blasphemous and impious opinions against the Creator" are leading many to ruin, "away from him who established and adorned this universe." The world is full of blasphemies, of course, but these opinions are appearing within the church, claiming the right to be heard. "They speak the same language we do, but intend different meanings." They operate with "specious argumentation," "falsifying the Lord's words" as "wicked interpreters of genuine words." Such proceedings must be exposed and refuted, along the lines of the previously mentioned illustration of chopping up and reassembling lines from Homer's poetry.

But it is not just a question of logical procedure in interpretation for the sake of valid and meaningful discourse. The Gnostics have kept their teachings secret, refusing to expose them to the light of reason. They beguile the naive with intimations of possessing the secret plot of Scripture. With his historical-critical research, Irenaeus will now bring these secret teachings of knowledge, falsely so-called, to public awareness. At the end of the tedious first volume, after listing countless variations of Gnostic mythology, Irenaeus claimed success in this: "the very manifestation of their doctrine is a victory against them"

(AH I,31,3), since surely the absurdity and incoherence of their many myths would not withstand public exposure and rational scrutiny. Refuting the Gnostics did not prove, however, to be quite so simple. Recalling Hoskyns's thoughts regarding the vulnerability of John's Gospel to Gnostic takeover, we have to imagine a situation in which the early catholic church had neither an acknowledged canon of Scripture, nor a definite Creed, nor a method of inter-pretation, that is, dogmatic theology.

There is justice to Irenaeus's complaint:[87] "We have nothing in common with them in doctrine, morals or daily conduct. But they use the Name [of Jesus] only to veil their own wickedness." How was this charge convincingly to be established and sustained? The question of authoritative Scripture and the primacy of plain-sense interpretation will have to be settled; Irenaeus, as we shall see, is really the pioneer theologian on these questions. But solutions to these burning questions of canon and hermeneutic require a vision of the whole body of Christian doctrine, an insight into its centrally important con-cern. "Nearly all the heretical sects, many as they are, speak of one God," even though "they alter Him," thereby showing themselves to be "ungrateful to Him who made them, just as the pagans [do] by idolatry" (AH I,22,1). Simplistic appeal to "one God" therefore resolves nothing. Theology has to probe, test, question, reflect, and understand the "why" of God's ways to tell of the God who is one. It has in this way of rational understanding to demonstrate the unity of God's works. The question, Why? really seeks and discovers the *one-ness* of God in His works narrated in the Scriptures. Knowledge of God does not come about by supplanting the scriptural narrative of the creation and redemption of the world with new myths, but rather by putting the systematic question, Why? to Scripture's storyline. Under the press of the Gnostic assault, the "plot" that Irenaeus consequently discovered was the "thought of a total economy [*oikonomia*, literally, household management, that is, plan of salva-tion, providence] of God for humankind, centered on Jesus Christ . . . who recapitulates [Greek: *anakephalaios*, literally, puts the head back on, that is, repeats and corrects] humankind's whole history and whole being."[88]

The "whole" that Irenaeus envisioned has Pauline precedents in passages like Ephesians 1:9-11, that is, the plan of God, hidden before the ages but now made known, that God out of love would freely create and redeem a world in Christ and for Christ, so that there would be a creation to enjoy His love. The "center" of this history is the God-man Jesus Christ, who by His life in the flesh accom-plished the perfect humanity that God intends for all and in just this way has made it known. Irenaeus thus conscientiously and exclusively sources theology in *revelation*, "for the Lord taught us that no man is capable of knowing God, unless he be taught of God; that is, that God cannot be known without God: but that this is the express will of the Father, that God should be known. For they shall know Him to whomsoever the Son has revealed Him" (AH IV,6,4).

But this knowledge of God in revelation is not dumb repetition; it comes from inquiry into the unity of the economy, from grasping how the narrated deeds of God hang together to form a coherent plot centered in the recapitulation in Christ.

> Knowledge of God does come about, however, by bringing out more fully the meaning of whatever was said in parables and adapting it exactly to the doctrine of the Truth; and by explaining God's dealings and Economy, which He made for the sake of the human race; by making clear that God was long-suffering . . . by announcing *why* one and the same God made some things temporal, others eternal . . . by understanding *why* God, who is invisible, appeared to the prophets, not under one form, but differently to different prophets; and by indicating *why* several covenants were made with the human race; by teaching what the real nature of each of the covenants was; and by searching out *why* God consigned all things to disobedience that He may have mercy on all; by acknowledging gratefully *why* the Word of God became flesh and suffered . . . by unfolding as much as is contained in the Scriptures about the end and the things that are to come . . . *why* God made the Gentiles, who were despaired of, joint heirs . . . by proclaiming how this mortal body will put on immortality. (AH I,10,3, emphasis mine)

Dogmatic theology systematically poses to Scripture the question, Why? This questioning treats the various scriptural deeds ascribed to God as the intentional works of a single mind for a self-consistent purpose, yet at the same time divine works, qualified by the apophatic rule. Referring to Schoedel's interpretation of AH II,25-28, Donovan writes, "God transcends ordinary ways of thought. Gnostics err by not recognizing this aspect of transcendence and proffering explanations of the humanly inexplicable."[89] The Gnostics neglected the notion of divine simplicity as a *rule* for reverence and deference in speech about the unique being and act of the One who is creator of all that is other than Himself, in part, of course, because in their ontological dualism they did not take God as the creator of matter. By the same principle, posing the theological question, Why? does not imply achieving full and satisfactory answers this side of the eschaton, only sufficient understanding to know God in distinction from idols and demons who would mislead. As T. F. Torrance has rightly noted, formulations of belief for Irenaeus "were not doctrinal propositions connected together through a logico-deductive system of thought, but assertions of belief that are organized from beyond themselves by their common ground in the apostolic deposit of faith and ultimately by the self-revelation of God in Jesus Christ, the one incarnate truth of God from which all evangelical truths flow. . . . having regulative force in themselves in so far as they were rightly related to that truth and serve its supreme authority."[90] The kataphatic theology of the economy is thus qualified by an apophatic rule that we speak of God as befits His uniqueness, transcending the limitations that attend the creature.

Irenaeus's *magnus opus* accordingly concluded with the following words about the wisdom of God by which He brings all things to their goal in His kingdom: "Then there is one Son, who accomplished the Father's will, and one human race, in which the mysteries of God are accomplished, which angels longed to behold. [But not even angels can] search out the wisdom of God, by which what he had fashioned is perfected by being conformed and incorporated with the Son—or how that his offspring, the first-begotten Word, could descend into his creature, that is, into what he had fashioned, and be contained within it—and that the creature again should lay hold on the Word and should ascend to him, passing beyond the angels, and be made [anew] according to the image and likeness of God" (AH V,36,3). Theology cannot ask or answer the question, How? as the Gnostics illicitly pretend. The question is literally out of bounds in regard to the being and act of God, the creator of all that is other than Himself. Theology is limited to the questions, What? and Why? But that limitation is not cognitively idle, since it directs believers to the critical discernment of what is to be identified as divine and who is to be addressed as divine.

Thus Irenaeus praises the revealed divine wisdom, the plan or economy of the world, decreed in Christ before time and executed in time by Christ as this Word made flesh, actualized. We can see this wisdom, when by faith we acknowledge with the biblical monotheism of the Scriptures: there is *one* God, *one* human race, *one* incarnate Son in whom the creation of the human race is perfected, *one* destiny of being conformed to Christ and thus created anew in the image and likeness of God by the Spirit of God in the resurrection of the dead. In a word, the world exists as *one* divine plan of salvation. God made the world, and especially humanity, for fellowship with Himself. Coming to the love of God is the purpose of creation. For "the glory of God is the life of humanity, and the life of humanity is the vision of God" (AH IV,20,7): "Against the gnostic dissolution and separation of God and the world, against the division of Christ [into human and divine parts], of man and of salvation history, Irenaeus now resolutely sets the idea of the unity of God, Christ and salvation. In this connection he develops the idea of a universal *oikonomia*."[91]

The Economy of God

Irenaeus's idea of the economy of God is meant to provide the plotline, then, of the whole biblical narrative: "the beginning, the middle and the end, the entire divine economy and the operation which is directed to humanity's salvation . . . the foundation of our faith" (AH III,24,1). It is for Irenaeus an implication of exclusive biblical monotheism, just as Justin had found in the Hebrew Scriptures. Frend writes that, for Irenaeus, "God was one; that unity penetrated the whole creation and all human history. Moreover, Irenaeus' monotheism was Hebraic rather than Greek and his sense of time was linear, not cyclical; God was active in creation which came into being at one point in time and ended at another."[92] Change, then, is the order of the day here below. Radical conversion is standard operating procedure. "How, then, are the sick to be made strong? and how are sinners to repent? Is it by persevering as they are? or on the contrary, by undergoing a great change and reversal of their previous behavior?" (AH III,5,2). Why, to be changed "is the goal of the human race that has God for its inheritance [to be] washed and cleansed from everything pertaining to death and [to] come to God's life" (AH IV,22,1). God is leading His creation to salvation, and Jesus Christ is the deed and revelation of this lordship of God by which God directs history to its goal. Cyril Richardson nicely captured Irenaeus's endeavor here "to describe the creed as an epic and the dogma as a drama. The Son of God worsted the ancient enemy [the devil] in fair fight, thus redeeming mankind from its slavery. . . . [Faith in this] certainly for Irenaeus means the acceptance of sound belief, but in the sense of joyful turning to God, not simply correct information about him. . . . [For believers become part of the story in that] God redeems nature by nature and through nature. . . . God has redeemed his own dear universe and not simply provided a way of escape from it. And so at the end of the drama the world which came from God will visibly return to him again."[93] The very world on which the cross stood is the object of God's creative and redemptive love. Just so, this world is not to be conceived as a static system, let alone as a cosmic tragedy, but rather as a history of salvation in which "the world that came from God will visibly return to him." As in Justin, the prophetic eschatology of the Old Testament so powerfully expressed in Irenaeus is *realistic*. The Pauline "redemption of our bodies" is affirmed. Resurrection of the dead provides the chief image of salvation. The horizon of salvation is cosmic and universal, not restricted to a sect of pure believers escaping to heaven. Hell exists in order to be emptied. Redemption is predicated of creation. The glory of God is a living human being.

Jesus Christ is the key to the understanding of the whole; He is the revelation of the mystery of God's plan as we see in Him the *recapitulation* of the whole. "There is therefore one God the Father . . . and one Christ Jesus our Lord, who comes through a universal plan and recapitulates all things in himself. But in every way he is also a human, a creation of God; he, therefore, recapitulated humanity in himself" (AH III,16,6). Corresponding then to "economy" is another key idea in Irenaeus, recapitulation (Greek: *anakephalaio*—Rom 19:9; Eph 1:10; literally, "to put the head back on"). Recapitulation is the soteriological idea that Christ saves by reuniting humanity in Himself as the head to the body, that is, according to the great exchange in which Christ in His own historical passage through cross to glory wrests guilty, dying human nature from its lost state in Adam and re-creates it to be directed anew by the Spirit. In principle, Christ accomplished this recapitulation of humanity on the cross when He died for all and emptied hell. Now through the gospel and sacraments, the Spirit is working out in history the reunification of humanity in Christ, under Christ, the head of the body, which is His church. Notably, the Spirit is necessary to salvation in this understanding of recapitulation; the Spirit is not merely a subjective principle bearing private witness to an objective reconciliation, but rather comes and imparts the very gift of God's eternal life that brings about a new state of being. "God will be glorified in his creation, shaping it to be the same form as, and similar to his own Son" (AH V,6,1). So the plan of God is being realized by recapitulation: taking on Christ as Head by joining His body, the temple of the Spirit.

The difficulty in this theological thinking, evident in the conflict with the Gnostics, is how to make some sense of the negative reality of sin, the harsh pedagogy of the law, and the cruel tyranny of the devil. Gnosticism's attractive but false solution to this problem was dualism. Man was not culpable being, lost to God and in need of forgiveness and renewal, but rather an innocent victim of hostile angels and repulsive matter—just as the existence of this world is a cosmic tragedy. But Irenaeus found his theological solution to the enigma of evil in the Pauline text, "For God has imprisoned all in disobedience so that he may be merciful to all" (Rom 11:32). This thought became the key to the meaning of salvation history for him, for it allowed him to integrate the negative role of human sin and the old covenant of law that constrained it into the overriding, utterly good purpose of God. "God was magnanimous when, before humanity's failure, he foresaw the victory that he would give it through the Word . . . [for God] had in advance established and prepared the means of deliverance" (AH III,20,1). Jesus Christ is not God's second thought, so to say. From the beginning of creation, the Word of God intended to become the man Jesus Christ, and in Jesus Christ bring lost humanity to God's glory by bestowing the Spirit. This is the mystery of the plan of God, hidden from the ages, but now revealed in the gospel.

Notice what is taking place in this reflection. Theology is thinking strictly about the reality of God on the basis of Jesus Christ, that is, on the basis of the event of the Son's incarnation and the sending of the Spirit upon the church. Jesus Christ is not then the symbol of a God who may be something very different, as per a theory of divine *accomodation*. Jesus Christ is the actual event of God in coming to us, the decisive, determinative moment in God's life with the creation as God moves in to redeem what is lost, as per the theory of the christological *communication of idioms*. The point of most other ideas about God is precisely the opposite of incarnation; that is, it is about how to escape this world to the God beyond, how to transcend time and be rid of the body with its spatial limitations, how to be perfectly powerful, impassible, invulnerable.

For such theology, incarnation could at best be conceded as a necessary *accommodation* for the purposes of communicating with earthbound beings. Against this philosophical monotheism of the Platonists, Irenaeus emphatically reiterated the christological paradoxes that he had learned from Ignatius, for example, that in Christ "the impassible became passible." Rhetorically this *communication of idioms* offends the Platonic axiom that God cannot "suffer," while yet admitting some kind of truth to it. The Pauline teaching to which Irenaeus appealed implies that God patiently suffered the human rejection of His lordship. God allows Himself to be rejected—supremely at the cross of His Son. To be sure, this is a unique and divine suffering, the holy suffering of the one God who is uniquely and truly the Lord. Divine suffering then would not mean that God's essence is mutable, that is, that God is substantially changed into something else against His will, for example, the way that you and I will be changed into dust and ashes if someone kill us. That is the suffering or mutability that ontologically attends creaturehood. But divine suffering is spiritual, since God is Spirit. Divine suffering is an implication of the holy passion of divine love, the ontological cost of divine love, in that God freely chooses to be, as it were, personally vulnerable in the way that lovers always are: His name mocked, repudiated, scorned, hated. Such suffering God in patience endures, the Apostle states, in order to overcome all creaturely exploitation and abuse and replace it with the eternal rhapsody of love for all by means of the great exchange. "For you know the generous act of our Lord Jesus Christ, that though he was rich, yet for your sakes he became poor, so that by his poverty you might become rich" (2 Cor 8:9). God is not mutable in His divine essence, but certainly is so, according to the concept of exchange in the economy: in His divine person, for example, *kai ho logos sarx egeneto*, "the Logos *became* flesh." Whether Irenaeus completely broke through to this insight on the level of theological conceptuality is debatable. But clearly he struggled in this direction. He sensed that the God whose being is love can suffer spiritually, in a way that is holy and divinely "fitting," for this is in fact what has happened in the cross of Christ. The love of Christ shows itself in and as divine generosity of being that can freely undertake suffering for the sake of another.

Yet God's holy suffering by itself is not the gospel, any more than the cross of Jesus would redeem without the resurrection. It is only good news in the role it plays in the larger story of how God is creating the world and us in it anew and anew on the way to the best of all possible worlds. God is at work changing the world. The offense is doubled in the manner God has chosen to do this. Irenaeus sees that God is changing us, and through us the world, not by externally manipulating history, but by personally participating in it. Redemption is not the wave of a magic wand. It is not the pronouncement of a fiat. It is what transpires in personal encounter with Jesus Christ through repentance, faith, and the new obedience: "The Lord, therefore, redeems us by his blood and gives his soul for our souls and his flesh for our flesh; he pours out the Father's Spirit to create unity and communion between God and human beings. He brings God down to humans through the Spirit, and at the same time raises humans to God by his incarnation" (AH V,1,1). Not only then can we say that God suffers spiritually for Irenaeus; we can also say that the finite creature is capable of the infinite God. Reporting on Antonio Orbe's research, Mary Ann Donovan writes that Irenaeus "reworks the philosophical definition when he considers human perfection. He replaces 'capable of thought and science,' with 'able to tend to the perfect Father' (AH V,1,2) and capable, according to the flesh, of a divine life."[94] This represents a far-reaching revision in anthropology: human nature admits of a historical process, the coming of new life in God that ensues from the encounter with Jesus Christ. The "entire economy may be summarized as the modeling of human clay in the image and likeness of God"[95]—creation, as it were, is eschatological, for the Logos became what we are so that we may become what He is (AH V, preface). "This is why the Word of God became man, and this is why the Son of God became the Son of man, that humans might possess the Word, receive adoption and become children of God" (AH V,10,1).

The redemption worked by Jesus Christ, then, is nothing but the redemption of the creation gone astray and thus its creation anew. In Jesus, creation is liberated *from* its bondage to death and sin and liberated *in order to* find fulfillment in fellowship with God. "In Irenaeus' view there is a strict connection between creation and redemption, or better still, the world was created for the sake of the Redeemer and redemption. This link becomes explicit when the Creator and the Redeemer are identified with the person of Christ."[96] Peter C. Phan points to a text in which Irenaeus writes, "Since indeed [Christ] preexists as the Savior, it was necessary that what should be saved should also be called into existence, in order that the Savior should not exist in vain" (AH III,22,3). *The world was created in order to be saved.* From all eternity, the Son of God determined to become flesh, and having come as Jesus, to remain Jesus forever and ever, bringing all creation into harmony with this love. Now the mission of the Holy Spirit is effecting the obedience of faith among the nations. The *ecclesia catholica* is itself an expression of Jesus' obedience of faith on the earth. "This preaching and this faith" is what the church believes, "as if she had but one soul and one and the same heart; she preaches, teaches, and hands them down harmoniously, as if she possessed but one mouth" (AH I,10,1).

How is this change worked out according to Irenaeus? It is worked out in the first place in the history of Jesus, in the human nature of the Son of God. We now return to the important concept of recapitulation, which is how Irenaeus envisions the connection of creation and redemption in the person and work of Jesus. Against every Gnostic idea that the earthly Jesus is merely the neutral instrument of an otherworldly spirit, the notion of recapitulation refers to the saving significance of the life and death that Jesus actually lived and died: "If he only appeared as though he were flesh, without actually having become flesh, then his work was not true. But he actually was what he appeared to be, namely, God, recapitulating in himself the model of humanity formed long ago, in order to kill sin, destroy death, and give life to humanity" (AH III,18,7). It helps to have in mind here the Pauline text that inspired Irenaeus, from Romans 5:12, where the Apostle contrasts the disobedience of Adam to the obedience of Christ. The idea is that Jesus is the New Adam in whom the human creature that God intended is realized and made possible for and in all who believe in Him. Adam by disobedience had brought ruin upon human nature. But now Jesus' life of obedience to God, perfected in suffering love for the sake of the lost and guilty children of Adam, "recapitulates," that is, re-lives, the whole human life before God from birth to death. In this very act, human nature is being brought back in this one representative life under its true Head, the Word of God. In Jesus' life of perfect love, human nature is thus re-created. For "the saving Word has become the very thing that had perished, that is, humanity, and has produced through itself that participation in itself and the discovery of humanity's salvation" (AH IV,14,2). "The Word of the Father and the Spirit of God, united with the ancient substance of the creation of Adam, made a living and perfect man, receiving the perfect Father" (AH V,1,3). This obedience of Jesus Christ is the new event of the New Testament, through which the eternal Word of God established His supremacy over humanity, "constituting himself head of the church [that] he might draw all things to himself at the proper time" (AH III,16,6).

How does this new creation of humanity in the person and work of Jesus Christ becomes ours as well? At this point one has to talk about the Holy Spirit and His instruments: the preaching of the gospel and faith, the sacraments, the church. Yet a few comments about Irenaeus's anthropology are needed to make this clear. It is part of the very structure of creation, for Irenaeus, that to be human is to be led by the Spirit of God to the Word of God. God really created humans for Himself, for communion with God. Eternal life of love is the very goal of creation and the true orientation of created being. The leading of the Spirit of God, in Irenaeus's conception, is the very life of the human soul and body, the linchpin of his conception of created human nature. Apart from the Holy Spirit, the human dies spiritually, then physically, then eternally. Contemporaries of Irenaeus made an anthropological distinction between spirit and soul on basis of the putative distinctive in Genesis 1:26 between image and likeness: "Then God said, 'Let us make humankind in our image, according to our likeness.'" Gnostics especially associated one term, "image," with the merely human psyche and the other term, "likeness," with the divine spark, the element of spirit. Irenaeus took up this exegetical convention in a fundamentally different way. "Image (*eikon, imago*) he takes to be constituted by the human body and soul, whereas likeness (*homoiosis, similitudo*), the supreme gift of the

Spirit."[97] This scheme denies the immortality of the soul in itself and asserts its necessary relation to the body: human being is essentially a unity of body and soul. But this fragile, created, essentially mortal compound of body and soul sustains its unity of body and soul and lives just because and only because it lives under the Holy Spirit who leads it to God in His Word. If the Holy Spirit departs, left to itself, the human being begins to fall further and further from God back into nothingness, to death and disintegration.

Irenaeus therefore refers the second term in the scheme not to the human spirit, the Platonic mind, or the Gnostic spark of divinity. He refers it to the very Spirit of God under whom the human person ought to live in love to God as its true goal. When Adam lost the likeness of God after the Fall, what he lost was the Spirit of God, not as some extrinsic, extra gift, but as something intrinsic, essential to his true humanity. That is why Adam is a failure in being who finally perishes. This, it seemed to Irenaeus, was the meaning of the first three chapters of Genesis. In Christ, this situation has been reversed. As a human being, Christ was anointed with the Spirit forever, and the Spirit subsequently led Him through every trial to the completed life of righteousness. Now the exalted Christ sends that same Spirit to all His people, renewing in them the image of God. "The flesh taken as an inheritance by the Spirit forgets what it is and takes on the character of the Spirit and is conformed to the Word of God" (AH V,9,2). The Spirit in turn renews believers in the image of God. For the Spirit is a "down payment," "gradually accustoming us to grasp and bear God . . . [something] accomplished not by discarding the flesh, but by the communication of the Spirit" (AH V,8,1). The Spirit as down payment points believers to the future of God, the coming of Christ in glory, the transformation of reality, the resurrection of the dead. This will be the "true Sabbath of the just, in which they will have no earthly work to do, but will have a table prepared before them by God . . . the times of the Kingdom, when the just, rising from the dead, will reign, when the created order will be made new and set free, and will produce an abundance of all kinds of food, from the dew of heaven and of the fertility of the earth . . . [even] the animals, using the foods which come from the earth, will be peaceful and harmonious with each other, and perfectly subject to man." The realism of the eschatology indicates that from the beginning this earthly creation was meant for redemption and that redemption is the perfection of this earth. That is God's astounding plan that becomes visible in Jesus Christ, understood narratively as the recapitulation of humanity.

Because Irenaeus presses conventional ideas about divine and human nature with his teaching of recapitulation in Christ, he anticipates the future of Christology. The Logos, he teaches, "joined and united humanity with God. For if a human being had not conquered humanity's enemy, then that enemy would not have been overcome justly; but at the same time, if God has not bestowed salvation, our possession of it would not have been secure" (AH III,18,7). Abstractly speaking, then, both natures are thus needed for the work of redemption, but for

Irenaeus "the Logos is in a living relationship with the flesh he has assumed."[98] We do not accordingly have in Irenaeus any picture of a demigod occupying a human body, a monstrosity that would be neither fully God nor fully man, nor have we a picture of an autonomous human personality cooperating with God to a high degree. Irenaeus speaks christologically in the categories of the Logos and the *sarx*, the flesh, as inspired by John 1:14 and required by his anti-Gnostic polemic. Technically this is what scholars designate a Logos-Sarx Christology, in distinction from a Logos-Anthropos Christology, where the word "anthropos" explicitly includes the soul in the humanity that the Logos took on. But it would cohere with Irenaeus's whole line of thought if we explained that the human soul of Jesus is neither replaced by the Logos nor, as it were, coerced by the Logos. Rather through every stage of Jesus' life, Jesus' human soul freely obeyed God because the love of the Holy Spirit filled Him with the confidence that truly He is God's beloved Son, well-pleasing to Him (Luke 10:21). Jesus is the New Adam. As the New Adam, He is the "Word made flesh." In Jesus' total life of free and radical obedience to His Father in the power of the Spirit, the Word became flesh. When we think this way about Jesus and God, that is, *being* as they *act* in the economy, then our theological knowledge must rise to *trinitarian ontology*.

The Rule of Faith and the Trinity

The Gnostics with their fanciful methods twisted and turned texts inherited from Israel and the apostolic age, or introduced books alleging new revelations or secret traditions. But, Irenaeus responds, none of this agrees with baptism, that is, with the name of God by which and into which believers are baptized, the God for whom Christians live new lives and for whose name they are willing to die as martyrs. The Gnostic doctrines contradict the baptismal rule of faith in the Father, the Son, and the Holy Spirit. The baptismal creed in turn judges doctrine and life; it becomes the fitting standard by which to discriminate between faith true to the gospel and imposters. "They lead away from the Truth into captivity those who do not guard a firm faith in the one Father Almighty and in one Jesus Christ, the Son of God" (AH I,3,6). But "anyone who keeps unchangeable in himself the Rule of the Truth received through baptism will recognize the names and sayings and parables from the Scriptures, but this blasphemous [Gnostic interpretation] he will not recognize" (AH I,9,4). Irenaeus does not mean that one and the same creedal formulation exists everywhere. "Though the languages throughout the world are dissimilar, nevertheless the meaning of the tradition is one and the same." All the church believes, as Irenaeus phrases the creedal tradition, "in one God the Father Almighty, the Creator of heaven and earth and the seas and all things that are in them; and in the one Jesus Christ, the Son of God, who was enfleshed for our salvation; and in the Holy Spirit, who through the prophets preached

the Economies, the coming, the birth from a Virgin, the passion, the resurrection from the dead, and the bodily ascension into heaven of the beloved Son,
Christ Jesus our Lord, and His coming from heaven in the glory of the Father
to recapitulate all things and to raise up all flesh of the whole human race, in
order that to Christ Jesus, our Lord and God, Savior and King, according to
the invisible Father's good pleasure, every knee should bow . . . [and that He
should exercise judgment]" (AH I,10,1). The rule of faith is authoritative, not
because of uniform formulation, but because of one God in three Persons (as
it was finally defined) to whom it directs the faith of the church, that is, where
the faith comes with baptism into Christ.

Three features of the rule of faith, according to Irenaeus, are noteworthy.
First, the Holy Spirit is the subject who is proclaiming the saving deeds of
the Father and the Son. The Spirit is not a pious but empty name, serving to
privilege private feeling in individual hearts as if divine. The Spirit is the Spirit
of Jesus and His Father, the real, operative divine Agent at work in the spread
of the gospel to evoke the life of the church. Second, the purpose clause of
the whole confession of faith points to the eschatological glory of Jesus and
the judgment of the living and the dead. And third, all this talk is located in
the reality in which we live, the Father's world, "the earth and the seas and all
things that are in them." The rule of faith in every connection is *trinitarian*: it
describes this one world as one history of salvation in which we must speak
of God in three distinct but strictly coherent, interrelated ways of being and
acting, the one God of exclusive biblical monotheism.

In connection with Irenaeus's use of the baptismal creed as a standard of
doctrine, we may also mention the Eucharist, in that baptism was understood
as admission to the Lord's meal. As with Ignatius before him, the Eucharist is
the reality of *koinonia* with the crucified but risen Christ. "If this mortal flesh
is not saved, then neither did the Lord redeem us by blood, nor is the cup
of the Eucharist the communion of his blood, and the bread that we break
the communion of his flesh" (AH V,2,2). Knowing what we know about the
culture in which Irenaeus lived, this theological affirmation of the significance
of flesh is nothing less than astonishing. The reality principle in Irenaeus's theology denies that creatures have life in themselves, that the soul is immortal
by nature; instead they are flesh and blood, perishable. Just so and only so are
they valued by the eternal God and Creator. "Our survival forever comes from
[God's] greatness, not from our nature," he writes, so that we "may not wander
far from the true conception of the reality of things" as do the Gnostics (AH
V,2,3). True life depends on Christ, who brings God's life to flesh and blood, so
that feeding on Him at the Eucharist is a matter of life and death. In addition
to the rule of faith deriving from baptism and the antidocetist reality principle
of the theology of the martyrs, Irenaeus can maintain that "our thinking is
consonant with the Eucharist and the Eucharist in turn confirms our thinking":

"Just as bread that is produced from the earth, receiving the invocation of God is no longer ordinary bread, but the Eucharist, consisting of two elements, earthly and heavenly, so our bodies, nourished by the Eucharist, are no longer corruptible, having the hope of the resurrection" (AH IV,18,5).

Such a standard of doctrine entails also a standard for living. In the historical event of Christ the human being's obedience, "God recapitulated in Himself the ancient formation of man, that He might kill sin, deprive death of its power and vivify man" (AH IV,18,7). By contrast, historical life in the body and society for the Gnostics is generally without ethical not to mention theological significance. The Gnostics exempt themselves from the ethical conflict between biblical monotheism and pagan culture and thus from any danger of martyrdom: "Food sacrificed to idols they eat without scruple. . . . They are the first to assemble at every heathen festival held in honor of the idols. . . . Some do not even abstain from the spectacle loathsome to God and men where men fight with wild beasts and each other in homicidal fashion. . . . Carnal things, they say, must be given to the carnal, and spiritual to the spiritual" (AH I,6,3). "They claim that deeds are good or bad only because of human opinion" (AH I,25,4). While some rationalize licentiousness because the bodily life is ethically irrelevant, others seek liberation from the passions and "preach abstinence from marriage and so make void God's pristine creation, and indirectly reprove him who made male and female for generating the human race" (AH I,28,1).

In short: different Christs, different salvations, different ethics. This conflict pressed Irenaeus to develop further the implications of the gospel's trinitarian rendering of God. The variegated Gnostic myths about divine emanations from the Pleroma so appalled Irenaeus that it liberated his thinking about the Logos from residual mythological connotations in Platonism, as Jenson rightly notes:[98] "The angels neither made nor formed us, for only the Word of God has the power to make an image of God, not angels or anyone else, no power far removed from the Father of all things. God had no need of such beings . . . as though he had not his own hands. The Word and the Wisdom, the Son and Spirit are always present with him. By them and in them, he freely and independently made all things" (AH IV,20,1). This means, first of all, that the biblical dividing line of creator and creature is being drawn. "God differs from man, in that God indeed makes and man is made; and truly He who makes is always the same; but that which is made must receive both beginning, and middle, and addition, and increase" (AH IV,11,2). Irenaeus describes the one true ontological divide: "But the things established are distinct from Him who has established them, and what have been made from Him who had made them. For He is Himself uncreated, both without beginning and end, and lacking nothing. He is Himself sufficient for Himself, and still further, He grants to all others this very thing existence; but the things that have been made by Him have received a beginning. But whatever things had a beginning, and are liable to dissolution, and are subject to and stand in need of Him who made them, must necessarily in all respects have a different term [applied to them] . . . so that He indeed who made all things can alone together with His Word, properly be termed God and Lord" (AH III,8,3). God *together with* His Word and Spirit (see AH IV,20; 1:487 or *Apostolic Demonstrations* 47) then is related by Irenaeus to the world as creator to creature without any other ontological mediators between them. The line of division is drawn between creator and creature (not, say, between being and becoming, or impassible and changeable, regarding these familiar binaries of Greek philosophy instead as first of all intra-cosmic polarities). Accordingly, the Word and the Spirit are Creator, not creature, whose being *and becoming* transcend all we can know or imagine within our created world with our finite minds. But it follows, as the preceding italics indicate, that God Himself is from eternity not simply self-identical in substance, but is also internally related as persons by love, that is, living a life, not being a thing. To be sure, such a divine "life" is unique, ineffable, incomparable. Yet divine "simplicity" turns out in this case not to be so simple a concept at all, since what it describes is internally and irreducibly complex.

Love is alive. It is indeed striking how Irenaeus lifts up the biblical depiction of the Johannine Logos as an active agent in providence in relation to humanity: "at one time conferring with His creature, and at another propounding His law; at one time, again, reproving, at another exhorting, and then setting free His servant, and adopting him as a son; and, at the proper time, bestowing an incorruptible inheritance, for the purpose of bringing man to perfection" (AH IV,11,1). If for our salvation this latter is definitive for the biblical depiction of the Logos as *incarnate*, then it is the biblical story of the baptism of Jesus that determines Irenaeus's thinking about the Logos. This defines not only the Logos's active relation to humanity in the Incarnation, but also His relations to the Father and the Spirit: "In the name of Christ is implied, He that anoints, He that is anointed, and the unction itself with which He is anointed. And it is the Father who anoints, but the Son who is anointed by the Spirit, who is the unction . . . pointing out both the anointing Father, the anointed Son, and the unction, which is the Spirit" (AH IV,18,3). This is the deep reason why the very structure of gospel revelation is trinitarian: "Thus therefore was God revealed; for God the Father is shown forth through all these [operations], the Spirit indeed working, and the Son ministering, while the Father was approving, and man's salvation being accomplished" (AH IV,20,6).

Thus the truly astonishing thought to which Irenaeus came, explicitly for the first time in Christian theological history, is that of an eternal trinitarian life of God that constitutes the ground of God's economy as free act of love: "In the beginning, therefore, did God form Adam, not as if He stood in need of man, but that He might have [someone] upon whom to confer His benefits. For not alone antecedently to Adam, but also before all creation, the Word glorified His Father, remaining in Him; and was Himself glorified by the Father. . . . Nor did He stand in need of our service when He ordered us to follow Him; but He thus bestowed salvation . . . for He is rich, perfect, and in need of nothing. . . . As much as God is in want of nothing, so much does man stand in need of fellowship with God. For this is the glory of man, to continue and remain permanently in God's service" (AH IV,14,1). Irenaeus for the first time reasons from the *economic* trinity, the God revealed in the gospel, to the *immanent* Trinity, the God who from eternity to eternity is the love of the Father and the Son in the Holy Spirit, a plentitude without limit. So the "Word, namely the Son, was always with the Father, and that Wisdom also, which the Spirit, was present with Him, anterior to all creation" (AH IV,20,3). Just so, God is antecedently a perfectly fulfilled life, not in need of any kind, but free to innovate. Not that we can fathom this eternal, immanent Trinity, or that we should speculate about it. The knowledge of God as Father, Son, and Holy Spirit, Irenaeus explains, is not a knowledge of God's greatness (that is, infinity), but rather of "His love. He is always known through Him by whose means He ordained all things. Now this is His Word, our Lord Jesus Christ" (AH IV,20,4). But the inference of the eternal Trinity makes clear that the economy did not have to be so, that God chose freely to have a world, at the knowing cost of the Son's incarnation and death.

The Gnostics imagine that "they have discovered another god beyond God," but in fact

> they have dishonored and despised God, holding Him of small account, because, through His love and infinite benignity, He has come within reach of human knowledge (knowledge, however, not with regard to his greatness, or with regard to His essence—that has no man measured or handled—but after this sort: that we should know Him who made, and formed, and breathed in us the breath of life, and nourishes us by means of the creation, establishing all things by His Word, and binding them together by His Wisdom, this He who is the only true God); but they dream of a non-existent being above Him, that they may be regarded as having found the great God, whom nobody [they hold] can recognize as holding communication with the human race, or as directing mundane matters. (AH III,24,2)

Irenaeus thus anticipates the later distinction of mature trinitarian theology between God's infinite, unknowable essence and its true expression by the three concrete persons made known in the gospel. By this he distinguishes a true apophaticism (the doctrine of simplicity, taken as a rule, that we are to speak of God's unique being as the One who infinitely transcends all our possible knowledge of that being). This is to take the notion of "divine simplicity" as a rule, a stipulation to speak of God as befits the One whose being and act are to create all things other than Himself. Such an apophaticism is *based* on the self-revelation, the kataphaticism of the tri-personal life of the God of the gospel as an implication of it. Such a knowledge of God "beyond being" is far removed from Platonic mysticism, which reasons from the inadequacy of anything finite truly to express the infinite to the reification of a divine Nothing—the nihilism from which Hegel thought God had to distinguish Himself by self-negation into the world, the nihilism that Nietzsche mistakenly but plausibly found imbedded in the (liberal Protestant) Christian doctrine of God. But we have seen that Irenaeus regards the creature made in God's image to be "fit" for God, capable of God, *finitum capax infiniti*.

For the same reason—that God as Triune is immanently capable of becoming in the eternal begetting of the Son and breathing of the Spirit, that human being as God's creature is created by nature capable of divine life—Irenaeus had vigorously rejected the christological docetism of the Gnostics who variously taught that the Logos "passed through Mary as water passes through a tube" or that he "descended in the shape of a dove at his baptism" and then departed before the crucifixion. They held such a view on the grounds that the Logos "remained impassible—inasmuch as he is inapprehensible and invisible [so] it would be impossible for him to suffer" (AH I,7,2). Against this Irenaeus maintains Ignatius's christological paradox: "Jesus who suffered for us, who dwelt among us, this very same one is the Word of God. . . . Flesh is the ancient handiwork made by God out of the earth as in Adam. But it is this which John points out that the Word of God truly became" (AH I,9,3). For the Gnostics, "knowledge is the redemption of the inner man. And this redemption is not corporeal, since the body is corruptible. . . . Redemption too must be [only] spiritual" (AH I,21,4). Against the Gnostic idea of redemption of the divine spark by liberation from the flesh, Irenaeus, thinking out the reason for the Incarnation, develops the soteriological idea of the great exchange between God and humanity in Christ: "He would become the Son of man for this purpose, that man also might become the son of God" (AH III,10,2); "He who was the Son of God became the Son of man, that man, having been taken into the Word, and receiving the adoption, might become the son of God" (AH III,19,1). "The Word of God, our Lord Jesus Christ, who did, through His transcendent love, become what we are, that He might bring us to be even what He Himself is" (AH V, preface). This notion that in Christ God and humanity exchange properties to form a new unity, so that man who cannot save himself can be saved (see AH IV,18,2), is formulated against the Gnostics' view of salvation (see AH III,11,3).

These considerations finally led Irenaeus to reflect upon the question of why God chose this way of the Incarnation to achieve human salvation. God did not have to adopt this course. He never had to have a world. He could have saved humanity by a sheer miracle. Why then incarnation and cross? In part, Irenaeus says, it was to show that the redeemer of humanity is the same God who made the earth and humanity upon it, the one and true God. The Redeemer is the Creator, and what is redeemed is nothing other than the creation. That is made clear in the very fact of the Incarnation. But the chief reason for the Incarnation is the idea of salvation as eternal life in communion with God: "The glory of God is a living man; and the life of man consists in beholding God" (AH IV,20,7). The goal of salvation is *theosis*, "divinization": "By their continuing in being through-out a long course of ages, they shall receive a faculty of the Uncreated, through the gratuitous bestowal of eternal existence upon them by God" (AH IV,38,3). What would be the alternative? The depth of the Gnostic hatred for the one true God, according to Irenaeus, is found in their contempt of God's law, not merely in its moral sense as an expression of God's will for them as embodied and social creatures on the earth whose disciplined lives are to lead them to theosis, but indeed chiefly in its judicial sense, as the expression of God's wrath against sin and God's judgments in history: "That they might remove the rebuk-ing and judicial power from the Father, reckoning that as unworthy of God, and thinking that they had found out a God both without anger and [merely] good, they have alleged that one [God] judges, but that another saves, uncon-sciously taking away the intelligence and justice of both deities" (AH IV,25,2). The Gnostics dualize law and gospel and so sunder the canonical narrative.

To be sure, this final insight of Irenaeus leaves hanging the tremendous ques-tion of the role that God's wrath and other evils play in the plan of God. The question of *theodicy* arises at the heart of biblical faith, which from the first chap-ter of the first book of the Bible insists that God the Creator is all-good, all-wise, and all-powerful and so evil only to the evil. The rule of faith insists on the one God, the almighty Father who creates, redeems, and fulfills one world though the missions of His Son and Spirit. This unity, however, does not *yet* exist (except in faith) and thus cannot be seen *until* the fulfillment of the creation. It is a rule of *faith* in the *revealed* God of the gospel against a backdrop of God's continuing *hiddenness* in evil and chaotic events that afflict the creation—the very evidence to which Gnostics always plausibly enough appeal against orthodoxy's affirma-tion of the goodness of creation. In that the resurrection of the Crucified informs us, we rightly hope to see the hell that He endured for us defeated eternally. Platonism on the other hand thinks to save God from any suspicion of responsi-bility for evil by denying that the good God is responsible—a seemingly attractive move, which comes at the cost of diminishing God's creative power and regard-ing this material world as incorrigible beyond redemption. The great creedal decisions of ecumenical Christianity affirmed the God who spared not His own Son, God the Father who in the person of His Son "stretched out His hands in suffering in order to free from suffering." Gnosticism was in principle defeated by the strength of Irenaeus's trinitarian dogmatics, which led the church to a new appreciation of the unity of God's works and the singularity of God's purpose. Thus to this contest of philosophical and biblical monotheism we next turn.

CHAPTER 5
The Confrontation of Biblical and Philosophical Monotheism

Emergent Trinitarianism issued in a new understanding of deity in relation to the philosophical theology stemming from Plato's critique of Homer.[1] Platonism had never attained to the transcendence of God as creator of everything other than God since it has not understood the true immanence of God by His incarnate Word and Pentecostal Spirit at work to bring in the kingdom. Instead, Platonism thought of the transcendence of God as the general superiority of mind over matter and thus interpreted God's immanence by means of mediating beings, preeminently the Logos. But with the gospel, "God" is not to be understood philosophically as intellectual or super-intellectual substance or nature, essentially characterized by the method of negation as ineffable, incomprehensible, immense, immortal, and so on. Taken on its own terms, this reasoning of natural theology inevitably leads to the false infinite of the dualistic *finitum non capax infiniti* dogma, which removes God from human reality contrary to the depiction of God in biblical narrative.[2] With the gospel, the word "God" (in the sense of the unique divine nature or singular deity) is to be understood relatively, that is, from the Trinity's eschatological office as the creator of the creation, not absolutely, as if we gained any positive insight into the being of God in and for itself by way of negation of the world's supposed imperfections. For the God of the gospel is not essentially creative, but essentially self-communicative, thus the God who comes to be related to what is not God freely and decisively, not essentially or necessarily.

But from this actual free and decisive relation to what is, the nature of God is to be conceived dynamically as that perfect harmony of power, wisdom, and love that can be so related as its creator to everything that is other than God. These divine attributes or perfections of power, wisdom, and love are appropriated respectively to the Father, the Son, and the Holy Spirit as the *proprium* of each in their indivisible relations ad extra to the creation. It is as such a living *harmony*[3] and not a dead self-sameness that the perfect being of God is dynamically one, ineffably complex, creation's Alpha and Omega, infinitely beautiful and eternally engaging, indeed "simple" but not like a rock, rather like an irreducibly complex organism. The divine nature of the Trinity is to be conceived rigorously as the eternal *Life*, the glorious freedom of the Father for the Son and the Son for the Father in the love of the Holy Spirit, radiant for us in Jesus Christ because by His harrowing of hell this divine life comes to include those otherwise lost to God. The Holy Trinity is the *living* God, who *gives* a share in His own life to others and so makes all things new. *To be this living God is ever concretely to give.* In this chapter we trace the confrontation of biblical and philosophical monotheism just sketched through Origen up to the Arian crisis.

The Problem of Christianity and Platonism

What are the problems created by the resort to the philosophical Logos doctrine that we noticed in Justin Martyr? We saw at points in Justin the appearance of the scheme of Absolute God-mediating Logos-visible world, where the world is the third member of a cosmic system without beginning or end.[4] This scheme derives from so-called Middle Platonism.[5] In the Greek-speaking East, *Middle Platonism* was the very air that the thinkers of the early church breathed, as axiomatic as the scientific worldview is to us today. Thus it was inevitably the source of ideas or concepts with which to make intelligible to themselves the difficult paradoxes of the gospel narrative, such as Ignatius's "the impassible became passible." The difficulty here is a subtle one. Like any other form of human reason, theology will employ familiar images and concepts to render intelligible what is new and unfamiliar. This is an inherent and inescapable facet of finite understanding, which is not dangerous or misleading when it is recognized for what it is and remembered that the purpose is to understand the unfamiliar in its own right, not simply incorporate it into comfortable, conventional thinking. The danger to the gospel of the resurrection of the Crucified occurs then when it is devoured rather than illuminated; this happens when it is incorporated into some other scheme of reality, rather than being permitted to critique and revise such schemes in the very process of being made intelligible by their terms. The course of thought that led to the articulation of the doctrine of the Trinity is exemplary of this perennial hermeneutical difficulty in theology.

Only in the course of time would hidden incompatibilities of the Platonic conceptual scheme with the gospel come to light, and even this eventual parting of the ways is not properly understood until we see why, of all the available philosophical positions in the Hellenistic world, the early Christian thinkers found Platonism most congenial.[6] Eric Osborn refers to "certain stock texts of Plato . . . that permeate early Christian thought" on God as the "ineffable Father," the "cause of all good," "holding the beginning, end, and middle of things on the path of nature and law."[7] In De Vogel's summation: "Platonism shared with Christianity a few basic views which might be described as follows: a) that visible things are no primary reality, existing by and through themselves; b) that by their imperfections visible things point to and require a perfect and absolute reality, primary being and founded in itself; c) that this invisible reality is of an infinitely higher significance and value than that of visible things depending on it; d) that this fundamental fact has to rule our life and conduct; e) that it implies the infinite value of the human soul, and therefore, of the individual person." In addition to these doctrinal affinities, Platonism provided "a rational form of expression, which by Christians could be recognized as being in accordance with what they had learned from Scripture, but at the same time as deepening and confirming their Christian belief."[8] Thus the problem of Christianity and Platonism is complex. Both are critiques rendering the existing reality and/or its appearance dubious. Platonism, however, thinks of the dubiousness of the visible within the static framework of an eternal cosmos, while Christianity renders the present establishment of things dubious by expectation of a new creation through the gospel of the resurrection of the Crucified. Thinking out this affinity, and this difference,[9] by tracing the rise of Trinitarianism is the task of this chapter.

Overview of Trinitarian Doctrine and Trinitarian Errors

We can note in a preliminary way that the Absolute God-mediating Logos-visible world scheme Justin borrowed creates a problem for the doctrine of God: without the Spirit as the third member of the triad to mediate the love of the Father and the Son, we are not thinking of the *immanent and eternal* Trinity, the God who *is* the love of the Father and the Son *in the Spirit*, that is, God for God and to God *in God*, as the one, eternal Life antecedent to any act of creation. As we read, Irenaeus laid it down as a principle: the "Word, namely the Son, was always with the Father, and that Wisdom also, which is the Spirit, was present with Him, anterior to all creation" (AH IV,20,3). If we cannot think of this intrinsically fulfilled divine life "anterior to all creation" as completed in its own third, we cannot in turn think of a *free* decision to create the world from nothing out of superabundance of *love*. God and world otherwise become linked in a system of necessary relations. The cosmos becomes the necessary third of the Absolute and its Logos. But the God of the gospel is engaged *freely and not out of any need* to bring about His reign of *love* through a *history*, that is, by the gift of His Son and mission of the Spirit in the project of *eschatological creation*.

The use of the philosophical concept of the Logos also created several christological problems. Since the function of the philosophical Logos is to lend rational form to unorganized matter, the tendency in Christology will be for the Logos to substitute for the human soul of Jesus, as if in the Incarnation the Logos appropriated a physical body as its puppet through which to communicate with mortals, displacing the natural human psyche. Consequently, we get a Jesus who is neither really God (the Logos in Platonism is God's next best, His duplicate or replica) nor really human, lacking a human soul, but a kind of hybrid. By the same token, this Jesus' function is less to redeem the sinful soul and dying body for the coming Reign than to moralize within the existing establishment of things. Jaroslav Pelikan asks in this connection, "Was the work of Christ to be thought of as having accomplished the reconciliation between God and the world or as having disclosed a reconciliation that had actually been there all along?"[10] The latter narrative tends to turn Jesus into the puppet of the Logos's timeless truth (usually some moral that we have forgotten or neglected) and so robs saving significance from Jesus' *particular* life of mercy for sinners and shameful death in solidarity with them. But the theological rationality of the latter must be probed in the particulars—lest Christ have "died for nothing" (Gal 2:21). As we have seen, Christology that is deeply, profoundly antidocetist is not merely insisting that Jesus had a body, or that Jesus had a soul, but that the public obedience of Jesus in His body made complete by death on the cross is what accomplishes human redemption at the turn of the ages, the dawn of the new creation. The creedal theology of the ecumenical councils, as we shall see, was concerned with the gospel's proclamation of *the man Jesus as God's redemptive act of self-giving love*, just so and *only so* the Word who is God eternally now *incarnate*, the love of the Father for the Son turned by the Spirit to the world in Jesus Christ, proclaimed in the gospel, gathered as the church to be harbinger of the Beloved Community that is the eschatological goal of creation.

It may help here if by way of anticipation we ask at the outset what kind of ontologically realistic *description* of (not metaphysical speculation about) God we get—and what is excluded—when we analyze the gospel narrative in the way of the creedal theology of the ecumenical councils. For the Nicene fathers, the divine *apatheia*, or God's *substantial* impassibility or immutability (meaning that God is the One Nature, simple and uncompounded, that *cannot* morph, so to say, into some other substance or disintegrate into some more basic elements) consists in freedom from "passion," in the sense of being overwhelmed by emotions caused or motivated by something external to the self. God is not like Zeus, who gets jealous and spiteful when Hera takes another lover! (One might think by way of comparison of the prophet Hosea's preaching of God's anger at adulterous Israel, but witness the decisive text in which Yahweh declares that He is not like a jealous husband who comes to destroy, but rather like a holy love that will find the way to redeem, Hos 11:8-9.) The Nicene theologians shared Platonism's rational critique of such mythological depictions of God for representing God like a creature as subject to forces other than self. Such representations are unworthy of true deity. Yet, at the same time, they consistently interpreted God's freedom from passion as the "impassible passibility" they saw in Jesus' way to the cross in the Gospels of Luke and John or the Letter to the Hebrews: as freedom for love, as philanthropy. Eric Osborn, drawing upon J. C. McLelland, has rightly stressed in this connection that we "need to recover the positive meaning that negative theology had for the early Fathers; 'Immutability asserts God's trustworthiness, impassibility his moral transcendence, anonymity his eminence beyond our linguistic and conceptual categories.'"[11] Likewise Joseph M. Hallmann, following Prestige, affirms: "God's impassibility expressed moral transcendence. God is 'incapable of being diverted or overborne by forces and passions such as commonly hold sway in the creation and among mankind.'"[12] Making this move to profoundly qualify the apophatic tradition with kataphatic affirmations of the gospel narrative, we may then say that God as self-caused or self-motivated creator of all that is not God is full of "passion" in the sense of self-motivated, creative, value-bestowing love. If in fact the church fathers so interpreted divine freedom, it is because they came to their idea of the eternal life that God lives by reflection upon the three agents interacting in the gospel narrative and used Platonism's negative theology and its concepts in that kataphatic light.

Of these three, only the Son is incarnate, yet fittingly He is this Incarnate One as sent by His Father and empowered by their Spirit. He exists among us in the act of obeying His Father's will by the power of the Spirit. The Father sends and gives, the Son obeys and surrenders, while the Spirit mediates these actions of the Father and the Son in mutual love so that they come to include the weak and the godless (Rom 5:6, 8) in the sphere of time and space. In the story of the Baptism of Jesus and Testing by Satan in the Wilderness, standing as a heading over the ensuing gospel narrative as if to introduce the cast of characters, we are given this picture of the Father and the Son in the unity of the Spirit. Consequently, the gospel narrative turns and twists on what transpires between these three so that in the end *the entire event* telling the love of the Father and the Son accomplished in the Holy Spirit now including us *is* the living God of the Bible in the event of the coming of His reign. This narrative describes God's being in its self-communicative action; it is neither theoretical comprehension of the ineffable Life nor merely a way of speaking about it accommodated to our finite comprehension. This reflected narrative denotes rather the Life that the doctrine of the Trinity *describes*. If that is so, there are a number of interpretive possibilities that are excluded, namely, *modalism, tritheism,* and *subordinationism.*

The first thing we have to say in describing the actors as rendered in the gospel narrative is that the divine characters that here appear are depicted as real, distinct agents, not signs of something else. The decisive action in the narrative is what happens among them, that is, when Jesus, obeying His Father, dies as a ransom and the Father, acknowledging this love of the godforsaken Son for sinners as His very own, raises Him for their justification, then promises life for the dead and salvation to the world by sending the Spirit in His name. While Jesus as the Crucified is the parable of God who hardens or opens hearts to faith as the Spirit wills, to those who come to see Him in faith as the Christ, the Son of God, the saving action that transpires among the three is not some kind of symbol pointing to something else above and beyond the narrative. It is thus a kind of unbelief appearing in the guise of theological interpretation when the three are treated as transitory symbols of a supernatural reality not identical with them. For faith, however, the gospel narrative cannot be taken as a theatrical performance by an actor donning masks, who in reality does not personally identify with the role. Father, Son, and Spirit are not to be taken as various masks that God (who would be in this case some unknown fourth thing) dons as suits the mood or occasion, appearing the Father at one moment, as the Son the next, or as the Spirit a third time—how, then, as at the baptism of Jesus, all three at once?

The fictive interpretation of the threefold appearance in the gospel narrative is called *modalism*, that is, the doctrine that God is not really the *personae* Father, Son, Holy Spirit but only appears to us in these roles as "modes" temporarily assumed. Historically there were two types of modalism that differed in their practical effect. Dynamic modalism in the West wanted in a simplistic way to emphasize the divinity of Jesus so that His saving significance was secured. Monarchical modalism in the East wanted to preserve the Father from the suffering that the Son experienced, and thus regarded the Son and also the Spirit as temporary, delimited manifestations of the Father.[13] In either case, as a reading of the gospel and ontological description of the divine agency depicted in it, modalism is a major blunder, a categorical misunderstanding, the very first deviation excluded by incipient trinitarian theology.[14] These three, Father, Son, and Spirit, are distinct though mutually defining agencies in God's one life, not three roles played by another, fourth unknown God the Actor hidden behind the masks. These three are God appearing as God truly is in and for Himself, since the God of the gospel cannot be conceived to deceive in what faith understands as His self-imparting revelation for us and our salvation. Deception would in this case imply a fatal self-contradiction in

God. In fact, to affirm the possibility of such deception in the form of modalist theology would be unfaith in the gospel appearing in the form of false belief.

Affirming that, however, does raise an alarming question. If God is three, how is God one? In rejecting modalism, have we stumbled somehow into polytheism? Does God have to start a conversation, negotiate, broker, and bargain for a consensus within God before resolving to do something as God? Talk about mythology! How then are we to grasp the true and divine unity of the three persons? Ruled out from the start is any notion of three individual divinities who have only an *external* relationship to each other, as if the Father, Son, and Spirit could be taken as three individuals accidentally connected, not belonging to one another in an essential bond of social relationships, but rather like hagglers at the market having to consult, negotiate, contract, cooperate, and possibly quarrel. Karl Barth speaks from the Western tradition (which has always shared the concern, if not the error, of dynamic modalism and tends toward a psychological view of the Trinity, that is, that the "persons" are not so much like agents in community as operations of divine mind): "Can we really think of the first and second persons of the triune Godhead as two divine subjects and therefore as two legal subjects who can have dealings and enter into obligations with one another? This is mythology, for which there is no place in a right understanding of the doctrine of the Trinity as the doctrine of the three modes of being of the one God."[15] *Tritheism* would certainly be a *polytheism* in violation of biblical monotheism's conviction that God is the *one* creator of all that is not God.

Yet John Meyendorff, speaking for the Eastern theological tradition, counters Barth's accusation with a simple reiteration of the basic fact to be interpreted: in the gospel "the incarnate Logos and the Holy Spirit are met and experienced first as divine agents of salvation, and only then are they also discovered to be essentially one God." Citing Theodore de Regnon, Meyendorff points to divergent metaphysics behind Eastern and Western construals of the Trinity: "Latin philosophy considers the nature in itself first and proceeds to the agent; Greek philosophy considers the agent first and passes through it to find the nature. The Latins think of personality as a mode of nature; the Greeks think of nature as the content of the person."[16] It is clear then that the present study adopts the Eastern approach, insofar indeed as the Regnon thesis is historically correct (it may not be[17]). If that is so, Western theology might well ponder whether the revision of metaphysics by the gospel was advanced more consistently in the East. For here an agent is not understood as the exemplification of a generic class, whose particularity would then be pure idiosyncrasy. Rather idiosyncrasy reveals certain being or nature as capable of the personal, as fundamentally social.[18]

All, both East and West in the ancient church, expressed horror at any thought of tritheism. The later Nicene theologians of the Greek East were accused of tritheism, or at least a conceptuality vulnerable to it. They called the Son *homoousios* (of one being) with the Father, and insisted at the same time these two were distinct *hypostases* or *prosopoi* (*personae*). Against them, it was argued that, in spite of good intentions, talk of two distinct persons of necessity posits two individual entities in the class of divine being or substance, limiting each other, and so ending up with two finite gods—an impossible contradiction of monotheism, even a reversion to polytheism. How did the Nicene theologians of the East respond to this criticism? With "strong Trinitarianism," that is, the theory in which "(1) Father, Son, and Spirit are conceived as persons in a full sense of 'person,' that is, as distinct centers of love, will, knowledge, and purposeful action (all of which require consciousness), and (2) who are conceived as related to each other in some central ways analogous to, even if sublimely surpassing, relations among members of a society of three human persons."[19] Each of the three is its own individual, subsistent existence, yet only in being *internally related* as the agent it is to the other two, and so each living as the agent it personally is by mutual indwelling (*perichoreisis*) of love.[20] Thus they meant not a relation that is accidental to a self-sufficient substance (like, say, being an American would be the accidental property of *homo sapiens* as such), but rather a relation that is essential to each one's own concrete and personal existence, where existence and essence are not otherwise differentiated than by these very relations, but indeed rather cohere because of them.

Accordingly, the Father is not Father for Himself but the Father of Jesus His Son, apart from whom He cannot be the Father at all. Jesus is not Son for Himself but the Son of the God of Israel, apart from whom He cannot be the Son at all. It is in this mutual relation mediated by the Spirit that the Father and the Son each exist in His own concrete way yet for each other in love. The divine love unifying the Father and Son, moreover, is not an accidental quality of the Father or the Son, an emotion they happen to have, or a contingent affection that may or may not be elicited by a chance encounter, but rather is the Holy Spirit, who exists in giving the Son to the Father and the Father to the Son. These two dwell in one another by the Spirit and in this way constitute a single but complex, internally differentiated life that is creator and redeemer and fulfiller of everything else. The eternal divine nature or reality is not to be thought of as an underlying Lockean substance, "I know not what," but as analogous to *life*, not stuff nor even consciousness. This Trinity is the *living* God.

If this is right, tritheism was only a theoretical danger in the ancient church. Subordinationism was the real alternative to modalism. Subordinationism is the opposite form of deviation from modalism, though it shares the same aversion to the capacity of the living God for the creature. Modalism thinks that the distinctions in God are not real, that Father, Son, and Holy Spirit are only temporary masks worn by God as some fourth unknown thing, of whom then we can never truly be sure. Modalism wants to preserve the divine unity at the expense of the divine distinctions. Subordinationism reflects the opposite impulse: it wants so much to maintain the personal distinctions between Jesus and God that it falsely conceives the divine unity as a unity founded on the superiority of the Father in being. In relation to God the Absolute Father, so to say, the second and third persons are replicas, intrinsically diminished as such, divine only by near association with the Father. Thus they are ontologically subordinate, conceived of as divine in lesser degree.

Subordinationism distinguishes between Father on the one side and the Son and Spirit on the other so sharply that it thinks of the three persons on a descending scale of degrees of divinity, with the Father being God absolutely, but the Son and the Spirit only relatively. The Father's superiority is to posses divinity like a substance possesses an essential quality, as in "man is the animal having mind"; there can only be one nature that is the genuine possessor of an essential quality (if we said baboons have minds, we would be saying that baboons are human), and if we are monotheists, then it seems that the Father is the one genuine possessor of divinity. In subordinationism, the Son and the Spirit participate in this essential quality of deity that is the Father's, not then by nature but by gift, by grace, by adoption, by creation. Subordinationism appealed because it seemed to solve difficulties on either side as the middle way between modalism and tritheism. It proved to be an instructive failure. It brought to the surface the deep, latent cleavage between two kinds of monotheism.

In distinction from ontological subordinationism that can imagine the Father existing all alone, and then adding on a second and a third replica, the orthodox Nicene theologians, as we shall see, conceived of a primacy in the eternal sequence of divine life. This primacy naturally belongs to the first person; it is simply the personal property or internal relation characteristic of the Father, which is to be the Unbegotten who begets the Son and spirates the Spirit. Origen's concept of "eternal generation" of the Son by the Father begins the necessary revision of metaphysics by conceiving of the eternal God as the living God, who lives in the temporal and so also eternal, act of self-communication.

Two Kinds of Monotheism: The Living God of Radical, or Exclusive, Monotheism

The living God of the Bible is the One who is passionately concerned with creation, especially with humanity, specifically on behalf of the poor, the lost, those helplessly enslaved under the antidivine powers of sin and death, as figured in the devil. This biblical narrative of the creating and redeeming God of the creation fallen under the sway of antidivine powers finds itself not infrequently in mortal conflict with other images or ideas or narratives of divinity, representing different interests and serving projects other than eschatological creation. Citing Philippians 2:6 in the opening chapters of his *Exhortation*,[21] Clement of Alexandria at the turn of the third century contrasted the God of the gospel who became human and servant of all (EX I:174) with "the mysteries of the atheists. And with reason I call those atheists who know not the true God, and pay shameless worship to a boy torn in pieces by the Titans" (EX II:177). This latter, not atypical piece of Platonic criticism of the myths of the gods seemed to play well for Clement, the Christian apologist seeking to commend to his generation the Christ who "counted not equality with God a thing to be grasped, but emptied himself and became obedient, even to death on a cross." Yet could not these "atheists" by the same token have asked Clement about his Christian God who spared not His own Son—but handed Him over to the torturers? Philosophical criticism of pagan mythology could turn with equal vengeance upon the Christian narrative; in fact, it quickly did. As early as the year 165, for example, we find the pagan essayist Lucian ridiculing the absurdity of the Christian superstition in the same rationalistic spirit of the philosophical critique of mythology: "[Christians] worship that great one, the man who was crucified in Palestine, because he introduced this new religion into life. . . . [What a religion!] The poor wretches have convinced themselves that they will be absolutely immortal and live forever, and in consideration of this they despise death and commonly offer themselves of their own accord [for martyrdom]; and besides this, their first lawgiver persuaded them that they are all brethren, when once they have transgressed and denied the gods of the Greeks, and pay worship to their crucified sophist, and live according to his laws."[22] The notion of a unique incarnation of God in a particular human being, focused no less on the shocking and seditious image of the Crucified, could be criticized by philosophical monotheism with as much justice as any pagan myth of "a boy torn in pieces by the Titans." The biblical narrative was as full as Homer with tales that seemed "unworthy of the gods."

This raises the very interesting question, What is worthy of God? How might we know? Do human beings as rational beings created in God's image have the capacity, independent of the gospel, to grasp enough of the true, the good, and the beautiful to know and to judge what is and what is not worthy of God? Can they recognize rationally as creatures what does and what does not qualify any candidate for the title "Creator"? Is there an analogy or proportion or relation between the creature and the Creator by which the rational creature can discern what is "fitting" for God? Or, in the fallen world, is the human status as the creature made in the image of God something made known by the gospel, that is, by incorporation into Christ, the new and true Adam and image of God?

Platonism, thinking of God in analogy to the operations and perfections of mind as opposed to body, seemed to many Christians to offer the exalted notion of God *as immaterial Mind*. In the case that determined the question for the future of Western theology, Augustine, mired now in Gnostic, now in Stoic conceptions of the deity as a highly refined but all the same material part of the cosmos, learned from "the books of Platonists" that "the soul of man, although it bears witness of the light, is not the Light."[23] This led the searching Augustine to "return to my own self . . . into the depths of my soul . . . [to see] the Light that never changes casting its rays over the same eye of my soul, over my mind . . . Eternal Truth, true Love, beloved Eternity . . . [even though] it has no extension in space."[24] Augustine's meaning is that all insight into truth presupposes Truth, all love presupposes the Good, all meaningful passage in time presupposes Eternity. Without these immaterial lights, the mind wanders aimlessly in darkness, never knowing this from that, nor true love from passing attraction, nor destiny from distraction. To operate at all, the human mind in time presupposes the intellectual lights of Truth, Goodness, and Beauty—even though, as immaterial ideas, these are not themselves objects appearing in time and extended in space but only as ideas that enlighten the mind in its acts.

So a notion worthy of God's kind of reality seems to arise from the soul's self-reflection on the intellectual light by which the mind operates to know, to love, and to enjoy anything at all in the world. God is like the physical light that enlightens the eye to see; God is source of the intellectual light by which the mind operates. God is not refined matter, the higher part of the cosmos, "extended through all space to infinity,"[25] as Stoics think. Rather "all finite things are in you [O God], not as though you were a place that contained them" but rather like the sunlight that makes things visible, or the intellectual lights of truth, goodness, and beauty by which the mind understands, loves, or enjoys what the eye sees. Hence all visible things exist in *God's creative envisioning and willing of them*. Since God is *creator*[26] of all that is not God, all other things "are fit and proper not only to the places but also to the times in which they exist," since, as Augustine prays to God, "you abide forever and cause time to come and go."[27] God is the creative Mind that in an eternal act chooses a possible world and actualizes it as the meaningful sequence of events destined for the Reign. This creative action determines all that is not God by foresight and superintendence.

Clearly Platonism helped Augustine to conceive of the God of Christian revelation worthily as the transcendent creator of the cosmos, not the highest kind of being within a cosmic system that as such would also contain and limit Him. Augustine does not stop here, however. Taking up the writings of the apostle Paul, Augustine finds himself "chastened" to wonder anew over what notion of God is worthy of the One who, "though he was in the form of God, did not regard equality with God as something to be exploited, but emptied himself, taking the form of a slave, being born in human likeness. And being found in human form, he humbled himself and became obedient to the point of death—even death on a cross" (Phil 2:6-8).[28] Of this creative deed there is nothing in the books of the Platonists. So perplexity deepens. Do Christians as new creations of this latter grace, instructed by the God who was not ashamed of the virgin's womb, think a "revolution" in the highest, noblest conceptions of divinity, corresponding to the highest, noblest conceptions of humanity, as in the very Platonism that helped Augustine to think of God in analogy to

the light of the mind? In his unjustly forgotten *magnum opus*, Charles Norris Cochrane so argued. Augustine's breakthrough in conceiving "substance as
spiritual" happened when at last he grasped that "so far from being ultimate,
'form' and 'matter' alike were merely figments of the human mind . . . the
spectacles through which men saw the corporeal or object world." This insight
liberated him from the "delusions of materialism and idealism" to make the
revolution "complete."[29] The conception of the human as "an expanding egoism
that accepts the empirical or contingent self as independent and cherishes it to
the exclusion of all else" was left aside[30] with Augustine's acceptance of "trinitarian Christianity, [by which] he identified himself with the effort of the thought
initiated by Athanasius."[31] The thought of the "incorporeal, infinite, absolute"
being of One who creates all that is other than Himself in thinking and willing
them to exist surely was aided by "reading these books of the Platonists." But,
as Augustine went on immediately to acknowledge, in them he found nothing of grace, charity, incarnation, or Christ as savior.[32] In fact, it is this latter
God of the gospel whom Augustine begins to think with the help of Platonic
conceptuality. And here indeed Augustine articulated the breach caused by the
resurrection of the Crucified: that God is creator in the radical sense of *creatio
ex nihilo* is not a proposition available to Platonic philosophy and was in fact
resisted by it. But this is Cochrane's "revolution" by which Augustine demythologized *Roma Aeterna* and subordinated its peace by the sword to the victory
peace of Him who had been crucified on an imperial stake. Whatever subtleties
separate Augustine from the Eastern theologians primarily studied in this book,
he grasped the fundamental confrontation of the two kinds of monotheism as
profoundly as any.

"Early Christian thinkers . . . seized upon the idea that the universe was created
in both matter and form out of nothing as absolutely basic to belief in the one and
only God," writes Torrance. "It is highly significant, however, that their real starting
point for the doctrine of creation . . . was the mighty act of God in raising Jesus
Christ from the dead, for it was there that the absolute power of God over life and
death, over all being and non-being, was uniquely exhibited."[33] Frances M. Young
likewise points out that creation out of nothing "was not just a doctrine about the
world. It was doctrine about God. For it meant that God was no longer conceived
as ontologically intertwined with the world. . . . Nor was he simply the active principle in relation to the passive principle. God became independent of the world
as its sole *arche*, its 'sovereign' as well as its 'beginning.' Furthermore, God was not
subject to necessity but free, and that was a better and more biblical grounding
for his transcendence and impassibility than a mere adoption of Platonic axioms."
Indeed, it was the doctrine of creation out of nothing that finally forced the question about the Logos: Is "the Logos 'out of God' or 'out of nothing'?"[34]

H. Richard Niebuhr described the biblical reevaluation of the theological
metaphysics antecedent to the coming of Christ as "radical monotheism," that

is, the "assurance that because I am, I am valued, and because you are, you are
beloved . . . the confidence that whatever is, is good, because it exists as one
thing among the many that all have their origin and their being in the One—
the principle of being that is also the principle of value." Monotheism is "less
than radical," Niebuhr continued, "if it makes a distinction between the principle
of being and the principle of value; so that while all being is acknowledged as
absolutely dependent for existence on the One, only some beings are valued as
having worth for it; or if, speaking in religious language, the creator and the God
of grace are not identified."[35] But the God of grace is identified with the creator
God, if Christ is the Son of God, and by this *homoousios* distinguished from the
philosophical One as well as from the Gnostic Other.

In this connection, the canonical narrative from Genesis to Revelation tells
of a life-and-death struggle of the one true God for human allegiance against
idols that claim them and demons that enthrall. According to radical monotheism
one cannot love both the God of Moses and the God of Pharaoh, both God and
mammon. As Gerd Theissen explains: "The one and only God of the Bible is a
God of those who have escaped, of fugitives and exiles, the deported and prisoners of war. This God may not be detached from the stories about him: the stories
of the homeless Abraham, the fugitive Jacob, the enslaved Israelites in Egypt, the
oppressed tribes in the period of the judges. . . . If we detach him from this history, he soon becomes the God of the rulers."[36] Thus this first commandment of
God requires exclusive allegiance to the God "who brought you up out of the
land of Egypt, out of the house of bondage." Elijah demands that the people of
Israel choose whether they will serve Yahweh or Baal; they cannot have both, say,
Baal for nature and Yahweh for history, for it is Yahweh the liberator who makes
the rain to fall on the earth as well as kings to fall from their thrones. *The world
is not "nature" on which grace may dance as on a stage, but a history of salvation,
including "nature" as well. Nature too is historical, coming into being in an act of origin
and destined for a glorious redemption.* So Israel's radical monotheism projected its
experience of salvation by exodus from Egypt back upon the origination of the
cosmos, just as Torrance argued that creation out of nothing was exhibited by
the resurrection of Jesus from the dead.[37] Nor do the prophets allow the people
of Israel to perceive in the disasters of conquest and exile the defeat of a tribal
deity by enemy gods. Jeremiah, Ezekiel, and Second Isaiah all teach instead that
Yahweh, the only true God, had given over His own people for their faithlessness,
that yet again for the honor of His own name, Yahweh will redeem Israel. In the
same way, it is none other than His Father who hands Jesus over into the hands
of sinners and the power of darkness, who will on the third day raise Him again
from out of their grip. In the same way Paul the Apostle rejoiced over his Thes-
salonian converts who had "turned to God from idols, to serve a living and true
God, and to wait for his Son from heaven, whom he raised from the dead—Jesus,
who rescues us from the wrath that is coming" (1 Thess 1:9-10).

Therefore, no one can serve two masters. One can only love God with one's all, and accordingly be *converted* to a corresponding new life. This converted life rejects all coveting, since the Lord of nature generously provides for the life He creates. This converted life practices love of neighbor as oneself, since the Lord of history values all His creatures equally and providentially casts that needy other into one's path to love as oneself. Jesus tells the scribe who professes the double-love commandment, "You are not far from the kingdom of God!" (Mark 12:34). Ethically speaking, Jesus' proclamation of *the reign of God* tells that the Lord, the God of Israel, who commands what He wills, is about to give all that He commands, putting that First Commandment into universal and visible effect. In anticipation of that, Jesus' message requires the repentance of *conversion* in values, total trust, and new lives of discipleship. Theissen notes in this connection how the command of *exclusive allegiance* to Yahweh effects radical monotheism's critique not only of vulgar polytheism, but also of the "syncretistic monotheism" of Hellenistic Judaism and the "philosophical monotheism" of the Platonist school of the intertestamental times and following. Despite resemblance to biblical monotheism, Theissen stresses, these latter views lack the "radical call to *conversion*" that is ethically essential to the message of the biblical God. Indeed, their tendency is to regard "all the gods as identical and simply as a manifestation of one and the same deity. One could therefore be a philosophical monotheist, but in practice worship many gods and continue to practice what they required."[38] Unlike biblical monotheism, then, philosophical monotheism leaves the world as it is. That is the point. It is a justification of the present establishment of things. It is the theology of the world as it is, mystified as eternal, *Roma aeterna*, but in reality *civitas terrena*. Biblical monotheism is the theology of the world to come that has broken into the strong man's house. The gospel message of exclusive monotheism summons to *conversion*, to "crucifixion to the world" (Gal 6:14) and new life in the Spirit. "These people who have been turning the world upside down have come here also!" (Acts 17:6). But the divergence is even more profound than this.

Bear in mind Theissen's comment that "the God of the Bible may not be detached from the stories about him." The God of the Bible is truly God, not in being aloof from the world of time and space, but in being free for it, to participate in it, to overcome its resistance to His will and accomplish our ethical conversion from within its natural structures and historical processes that are themselves effects of His historical providence. This God is the God who cannot be detached from the name of, the story about, the flesh of Jesus Christ. God's own being *is* in this *coming* of Jesus, once for all in Galilee, but now wherever and whenever the Spirit pleases by the proclamation of the resurrection of the Crucified, through which God draws near to repentance and faith and at the same time withdraws from hearts that are far from Him. God *is coming*, who cannot be detached from the particular story of Jesus' sending, its collision with the antecedent world in the cross, Easter vindication, and final destiny. This particular story further indicates that God is not in the business of stabilizing the status quo ante, but rather in the business of "choosing what is foolish in the world to shame the wise; choosing what is weak in the world to shame the strong; choosing what is low and despised in the world, things that are not, to reduce to nothing things that are" (1 Cor 1:27-28).

Jesus' ministry of the reign of God provoked the acute question, as we noted in Mark 2, By what authority do You do these things? Who do You say that You are? Likewise, from Pentecost, the church's worship, mission, and common life together in Jesus' name raise the *same* question: Who or what is the God in whose name you gather, worship, baptize, evangelize? This *krisis* of episte-mology brought on by the resurrection of the Crucified consequently entails a revision of the antecedent metaphysics, if the legitimate concern of metaphysics is to articulate what ought to be loved above all by identifying what in truth concerns humanity ultimately. The early catholic church, as we are seeing, is answering: God is the Father who out of love sent His own Son, the Son who out of love gave Himself into the hands but also in the place of enemies, the Spirit of this Father of the Son let loose on the earth to make out of rebels beloved children, and so manifest already now in the reign of God. By 177, Athenagoras could ask with rhetorical flourish, "Who, then, would not be aston-ished to hear men who speak of God the Father, and of God the Son, and of the Holy Spirit, and who declare both their power in union and their distinction in order, called atheists?"[39] Despite the Platonic, subordinationist cast, here the Trinity is being articulated as the God of radical or exclusive monotheism, antic-ipating the *homoousios* of the Nicene Creed, since this God cannot be detached from the story of Jesus, not in His temporal economy, nor even in His eternal life.

Two Kinds of Monotheism: Divine Simplicity

What was the alternative in seeking a worthy conception of God? Let us undertake a generalized sketch of the theological thinking of so-called Middle Platonism.[40] By this time in history, Platonism had evolved from the body of Plato's writings[41] and elements of Stoicism. It was explicitly religious in ori-entation and well on the way to the Neoplatonism of Plotinus.[42] The wider context of this development was an age in which social and political life was sorely stressed by sweeping change. For intelligent people the old religion of the Olympic gods of Homer, the Delphic oracles, and the civic sacrifices[43] had lost its power to hold the world together, and became the object of philosophi-cal criticism as a new program seeking a religious alternative: "on the one hand, the critical attitude toward the traditional representations of the gods, and on the other, the development of a metaphysical system that is independent of the

Olympian pantheon."[44] Everything seemed adrift in a sea of change.[45] Lietzman characterizes the mind of this age this way: "the increased elevation of God above the present world and its material character, and, in connexion [sic] therewith, an inclination to fantastic developments of the conceptions of daemonic intermediate beings, conceptions already present in Plato; detailed discussion of the problem of divine providence and divine righteousness; the assertion of the immortality and personal responsibility of the soul; the doctrine of its share in the divine being; and occasional traces of a mystical tendency. Ethics are developed under Platonic influences: 'to become as similar as possible to God.' Allegorical exegesis was frequently employed"[46] to find a usable tradition in the old texts.

In this context, what philosophers experienced in the act of thinking was the power of the human mind to transcend bodily limitations of time and space, to ascend from the apparent and dubious world of becoming to contemplation of the eternal ideas that populate the realm of being. What a tremendous experience of power this must have been, what a source of religious awe! "The human mind as a part of the cosmic god: a revolutionary and fascinating thought."[47] In light of this intellectual act of self-transcendence, all reality divides into the intelligible and the sensible, so that spirit or mind whether of God or angels or humans inhabits one side of the divide and whatever is material lies on the other. Thus divine and human mind share in a common ontology, separated in degree but not by kind. How does the limited human mind, now imprisoned in a body, arise to God as pure Mind? If "essential reality develops though incremental layering, the essence of that reality should logically be uncovered by taking away the layers of sensible and intelligible attributes. The apophatic method was just such an epistemological tool. To arrive at the essential knowledge of any entity, including the Ultimate One—God, it was necessary to subtract, abstract or negate layered attributes until one arrived at its essence."[48] The so-called negative theology that thus emerges required in turn criticism of the poets' tales of the gods for representing the divine in an unfitting way under "layers of materiality." This task of demythologizing was begun by certain of the pre-Socratic philosophers, Heraclitus especially,[49] but Plato transformed it into a thoroughgoing program in book X of *The Republic.* Plato argued there that poetic imitation, exemplified in Homer, is at third remove from truth: a copy of a copy of a copy (artistic representation of a material object that has its form as copied from an eternal idea). Such confused and distorted representations depict the gods acting unjustly. But philosophy, gazing directly on the form of justice with the intellectual eye of the mind, sees that the "gods never neglect anyone who eagerly wishes to become just and who makes himself as much like a god as a human can by adopting a virtuous way of life."[50] This is the gravamen of Plato's rationally purified theology.

More generally, philosophical thought delivers the human mind from the thrall of this bewildering world of ever-transitory sense experience to discover and participate in its eternal, rational ground, the forms or ideas of things.

Sub specie aeternitatis, the philosopher perceives the necessity of things in the material world when she penetrates the appearances to grasp the essences of things and their necessary relations, thus glimpsing the ultimate harmony of the cosmos. Physical sensations and poetical imitations of them enslave the mind in the world of change and subject it to its flux. But rational contemplation of what is really real, above and beyond all change and becoming, exalts the thinker beyond this apparent world and satisfies the desire to understand why things must be as they are. In rational contemplation of purified concepts, the philosopher even may be said to participate in eternity, no longer a slave, tossed here and there by every new sense experience, without any knowledge of the abiding form of reality, not only suffering in the body but above all suffering the indignity of a confused mind enslaved to the affections and passions of the body. Human thought is thus akin to the divine, and through thought human beings become "most like God," under the assumption that God is eminently Mind, and God as Mind eminently exists, indeed exists most truly of all.[51]

Recall that "the biblical worldview divides reality into the uncreated and the created rather than the intelligible and the sensible,"[52] and recall as well that a theology that finds reality to be the good creation of God "from nothing" will incline to a kataphatic theology of God as the fullness of being capable of self-expression in created things in contrast to the apophatic theologian who tends ever more radically to think of God as beyond being (or even as nonbeing).[53] The grounds for a "confrontation" between the two monotheisms, tactically allied in the criticism of myth and polytheism, now become clear.[54] What is the price Platonism pays for its program of insatiable demythologizing? "Through Plato reality is made unreal in favour of an incorporeal, unchangeable other world that is to be regarded as primary. The ego is concentrated in an immortal soul that is alien to the body and captive to it. 'Flight from the world' is a watchword that actually occurs in Plato."[55] This "nihilism," as Nietzsche would judge it, is indeed a religious motive in Platonism, if not the whole story. More positively expressed, the goal now becomes "assimilation to god as far as possible" by an ascetically conceived virtuous way of life here and now, not just in the beyond.[56] The experience of freedom in thought by the philosopher still bound to the body was ascribed to God as Mind wholly and purely.[57] God is immaterial. God is not made of matter. The only other possibility is Mind. God is the pure act of thought, mind purely contemplating itself, existing simply in blissful self-satisfaction. God is the same forever effortlessly and by nature. It is divine nature to be in this effortless way utterly self-absorbed. Rightly so! Whatever else would or could attract God's eye? This philosophical conception of supreme, highest divine being as Mind was articulated by Aristotle: the "first unmoved mover is accordingly the first and most beautiful being; it moves because it is the goal of love and longing. . . . Grasped in thought, *noeton* is the highest form of being, incorporeal, pure actuality, *energeia.* Its actuality consists

in intellectual comprehension; thereby the object of this is identical to its performance: 'thinking of thinking,' *noesis neoseos* is the most blessed existence, the
highest origin of everything. 'This is the god.'"[58] God is ontologically simple.[59]

Does the Platonic program, as hinted, contain within it the seeds of its own
cancellation? Thinking that God is mind or even that God is existent or real,
a being, is still to think of God in objectifying ways, as a phenomenon of this
world and so not as truly simple. Historically it is a fact that negative theology
was driven by an insatiable quest to attain to "God beyond God"—beyond
being as well as becoming, beyond mind as well as matter—to the point where
God becomes indistinguishable from nothing. That is perhaps, as Robert Jenson argued in *God after God*, the real outcome in atheism of the historical
journey of negative theology through Western civilization, as we shall see in
the next chapter. There is, as we have argued, a proper use in revealed theology
for the notion of divine simplicity, just as there is a proper role for apophatic
reflection within a fundamentally kataphatic approach to theology. Here simplicity is taken as a rule for speech, not as an ontological insight (which would
be the reification of a negation). In that case, the rule serves to direct faith
to the unique and incomparable creator God and not even to the doctrinal
formulations by which He is identified. "Dogmas can—and indeed must—constitute the pointer terms for the *via negativa*" when the point of negative theological reflection is "to set down and clarify beliefs" by showing that beliefs are
about God, not themselves God. This critical reflection also protects against
any demand to "obeisance to formulas and those who authorize them."[60]

Likewise, the notion of divine nature as simple or immutable *in relation to*
the created world, and as such an attribute of the common nature possessed by
and distinctly energized in each of the internally related persons of the Trinity,
can and indeed may be utilized by revealed theology, if the appropriations are
taken seriously. Here simplicity is nothing but a concept for "the notions that
[God] is completely independent of and sovereign over all things"[61] as the
creator of all that is not God, and as such something that can never in all eternity be communicated to creatures. In other words, we are to arrive at a theological notion of divine simplicity of nature relatively, from the revelation of
God as eschatological creator, not by the attempts of the creature at self- and
world-transcendence. As *this* rule version of divine simplicity is derived from
knowledge of God as creator, and thus in relation to the contingent world of
creatures, it actually does not tell us anything about God's nature in itself.
We cannot come to Aristotle's thought of Mind thinking itself as if this were
an adequate insight into divine nature as *actus purus*. It only says that divine
life that gives life to all others is simple in relation to us who receive life.
Rather such simplicity is, in relation to itself, complex; it is the anticipated harmony of power, wisdom, and love that does not yet correspond to the world's

experience. This harmony is therefore believed, often in the face of crushing appearances to the contrary from within an unfulfilled, still groaning creation.

The foregoing reflection and differentiation are important, because in the philosophical sense of simplicity, God has no choice but to be self-identical; God's nature as simple causes God to exist in such and such a way that God cannot violate without ceasing to be God. But in the theological sense, simplicity indicates that God, manifesting true transcendence in being by becoming, that is, by freely deciding to create a world from infinite possibilities, is immutably faithful to this decision as to His own self-determination. Beyond that relative simplicity, there is a mysterious complexity that attends the divine life in coming to that free and self-involving decision to create, redeem, and fulfill a world. All this history of God is not an "automatic" expression of an intrinsically simple nature, but rather the divine counsel of the Trinity of persons to actualize in the history of salvation a conjunction of perfect power, wisdom, and love.

How by contrast is the Simple related to the world in philosophical monotheism? How is divine simplicity to be related to the visible world of matter, multiplicity, and change? There must be some relation, since the human mind can raise the question. This questioning presupposes some connection, some relation. Must not the rational soul that would flee to God also have come from God? How did this come about? Was it the tragic fall of which the Gnostics speak? If not, how can the cosmos be understood as the positive expression or emanation of the divine? The notion of God as pure Mind contemplating itself in eternal simplicity could suggest the further picture of God speaking His Mind, so to say, externalizing an immanent thought as a near replica, the Logos. This picture seemed to introduce dynamism into the conception of the deity. Yet attribution of self-reflection or self-consciousness to God was often felt to be too anthropomorphic, allowing an element of duality to threaten the philosophical idea of God's simplicity of being. A gap, so to say, emerges here that is never successfully resolved. In that case, God, strictly speaking, is and remains the pure act of being as self-contemplating Mind; the Logos of God is not strictly speaking God Himself, but a first copy or replica of God, oriented in the direction of the cosmos, a "second god." The Logos exists then as the mediator between the absolute God of pure being and the changing human world of becoming. This Logos lends law, order, and rationality to the world of becoming, and so is the link of human minds to the divine.

Interestingly, we can best illustrate the philosophical doctrine of the mediator Logos with a citation from the Alexandrian Jew Philo, a contemporary of Jesus and Paul, who influenced early Christian theology, especially in Alexandria. "And the Father who created the universe has given to his archangelic and most ancient Word a pre-eminent gift, to stand on the confines of both, and separate that which had been created from the creator. . . . And the Word [says], 'And I stood in the midst between the Lord and you,' neither being uncreated as God, nor yet created as you, but being in the midst between these two extremities, like a hostage, as it were, to both parties: a hostage to the creator, as a pledge and security that the whole race would never fly off and revolt entirely, choosing disorder rather than order, and to the creature, to lead it to entertain a confident hope that the merciful God would not overlook his own work."[62] This vivid depiction of the Logos links God and the human mind in the structure of the cosmos. Yet this Logos is expressly not the Creator, but a creature, the first angelic or mediating creature standing between the absolute, unchanging God and the human world of flux. Philo was the first to fuse the Logos of Middle Platonism with the *Dabar* and *Torah* of the Hebrew Scriptures and the late personification of God's wisdom, the *Sophia* of Proverbs 8. As the biblical Wisdom literature itself demonstrates, there is a legitimate interest of faith at work here, namely, the attempt to understand the universality of Israel's covenant God as creator of all,[63] or vice versa, the attempt to understand that all of reality is the creation of the one God of the Exodus and the covenant. Jews and Christians *had* to ask, as Pannenberg has rightly insisted, whether the acknowledged wisdom of the Greeks is not finally the wisdom that comes from the God of the Bible.[64] Precisely because of their belief in one God, Christians were required at least to wonder, as Justin Martyr following Philo actually claimed, whether "Christ is the First-Begotten of God, and . . . the Logos in which every race of man partakes. Those who lived in accordance with Logos [reason, law, wisdom] are Christians, even though there were called godless . . . such as Socrates and Heraclitus" (*1 Apol.* 46). For the God of Jesus Christ cannot be understood as the mere tribal deity of Christians but must be conceived as the one true God of all.

As justified in intention and as plausible as the ready identification of the one God of the Bible with the simplicity in being of the God of the philosophers seemed, the philosophical conception of mediation by the Logos serves a very definite but, from the biblical viewpoint, very false interest. One aspires to union with the God of philosophical monotheism in order to become indestructible as God is thought to be by removal from relationships with others and the world and indeed one's own body rather than by conversion and reformation of the world. The hope of philosophical theosis is not to become united with the God "who became flesh and dwelt among us" and through Him to be reconciled with others in a renewed creation in the "mystery" of its redemption: "We will not all die, but we will all *be changed*" (1 Cor 15:51, emphasis added). This latter is the purpose of that Logos who became flesh forever and ever in Jesus Christ. Strictly speaking, Philo's Jewish idea of the merciful Father who created the world and will not disregard it is also in tension with philosophical monotheism. It is a carryover from Philo's Jewish piety. To call the God who is God in pure self-contemplation "Father" is a curious honorific, too anthropomorphic by far to survive for long the dialectic of negative theology. The honorific is historically understandable. Hellenistic

Jews like Philo, and then Christians, found in Platonism an ally against popular religion, superstition, and the more sophisticated fatalisms of the Stoics and Gnostics, as well as an aid in making their own faith intelligible. With the help of allegorical exegesis, they were able to execute, as it seemed to them, a saving interpretation of the anthropomorphic depictions from their own Scriptures of a God who arbitrarily seemed to love this one and hate another, to grow wroth and sometimes even to repent.

The ambiguity of this alliance only became clear in the course of time, beginning with Origen of Alexandria who published the first *systematic theology* in Christian history, *On First Principles*,[65] around the year 225. By "systematic" theology one denotes the "construction of a coherent and organic whole," taking up the "doctrines handed down in the rule of faith" as *first principles* along the lines of an Aristotelian deductive science.[66] A theology that could strictly be designated "systematic," deriving its axioms from revelation, now replaces philosophy's uncertain speculations. Indeed, the new discipline of systematic theology thus fulfilled philosophy's aspiration for a system of thought unveiling the intelligibility of the world by reducing it to its true causes or first principles. This was Origen's project. In exemplary fashion *On First Principles* manifests the struggle between biblical and philosophical monotheism, that is, between a static, vertically oriented view of reality as a great chain of being that can be known a priori by intellectual analysis on the one side and the idea of reality as the history that is realizing God the creator's plan of salvation made known in the gospel of Christ. Origen tried to synthesize these two monotheisms by pouring the new wine from Scripture into the old wineskins of philosophy, an endeavor that brought the true conflict between the contending monotheisms into articulate awareness. For just that reason, Origen of Alexandria is of monumental significance. We will, however, first appreciate his great contribution to the development of trinitarian doctrine in the notion of the Father's eternal generation of the Son, a consideration that demonstrates his fundamentally orthodox intention (centuries later Origenism was condemned as heretical), however unsuccessful his synthesis must finally be judged.

Eternal Generation

Prior to Origen no one knew how to conceive of something derived or "begotten" as truly divine. To be begotten seemed to be an equivalent notion to being created, passive rather than active, product rather than production. It was Origen who worked out for future theology the crucial concept of the *eternal generation of the Son* from the Father's being. Citing from Rufinus's (somewhat suspect, but for our purposes serviceable) Latin edition of *On First Principles*:

> Can anyone who has learned to regard God with feelings of reverence suppose or believe that God the Father ever existed, even for a single moment,

without begetting this wisdom . . . ? [It] is absurd and impious, that is, either that God should advance from being unable to being able, or that, being able, he should act as if he were not and should delay to beget wisdom. Wherefore we recognize that God was always the Father of his only-begotten Son, who was born indeed of him and draws his being from him, but is yet without any beginnings. . . . [We could utter] impiety against the unbegotten Father himself, in denying that he was always a Father and that he begat the Word and possessed wisdom in all previous times and ages. . . . It is impious and shocking to regard God the Father in the begetting of his only-begotten Son and in the Son's subsistence as being similar to any human being or other animal in the act of begetting; but there must needs be some exceptional process, worthy of God, to which we can find no comparison whatever . . . how the unbegotten God becomes Father of the only-begotten Son. This is an eternal and everlasting begetting, as brightness is begotten from light. (FP I:2:2-4)

Notice in the passage how Origen combines thoughts previously considered mutually contradictory: apophatic immutability of the divine and simple substance of the deity qualifies the kataphatic Father's generation of the Son. In other words, just because God is immutable, Origen argued, God never began and never ceased to beget His own Son. "But I consider that there is no evening in God, nor any morning, but time coextensive, so to speak, with his unbegotten and eternal life, in which the Son was begotten."[67] Divine simplicity is used as a rule to qualify the notion of begetting and being begotten as an eternal and ineffable generation.

Origen here grasps something that had eluded earlier Christians, whose imaginations had been captured by the Middle Platonic metaphor of the divine Mind and its externalized replica, the Logos, as we saw in Philo and Justin. But Origen criticizes the "arbitrariness and lack of consideration of the many who, when so many names are attributed to him, pay attention only to the title 'Word,' without examining why the Son of God was ever recorded to be the Word of God in the beginning with the Father, through whom all things came into being."[68] Acutely, Origen has noticed that in the Bible the dominate gospel language for the relation of Jesus to God is the analogy of son to father, which language designates personal realities constituted by social relations, not processes of mental life like Mind and its external articulation or expression in Word. He realized accordingly that it is impossible to speak of an eternal Father without also speaking simultaneously of an eternal Son, since one becomes a father only in having offspring. If there is no eternal Son, there is also no eternal Father, hence the necessary implication of an eternal generation in the life of God. This was Origen's great discovery. Does this eternal dependency in being, however, make the Son inherently inferior? Is there ontological subordination in the divine life?

Origen's proper theological concern is to maintain the personal difference between the Father and Son; commenting on John 14:28, "The Father who sent me is greater than I," he expounds the difference this way: "We say that the Savior and the Holy Spirit transcend all generated beings, not by comparison, but by an absolute transcendence." Thus the Son and the Spirit are greater than creatures not by any measure of degrees of holiness or divinity, but differ in kind. Having said that, Origen immediately continues: but the Savior "is transcended as much and more by the Father, as he and the Holy Spirit transcend other beings."[69] The Father then would seem to be greater than the Son and Spirit, not by degree but in kind. In *Contra Celsum*,[70] Origen grants "that there may be some individuals among the multitudes of believers who are not in entire agreement with us, and who incautiously assert that the Savior is the Most High God." This is a reference to the popular modalism, which in its eagerness to say that Jesus is God, obliterates the equally biblical insistence that the Son is not the Father, nor is the Father the Son. Origen continues: "We would not therefore make Him who we call Father inferior—as Celsus [a Middle Platonist critic of Christianity] accuses us of doing—to the Son of God" (CC VIII, xiv:644). Origen here clearly affirms in some sense the Father's superiority in rank or sequence as a superiority also in being, a difference in kind. There is ontological subordination in the life of God.

Consequently, one might argue, as Schleiermacher influentially did two hundred years ago at the fonts of liberal Protestant theology, that the very notion of the Son's eternal generation is suspect of incoherence: "If it means anything at all [it] must at least indicate a relationship of dependence" so that, if "no relationship in which the Father stands to [the Son] can be adduced as a counterweight, undeniably the power of the Father is greater."[71] Indeed it is so, Schleiermacher alleged, drawing the bead squarely on "the idea of Origen, that the Father is God absolutely, while the Son and Spirit are God only by participation in the Divine Essence—an idea which is positively rejected by orthodox church teachers, but secretly underlies their whole procedure"[72] in following Origen's idea of eternal generation. The point of this cunning critique by the father of liberal Protestantism is not to correct Origen's ontological subordinationism in an Athanasian way, but rather to expose the orthodox teaching of the trinity of persons as something unseemly, unfitting, unworthy of divine simplicity: "When it became necessary to speak of a plurality or distinction in God, unconscious echoes of what is pagan could find their way in."[73] The insinuation is that Origen's strong distinctions between the persons is a relapse to pagan polytheism; in reality, as previously noted, Origen's insistence upon the real difference in person between Jesus and His Father is what is biblical, and the elimination of this difference in the name of monotheism is what is wittingly or unwittingly "pagan" metaphysics deriving from Plato and his theological followers. Schleiermacher's true target is the distinction of persons as something real in God.[74] This attack reflects

Schleiermacher's own Sabellian-modalist view[75] that the only matter of abiding interest in the misguided ecclesiastical doctrine of the Trinity is the christologi- cal need to "equate as definitely as possible the Divine Essence considered as thus united to human nature with the Divine Essence in itself,"[76] that is, to assure that in Jesus' human consciousness of God we meet God as a veritable cause meets a singular effect. The "main pivots" of the "being of God in Christ" and "in the Christian Church" through the Spirit are thus concluded to be "inde- pendent of the doctrine of the Trinity"[77] of persons.

The Sabellian, or monarchical-modalist, thought is of the transcendent God the Father as cause and Son and Spirit as God for us in temporal dispensations as effects. These latter are masks worn by the heavenly Father in this relation or that, but do not apply to God's relation to God. Origen in fact knew just this view and rejected it: "They suppose that the Son of God is a fatherly utter- ance expressed, as it were, in syllables, and so if we examine their position pre- cisely, it does not accord him a distinct existence and does not clearly define his essence. It is indeed impossible, at the outset, to understand how a word proclaimed can be a son. Let them proclaim to us as God the Word a word having its own life; either it is not distinguished from the Father, and for this reason does not have a distinct existence and so cannot be a son, or it is so dis- tinguished and is endowed with its own essence."[78] For Origen, the Son *exists* in His own right as a distinct person precisely in eternally deriving His divine nature or being from the Father, reflecting the definite order in God: *pater est fons divintatis* (the Father is the font of the deity). As the Father's person has its real eternal existence as the font of deity, so the Son's person has its real exis- tence as the One begotten of the Father. Consequently, in the gospel we meet not mere passing effects of God in time, but the eternally abiding personal agents of Jesus and His Father "as two, considered as persons or subsistences [though] one in unity of thought, in harmony and in identity of will" (CC VIII, xii:643-44). Origen's problematic subordinationism inadequately relates these truly distinct persons by conceiving of divinity as a property possessed by a substance, a quality properly belonging to the Father as the Absolute God, and shared in turn with the Son and Spirit. In spite of this remnant of unrevised Platonist metaphysics, it was Origen's great contribution biblically to insist on the real personal existence and thus true distinction of the Father and the Son. We meet these agents in the narrative of the resurrection of the Crucified and thus relate the two in terms of an eternal generation as the basis of their historical interaction in time. This development in doctrine aptly reflects the starting point of the gospel narrative in antidocetic Christology, that is, that the incarnate Son and His heavenly Father stand over against each other, so that their relation of mutual love is one mediated by the Spirit in the dramatic history culminating in the resurrection of the Crucified.

The problems of ontological subordinationism, however, were real. Origen's breakthrough in understanding the eternal generation of the Son continued to rely on the Platonic Logos scheme, since Origen knew no better way to conceive of the unity of the three than as three possessing a quality (for example, omnipotence) in descending levels.

> The God and Father, who holds the universe together, is superior to every being that exists, for he imparts to each one from his own existence that which each one is; the Son, being less than the Father, is superior to rational creatures alone (for he is second to the Father); the Holy Spirit is still less, and dwells within the saints alone. So that in this way the power of the Father is greater than that of the Son and of the Holy Spirit, and that of the Son is more than that of the Holy Spirit, and in turn the power of the Holy Spirit exceeds that of every other holy being. (I:3:5).

Notice in the above statement how the fatherhood of God is related, first of all, not to Jesus His Son, but to the universe, at the head of which the Father rules by virtue of a divine quality, omnipotence; thence in descending rank comes the Son who as Logos rules rational beings, and finally the Spirit whose work is restricted to the saints and other holy beings. We can wonder: How is the Spirit's rule in the saints anything additional to the Son's work? Origen is trying to fit the biblical data into a framework that ill supports it. "Using the Platonic scheme, Origen assigns the imperial Logos-Son the role of linking God and creation. For purposes of cosmology the Logos-Son was adequate. A second link between God and the cosmos fit only clumsily. . . . The Spirit is now a double for the Logos."[79] As in Middle Platonism, the cosmos, as it were, wants to be the third member of the triad. Origen's project founders on the internal contradiction of the two monotheisms that becomes visible just because of his attempt to synthesize them. But this also hints at what we shall see in conclusion: it is only the confession of the co-equal personhood of the Holy Spirit at Constantinople that breaks decisively with the Platonic scheme in the direction of Scripture's eschatological creation.

Origen wants to think *both* of the eternal relation of the Father and the Son that he learns about from the Gospel of John *and* of the absolute God related to the cosmos by the principle of Reason that he learns from Middle Platonism. Origen felt precisely this tension and opined that God has always had both, both His Son and His world. In philosophical monotheism, we may recall, the divine is *conceived as the supreme aspect of the all-embracing world order, or cosmos,* the whole system of being and becoming without beginning or end. Here God is not the free creator of a world other than Himself, but is represented in the element of divine intelligence within the world system over against chaotic rude matter, which is equally eternal. Within the cosmic system, God can only relate to the lower levels of being through a descending series of mediators: His Logos that is the rational order of the world, His Spirit that is the holy eros that moves the angels and prophets who are messengers to humankind, and finally the rational souls of human beings that ought likewise to rule over their material bodies as microcosms of the hierarchical world system. Salvation in this scheme will then tend to be understood essentially as law and order, the rule of the soul over the body, and the corresponding stabilization of the social hierarchy. The earthly is to order itself as a copy of the heavenly. To the extent that Christianity adopts this philosophical monotheism as its frame of thought, Jesus will be conceived as the definitive revelation of God's moral will, which is the same moral law as human reason naturally knows. Both in Jesus' teaching and by the dramatic example of His life, death, and resurrection, Jesus is taken as a divinely authorized moral model to follow. Jesus becomes a superior Socrates, or an effective Socrates, a "Socrates for the people." The gospel becomes monotheism and morality with a dash of holy eros, represented in pictorial form that is able to move the masses. Origen of Alexandria's unstable synthesis, contrary to his best intentions, allowed this possibility of understanding Christianity as "Platonism for the people" (Nietzsche). Arius and his followers would attempt radically to realize it in the name of the theological axiom of divine simplicity.

Systematic Theology as Systematic Apologetics

Yet we would do an injustice if we left matters there. Who was this man? Origen of Alexandria's life began and ended under the dark cloud of persecution. For the crime of being a Christian, his father was murdered by the Roman state when Origen was a boy of eleven years. At the end of his life, Origen was imprisoned and tortured for a period of three years for the same crime as his father. Though he survived the imprisonment, his health was broken and he died shortly after his release. One of the most stirring of his voluminous writings was *Exhortation to Martyrdom*, written to inspire courage in confessing Jesus as Lord when unanticipated persecution suddenly fell upon the church: "We know that, since we have been persuaded by Jesus to abandon idols and polytheism which is really atheism, the Enemy [the devil] cannot persuade us to accept idolatry; but he tries to force it upon us . . . to make either martyrs or idolaters of [us]."[80] But "to those [of us] who are beheaded for the sake of Jesus, let us confess the Son of God before men and that the gods are not gods. He who will have had witness borne to Him, will in return bear witness to us before God and His Father."[81] Origen's passionate, personal loyalty to Jesus, the Scriptures and the church, indeed to the creedal "rule of faith,"[82] is beyond doubt. He suffered as a confessor of the faith. The theology of the martyrs was latent in his work.

In spite of that, we can feel the exuberant mood of third-century Christianity. The persecution Origen endured at the end of his life was one of the last, desperate outbursts of reactionary paganism. Throughout Origen's theological career, Christianity was becoming a success in the world.[83] The witness of the martyrs had exposed the weakness of power. The moral reform of personal life, which the philosophers demanded but never accomplished on a mass scale, was becoming reality in mass conversions to the faith and in the new lives of ascetic discipline that converts embraced. The unity that the state tried to impose on diverse peoples was being freely embraced and expressed in the worldwide *ecclesia catholica*. The Gnostic temptation to world-denial was fading. Alongside Christianity's rise, the Neoplatonic affirmation of the ultimate harmony of the cosmic system was becoming attractive. The confident mood of optimism accordingly is palpable in Origen; he intuited that Christianity, begun as a tiny persecuted sect only two hundred years before, was on the threshold of conquering his world, as indeed it was.

At the end of his great apologetic work, *Contra Celsum*, Origen thus taunted his pagan contemporaries, writing that "even the barbarians, when they yield obedience to the word of God, will become most obedient to the law, and most humane; and every form of worship will be destroyed except the religion of Christ, which will alone prevail. And indeed it will one day triumph, as its principles take possession of the minds of men more and more every day" (VIII, lxviii:666). Even the negative fact of the suffering of the martyrs fits into an overall optimistic picture of the progress of the human race: since it was "the purpose of God that the nations should receive the benefits of Christ's teaching, [providence] has extended day by day the Christian religion, so that it is now preached everywhere with boldness, and that in spite of numerous obstacles that oppose the spread of Christ's teaching in the world. . . . All the devices of men against Christians have been brought to naught; for the more that kings, and rulers, and peoples have persecuted them everywhere, the more have they increased in numbers and grown in strength" (VII, xxvi:621).

Now that Christianity was winning the world, however, the question arose: How shall it lead? How shall it positively evaluate the world that it is on the verge of winning and direct it for better? How shall it integrate the theology of the philosophers with the theology of the martyrs? Origen's systematic theology anticipated the victory of Christianity that would now take over the function of philosophy, with first principles based on Scripture rather than uncertain speculations of reason. Origen pioneered this endeavor and in the process gained stature as the intellectual giant of his day. In the process, he won respectability for Christianity among the intelligentsia of the third century. Whereas the second-century apologists like Justin were on the defensive, Origen has passed to the offensive. *Contra Celsum* is a massive work, not easily summarized. Celsus was a pagan, Platonist writer[84] of the second century, who was evidently acquainted with the writings of Justin Martyr, for he wrote his attack on Christianity as a refutation of Justin.[85] "How could God be said to have made the world? Was the Christian doctrine of creation breaching God's transcendence and making God directly responsible for the evil inherent in materiality?"[86] Watson concluded his interpretation with the words: "Celsus had been trying to protect the transcendence of God [as Mind, not as creator] by insisting on intermediaries since it is not fitting for God to be too closely involved in the making of the universe." Citing Trigg, Watson concurs: "Although he embraced cultic polytheism, Celsus was arguably a more consistent monotheist than Origen, who considered the Logos a second God. Celsus reconciled philosophical monotheism to traditional pagan polytheism by identifying the pagan gods with the daemons of Platonism."[87]

Several generations later, Origin took up Celsus's attack and responded to it. In refuting Celsus, Origen articulated his Platonized Christianity of monotheism and morality. Celsus had defended traditional pagan worship against Justin's criticisms and recommended "divinely inspired poets, as [Celsus] calls them, and wise men and philosophers." Consider how Origen responds to this challenge:

> Whether Orpheus, Parmenides, Empedocles, or even Homer himself, and Hesiod, are the persons whom he means by "inspired poets," let any one show how those who follow their guidance walk in a better way, or lead a more excellent life, than those who, being taught in the school of Jesus Christ, have rejected all images and statues, and even all Jewish superstition, that they may look upward through the Word of God to the one God, who is the Father of the Word. . . . Such indeed was the abounding love that [the Logos] had for men, that He gave to the more learned a theology capable of raising the soul far above all earthly things; while with no less consideration, He comes down to the weaker capacities of the ignorant men, of simple women, of slaves, and in short, of all those who from Jesus alone could have received that help for the better regulation of their lives that is supplied by His instructions in regard to the Divine Being, adapted to their wants and capabilities. (VII, xli)

All the features of Platonized Christianity are evident in this citation: the understanding of salvation as moral improvement and of the church as a "school"; the understanding of idolatry not as expressing carnal self-reliance but rather as devotion to materialistic images, that is, idols taken as misleading earthly copies of transcendent realities; the subordination of the Logos to the supreme God whom He represents to humanity and to whom He leads humanity; the dualism of the learned, who rise up to rational theology, and simple believers who listen literally to Bible stories; and so on. Origen, it seems, defends Christianity against the criticisms of the Platonist Celsus by transforming Christianity itself into "Platonism for the people!"

This apologetic aspect of Origen's complex thought will have important effects for the future. One is christological. Origen tried to defend Christianity against Celsus's criticism that it is absurd to think that the "Christ of God should suffer things most base and dishonorable." Origen quotes Celsus, who wrote, "But pray, if the prophets foretold that that the great God . . . would become a slave, or become sick, or die, would there be therefore any necessity that God should die, or suffer sickness, or become a slave, simply because such things have been foretold? We need not therefore inquire whether a thing has been predicted or not, but whether the thing is honorable or not, and worthy of God. . . . How then can the pious mind admit that those things that are said to have happened to [Christ], could have happened to one who is God?" (VII, xiv). The inadequate answer Origen gives to this question, which would have negative implications for centuries to come, was *to separate if not quite divide the two natures of Christ.* "Of this [divine] Being and His nature we must judge and reason in a way quite different from that in which we judge of the man who was seen in Jesus Christ" (VII, xvi). According to Origen, Celsus falsely supposes that Christians teach that "it is the body of Jesus extended on the cross and slain which we call God rather than his divine nature, that it was as God that Jesus was crucified and slain" (VIII, xlii). But this supposition of Celsus, according to Origen, is erroneous. Jesus suffered, he emphasizes, as a man (that is, as a physical body), not as God. At the same time, Origen emphasizes that as God, Jesus never felt any fear or doubt or confusion (that is, in that the Logos dominates Jesus' soul, if not replaces it). In this way the gospel's rhetorical paradox—recall Ignatius's "the impassible became passible"—is rationalistically explained away and robbed of its power as parable of the becoming of God in His coming to us. In less apologetic works,[88] Origen could find his way back to a kind unity of person, not "two such figures, but one," in that the "soul [of Jesus] is blended with the Holy Spirit"; yet he also regards this kind of unity not as christologically unique to Jesus, but as exemplary in Jesus and as such possible "for each of those who are saved"[89] in accordance with a moralistic-ascetic idea of salvation as progressive divinization. Origen thus reasons christologically in a way that at once anticipates Apollinarius (for whom the Logos replaced Jesus' human soul) and Nestorius (who could not unite the divine and human natures into one concrete, personal reality). These christological problems return with a vengeance in the period between 381 and 451 (but fall outside the scope of this study).

For this very reason Origen's unstable synthesis, or more precisely the Origenism of his latter-day disciples, had eventually to be condemned as heresy with the unhappy result that many of his works were destroyed or lost. To judge Origen personally as a heretic would be a terrible injustice; he felt himself and truly was loyal to the theology of the martyrs. Nevertheless, his attempt to integrate the Neoplatonic philosophy that was emerging in his optimistic age to the Christian message ended, as often is the case, with the tail wagging the dog. Not only did that eventually create the christological problems just mentioned.

The underlying issue is the question put by Celsus about the essence of God: What makes God God? How do we decide among candidates for deity which is truly or really God? What attributes are divine? What is worthy or fitting to say about God? The question is a good one, even if Origen all too uncritically took over the Platonic answer of negative or apophatic theology as though it provided some kind of positive insight rather than being a confession of ignorance and rule for reverent speech. But without further ado, Origen enunciates: "The great God is in essence simple, invisible, and incorporeal, Himself pure intelligence, or something transcending intelligence and existence . . . apprehended by no other means than through the intelligence that is formed in His image" (CC VII, xxxviii). The intellectualist bias in this passage is as evident as it is self-deceived. What is an essence transcending intelligence and existence yet something to be apprehended by no other means than intelligence? It is really nothing but a confession: I do not know what God is. God's essential being is here conceived by means of so-called "alpha-privatives," that is, negations of whatever belongs to the order of space and time: *not* multiple, *not* visible, *not* bodily, *not* mixed with matter, *yet* somehow thought to be akin to intelligence in the way mortals are intelligent. But why should intelligence prove the exception to these negations? Or why should conceptions of the divine as Not Anything prove any less anthropomorphic than sensual images? Aren't they, as in Nietzsche's withering criticism, just all-too-human expressions of world-weary alienation, the ascetic reification of nihilism?

On this question philosophical and biblical monotheism diverge subtly, though with immense consequence. Against the iconoclast whose real source lies in the Platonic traditions of philosophical monotheism and divine simplicity, Luther instructs Karlstadt first to remove the idol of the heart that is trust in one's own works rather than trust in God's care.[90] The God whose care can be known and is worthy of trust is the One ontologically Other as creator *ex nihilo*. Yet this God is God in such a way that the being or nature of God in the trinitarian conjunction of power, wisdom, and love is truly if not yet exhaustively expressed in space and time as the being of God for us in Jesus Christ. *The attributes of the divine as creator in relation to all that is not God are not negations of the creation but the conditions of its possibility as eschatological creation, for they are the eternal properties of the Father and the Son in the unity of the Spirit*, that is, the power, wisdom, and love harmoniously enacted in the life, death, resurrection, and destiny of Jesus Christ. As Jüngel puts the anti-Platonic point in an exposition of Karl Barth's new appropriation of the doctrine of the Trinity: "If revelation as God's being-for-us is to be taken seriously, then in Jesus Christ God's being *must* become visible and *be able* to become visible."[91] God's self-objectification is not then itself subject to Celsus's objection that it too is an *idolatrous* contradiction of God's simplicity of being, for as self-revelation it *is* the *iconic moment* of the eternal movement of the event of God's triune being: iconic, not idolatrous, in that it now comes to be and to act in space and time as savior of the helpless. But what is God's "being able," this potency, this power of the All-Powerful to become visible, objectified, even crucified in order to save? One might better speak in Christian theology of *divine complexity*!

For philosophical monotheism, what makes God God is that God is simply and solely unoriginate, pure actuality without any unactualized possibilities but perfectly that which it is, without origin or goal, underived from any other source but itself the source of all other being. As Paul Tillich influentially argued this case in the recent past, God is not a being among beings, but Being itself, the power of being in all that exists: "God is his own fate; he is 'by himself'; he possesses 'aseity.'" What makes God God is such unoriginate being, taken as absolutely simple, thus as absolutely stable and self-identical and so imperishable, *das Unbedingt* (the Unconditioned). God as such is to be thought of as "ground" of being and as such the "power" of being to resist nonbeing at work in all other existences. Yet, as Tillich forthrightly drew the implication, this means that "grave difficulties attend the attempt to speak of God as existing," since this "makes God a being whose existence does not fulfill his essential possibilities . . . [as] in everything finite. God ceases to be God, the ground."[92] For this reason the apophatic God can only be a "concrete" concern for us by virtue of the "structure of being," that is, by Tillich's equivalent of the Logos-mediator in the scheme of classical Platonism. "God must be approached cognitively through the structural elements of being-itself. These elements make him a living God, a God who can be man's concrete concern." Since we can predicate nothing concrete from the realm of finite existence to being-itself, it is the mediating structure of being that "enables us to use symbols which we are certain point to the ground of reality." This symbolization is possible, since per the great chain of being, the "symbol participates in the reality of that for which it stands."[93] Jesus as the Christ is such a symbol of the Logos, which is Being itself in its meaningful structuring of reality, the power of ordering chaos and so resisting nonbeing. So Jesus as a symbol is a symbol of a symbol that is the ultimate reality symbolizing itself.

Tillich was to an extent justified in these seemingly audacious claims. He joined dialectically in the atheistic protest against nineteenth-century liberal Protestantism: "God became a 'person' only in the nineteenth century, in connection with the Kantian separation of nature ruled by physical law from personality ruled by moral law. Ordinary theism has made God a heavenly, completely perfect person who resides above the world and mankind. The protest of atheism against such a highest person is correct."[94] Interestingly, Trinitarianism could share in this "atheistic" critique of Schleiermacher's unitarianism of the First Article, if it could appropriate Luther's tension between *deus absconditus* (God hidden in the course of nature and history) and *deus revelatus* (God revealed in the gospel narrative of Christ, taken as promise of inclusion in the Beloved Community, which the Trinity antecedently is). Rather more resembling Origen's (and Schleiermacher's!) systematic apologetics, however, that is not the solution Tillich sought. If we think that God is God as simply and solely unoriginate, and regard this as the bedrock intuition of natural piety clarified into a theological insight, we can never think that God the Father essentially and eternally begets His own true Son. Tillich indeed regarded the strictly trinitarian notion, even taken as symbol, as blasphemous. "The one thing God cannot do is cease to be God," either eternally in begetting the Son, or in time by the free act of the creation of a world, let alone by the incarnation of the only-begotten God. In this immediate connection, Tillich again forthrightly drew a daunting conclusion: "It is meaningless to ask whether creation is a necessary or contingent act of God."[95] It is meaningless because any God who would be capable of a free decision, hence also capable of time and space, would cease to be God as the ground of time and space.

This discussion of an influential contemporary theologian in Origen's tradition of Christian Platonism indicates that the issue between it and the renewal today of classical Trinitarianism following Karl Barth is the root idea of God as essentially unoriginate and simple. For Platonism, God *is not* His Word, but is represented by it, the "symbol" arising as an expression of the experience of grounding. For biblical faith, God *is* His Word, the Father who eternally generates the Son and in time sends Him to become a participant in the creature's world in order to bring the world of creatures forward to God's eternal kingdom. Of course, for biblical faith also God is eternal, but eternity is likewise understood quite differently than in the Platonic tradition: eternity is the final victory of the reign of God; God's own eternity is the project God freely undertakes and realizes in the creation, redemption, and fulfillment of the world. The One who is eternal does not stand impassively still, ultimately unknown above time at the top of the chain of being (or, as Tillich prefers, beneath it as its ground), nor remain like an engineer at the beginning who once set things in motion but then left them to themselves. The One who is eternal shouts with victory at the fulfillment of history, *Behold, I make all things new!* Eternity in biblical faith is the gospel victory of the reign of God, the accomplishment of the *future* that God has willed from the beginning for His creation in redemption and fulfillment. Eternity is the eschatological creation. God is not merely, then, certainly not exclusively to be thought of as the originative principle of all things, but as the true creator of time and space and all therein. God is the One who will show Himself to have been the all-determining reality at the culmination of eschatological creation (Rom 8). God demonstrates God's deity by the coming of His kingdom, the consummate act of new creation, the resurrection of the dead—this demonstration is what eternity is. The final word about God is not silence before empty transcendence, but the creaturely echo of the word of God, who makes all things new. Eternity is the concrete infinity of the love revealed in the Father and the Son by the Holy Spirit. So the church rightly sighs and sings: "Finish then thy new creation, pure and spotless let us be; let us see thy great salvation, perfectly restored in thee! Changed from glory into glory, till in heav'n we take our place, till we cast our crowns before thee, lost in wonder, love and praise!"[96]

The early Pannenberg impressively noted this differentiation: The "biblical God is indeed also the origin of present reality, but the manner and way in which he is this is already decisively determined by the fact that his essence is not exhausted in this function. God, as the origin, is never merely the invisible ground of present reality, but the free, creative source of the ever new and unforeseen. This essential characteristic of the creator and of his historical acts is unambiguously revealed for the first time by the resurrection."[97] The theological concept of God's eternity is thus to be gained by means of reflection on the promise of God narrated in the resurrection of the Crucified, which, as previously noted, entails conversion to a new life of faith based on it, not simply resistance to nonbeing. It is in this light that the idea of the eternal generation of the Word is intelligible and apt, because the God of the resurrection, who can and does grant a share to the dead of His own eternal life, must be conceived as essentially out-reaching and self-communicative. God *is* His Word, God *is* His Spirit, and just so God is infinitely able to share divine life with creatures in, as it were, the project of an *achieved* or *realized* eternity that is not *simply* (but rather *complexly*) identical to what God had ever been.

It is, once again, the ambiguous notion of simplicity that is at fault here, as if it can actually tell us something about God, so that we have to think of God as already fully actualized and just so recognized and valued as God. But "simplicity" in kataphatic theology can only mean that in relation to us God is freely but just so immutably self-determined to have mercy on all as the end for which the world was created. It tells us nothing about what possibilities for divine existence God rejects or reserves, only that the One who has infinite possibilities freely though wisely and justly uses them, as befits true God, to fulfill His sovereign purpose. The basis of this self-determination of God to share His life with creatures as a free act of love, as we have seen in Irenaeus and Jüngel, lies in the antecedent, not eschatological but protological eternity of the Trinity. There was a time before time, the divine time of the Trinity coming to the eternal decision and decree to create, redeem, and fulfill the world, just as there will be a time after time of the achieved eternity of the kingdom. Put otherwise, as Torrance rightly parses the matter,[98] God was not always creator (as Tillich teaches in his own diminished sense of creativity as grounding), but God was always Father of His own Son and Breather of His own Spirit, such that their "counsel," the Irenaean *oikonomia*, designates the "baffling and astonishing" (Torrance) self-determination of God *to become* our God through the history of this world, not any another.

Returning now to Origen, who tried to synthesize two contradictory ideas of the Logos, one being the communicative self-expression of the free creator of the world and the other being the rational order of the eternal cosmic system. He made this attempt at synthesis by positing the eternity of creation. God eternally begets His Logos, said Origen on the one hand, for the God of the Bible cannot be without His own self-communicative Word. Nevertheless, this Logos is the second, subordinate deity by which God, as through a mediator, forms and governs the world, keeping His distance. Both conceptions are true, Origen thought, in that God has never not had a creation. Creation then is as eternal as is the Creator. Not this visible world of matter, to be sure, which Origen speculated, was subsequently created as a repository and purgatory for spirits fallen from a first, celestial creation. In any event, God eternally begets the Logos, because God eternally creates a world for which He needs the Logos as intermediary. How could we imagine the God of the Bible, Origen asks, ever having been idle? without a creation? in some time before time? The system of God, Logos, and world must always have been and so always will be. Origen also speculates that when this present world cycle is finished, God will start it all over again.

Positing an eternal creation this way, Origen lost something of critical importance to biblical faith, as Augustine discerned. When the sense of the uniqueness of unrepeatable history is obscured, the radical distinction between God and human being as between creator and creature is also being blurred. The Logos as a mediating being can exist, so to speak, in the ambiguous zone between creator and creature, God to us but creature to God. The Holy Spirit is in reality superfluous since the cosmic system of God, Logos, and world endures forever through all apparent permutations. What is lost in this is the painful burden of the uniqueness or singularity of events, and so the ethical urgency of historical time-and-space as creation, that is, what Josiah Royce once called "the hell of the irrevocable"[99] that appears when the history of this natural world is taken as the sole field of the human encounter with God. Origen's optimism comes at the price of mitigating the decisiveness of history. At the end of long purgatory, as Origen imagines, universal *apokatastasis* forgives all and forgets all—and then the whole damn thing starts all over again. The whole tragicomedy with African slave trade and Christians thrown to the lions and the Holocaust of the European Jews recurs once again, only to be forgotten and forgiven and repeated ad infinitum. It is true that such speculations were cautiously entertained by the historical Origen and never pronounced as his definite teaching. But we see in the later developments of this impulse why Origenism, as a doctrine of salvation, had eventually to be rejected as a heresy. [100]

In Origen's own lifetime and immediately thereafter, however, his theological synthesis won the mind of the church because it mitigated the conflict between the gospel and Platonism on the cusp of Christianity's cultural establishment. Origen had reconciled Athens and Jerusalem. He had pointed the way in which Christianity could inherit Hellenistic civilization, reform it, and renew it. Every self-respecting Eastern Christian thinker for the next several generations was an Origenist. So in the decades following Origen's death, Origenism became the standard theology of the Eastern church. It was an ambiguous mélange of philosophical monotheism, allegorical exegesis of the Bible, the legacy of the martyrs transformed into ascetic moralism and the political triumph of the church, a system of thought at once claiming to fulfill philosophy and at the same time newly framing its questions and inquiry on the basis of Platonic traditions of thought. Jesus now appeared as the One who revealed God's will and demonstrated obedience to it, the pioneer blazing a trail to follow. Arius then asked fairly enough: Isn't Jesus a creature like us, such that we can imitate? However else could He help us?

Arius as Consistent Platonist

In the light of the foregoing, a *consistent* Platonism would be one that eliminates the gospel's critique of epistemology and revision of metaphysics in favor of a consistent interpretation of the gospel within its own conceptual framework.[101] Origen's synthesis from this perspective was ambiguous.[102] It could be developed in either direction. "Eternal generation" can and did lead on to the doctrine of the Trinity. The absoluteness of God the Father could and did lead to Arianism. In the period immediately following Origen, two controversies occurred that foreshadowed these developments. The first involved Origen's pupil and successor at the Catechetical School in Alexandria, Dionysius, who became that city's bishop in 247 until his death in 264. He became involved in controversy with a group of "Sabellians" in Libya, who taught "that there was only one God, that He had appeared on earth physically in Jesus Christ."[103] In the desire to say that Jesus is God, these Sabellians ignored the personal difference between Jesus and His Father. Against this modalism, Dionysius defended the idea of the unique personal reality of the Logos, that "the Son of God was not identical with the Father, but was another being [*hypostasis*] as different from the Father as the vine from the vine-dresser, as the boat from the boat builder."[104] With these admittedly "clumsy metaphors of vine and boat," Dionysios defended the personal reality of the Logos, albeit at the apparent cost of depicting Him as a creature. As a result of this controversy, the word *hypostasis* became associated with extreme and consistent subordinationism. It is interesting to note that almost one hundred years later, the Arians appealed to Dionysius's theology to justify their own doctrine that the Logos is a creature. Athanasius tried to defend Dionysius (who in fact modified his teaching and corrected his polemical overstatement that the Logos was a "creature"). But Basil the Great's comment is probably more incisive:

I do not admire everything that is written [by Dionysius]; indeed of some things I totally disapprove. For it may be, that of the impiety of which we are now hearing so much, I mean the Anomeon [radical Arianism of Eunomius, which says the Logos is positively unlike the Father], it is he, as far as I know, who first gave men the seeds. I do not trace his so doing to any mental depravity, but only to his earnest desire to resist Sabellius. . . . He is carried away unawares by this zeal into the opposite error. . . . He is not satisfied with laying down a difference of hypostases, but must needs assert also a difference of substance, diminution of power, and variableness of glory. . . . [Dionysius is found] to be disloyal to the homoousios, because of his opponent who made a bad use of it to the destruction of the hypostases. . . . Besides this, he uttered very unbecoming words about the Spirit, separating Him from the Godhead, the object of worship, and assigning Him an inferior rank with created and subordinated nature.[105]

In Basil's analysis we find beautifully expressed the Scylla and Charybdis of modalism and subordinationism through which trinitarian theology has to pass. It is important to grasp that neither error is somehow more philosophical or less biblical than the other. Both err in thinking that God as such cannot be internally differentiated, though they make this error in different ways. Modalism says that the persons are not eternal, only temporal manifestations of an eternally undifferentiated deity that stands behind these temporary masks donned in time and space. Subordinationism says that only the Father is truly eternal, and the Son and the Spirit are personally real only in the sense that any creature has come into being and is thus individuated.

The most sophisticated form of modalism is connected with the name of Paul of Samosota, who became the bishop of Antioch in 260. In the name of a more "biblical theology," he attacked Origenism and further developed the logical implications of modalism. He taught that as a uniquely created man through the virgin birth by the power of the Holy Spirit, Jesus is the Son of God, that is, "Son of God" is a human, not a divine, title. Thus the divine Logos is not by nature the Son of God, "but dwelt and operated in this Son of God [the Virgin-born Jesus] as if in a temple, the Logos appearing as another being clearly distinct from the man, Jesus Christ . . . revealed with the highest degree of fullness in Jesus."[106] By the same token, Paul of Samosota did "not regard this Logos . . . as an independent person . . . but as a form of God's operation, a manifestation of His being; in short, not a self-subsistent being (*ousia*) to be separated from God, but rather 'one in essence,' that is, *homoousios*."[107] Paul's teaching was rejected with horror. Here there is no real trinity of being, only a threefold revelation: "The Logos had no independent personality, but was only a term for a divine mode of activity [and] the way in which he dwelt in the man Jesus. Christ could only be conceived, on closer inspection, as a kind of exalted inspiration."[108] Paul loses both the Trinity in theology and the unity of person in Christology. As a consequence of this controversy, the term *homoousios* became associated with modalism, just as *hypostasis* had been with subordinationism. Both of the key terms in later Nicene theology thus entered the fourth century bearing the stigma of heresy.

These controversies form the immediate background of the Arian controversy. With the conversion of Constantine in 312, the persecution of Christians was banned. That dark cloud lifting, the inevitable but heretofore suppressed confrontation between the biblical and philosophical monotheism finally erupted into the open. It happened in the year 318 in Alexandria. Arius, formed by the Antiochene tradition (Paul of Samosota was bishop of Antioch), grew impatient like Paul before him with the zone of ambiguity Origenism threw around the Logos. Rightly invoking the biblical distinction between the Creator and the creature, Arius declared, "There was a time when the Logos was not." Not in earthly time, but in God's time, at some point in eternity the Logos was generated. Strictly speaking, it follows that the Logos is a creature, made out of nothing, who came into being. Only God the Father is unoriginate (*agenetos*). Whatever is begotten (*gennetos*) has a derived, originated existence. Thus the Logos, as *gennetos* (born, begotten), is something made (*genetos*, originated), a creature (see the discussion in Athanasius, *Against the Arians*, IV:149), not God, creator (*agenetos*). So against Origen's zone of ambiguity erected in the idea of eternal creation, Arius reiterates the sharp biblical distinction between creator and creature, denying the eternity of the world by which Origen tried to synthesize the two monotheisms, thinking of the eternal Son along with eternal world.

Arius publicized his doctrine with its plausibly biblical basis in rigorous creation theology in a popular poem, the *Thalia*, which according to Athanasius's report in *De Synodis* reads in part as follows:

> God Himself then, in His own nature, is ineffable to all men. Equal or like Himself, He alone has none. . . . Ingenerate (*agenetos*) we call Him, because of Him [that is, Christ, the Son] who is generate (*gennethentos*) by nature. We praise Him as without beginning because of Him who has a beginning. And adore Him as everlasting, because of Him who in time has come to be. The Unbegun made the Son a beginning of things originated; and advanced Him as a Son to Himself by adoption. He has nothing proper to God in proper subsistence (*hypostasis*). For He is not equal, no, not one in essence (*homoousios*) with Him. . . . There is full proof that God is invisible to all beings; both to things which are through the Son, and to the Son He is invisible. . . . There is a Triad, not in equal glories. Not intermingling with each other are their subsistences (*hypostases*). . . . Foreign from the Son in essence is the Father, for He is without beginning. Understand that

the Monad was; but the Dyad was not, before it was in existence. . . . It follows at once that, though the Son was not, the Father was God. . . . At God's will the Son is what and whatsoever He is. . . . To speak in brief, God is ineffable to His Son. For He is to Himself what He is, that is, unspeakable . . . for it is impossible for [the Son] to investigate the Father, who is by Himself. For the Son does not know [even] His own essence, for being Son, He really existed at the will of the Father. . . . It is plain that for that which has a beginning to conceive how the Unbegun is, or to grasp the idea, is impossible.[109]

"Polytheism has prevailed. Our opponents own a great God and a small God." So Basil the Great later characterized the teaching of the *Thalia* (Letter 243). Despite the correct biblical distinction of creator and creature he drew, Arius wished still to value Jesus *as if* God, God *for us* though not God to God as eternal Son to eternal Father.

Arius had indeed seen through Origen's false solution in the supposition of an eternal creation. Even if we grant that creation is eternal, the Logos would still be, strictly speaking, nothing but an eternal creature. The only possibility besides the divine, unoriginated existence is creation out of nothing. On the one side, Arius argues, it is not possible to imagine that God generates the Logos *from His own being.* That notion would introduce becoming and plurality into God's simple, self-identical nature or substance, which is impossible since it contradicts the axiomatic idea of God as unoriginate source of all else that is not God. Anything that is originated, in turn, cannot be true God. Since the Logos cannot derive from God's being, the Logos must derive from an act of God's will commanding something to arise out of nothing. So with rationalistic consistency, what reappears in Arius, even though under the veneer of the biblical theology of creation, is the by now familiar scheme of Middle Platonism. It moves under the ensuing pressure of the controversy, as we shall see, more and more in the direction of thoroughgoing apophatism. Arius in any case seems to think that God the Unorignate was always rational. When God decided to create the world, He made as His first creature an image of His own rationality, and gave to this being, the Logos, the actual work of calling forth the world and ordering it. The Logos is the mediator between mind and matter, being and becoming, spirit and flesh, ideal and real, the divine and the mortal. Therefore the Logos, eternal or not, is a creature. He is made, not begotten, out of nothing, not of the being of the Father. Thus Arius denied that the Son could be of the same being (*homoousios*) of the Father.

Are there profounder reasons why Arius denied this? Some revisionist historians have argued that Arius was motivated not by philosophical rationalism but by a soteriological interest. Arius was "insisting that the Son was Son by grace and obedience on the grounds that our salvation depended on his identity with us" in terms of coping with the same creaturely limitations of "willing, choosing, striving, suffering, advancing."[110] The objection to the *homoousios* then is that if the Logos is wholly divine, the victory of His life in the flesh is secured in advance, and would thus be without any force as an example or model for us. If a divine Logos is understood, it is impossible for the Logos Incarnate seriously to be tested and tried. The thesis seems plausible historically. But even if we granted such a soteriological motive in early Arianism, it would not meet the theological countercriticism that thinking of Jesus' soteriological meaning in terms of an example for us to follow is deficient. We could say with Luther than if Christ is creature, He too is in need of a truly divine savior and so cannot help us. One could hardly consider the Arian Christ as a savior of the lost, the perishing, the helpless, the sinful and bound. Rather, this Christ helps those who are willing and able to help themselves. Such a Christ is more a helpful inspiration and guide to those who have already decided to save themselves than a rescuer of those in despair of self. Athanasius, accordingly, never ceases to emphasize that the Arian's meager Christology corresponds to a meager view of salvation and grace and a serious underestimation of the antidivine powers of death, the devil, and sin.

Jenson describes the understanding of salvation entailed in Arius's claims from another angle: "It is plain that what moves Arius is the late-Hellenic need to escape time, to become utterly dominant. If we are to be saved, Arius supposes, there must be some reality entirely uninvolved with time, which has no origin of any sort and whose continuity is undifferentiated and uninterrupted. Just so, it is because Christ is involved with time that he will not do as *really* God: 'How can the Logos be God, who sleeps like a man and weeps and suffers?'"[111] As a version of the mediating Logos of Middle Platonism, Arius's Christ provides a bridge from here to the beyond, not the coming here of the beyond, with all that entails, also for the doctrine of God. Can we combine these two interpretations of Arian theological intentions?

R. D. Williams had patiently elaborated the "logic" of Arius's theology in this way by studying how predication is thought to work in the contemporary school of Porphyry, that is, how anything can be attributed properly to God. Predicating God, speaking properly of God—this is at the heart of the matter for kataphatic theology. For Arius the Son is not "proper" to God, for "divine properties are impersonal and eternal. Of course God 'had' Sophia and Logos, but they are qualities belonging to his substance." By this logic, to say that the Son is proper to the Father is actually to destroy the Son as a real, individual agent and reduce him to impersonal qualities. What is proper to God "relates only to a quality predicated of a substance."[112] Just as God the Father has His own proper qualities, so also the Son "has his own properties . . . other than the essential characteristics of the (essentially eternal) Father." That must be, because for Arius "the reference of 'Father' is the same as that of 'God': the eternal and self-subsistent source of all things. . . . To be Father is, *as it happens*, an identifying and thus inalienable characteristic of God, but it is not part of the 'essential' definition of God, since God as such, being self-subsistent, cannot be defined as to *what* he is by reference to anything else."[113] Arius would then be justified in saying, "God as God was not always Father," as the correlate of saying, "There was a time when the Logos did not exist." If the Logos, however, does really exist, like any other concrete reality or hypostasis that has come into existence, He must have His own set of individuating properties that cannot be those of the Father's hypostasis.[114] To speak of the Son being born out of the Father's essence contradicts the "pure spirituality or intellectuality of God"; it "fatally jeopardizes the divine simplicity and immutability, and implies God's materiality."[115]

What Williams makes clear in this patient analysis of Arius's logic is that Arius, more rigorously and clearly than most, "understood God to be the name of an individual spiritual subsistence," the one and only instantiation of the class "divinity," understood in terms of simplicity: "The simplicity of the divine nature is assimilated to the (necessary) indivisibility of a non-material individual."[116] Arius is attacking "the idea that Theos should be understood generically, so that 'God' is the name of a substance participated equally by Father and Son."[117] In the latter case, the word "God" is taken as title of an office, for example, creator of all that is not God, rather than a proper name of a special substance possessing the incommunicable quality of simplicity. As a result of this analysis, Arius's Christology can finally make real sense. "The Son's revelatory importance lies in being a maximally endowed creature who manifests at once the immense and unbridgeable gulf separating even the highest creatures from God, *and* the fact that God is not idle or indifferent, but wills to create (necessarily fragmented) images of his own life. . . . As a paradigm creature, Christ the Son exhibits perfectly what kind of continuities and what kind of discontinuities exist between God and creation."[118]

How did Arius come to hold these views? Arius, as mentioned, came from the school of Antioch (home of the apologist Theophilus and the modalist bishop Paul of Samosota) and was a pupil of Lucian, from whom he learned to think that "Biblicism that held fast to the simple word-sense" was the right theological method.[119] Arius consequently found many biblical "proof texts" that indicated to him that the Son, the Logos, or Sophia is a creature of God. Armed with this method, Arius became embroiled in conflict with a schismatic group of modalistic tendency in Alexandria, the so-called Meletians. These were rigorists like the Donatists in the West, who in the Great Persecution of 303–312 stood fast and thereafter were not disposed to be merciful to the many failed Christians who had denied their Lord but now wanted to return to the church. Close to the theology of the martyrs, these Meletians held that redemption depends on God's deification of the human body through the

Incarnation, a theory that in modern scholarship is sometimes called, less than kindly, the "physical theory of redemption." Lietzman describes it thus: "Our human bodily form represented in Jesus' bodily form, was combined with the entire and most exalted nature of God, without any sort of diminution, and was thereby withdrawn from the perishableness of the earthly."[120] So the martyrs participated in Jesus' own "impassible passibility" when persecuted and thus attained to His immortal life. But Arius turned against this understanding of redemption with his doctrine of the created Logos. For Arius, salvation does not consist in union with Christ the God-Man, but (as in a tendency we observed in Origen) in moral imitation of the created Logos who appeared in Christ to show us the path of self-salvation.[121]

Arius was rehabilitated soon after Nicea in 325, and his opponent Athanasius suffered multiple exiles during a fifty-year interregnum of so-called semi-Arianism. It is instructive then to make a few correlations with the political theology that attended the conflict.[122] One of Arius's most significant supporters was Eusebius of Caesarea, an imperial apologist who was appalled by the embarrassing outbreak of theological controversy at the very moment when Christianity was supposed to be triumphing as the religion of monotheism and morality that would save the Roman Empire. Eusebius is the author of the invaluable *Ecclesiastical History*, the first narrative of Christian history from the time of the apostles to the conversion of Constantine. The book was published right after the Arian controversy began. For the most part it tells the stories of the martyrs. Significantly, Eusebius *foresees the end of the period of martyrdom*. The book ends with Eusebius celebrating the conversion of Constantine as the fulfillment of Christianity, the cause for which the martyrs had not suffered in vain. Here emerges for the first time a Christian political theology of the symbiosis of church and state, a fully realized eschatology, buttressed now with an even more sinister implication of left-wing Origenist theology. Eusebius thinks that, as the Son is ontologically subordinated to the Father, so in the earthly order (whose salvation is to copy or imitate the heavenly order) the church of Jesus is to be subordinate to the state, the representative on earth of God the Father. There is a correlation here of God the Father with the state and God the Son with the church. That is no little clue to the sympathy for Arianism that simultaneously arose and why emperors would persecute the Nicene theology of Athanasius for the next fifty years.

As the Arian controversy spread, Eusebius expressed the exasperation of those for whom the main point of Christianity is monotheism and morality—not, as they view it, idle metaphysical disputes.[123] Of course, on examination Eusebius has his own metaphysics—of subordination. More profoundly, we can understand why Eusebius supported Arius in the controversy on the grounds that he was orthodox in intention but tragically misunderstood, even as he conceded that some of Arius's statements were needlessly extreme. As we have seen, the theological tendency of Origenism lies in a systematic synthesis of Christianity and culture. With perfect consistency, Eusebius welcomed Constantine as the fulfillment of the gospel, the veritable end of salvation history. Arius articulated this same tendency with stark theoretical clarity. Though some have recently challenged the older scholarly picture of such "inner connections between theological and political positions," it remains in its broad features essentially correct: "The history can be understood almost as well if for 'Arian' we read 'imperialist,' and for 'orthodox' 'ecclesiastical.'. . . Those for whom Christ was Lord and God defend the 'crown rights of the Lord Jesus' over his church, while those for whom he was a lesser being, however close to God, were more prepared to bow to the will of the emperor, as also God's vice-regent on earth."[124] In other words, the Arian scheme not only misunderstands the Son's relation to the Father. It also, indeed principally, misunderstands God the Father's relation to the world. It turns the God of the gospel into the ideologically mystified sanction of the way things are rather than the coming King who makes all things new.

Arius's teaching could not but provoke a reaction. The inarticulate sense of the received faith from the Scriptures, parsed by the baptismal creed, was that whatever reality the Father is, that the Son is also. An ontological line between Father and Son as between creator and creature was not acceptable. Such conceptually inchoate reaction against Arianism was the product of the fateful council of bishops summoned by the emperor Constantine to the city of Nicea in the year 325 to resolve the controversy, as we shall carefully examine in the next and final chapter. But we may conclude this chapter on the confrontation of the two monotheisms with R. D. Williams's crisp challenge to "Athanasius and his heirs," should they "still want to pursue the debate" on behalf of "Sonship" as indicative of a "grace [which] is a more pervasive transfiguration of the human condition": they will have to "struggle through the complexities of metaphysics" (what we have called the revision of metaphysics) in order to make intelligible their paradoxical notions of the eternal generation of the Son, the Word made flesh, the impassible becoming passible, and so on. "The nature of the Arian debate makes it clear that there are no short cuts."[125] But this much help can be gleaned from taking Arius's logic fairly and seriously: the alternative that is robust Trinitarianism proposes that the word "'God' should not be treated as a proper name: it is a shorthand for that life or agency or process constituted by the inseparable, reciprocally definitory terms of Father, Son, and Spirit, or source, issue, and response. . . . And as life or process, it is capable of taking into itself the processes of human lives, as a global context of meaning, nurture and growth." This is to say, as this chapter has argued, "that, ultimately, the borrowed logic of 'God' as a proper name and the native Christian sense of Jesus' reconstitution of the meaning of 'God' could not comfortably coexist."[126]

CHAPTER 6
The Holy Trinity as the Eternal Life

We have seen that the gospel of the resurrection of the Crucified inaugurating "the turn of the ages"[1] executes a critique of epistemology. The new starting point of faith in the God who gives life to the dead in turn issues in the canonical narrative of this world as God's eschatological creation, working therewith a corresponding revision of the metaphysics of "persistence" in favor of the metaphysics of "anticipation" (Jenson). Where and when faith in the crucified Jesus as the Christ, the Son of God, is created by the Holy Spirit, the world is being created anew. "Therefore, if anyone is in Christ, he is a new creation; the old has gone, the new has come!" (2 Cor 5:17). The revision of metaphysics is indicated by the creedal confession of the trinity of persons, the Father, the Son, and the Holy Spirit, as true God; just as in turn "true God" is now understood as the public office of the creator of everything else, God as author, agent, and goal of the scriptural narrative of the world as eschatological creation. The creator of everything other is God, and *the Holy Trinity is this God*. This is the chief dogma of evangelical and catholic Christianity as initially, confusedly articulated against Arius in the Creed of Nicea (325) and brought to completion after a long struggle at Constantinople (381); it is Christianity's chief dogma because it regulates the right reading of canonical Scripture, with respect to the authorial intention of the Holy Spirit to tell the world of the Son of the Father, and thus to indicate the right preaching of the true humanity of Christ, as that One of the Trinity who suffered for us and for our salvation. *Esse deum dare*—to be God is to give.

The Martyriological Background

After years of toleration in the course of Origen's century, old tensions reappeared with new fury in the Great Persecution from 303 to 312. According to Frend, during the time of Origen "there may have been no great differences in the beliefs of an educated pagan and an educated Christian, but there was a depth of cleavage in terms of ultimate allegiance. . . . [Christians] remained dangerous atheists, worshipping a man who had died a violent death as a rebel."[2] The Great Persecution came about as a deliberate campaign to reground imperial Rome in the old cult by halting the spread of subversive Christianity. It began in the year 303 and lasted with varying degrees of intensity until the conversion of Constantine around 313. In four successive edicts, the imperial government (1) confiscated Christian literature, destroyed churches, and legalized discrimination against Christians; (2) arrested the clergy; (3) required the clergy to sacrifice to the pagan gods; and (4) required all citizens to sacrifice to the gods.[3]

There is no doubt that this renewed experience of imperial persecution broke the spell of the optimistic synthesis of Origenism in which Athanasius had grown up. In fact, at the conclusion of his early theological manifesto, *On the Incarnation of the Word*, Athanasius attributed his theological achievement in it both to the study of the Scriptures and to "what we have learned from inspired teachers, who have been conversant with the [Scriptures], who have also become martyrs for the deity of Christ."[4] This latter is a direct reference to teachers who died in the Great Persecution. The total war undertaken by the state against the church disabused Athanasius of illusions about any permanent peace between the divine-human Christ and human constellations of power that take offense at His cross—so *On the Incarnation* begins with a theology of the cross, lifting up the epistemological critique attending Christianity's perennial stone of stumbling. What human beings "deride as unseemly"—recall the question of philosophical or natural theology about what is fitting or worthy to say of God—Christ "by His own goodness clothes with seemliness, and what men in their conceit of wisdom laugh at as merely human, He by His own power demonstrates to be divine, subduing the pretensions of idols by His supposed humiliation—by the Cross" (IW 1:3).

After almost a century of relative peace and progress in which Origen's synthesis of Christianity and Platonism had become common coin in the Eastern church, the rupture of the two monotheisms occurred over the co-equal deity of Christ, meaning not, as we shall see, that Jesus is divine (as possessing an identical essential quality), but that Jesus' divinity is the same as His Father's (as the numerically same reality). For Athanasius, the affirmation of the "deity of Christ" in the latter sense always entailed a simultaneous and corresponding de-divinization of the state, since the appearance of this one true Son of God on the earth dispossessed all other claimants in the minds and hearts of His people. Thus the theology of the martyrs came to life again in Athanasius, not only as an ethic, howsoever passionately held as in Origen, but as theology, that is, as the perspectival shift of faith in the resurrection of the Crucified with corresponding cognitive insight into God in His coming to reign in the world, whose Son became flesh, not as Caesar on his throne, but as Jesus hoisted on Caesar's gibbet.

Athanasius was present at the Council of Nicea as theological adviser to his bishop, Alexander of Alexandria, the ecclesiastical official who had first brought charges against Arius. Athanasius succeeded Alexander as bishop of Alexandria in 328 when his public life really began.[5] Though he was exiled many times subsequently by a succession of Arian-sympathizing emperors, victory for Athanasius's theology finally came after his death in 381, when the creed we customarily call the Nicene Creed (of 325) was validated in expanded and revised form at a council in Constantinople.

The Creed at Nicea 325

At Nicea the gathered bishops took up a local baptismal creed as the vehicle for their rejection of Arius's doctrine. This in itself is significant, because creeds, as we may recall from J. N. D. Kelley's investigations, originated as professions of faith to be made on the occasion of baptism: "Whatever other uses they may have been put to in the course of history, the true and original use of creeds, their primary raison d'etre, was to serve as solemn affirmations of faith in the context of baptismal initiation."[6] Specifying the initiate's faith in the Father, Son, and Holy Spirit, creeds served to identify both the person as a believer and the God in whom the person believes. Because this identification of the God of the gospel was their function, the tendency was for baptismal creeds to expand beyond the mere recitation of the trinitarian names by adding further bits of the canonical narrative in the form of "who . . ." clauses. These relative clauses narrate the history of the subject in order better to identify Him. Thus, the creed has the baptismal candidate recite, "I believe in God the Father, *who made* heaven and earth, *who is* the Father of His own only Son, our Lord Jesus Christ, *who* for us and for our salvation *came down* from heaven and was made man . . . and in the Holy Spirit, *who is* the Lord and Giver of life," and so on. In his acute study from 1983, Robert Jenson justified this expansion of the baptismal creeds that put them to new work as standards of doctrine, on the grounds that in "the Bible the name of God and the narration of his works thus belong together. The descriptions that make the name work are items of the narrative." Such "identifying descriptions" were needed in that (think of the difference between the God of Moses and the God of Pharaoh to which Theissen drew attention) "salvation depended precisely on unambiguous identification of . . . God over against the generality of the numinous."[7] In this way, the

trinitarian persons of the gospel narrative are concretely identified by recitation of their acts as known from canonical Scripture, and the expanded baptismal creeds in turn recite *in nuce* the one history of salvation that comes upon
the world from the Father through the Son in the Spirit. The Nicene fathers
thus seized upon what was already established custom in utilizing the *regula
fidei* of the creedal tradition, as we saw in Ignatius and Irenaeus:[8] these creeds
articulated belief that is "epistemically primary" (Marshall) for the church's
faith, spelling out what every initiate makes his or her own at baptism in order
to become and to remain a member of this community through continuing
time, in the present case, in the face of the Arian challenge.

Into such a baptismal creed, the Nicene bishops inserted anti-Arian statements as follows. First, after the words "only-begotten of his Father," they
added, "*that is, from the essence of the Father.*" This directly contradicted Arius's
assertion in his *Thalia* that the Logos "is not equal to [the Father], nor for
that matter of the same essence. . . . The Father is alien to the Son in essence."
Thus the Nicene fathers rejected "the principle tenet of Arianism, that the
Son had been created out of nothing and had no community of being with the
Father."[9] Next, the bishops added the words "*true God from true God*" in order
to reject all Platonic notions of the Logos as a second God, an external replica
or mirrored copy of the original, absolute God, with the related implication
that the Father is alone true God. This "clause had the effect of laying it down
that the Son was truly God in whatever sense the Father was God." Then they
added the crucial but unprecedented clarification "*begotten not made*," which
distinguished between *gennetos* (born, begotten) and *genetos* (generated, made)
by denying that what is begotten of the Father is something contingent, made,
or created. This distinction means that as God *is* Father, it belongs to His very
persona to beget, for no father can be without offspring. *The terms "father" and
"son," the fundamental analogue for the relation of God and Jesus in the canonical
narrative, are correlative.* They are lifted up to define doctrinally the relation of
God and Jesus as given in the gospel (not the Platonizing picture of Mind and
its Word). The real distinction between Father and Son in God, on the other
hand, simultaneously indicates an essential relation, as in Plantinga's "social
analogy," in the life of the one God.

With this, something truly monumental occurs. The tendency to think of
the relationship between God and Jesus in terms of a Mind and its intelligent
Word ordering its world is being revised. The biblical, kerygmatic proclamation of Jesus' relation to God as Son to Father is being reasserted as primary.
From now on, Jesus' particular Sonship as we know it from the gospel narrative is to govern thinking about the Logos of God, not vice versa. This excludes
the possibility of thinking that the Logos is akin to all the other mythological
sons of God, angels, and mediating beings, albeit first and best. From now on,
thinking in service of the gospel has to work this way: Jesus, whom we meet in

the gospel, is *revealed* as the unique (the only-begotten) Son of His Father. As such, the one persona Jesus, Son of God, *is* God the Logos, that is, God *as His own self-giving and self-communicating Word.* Let us note for emphasis with T. F. Torrance: "The homoousios holds not simply between the eternal Son and the Father, but . . . between Jesus, the incarnate Son, and the Father."[10] It is as the true human being that Jesus is, the man crucified *sub Pontio Pilato*, that He is the eternal Logos of His eternal Father. This means not only that the infinite is capable of the finite, that is, that the impassible God is capable of suffering without ceasing to be God, but that the finite is capable of the infinite, that mortal humanity is capable of being divinized without ceasing to be creature. But this latter consists in receiving a fitting share or participation in the eternal life that is the Trinity. To be God is to give; to be human is to be so gifted. How God is and can be this life-giving life is the mystery explored in this final chapter as the gospel's revision of the metaphysics of the fallen world.

Thus all three of the interpolations into the baptismal creed just listed led to the climatic statement affirming precisely what Arius had denied: the Son is of one being with the Father, the famous *homoousios* clause. At the end of the creed, the following anathema was pronounced: "But as for those who say, There was when He was not, and, Before being born He was not, and that He came into existence out of nothing, or who assert that the Son of God is of a different hypostasis or substance [*ousia*], or is *subject to alternation or change*—these the Catholic and apostolic church anathematizes."[11] With this statement, biblical monotheism reasserted itself against both the Origenist synthesis and Arius's consistently Platonic dismantling of it. Yet it must be conceded that the Nicene fathers of 325 reacted instinctively, that is, more on the basis of their inchoate sense of Scripture and the church's faith than with clear, articulate, precise theological reasoning. What no one fully realized at the moment (Arius was correct at least about this) was that introducing the idea of the eternal generation of the Son from the being of the Father indeed made God "subject to alteration or change" in a sense, even though the anathema explicitly denies this. Christian theology here, unwillingly perhaps but of inner necessity, violated the Platonic axiom that "since [divine being] is unique, transcendent and indivisible, the being or essence of God (*ousia*) cannot be shared or communicated. For God to impart his substance to some other being, however exalted, would imply that he is divisible (*diaipetos*) and subject to change (*treptos*)."[12] This formulation of an objection, of course, states precisely the riddle of the gospel paradox that we have considered in this study from the outset: Ignatius's "the impassible became passible," taken as God's real, not apparent, self-impartation in Christ. God-as-God-to-God is now turning to us, as such and not as another in some diminished form. Thinking this out would take the next fifty years, as we shall now see. In what sense can *both* the becoming of "the Word who became flesh" *and* the divine, immutable simplicity of this unique becoming be articulated clearly and properly formulated?

Of more immediate consequence was the fact that in this final anathema the words *hypostasis* and *ousia* were still being used as synonyms: those are condemned who assert that "the Son of God is of a different hypostasis or substance [*ousia*]" than the Father. Thus coupled with significant ambiguities, as well as bearing the seeds of a revolution in metaphysics, the Creed of 325 condemned Arianism. Notwithstanding, Kelly, using Athanasius's later arguments against Arius, rightly summarizes the sense of this rejection in three points. First, under the assumption that the divine three of the gospel narrative has been inchoate doctrine from the outset, "Arianism undermined the Christian doctrine of God by presupposing that the divine Triad is not eternal and by virtually reintroducing polytheism." Second, under the assumption that baptism delivered the rule of faith, Arianism "made nonsense of the established liturgical customs of baptizing in the Son's name as well as the Father's, and addressing prayers to the Son." Third, under the assumption that the canonical reception of the Hebrew Scriptures, and not the Gnostic repudiation of them, exposed the human predicament before God, Arianism "undermined the Christian idea of redemption in Christ, since only if the Mediator was Himself divine could man hope to reestablish fellowship with God."[13] Thus what is being denied is clear enough. But, as Kelly points out, it is not so clear precisely what the Creed of 325 affirms, particularly with the controversial neologism *homoousios*.

Does *ousios* here mean one entity, an individual substance, or does it mean one class of beings, one nature common to many individual substances? Is it a numerical one denoting something or a generic oneness of type or kind defining something? Is it the New Testament's *"ho theos kai pater,"* that is, the God who is the Father and as such the proper name for a single spiritual substance (albeit communicated to the Son and Spirit), or is it God as an adjective, that is, "the divine" for a kind of being or life? Is the Creed saying that Father and Son are two subjects in, as, or of one entity, or that two entities share one kind of divine nature?[14] It would take a protracted struggle, indeed the near triumph of an ever more sophisticated and radical Arianism, before the great theological labors of Athanasius and later of the Capaddocians worked out the early, anti-Arian reaction of 325 into the positive articulation of the doctrine of the three *hypostases* in one *ousia*. The actual creed produced at Nicea in 325 more asserted an outside boundary within which solution of the problem would have to be sought. Bearing in mind that a "solution" would be a more precise description rather than any kind of comprehensive definition of the God of the gospel, a solution would only come in 381 at Constantinople with the addition of the Holy Spirit as the divine third completing the triad of the one divine life. As we shall see, this addition clarified the sense of *ousios* as designating the numerically one, ineffable divine reality taken as a life co-equally lived by the three persons in virtue of their internal relations to each other.

But we are getting ahead of the story. For it was an embarrassing fact of history for the later opponents of Arianism that the anti-Arian decision of 325 did not last two full years. In the fall of 327, Arius petitioned for pardon to the emperor and in a private audience assured Constantine that he accepted the Nicene Creed. The emperor, wanting religious peace, took him at his word and wrote to the bishop of Alexandria, asking him to reinstate Arius. A synod of bishops that met in 327 "achieved a considerable amelioration and, broadly speaking, a revocation of many of the decisions of A.D. 325."[15] What accounts for this remarkable turnaround?

In the first place, Emperor Constantine himself. He above all wanted an end to theological controversy (he had called the council in 325 for that purpose) and at length apparently found the semi-Arian theology of Eusebius of Caesarea more congenial to imperial interests.[16] It had been Constantine himself, under the influence of a theological adviser of modalist tendencies from the Latin West, who introduced the term *homoousios* in 325. If he would now retreat from the term that he had introduced on account of its failure to end the conflict, who could oppose him? As Lietzman notes, "There really were no Nicene theologians [yet]. . . . All, including Arius, accepted the Nicene Creed and each read his own theology into it. What is more, the Emperor was content that it should be so."[17] It was only in 332, when the new bishop of Alexandria, Athanasius, refused to readmit Arius to the priesthood, that the dormant conflict burst into flames anew. For the next fifty years, the Emperors would more or less side with Arians, or more precisely, semi-Arians like Eusebius of Caesarea who strenuously opposed Athanasius and his followers. "The Eusebians calmly asserted their former, pre-Nicene, position [of moderate Origenism], paid due reverence to the Nicene synod by recognizing its condemnatory clauses, but refused to be forced into new and strange paths by the term *homoousios*."[18] In other words, they would deny the extreme and provocative language of the *Thalia*, but not affirm what this denial logically entailed in the term *homoousios*. Why?

The chief theological reason for the astonishing about-face in 327 was the ambiguity of the term *homoousios* itself. Properly speaking, the point of the term is to say that God does not have a Word or Spirit that is something other than God. But God *is* His Word and *is* His Spirit, in the *personal* sense that God cannot Himself *be* the Father except as Father of the Son, the Speaker of the Word, in the love of the Spirit. Arius himself, as we saw in the previous chapter, could in his own way—not personal but essentialist—agree: the Father has mind and spirit; these are qualities that He eternally possesses for Himself as an individual spiritual essence; these become externalized and replicated as genuine divine agents in relation to the world, when the Creator decided to create. In this way, Arius too could say that God *is* His Word and Spirit but just so continue to deny that this God has any *essential* relation to the ontologically inferior and individually separated *beings* of the Logos and the Holy Spirit, which are created and thus inferior replicas of the immanent or latent divine qualities. In this way Arius could loosely read his own ideas into the *homoousios* of 325. Gingerly ignoring the notorious denial entailed by Arius's actual convictions and affirmations ("There was when He was not"), Arius too could make peace with the conceptually ambiguous decision of 325.

As the post-Nicene theologians regarded full-fledged Arianism as a relapse into polytheism, they continued to regard Sabellianism as a return to Judaism.[19] So they worried that the un-nuanced assertion that the Father and the Son are the same thing, while thinking to exclude Arianism, instead in fact introduced modalism. Basil the Great wrote: "Sabellianism is Judaism imported into the preaching of the Gospel under the guise of Christianity. For if a man calls Father, Son and Holy Ghost one thing of many faces, and makes the hypostasis of the three one, what is this but to deny the everlasting existence of the Only Begotten? He denies too the Lord's sojourn among men in the incarnation . . . also the proper operations of the Spirit" (Letter 210).

Basil the Great accordingly persuaded Athanasius and his party of the ambiguity of the *homoousios* formula, in that it could be interpreted in a modalistic fashion, if careful attention to the distinction of persons were neglected.[20] Basil pointed out that an ally of Athanasius, Marcellus of Ancyra, interpreted the *homoousios* in a Sabellian way, "for he does not confess the Son in His proper *hypostasis*, but represents Him as having been sent forth, and as having again returned to Him from Whom he came," that is, that the Logos is a temporary, temporal manifestation of God the Father (Letter 263). This is "the teaching that God is one *hypostasis* that has three appellations, and one object (*pragma*) that has several names or presentations (*prosopa*). . . . [In fact,] Marcellus spoke of God as one *prosopon*."[21] Marcellus indeed could not understand why anyone spoke of the real and distinct subsistence of the persons. To him this sounded as if one "ascribed independent being to the Logos and the Holy Spirit . . . beside God the Father, each with His own personality." This would be tritheism, polytheism. Marcellus was thus a zealous advocate of the *homoousios*, in the sense that for him the Logos was simply and wholly God. Yet, ironically, the Logos was God in a temporal mask, for the Logos was not and will not always be God as God is eternally. There is then only an economic trinity of revelation, not a true, eternal trinity in God.[22] Marcellus "laid stress repeatedly on God's oneness, which in the course of the work of redemption, that is in the sphere of time, had unfolded into a trinity, and subsequently returned to the original unity."[23] Marcellus consequently asserted on the basis of 1 Corinthians 15:28 that Christ's lordship would thus come to an end. It was against this modalistic interpretation that the clause "and of His kingdom there shall be no end" was eventually inserted into the Constantinople revision of the Creed of Nicea in 381. Marcellus's Sabbelian-modalistic interpretation of the *homoousios* was thus excluded.

This exclusion implies that the Logos is hypostatically or personally distinct from His Father, not as a creature who was made out of nothing, but as the Son from the Father's own being, existing by the Father's own eternal act of generation. As such, the Son never began and will never cease to be, but exists as the same divine essence as His Father, differing only in the personal agency of this essence, as its receiver and returner, not its initiator and bestower. That is to say, the Father is God who begets, who exercises divinity as Giver. The Son is God who is begotten, who exercises divinity as Given (that is, Phil 2: not counting equality with God something to be held on to, He emptied himself). As we shall see, this nonmodalist interpretation of the true personhood of the Son (and the Father) can be carried through only when it is anchored in the true personhood of the Spirit. It is the Spirit who presents the Son to the Father and the Father to the Son, descending on Jesus at His baptism as a seal of the Father's love, presenting Jesus in his life's oblation to His Father in return. God as Giver, Given, and Giving, as Speaker, Spoken, and Hearing, as Lover, Loved, and Loving—each a real existing agency (*hypostasis*) of the one and same Life, thus enacting the one and same divinity (*ousia*) each in its particular way, *by* and *never apart from* the indwelling of the others. The Spirit is the hypostatic agent of this eternal indwelling in the divine life as, fittingly, also of our inclusion in time into the divine life.

Thus divine complexity is secured as description, though not definition, of the God of the gospel. The oneness of God then lies not in a generic concept of divinity, divine *ousia*, by which autonomous reason could philosophically secure its world and safely keep God distant in nebulous transcendence of the many here below. Nor, more subtly, is divine oneness some underlying essence, we know not what, of the three who breach our immanence in the gospel narrative to make us one with them in the Reign. Nor is the divine oneness some odd (privative, empty) property of the Father somehow shared with the Son and the Spirit.[24] The ineffable oneness of God is not comprehended (it remains eternally the mystery beyond finite comprehension) but truly apprehended as the Life of the three in the eternal and temporal presenting of the Father to the Son and the Son to the Father in love by the Spirit.

The unity of God, and of God with us, is the love of the Spirit. In his *Systematic Theology* Wolfhart Pannenberg writes in an Athanasian key: "The heavenly Father whom [Jesus] proclaimed is . . . so closely related to Jesus' own coming and work that it is by this that God is identified as Father. . . . Jesus is the Son inasmuch as it is in his message of the nearness of the royal rule of the Father, his subjection to the Father's will, and especially the function of his sending as a revelation of the love of God, that this God may be known as Father."[25] Moreover, the Spirit appears as "the medium of the communion of Jesus with the Father and the mediator of the participation of believers in Christ."[26] The love by which the Father gave His only Son, the love by which Jesus gave Himself into death for helpless sinners, and the love by which human resistance to God's reign is overcome—this manifest and effective divine love is no whim or happenstance but very God, the Lord, the creator Spirit. As these three, God is the one really real substance that alone can truly be called substance, since it lives as event without beginning or end yet as supremely capable of making beginnings and endings. None of this then is to deny divine nature or substance, as Western theology almost reflexively fears, but rather to conceive of immaterial substance not on the analogy of mental operations of a private mind, but rather as the public life of a society. It is thus rather rigorously to discover divine substance in and not apart from the trinitarian existence of God by the event of the coming of His kingdom. This in turn is just as rigorously a more biblical conception of the oneness of God: God's faithfulness to His promises "though time and its vicissitudes" by an "inner consistency" or "integrity" rooted "in the divine self-relation that . . . the Shema calls *echad*."[27]

There is in this to be sure a reason for anxiety. It implies that there is no transcendental guarantee for us above and beyond the God who truly gives and presents Himself in the gospel narrative. God cannot be located on a plane above the world, unaffected by how it all turns out, so that we will be saved no matter what. Rather God is the promised resurrection of the dead and the life everlasting, or God in fact falls apart and disintegrates; in fact, then, God would be, as it is said today, "dead."

Here we may also recall the conclusion of the last chapter, in R. D. Williams's words: "'God' should *not* be treated as a proper name: it is a shorthand for that life or agency or process constituted by the inseparable, reciprocally definitory terms of Father, Son, and Spirit, or source, issue, and response." That is to say, the tendency deriving from classical metaphysics is to think that some underlying divine substance—we know not what—that like a self-identical thing (think, say, of a rock) undergirds Father and Son, who are in turn its exemplars or instantiations or modes or appellations or appearances. In that case, however, we inevitably make unwarranted assumptions about the nature of this underlying substance (along the Platonic lines of negative theology somersaulting into pseudo-affirmations of the alpha-privatives as positive reality) so that it can perform the function of warranting God's transcendental status—the Trojan horse by which the unbaptized metaphysics of the fallen world are snuck in. Consequently, we are saddled with the Platonic problem: we cannot see why this immutable something should fittingly, not to say necessarily, express itself as the three persons of the gospel narrative. As a result, the Trinity becomes a mystery to be put on an altar and adored rather than the mystery of the world that is inescapably loved in spite of all.

The one substance of God, which surely is the irreducible and ultimate reality as faith affirms, is not to be thought of as something statically underlying a surface dynamism, as itself not in play. The Father gives His own being to the Son and the Son returns His own being to the Father in the Spirit whose being is to conduct this very exchange of being in love—so eternally as temporally. *God's eternal being is in becoming, for God is love;*[28] so also, fittingly, God comes into the time of His creatures, at hand though never in hand, for faith and love but never for the gaze that possesses and uses, in hope against hope. As Jüngel has put the point so well: "The doctrine of the Trinity is an attempt to think out the self-relatedness of God's being. It attempts to think out the self-relatedness of the being of God as Father, Son and Spirit, but it can only do this appropriately when it understands God's self-relatedness in his modes of being (not at all as a kind of ontological egoism of God, but rather) as the *power* of God's being to *become* the God of another."[29] This latter power is precisely the mediating work of the Spirit within the eternal life of the Trinity as also in time, when we take the Spirit hypostatically, publically then as the bond of unity, not privately as merely inward assurance.

Thus certain conceptual distinctions produced in this history of the gospel's encounter with Platonism between *hypostasis* (subsistence, a concrete way of existing) and *ousia* (essence, reality, substance, or being), between *aggentos* (unbegotten, unborn) and *agenetos* (unoriginated, self-existent)—enable us to think with some measure of clarity about both the distinction of persons in God and the unity of substance of God, provided, as we have been arguing, that we take them to denote God as Life not thing, as social not individual, as public not private. To adopt this terminology for purposes of conceptual clarity in ontological description does not entail adoption of any specific metaphysical baggage, as is often confusedly maintained. The terminology does not presume in itself and as such to say *what* God is, only *that* the creator of all other than Himself concretely lives the eternal life of the Father and the Son in the Holy Spirit. To this extent, it can and should be granted that *ousia* designates a reality, states a truth claim, that the Trinity is real (Bielfeldt). Christopher Stead concluded an important study by asking, "What is the point of stating that God is an *ousia* in the categorical sense, a substance?" He answers: "The statement is general enough; it leaves a number of options open. Its principle function, as I see it, is to claim that God is not limited or prescribed by our experience of him, but exists in his own right. . . . To characterize God as a substance is to stake a claim against reductionist theories that in effect represent God as dependent on the human experience that he is invoked to explain. In claiming that God is a substance we do not, I think, prejudge the difficult and controversial question of his relation to time and change."[30] Even if the categorical notion of substance, as per Aristotle or Porphyry, as the proper subject of essential predicates is therewith applied (analogically!) to God, it need mean, according to Stead, no more than to assert the nonreductionist *that* of God's being in such and such a way as theology goes on to explicate. Everything actually rather depends on how God exists as God and so becomes *truly, really* also our God. The gospel tells that the God who does not reduce to our need nor surrender to our abuse nevertheless comes to our aid in Jesus Christ. For this salvation Trinitarianism contends. But it would be wiser, we have urged, to think of the immaterial substance of the one God as the process of an internally related life rather than as an unchanging thing or as the private mental operations of subjective consciousness.

Theology of Redemption

The Holy Spirit exists as the agent of the love of the Father for the Son and the Son for the Father, including us in these relationships by the gospel. This inclusion takes form in the person by faith in God, love for one another in the community of faith, and hope for the world as the object of redemption. It was with such recognition of the divine *personhood* of the Spirit that the doctrine of the Trinity triumphed in 381 at the council of Constantinople. At Constantinople, the basic decision of Nicea in 325 was validated and extended further—not merely by the technical terminological formula of one *ousia* and three *hypostases* as such but by anchoring the one deity of the Father and Son in the mutual Exchanger of love, that is, in the person of the Holy Spirit. The triumph of Trinitarianism in this way is the theological story of Athanasius's career. Athanasius was not the most brilliant of the Nicene theologians. The two Gregorys from Cappadocia outshine their elder contemporary in this regard. But Athanasius was the greatest gospel theologian of early Christianity, in whom was combined "the astonishing vitality of [the apostle] Paul's ideas and also the genuinely Greek quality of the effort to know."[31] In him the soteriological passion and political-ethical backbone we have seen in the martyrological line running from Ignatius to Irenaeus revives. For Athanasius, the Christian message is the message of eschatological redemption in a new creation—not the monotheism and morality of Platonism. Salvation consists in loving communion with God—not chiefly law and order. "For [the Logos] was made man that we might be made God; and He manifested himself by a body that we might receive the idea of the unseen Father; and He endured the insolence of men that we might inherit immortality. For while He Himself was in no way injured, being impassible and incorruptible and very Word and God, [we] men who were suffering and for whose sake He endured all this, He maintained and preserved in His own impassibility."[32] Thus Athanasius formulates the soteriological principle of the redemptive exchange enacted by the "impassible passibility" of the Incarnate Word.[33] This formulation, crucially, is not taken as sheer paradox; the paradox is rhetorical, intended as the crisis of self-securing epistemology, opening up locked human minds to a new understanding of God and world, the revision of metaphysics.

For Athanasius, the redemption of the human person is what is at stake. So much is this concern for salvation the driving force that for years Athanasius did not even use the controversial term *homoousios* from the 325 council. The matter for him was hardly one of nitpicking logomachy but of "a two-fold movement, from God to man and from man to God," in such a way that "both divine and human activity in Christ must be regarded as issued from one Person." Jenson explains: "After initial hesitation, Athanasius found he could use *homoousios* as a slogan for his vision of God, to mean that the Father and the Son (and the Spirit) *together* make the one reality of God. The Godhead of the Son is not 'by participation' in *another's* Godhead; rather, 'the fact that there is the Son is a proper characteristic of the Father's being.'"[34] Indeed, the Father, the Son, and the Spirit *each* exist in relation to the others by virtue of a distinct role in the divine life-process. The unbegotten Father begets and breathes (spirates), the Son, is begotten but returns to His identity as Father, and the Spirit is breathed (spirated) on the Son, presenting the Father to the Son and leading the Son again to the Father. The soteriological significance of the Nicene *homoousios* lies close at hand: If Jesus Christ, the incarnate Son, is not true God from true God, then we are not saved, for it is only God who can save the creature that is lost to God, sold under the powers of sin and death; but if Jesus Christ is not truly man, then salvation does not touch our human existence and condition, so that we are won to God from within. "*Only God can save, but he saves precisely as man.*"[35] That is, the Impassible saves as, and by becoming, the passible. This theological principle of the redemptive exchange and its corresponding Christology defines the gospel as a message of salvation.

To understand that precisely, however, we must explore Athanasius's difficult notion of divine impassibility—"Himself in no way injured, being impassible and incorruptible." We have to examine carefully how the concept of impassibility is actually used in Athanasius. For Athanasius, the impassibility of God is a logical, analytic notion: God cannot be coherently conceived as liable by nature to any suffering that would disqualify His being as the one creator of all that is not God. In this sense, God is unchangeable qua the unique being that must be conceived to attend the One who is the only creator of all others. God does not morph into some other kind of being—the *only* alternative, according to the Bible, is creaturely being—without the universe losing its creator and all things dissolving back into nothingness. Given this fundamental differentiation of the Creator and the creature, it proves simply meaningless to ask whether God by nature feels physical pain. The question is absurd, a category confusion. Physical pain is a creature of God, indeed a good creature of God by means of which the nervous system of bodily organisms, in combination with instinct and experience, warns against those inevitable dangers to an organism's life to which mortals are by nature exposed. Creaturely life is essentially a gift that is bounded by the limit of mortality; pain is the marker of this boundary. The fact that pain—like any other good creature of God—can be misused to terrorize and destroy life is an important but distinct problem. The question under discussion is whether it is coherent to predicate pain to God by nature. The same kind of logical clarification is involved in asking whether immortality can be predicated, say, of the human soul. Physical pain, as a property of organisms, cannot be properly predicated of divine nature any more than immortality, as a property of the Creator, can in the abstract be predicated of a creaturely nature. The Christian faith insists upon this sharp distinction of divine and human natures and forbids, as per the later decree at Chalcedon (451), that they be confused or compounded.

How, then, might it be meaningful to ask about divine suffering? If He does not feel pain as a bodily organism, then presumably we could ask whether God suffers *spiritually*, that is, whether God can be subjected against His will to a will other than His own. Twentieth-century theologians have wanted to affirm something like this. The poignant words of Dietrich Bonhoeffer penned in a Nazi prison cell speak for many: "God lets himself be pushed out of the world on to the cross. He is weak and powerless in the world, and that is precisely the way, the only way, in which he is with us and helps us."[36] It is not, however, too fine a point to belabor that Bonhoeffer's elegant words speak of divine *permission*. Within a month, the same man approaching martyrdom wrote about himself to the same correspondent: "Please don't ever get anxious or worried about me, but don't forget to pray for me—I'm sure you don't! I am so sure of God's guiding hand that I hope I shall always be kept in that certainty. You must never doubt that I'm traveling with gratitude and cheerfulness along the road where I have been led. My past life is brim-full of God's goodness, and my sins are covered by the forgiving love of Christ crucified."[37] The atheists may be right that there is no God. But the Christian, as Bonhoeffer thinks, does not imagine that God ever suffers something against His own will, not even in the bitter fates of His chosen witnesses and martyrs. To imagine so would make the worst kind of atheist, that is, the religious atheist who lacks the self-knowledge or the courage to dispense with talk about God that has become essentially contentless. God would not be God if *finally* God has to submit to some other will—indeed, in that case, that *other* will would be God![38] To be God is to be the all-determining reality of all else, the Creator.

Just so, however, God can be conceived to determine Himself in long-suffering, permitting the evil will that opposes Him, in a decisive moment letting Himself "be pushed out of the world on to the cross." Here God suffers spiritual anguish, indeed also bodily pain, in the person of His Son, yet on account of His own will to love a hostile world. "This means that, contrary to some classical concepts of Necessary Being, God does suffer. But the trinitarian understanding does not deify suffering for its own sake or foster masochism. The rejected, crucified Other is also the resurrected and vindicated Other."[39] Anatolios asks in Athanasius's name: "If the Word simply 'equalizes' himself with humanity, how is his condescension our exaltation, how does his hominization amount to our deification, and how is his taking on a servant's form continuous with his mastery and emancipation of that form? In a word, how does the incarnation represent our transformation, unless the Word's taking on of humanity is simultaneously a transformation of our humanity into the likeness of God, and not a mere equalizing of God with humanity?"[40] The God who suffers with us also and indeed chiefly suffers *for us* and so will *demonstrate* His deity in the actual *fulfillment* of His promises, in the final *coming* of His kingdom.

We are skirting the problem of theodicy that had dominated modern theology at least since Leibniz, perhaps since the conclusion of Luther's treatise against Erasmus. There is no theological solution to the problem of evil in the merely pathetic notion of divine co-suffering. The theodicy of faith stemming from Paul's eighth chapter to the Romans points to the promised resurrection of the dead, the reversal of worldly injustices, and the public justification of the justice of God to the eternal comfort of every innocent victim of human and superhuman malice at the culmination of the project of eschatological creation.[41] God's will must finally prevail in this way, or we do not believe that God in the Christian sense exists whatsoever. That atheism is of course a human possibility. But it is not a Christian possibility, which, as the young lion Karl Barth once roared, is "altogether thoroughgoing eschatology" or it has nothing whatsoever to do with Jesus Christ.[42] The very concept of God the creator self-destructs if we imagine that God suffers against His own will, but the gospel of this God's saving incarnation requires that we affirm God's willingness to suffer for our sakes. That self-donation of love is the sense of the paradox of impassible passion. Before Athanasius, Origen in one of his biblical homilies (in felicitous inconsistency with his systematic theology) could ask and answer: "What is that passion that He suffered for us? Love is that passion. . . . Also the Father Himself and God of the universe, longsuffering, very pitying and compassionate, does He not suffer in some way? The Father himself is not impassible. If asked, He has pity and compassion, He suffers something of love."[43] And another disciple of Origen, Gregory the Wonderworker, posed the problem this way: "If by nature God is impassible, it follows that he can never suffer even if he wanted to, since his nature would then be doing what was contrary to his will."[44] Whatever we go on to think of divine nature, it must, if it is the God of the gospel, include in its infinite scope of possibilities also freedom to suffer, wisdom to suffer, love to suffer.

Biblically the long-suffering patience of God is meant to elicit human repentance. God does not have to suffer evil contradiction of His will, yet out of love He patiently allows sinners to continue in their sin—and this, in the very fact of willing a world populated with wills, albeit creaturely, other than His own. Such patience of God, on the other hand, bestirs the cry of the oppressed, those innocents who are victims of sinners who persist in their sin: "How long, O Lord! Stir up your power, and come!" At the outset of his theological career, Athanasius asked, How is God to resolve this dilemma? On the one hand, if God should intervene justly to punish the sinner, His own creation would also be destroyed in the act, and His love, expressed in patience for the purpose of repentance, would be frustrated. On the other hand, if God should in patience forgo the assertion of the right and condemnation of evildoers, then rebellion, violent chaos, and the powers of death would reign over creation, wreaking destruction, oppressing innocents. In either case, God conceived of publicly, in His office as Creator and Judge, would thus cease to be God. "What was God to do in his goodness?" (IW 6:7).[45] Such reflection on the so-called *divine dilemma*[46] can be traced back as far as the prophet Hosea (11:1-9).[47] Yet it was Athanasius, drawing especially on the apostle Paul (Rom 3:5, 25-26), who for the first time made this reflection central to the theology of redemption.

Following Paul, Athanasius saw in the cross of the incarnate Word the answer to the question of what God in goodness could do both to assert His righteous rule against sin and its lethal effects on the creation and yet to put the lost and sinful creatures in the right. It happened in "no other way save on the cross . . . [since] no other way than this was good for us. . . . For if he came to bear the curse laid upon us, how else could He 'become a curse' unless he received the death set for a curse? and that is on the cross" (IW 25:1-2). Furthermore, "he accepted on the cross, and endured a death inflicted by others, and above all his enemies, which they thought dreadful and ignominious and not to be faced; so that this also being destroyed, both he himself might be believed to be life, and the power of death be brought to naught. So something startling and surprising has happened" (IW 24:3-4). The astonishing thing is that, moved by irrepressible divine love, the Logos in a unique historical act took all human woe upon Himself. This does not happen to the Logos in a pathetic fashion (IW 6:7). The ground of this event is the holy God's love. God's holy love is not a whim. Holy love is the one God in the utter uniqueness of His own act and being, the Father for the Son and the Son for the Father. Love moves God to suffering in the sending of the Son, but not as something outside of God, but as God the Father moving God the Son to become God in a historically new way, God the Spirit justifying the ungodly and giving life to the dead. The Incarnation is this new and profound act of loving identification with hostile and perishing creatures, those rightly under the "curse." The Logos assumed a human body, then, not in order that He might merely hurt with

us, although surely the Logos did hurt in His own body when He was crucified, as also He hurt in His own soul, according to Athanasius, feeling the
"curse" of God. But the Logos suffered body and soul in order that human
beings who are helplessly lost under the power of the Rebellion (Satan)
might be claimed and healed. What astonishes Athanasius, then, is the spiritual willingness of divine love freely to suffer for another, indeed for someone who is lesser in dignity and even hostile. Athanasius is surely right to
think, however, that this act of God's suffering love in the Cross does not
and cannot mean that God suffers *finally*. Christ is risen! The Christ who
came in humility and suffering will come again in power and great glory
to judge all things, so Athanasius concludes *On the Incarnation*. God's will
for life, righteousness, and peace finally does not suffer defeat but triumphs
through apparent defeat for all and forever. So faith hopes.

The divine Logos cannot suffer physically and psychologically except by
virtue of assuming His own human body and soul. But because the Logos has
become the body and soul, Jesus, forever and ever, whatever the Logos experienced in Jesus is truly, inseparably, uniquely His own. Indeed, it must be so if
the soteriological principle of the redemptive exchange is to work. "For what
the human body of the Word suffered, this the Word, dwelling in the body,
ascribed to himself, in order that we might be enabled to be partakers of the
Godhead of the Word."[48] It is not a merely verbal ascription, a pious way of
talking, but a real communication of properties, a real exchange of conditions.
For what God the Word says, God the Spirit also effectively does. Unlike our
suffering, which most often is simply pathetic, God's suffering in the cross
of Jesus is a powerful manifestation of God's *apatheia*, that ambiguous word
taken from the philosophers that, baptized, now indicates the gospel God's
"selflessness," His divine power to suffer for others in love. In Jesus, freely
willed suffering of love triumphs on behalf of all creatures who suffer patheti-
cally, thus not by magically removing pain but by adding divinity to it and so
dispelling the terror of pain's apparent finality. The martyrs of Jesus do not
somehow become anesthetized. They are not rescued from the terrorists. But
they are clothed with triumphant divine courage of faith that overcomes the
world.

The entire development in theology here ultimately stems from the unre-
lenting paradoxes of the antidocetic Christology of the martyrs, going back to
the Gospel of John and its appropriation by Ignatius.[49] Athanasius expressly
recalls Ignatius's seemingly contradictory statement that Christ is both "originated and unoriginated, God in flesh," and wrote that "the blessed Ignatius
was right in writing that Christ was originate on account of the flesh (for He
became flesh), yet unoriginated because He is not in the number of things
made and originated, but Son from the Father." At the beginning of that magnificent early treatise *On the Incarnation of the Word*, Athanasius stated the

problem of interpreting this paradox. "What relates to the Word's becoming flesh," and "seeming low estate," he says, "Jews traduce and Greeks laugh to scorn." But the Word, to cite again a decisive passage, "not only Himself demonstrates as possible what men mistake, thinking impossible, but what men deride as unseemly, this by His own goodness He clothes with seemliness, and what men, in their conceit of wisdom, laugh at as merely human, He by His own power demonstrates to be divine, subduing the pretensions of the idols by His supposed humiliation by the cross" (IW I:1-2).

Athanasius could not have announced a more direct assault on preconceived notions of divinity in Greek philosophical monotheism. Greeks must be taught by the "impassible passibility" of the gospel to set aside their ideas of divinity as possession of qualities of invulnerability (as codified in the apparently self-evident axiom of divine simplicity); they must instead be instructed by the gospel to learn the true "cause of the bodily appearing of the Word of the Father. . . . [Although the Logos is] incorporeal by nature, and Word from the beginning, He has yet of the loving kindness and goodness of his own Father been manifested to us in a human body for our salvation" (IW I: 3-4). What is that true cause of the Logos's "seeming low estate" of which the Greeks are ignorant? It is love that moves God, but love that is intrinsic to God. It is love that occurs in the Incarnation, love that seeks, finds, and saves perishing humanity at the cross. This is the true glory of the eternal God. In Athanasius, the shameless, selfless—in this sense, "apathetic"—love of the God of the gospel appears with new clarity and force. For Athanasius sees in this revealed love the motive in all God's ways; it is this perception that forces Athanasius to go "beyond conventional Platonic descriptions of divine transcendence [to articulate] a doctrine of God who can become human and take to himself a human body."[50]

This theology of the martyrs—this, not some unbaptized remnant of Platonism—is the deep reason why Athanasius shies from any misleading or irresponsible talk about the suffering of God as mere pathos. Even in the Incarnation, even at the moment of death on the cross, the Logos never ceased to be God. The Logos suffered no change in His divine essence; He was not transmuted into something else. The Logos was not "changed into flesh and bones and hair and muscles and all the body . . . altered from its own nature" (AE 4). Rather the Logos strengthened, indeed divinized the weak human nature in and through the trial of sufferings to face them in a display of impassible passibility. That is why the incarnate Logos, the crucified and now risen Lord Jesus, can strengthen His martyrs in their trials. The blessed Apostles, Athanasius writes, "[and] the other Holy Martyrs were so bold as to think that they were rather passing to life than undergoing death. Is it not extravagant then to admire the courage of the servants of the Word, yet to say that the Word himself was in terror, through whom they despised death? But from that most enduring purpose and courage of the Holy Martyrs is shown, that the Godhead was not in terror, but the Savior took away our terror" (AA III:57). The terror hanging as a threat over mortal life is taken away because God personally participates with us *in it* through Jesus Christ. By the Holy Spirit God overcomes our sin and death *through* it. History has significance as the arena, so to speak, in which God's deity as the one true creator and redeemer is established by such *human* events of faith and witness. Until the kingdom comes, the martyrs in their own impassible passibility remain the paradoxical sign on earth of the presence of the reign of God, those who will not bow down to the idols. Their defiance of the threat of death is testimony of the victorious power of God. Indeed, for Athanasius the chief "proofs" of the risen Christ are the works He performs today in His martyrs.[51]

For Athanasius, then, "the cross has become the victory over [death]." The proof of this is that death "is despised by all Christ's disciples, and they all take the aggressive against it and no longer fear it" (IW 27:1). "He who has put on the faith of the cross despises even what is naturally fearful, and for Christ's sake is not afraid of death" (IW 28:2). Thus "many who were formerly incredulous and scoffers have afterwards believed and so despised death as even to become martyrs for Christ himself" (IW 28:5). The final vision of the seer in Revelation 21, which comforted martyrs hundreds of years earlier at the end of the New Testament age, could be placed as the motto over all Athanasius's theology: "Behold, the dwelling of God is with men. He will dwell with them and they shall be his people, and God himself will be with them; and he will wipe away every tear from their eyes." Athanasius naturally expresses this thought in the language of his own day and age, borrowing the idioms but not the concepts of the Platonic intellectual traditions. His motto actually reads, "God became man in order that man might become God." This motto of *theosis* does *not* imply loss of created nature or personal identity by mystical absorption into the deity. That would be undiluted Platonism.

But Athanasius's formula rather expresses the personal and communal notion of loving intimacy with God. His idea of divinization is an attempt to understand theologically the biblical promise of resurrection to eternal life in God's presence. For eternal life is nothing other than God's own unique substance, which is life, the life of the Trinity. To have eternal life, then, is to be divinized in the sense of participating, not substantially but personally, in God's triune relations. Such participation is given through union with Christ by the Spirit. One does not lose one's human nature or personal identity this way. Rather the human self is "clothed" with Christ's righteousness and "filled" with the eternal Spirit, which are "down payments" of eternal life. In fact, then, over against any Platonic idea of the immortality of the soul by virtue of its own nature as intellectually akin to the divine Mind, the theological idea of *theosis* thinks through the meaning of the biblical idea of resurrection of the body. The creature, who is essentially mortal, can live eternally only if God by grace bestows what the creature neither possesses nor has a right to: a true participation in God's own eternal life. In no way was Athanasius inventing a new idea, or importing some pagan idea, in the concept of divinization. He was formulating the soteriological rule that the gospel consists in the narrative event of mutual self-identification between God and humanity, between the sinful and perishing creature and the redeeming, life-giving Creator. This is what his motto means, "God became man in order that man might become divine."

What then is God's power, and how is it to be conceived? Athanasius put the Arians on the horns of a dilemma when he asserted radical monotheism's categorical distinction between the power of the Creator to give and the weakness of the creature in need. *Either* the Arians must admit that in worshipping the Logos—no matter how much of divinity they think Him to possess, no matter how much "like" God the Father they think Him to be—in fact they worship a needy creature, which would be not only pointless but also idolatry. *Or* the Arians should acknowledge that they introduce a plurality of deities, worshipping the Logos and the Holy Spirit alongside the Father, just as the Greeks used to worship Hermes and Apollo alongside Zeus. But that is polytheism. Athanasius realized that divinity is not in logical kind a quality whatsoever, something that one can possess in varying measure, as Arius thinks: God absolutely, the Logos and the Spirit relatively and by participation. What then is the almighty power of God, if it is not a quality possessed by a substance? Creative action, the power to give oneself to another in value—bestowing love—this is what the word "god" or "deity" denotes in respect to predicates like power. The basic ontological distinction between creator and creature sunders the self-evident truisms of classical substance metaphysics.[52] *Esse deum dare.* To be God is not to possess passively for oneself a quality, no matter how ineffable or exalted, but to be the person who is able and willing to give all to another, not as diminishment but as enrichment, not as death but as life, receiving in return only the acknowledgment of the gift. To be God is to be the Father of the Son and breather of the Spirit, whose essential giving is returned forever in the Son by the Spirit.

This singular divinity is exercised and so revealed in the action that originates and sustains, redeems and fulfills the world in the project of eschatological creation. God, deity, divinity is an *event of giving*, not a thing or a quality statically possessed by an empty, unknowable transcendence. God *happens* or God *is* not; God *comes* and *becomes* our God or God is—really—dead. God is God who at the end of history stands publicly revealed as the One who makes all things new. "One God" then means *monarchia*, one reign, one kingdom, one eternal glory, one saving history of creation and redemption and fulfillment. With this idea of the deity of God as the one sovereign creator who determines all things, Athanasius was able to enunciate both the distinction and the unity in God: "For there is but one form of Godhead, which is also in the Word; and one God, the Father, existing by Himself according as He is above all, and appearing in the Son according as He pervades all things, and in the Spirit according as in Him He acts in all things through the Word. For thus we confess God to be *one through the Triad*, and we say that it is much more religious than the godhead of the heretics with its many kinds, and many parts, to entertain a belief of the One Godhead in a Triad" (AA III:402).[53] If that is so, the issue for Christian theology is not whether we are theist or atheist, but whether we are trinitarian. The "one form of the Godhead" is the office of the Creator, but holding this title is the Father, who does all things through His own Word in the power of His own Spirit, that is, as the Triad. Each exercises the same creative power, but each according to its own personal characteristic, in the sequence "from the Father, through the Son, in the Spirit."[54]

As this Trinity, God is His own life eternally, antecedent to the creation as subsequent to its fulfillment. Athanasius thus appropriates the ideas of Ignatius, Irenaeus, and Origen. The Son's "generation is an eternal process; 'just as the Father is always good by nature, so He is by nature always generative' (*aei genntikos*). 'It is entirely correct,' he writes, 'to call Him the Father's eternal offspring. For the Father's being was never incomplete, needing an essential feature to be added to it; nor is the Son's generation like a man's from his parent, involving His coming into existence after the Father. Rather He is God's offspring, and since God is eternal and He belongs to God as Son, He exists from all eternity." Kelly explains: Athanasius's fundamental position then "is that the divine *ousia*, simple and indivisible, is shared at once by Father and Son. The distinction between them is real, and lies in the distinction between the Godhead considered as eternally activating, expressing and begetting Itself, and the selfsame Godhead considered as eternally activated, expressed and begotten."[55] God as Self-Giver and God as Self-Given (and God as Self-Giving). With this idea, the last piece of the puzzle falls into place. Even in the life of God, to be God is not statically to possess but ever to give and ever to receive and ever to return. The One who can create all things other than God lives eternally as Giver, Given, and Giving in the true and living "eternal return of the same."

Athanasius consequently is able to add a clarification, which does not rob the paradox of the Incarnation of its truth but only of unintelligibility. In Athanasius's trinitarian theology, the issue is, as Jenson notes, "not so much the 'status' of Jesus as about who and what God is himself."[56] Even when some have described the One, meaning the Father, as "unoriginated [*agenetos*]," they have not meant to say that the Son was originated, that is, created or made [*genetos*]. Rather they have meant to say that "the Father has no personal cause, but rather is Himself the Father of Wisdom [Sophia, the Logos, who is eternally begotten, *gennetos*], and in Wisdom has made all things that are originated" (DS 47:475). The christological paradox is true and truly understood, not when asserted as nonsense, *credo quia absurdam est*; but when it opens minds of creatures to the God who gives Himself in the flesh of Christ for their salvation as the God who is antecedently the eternal Son of His own Father. By the same token, it was from the beginning the paradoxical proclamation of Jesus as the crucified Lord that demanded the development of this new trinitarian understanding of the reality of God.

The creator-creature distinction, parsed by this trinitarian theology, became the decisive argument for the divinity of the Holy Spirit. "If the Holy Spirit were a creature, we should have no participation in God in him." But the triune God's purpose of salvation is fulfilled in the work of the Holy Spirit, the Lord and Giver of life. "The Father, through the Word, in the Holy Spirit, creates and renews all things."[57] How could the Holy Spirit not also be God, the third person of God's life? The Spirit is the agent of the new creation, who raised Jesus from the dead, the Lord and Giver of Life temporal as well as eternal. Therefore the Spirit too is creator not creature. Indeed, the very works of the Father and of the Son cohere in the Spirit's, just as salvation is not the stabilization of this world as it is, but its eschatological new creation by the Spirit who unites to Jesus' death and resurrection to deliver creatures to the Father's waiting arms. So "the Triad is in [the Spirit] complete. In him the Word makes glorious the creation, and, by bestowing upon it divine life and Sonship, draws it to the Father."[58] This is the *Spiritus creator* who "fructifies the economy of salvation by divinizing the saved."[59] The Spirit as also creator—not the private inward sanctifier of the pious, the impersonal source of inspiration by which they make themselves worthy of grace[60]—but as true creator by the Word of the Father of the new creation, secures Trinitarianism and overthrows the stabilizing metaphysics of the status quo ante. The triumph of Trinitarianism over the isolated, self-satisfied immutable shadow-Being of Platonism thus proved an ontological bombshell. The one God, the creator, redeemer, and fulfiller of all things, more than *exists* as self-identical; He ever *lives* as *internally related in love*. Robert Jenson emphasizes: "It is the Trinity as such—and not the Father as such—who is God. In the judgment of Athanasius' contemporaries, this insight was his great theological achievement."[61]

Lord and Giver of Life

In light of the soteriological concerns just discussed, the eventual revision of the creed from Nicea of 325 at Constantinople in 381 may be understood to authorize the worship of the eternal Spirit, together with the Father and Son, as the one triune God, the redeeming God of sinful and perishing humanity (Basil, HS I). The worship of the Trinity is, one must then stress, the end of salvation to which the doctrine moves, as if to say that true speech about the true God is finally doxological, the Spirit's own ecstatic anticipation already now in believers assembled for the eternal praise of the kingdom, at the victory feast of God and His Lamb. The Creed of Constantinople, 381, would much more deserve the title "Athanasian" than the Latin creed so named (which in reality developed some years later in the West and certainly was not written by Athanasius).[62] The Constantinople edition of the creed was and remains the chief doctrinal text of the ecumenical church; it "was admitted as authoritative in East and West alike from 451 onwards [Council of Chalcedon], and it has retained that position, with one significant variation in its text [that is, the Western interpolation of the *filioque* clause], right down to the present day. So far from displacing it, the Reformation reaffirmed its binding character and gave it a new lease of life and an extended currency by translating it into the vernacular tongues."[63]

When we compare the text of 381 to the earlier one adopted in Nicea in 325, we see that the "Constantinopolitan Creed" is in fact based on a slightly different creedal text. This is indicated by numerous, insignificant variations in detail.[64] The significant thing is that the *homoousios* of Nicea is retained, and the section on the Holy Spirit is expanded to describe "the Lord and Giver of Life, who proceeds from the Father, who with the Father and the Son together is worshipped and glorified." The doctrine of the eternal Trinity of persons is completed with the doxological acknowledgment, if not explicit confession, of the co-equal divine personhood of the Holy Spirit. Kelly concludes, "It seems clear that the [Constantinopolitan] council's primary object was to restore and promote the Nicene faith in terms that would take account of the further development of doctrine, especially with regard to the Holy Spirit, which had taken place since Nicea."[65] As Basil the Great, who was hesitant to call the Holy Spirit God in deference to the same reticence in Scripture's rhetoric, finally argued: "One, moreover, is the Holy Spirit, and we speak of Him singly, conjoined as He is to the one Father through the one Son, and through Himself completing the adorable and blessed Trinity" (Basil, HS 45). How did things come to this?

The *Homoiousions* and the *Homoousions*

It is evident from the preceding that during Athanasius's lifetime, that is, for the fifty years following the council at Nicea in A.D. 325, no one could have guessed that its *homoousios* would win the future of the church for Trinitarianism. "The great majority of bishops, while horrified by the bold statements of Arius, were too deeply entrenched in a pluralistic, mildly subordinationist trinitarian theology [stemming from Origen] to take kindly to the *homoousios*, with its wholly un-Scriptural flavor and its apparently Sabellian bias."[66] According to Lietzman, the Creed of Nicea's term *homoousios* was so fraught with difficulties that until 358 the term "never appears. . . . Nobody, not even . . . Athanasius used it as a test of orthodoxy. . . . The content of the Nicene declaration of faith exhausts itself in condemning Arius."[67] The Nicene council's notion of *homoousios*, as we noted, seemed to assert the opposite error to Arius's. It seemed to deny any real distinction between the Father and the Son, since it seemed to say they were one and the same thing. How can the Father and the Son both be the one and same reality, yet really distinct and individual?

The resistance to the *homoousios* had been led by Arius's defender, Eusebius of Caesarea. In fact, he was also present at Nicea in 325. There he had reluctantly agreed to sign the creed out of deference to the emperor's wish for religious concord. But he soon began an influential campaign against the concept, as he sought Arius's restoration. We can discern his objection already in a letter that Eusebius wrote immediately after the council that tried to explain and justify his assent at the Synod. In it, Eusebius drastically reinterpreted the creed's innovative and offensive term *homoousios*. Close reading of the letter's vague language reveals that Eusebius presupposed an Origenist understanding of the Logos as the first, unique, incomparable replica-creature of the Father, divine by close association with the latter. Indeed, Eusebius as much as admits that he accepted the term *homoousios* at the council as only a pious term of honor, not as an accurate ontological description of the Logos's relation to the Father. Thus Eusebius claims that the council had understood *homoousios*

> to indicate [the Logos's] being of the Father, but not as if he were a part of the Father. So I agreed to subscribe to this in the sense of the pious teaching that declares that the Son is of the Father, but not as being a part of his essence. So I agreed to this idea, not rejecting the word *homoousios*, having before me the aim of peace, and that of not falling away from the sound doctrine. In the same way I accepted the phrase, "begotten and not made," since they alleged that "made" is a term shared with the other creatures of God which came into being through the Son, which the Son is in no way like, since he is not a work of God comparable to those things which came into being through him, but is of a nature superior to everything made, which the divine oracles teach was begotten of the Father, the manner of his generation being ineffable and indescribable for every nature that came into being. So the phrase, "the Son is *homoousios* with the Father," stands up if properly examined—not in the manner of bodies or similarly to mortal animals, nor by division or cutting up of the essence—*nor by any suffering or alteration or change of the essence and power of the Father*, for the unbegotten divine nature of the Father is free from all these things. . . . The Son of God bears no similarity with the creatures of God that came into being, but is in every way *made like* only to the Father who begot him.[68]

The position that Eusebius defends here is that the Son is "made like" the Father as a replica or image of him. This so-called semi-Arian position came to be called *homoiousios*, the slight insertion of the single Greek letter *iota* changing the meaning of *homoousios*, "of the *same* being with the Father," to that of "a being *similar* to the Father." What difference does an iota make?

The religiously indifferent and believers who are anti-theological have for centuries made sport of the fifty-year dispute that followed over this little iota.[69] But we can see in the foregoing statement of Eusebius that this iota stands for philosophical monotheism's religious dread of introducing even a whiff of becoming into the being of the Father that in all religious seriousness is taken as absolute, Tillich's *das Unbedingt*. The Logos is only *like* His Father in being His replica or copy so that He can do the dirty work on behalf of the Absolute. Therefore relationship, love, movement are *not* to be introduced into God's very being, which is God by virtue of being totally self-identical. That is precisely Eusebius's (indeed all Platonic theology's) apophatic point, that is, to preserve God as the perfect being from any kind of involvement in becoming. Evidently enough, the Nicene doctrine of the *homoousios* contradicts that by involving the Father's being in the Son's incarnation by virtue of its identity with the latter. Jenson comments: "The Son is not an entity originated outside God by God's externally directed choice. . . . [Rather] there *is* a differentiation within God. . . . *To be God is to be related*. With that the [Nicene] fathers contradicted the main principle of Hellenic theology."[70] What difference does an iota make? A great deal of difference in our conception of God and His relation to the world. God is not the still silence before the world began—and for that matter ever since. God is the ever-abundant eternal love that called the world into being, speaks the world along its way, and will bring it to fulfillment in His company at the victory shout, "Behold, I make all things new!" For such reasons the Nicene theologians could not accede to an understanding of the Son as an external replica *like* God the Absolute Father, no matter how close and how precise an image—which is what Eusebius imagined and indeed required with his single little iota.

Eusebius was not a great mind. He still wanted to call his absolute, unrelated, unoriginate deity "Father." He did not perceive the inconsequence. A politician acting like a theologian, he was attempting to find middle ground between Arius's consistent, rationalistic left-wing Origenism and the (to him) disturbing implication of the *homoousios* of the Nicene Creed, that is, of predicating in any sense whatsoever "alteration or change in the essence or power of the Father."

It was only years later that the term *homoousios* regained currency, in reaction against the polemics of radical neo-Arianism represented by Aetios and Eunomius, who developed further the Platonic dialectic of negative theology inherent in Arius's stance. Gradually *homoousios* emerged as the slogan of Trinitarianism that effectively excluded the subtler error of semi-Arianism as well as that of the increasingly radical Neo-Arians or "Anomians" (the Son is *"unlike"* the Father), as they were called. These argued that the "idea of God is so far above the very idea of causality that we cannot even say He is the cause of His own being. Hence each and every causal relation within the divine nature must be abolished, nor is it possible to speak of "begetting" within God's being. Accordingly, God remained for all eternity unbegotten in His nature. Similarly, a begotten being was for all eternity something different in substance from God, and all talk of the *homoousios* or *homoiousios* was vain."[71] With this turn of events, the erstwhile enemies, the *Homoiousians* following Eusebius and *Homoousians* following Athanasius, found themselves aligned on a common front, alike under Anomian attack by a consistently Platonic theology of the absoluteness of God that found political expression in the campaign of the emperor Julian the Apostate. "Now, and really for the first time now, the Nicene formula, with its crucial term, *homoousios*, came into the forefront of the dispute."[72]

During this period in the fifties and sixties of the fourth century, Athanasius retrieved the concept *homoousios*. In his treatise *De decretis*, he undertook a detailed analysis and defense of the creed of 325. He explains that the term *homoousios* means nothing but to affirm the ineffable eternal generation of the Son, "God from God, Light from Light": "Since the generation of the Son from the Father is not according to the nature of men, and [is] not only like, but inseparable from the essence of the Father, and [since] He and the Father are one . . . and the Word is ever in the Father and the Father in the Word, as radiance stands toward light . . . therefore the Council, as understanding this, suitably wrote *homoousios*."[73] Notice how the notion of divine simplicity works in this passage merely as rule to deny that generation in the deity is like generation in creatures; it does not pretend to give some positive ontological insight, as with the Anomians cited above, asking us to imagine a God beyond causality. Consequently, we have in this passage of Athanasius an acute anticipation of the eventual theological solution: the eternal generation of the Son expresses *essentially what the Father is*, the ungiven Giver. It belongs to the Father's own personal identity that He eternally generates His own Son of His own being. This formulation expresses both distinction in person and continuity in being. On the other hand, the formulation shows what little sense there is in predicating of the unchanging, absolutely immutable and unrelated divine being of the Anomians the name "the Father," since, as Athanasius argued with no little force, a father must by definition beget offspring. With the Arians, the term "father" functions not as a name based on a proper characteristic, "God is the Father of His own Son," but as an honorific metaphor, "God is like a father, preeminently, perhaps, to Jesus, but in principle to all His creatures." But if God is indeed eternally and truly the Father, then there is an eternal begetting of His own Son. The Son in that case is *of the same essence* as the Father, just as God's eternal being lives *in this true but ineffable becoming*.

There was movement also from the side of the Homoiousians, who were awoken with a shock by the brief reign of Julian the Apostate in 361–363. If we recall the imperial triumphalism of Eusebius of Caesarea and the general tendency of semi-Arian theology to subordinate the church to the empire, interpreting the conversion of Constantine as bringing an end to the theology of the martyrs, we can imagine their disillusionment at Julian's attempt to re-paganize society. But even more telling was the kind of paganism that Julian sought to reinstate. His was a mystical version of Neoplatonism, not some crude and primitive mythology; it thus resembled the Platonic dynamics of negative theology in Arianism all too closely. For Julian, "the Divine Word was not to be identified with [the man] Christ but with the power and glory of King Helios, the Sun."[74] Lietzman thus characterizes Julian: "Well did he know that this religion of his was not purely and simply that of the ancients, but he held it was identical in essence. He looked at the myths and the cult-ceremonies through Neoplatonic spectacles. . . . This philosophical theology of myths [was] a theology that was, in the end, nothing more than the monotheism of the silver age of the ancient world pressed into forms modeled on Plato. King Helios is Aurelian's empire-god elevated into the world of Plato's ideas. Julian confided his plans to this god's care."[75] The very philosophical monotheism that Origenism had sought to harness for the gospel now unmistakably showed its true colors. Its Logos could never be fully identified with the Crucified, just as its Logos could never be fully identified with the Absolute. In Julian the spirit of the past seeking "grounding" in the structure of an eternal cosmos arose against the Spirit of the kingdom that comes. True deity, in Platonism's view, could never be the free and freedom-making Spirit of the crucified Jesus and His Father who gives life to the dead and calls into being worlds as yet unknown. The choice between the two monotheisms was manifest for all to see.

The shock was not lost on Basil the Great. This eldest of the Cappadocian theologians came out of moderate Origenist schooling, with a deep appreciation for Hellenic culture but an even deeper commitment to the wisdom of the gospel. Basil once remarked autobiographically: "Much time had I spent in vanity, and had wasted nearly all my youth in the vain labor that I underwent in acquiring the wisdom made foolish by God. Then once upon a time, like a man roused from deep sleep, I turned my eyes to the marvelous light of the truth of the Gospel, and I perceived the uselessness of "the wisdom of the princes of this world, that come to naught" (Letter 223). It is a fascinating circumstance of history that as children, Basil and Julian (the latter-day Apostate) were schooled together in the best Hellenic fashion. They even studied the Bible together as schoolboys. Thus Basil knew that Julian knew very well what he was rejecting and why he was rejecting it. After Julian's death in battle, the new emperor's continued support of Arianism, coupled with the rise of the radical neo-Arian theology of Aetius and Eudomius, disabused once and for all Basil, his young brother Gregory (of Nyssa), and their friend Gregory (the Theologian, of Nazianzus) of the confident synthesis of Origenist theology. Julian's apostasy to Neoplatonism made "semi-Arianism" of the type represented by Eusebius of Caesarea an impossibility for them. As a result, Basil began to make overtures to Athanasius, imploring him to reach out to the many sympathetic Homoiousians, who could be won over to the doctrine of the *homoousios*, if only it were clearly distinguished from Sabellian modalism. Athanasius did just this in the treatise *De Synodis*, where as always he firmly rejected Arianism but also addressed the Homoiousians as "brothers" who could be persuaded to the truth. "Those who accept everything else that was defined at Nicea," he wrote, "and doubt only about the *homoousios*, must not be treated as enemies, nor do we attack them as Ario-maniacs, nor as opponents of the Fathers, but we discuss the matter with them as brothers with brothers, who mean what we mean, and dispute only about the word" (DS 41).

The Failure of Biblicism

A further factor that led to the convergence between Athanasius and the Cappadocians was the failure of biblicism to solve the problem. By biblicism I mean the attempt to bypass logical, hermeneutical, and metaphysical questions probing the truth-value of Christian beliefs by direct appeal to arbitrarily selected texts of Scripture. In fact, the only right use of Scripture for purposes of theology is the one that passes through such questions in critical dogmatics. The attempt to short-circuit this rigorous examination is obscurantist, authoritarian, and Christianly speaking, self-defeating. Recall how Eusebius wished to continue to call God "Father" and complained that he only wanted to avoid unscriptural language. Eusebius was the first of many to argue that *both* Arius's *Thalia and* the Creed of Nicea contained "non-Scriptural terms, from which has come almost all the disorder and confusion of the Church."[76] Yet the question goes begging. We must ask Eusebius: Father of whom? And more generally, What gospel (Gal 1:6-9) or rule of faith (Gal 6:15-16)? Which Christ (Mark 13:5)? Whose Spirit (1 John 4:1)? Apart from critical dogmatics—the discipline of Irenaeus, now again exemplified in Athanasius—the Bible is putty in the hands of self-proclaimed prophets ("enthusiasts"—literally, those "full of God," in Luther's colorful expression, "as if they had swallowed the Holy Spirit, feathers and all").

The point is that one can easily manipulate biblical language to give expression to fundamentally divergent views of salvation from that parsed by the baptismal creed, telling of some other deity than the one God who is determined by His incarnate Son and Pentecostal Spirit to redeem His creation and bring it to fulfillment. Biblical language itself requires this theological rule for determining the correct sense of it. Recalling that the devil quoted Scripture to tempt Christ, and that Paul the Apostle quoted Greek poets and philosophers, Athanasius in *De Synodis* affirmed that even if one "uses terms not in Scripture, it makes no difference" if the meaning is true to the sense of Scripture. Likewise, if the heretic "uses scriptural terms," he is only all the more dangerous because of it (DS 39). The semi-Arian party had early on tried to end the controversy by evading the critical dogmatic question of the Logos's relation to the Divine with a pious appeal, as it were, to "whatever the Bible says": "For all that has been delivered in the Divine Scriptures, whether by the Prophets or the Apostles, do we truly and reverentially both believe and follow."[77] Years later the neo-Arians used the same biblicist tactic to censure theological vocabulary, arguing that "no sermon was to be delivered and no question was to be raised about *substantia*, called *ousia* by the Greeks. The same was to hold good about both *homoousios* and *homoiousios*, for there was nothing about either of them in the Bible, and both went beyond human understanding."[78] Such biblicism, whether in the hands of the theological Left or Right, is a sub-evangelical alternative to theological understanding and an uncritical evasion of intellectual responsibility in Christian thought. Eschewing critical thinking, it leaves the church to the self-proclaimed prophets.

Indeed, appeals to an apparent *sola scriptura* effectively sided with Arianism against the Nicene theology. That became evident a few years later in 358 in Ancyra, when the neo-Arians formally condemned the Nicene formula *homoousios*.[79] The year 359 brought the prohibition of the term *ousia* from theology, deciding that it sufficed to say that "the Son is like (*homoios*) the Father in everything."[80] The emperor continued to press for a definite end to the controversy, which next led to the formulation: "We reject *homoousios* and *homoiousios* as contrary to the Scriptures, we condemn *anhomoios*. Our formula runs, 'the Son is similar to or like (*homoios*) the Father.'"[81] The Creed of Ariminum (360), which became historically significant as "the last of the Arian Creeds, and the longest-lived since it survived among the Germanic [Goth] Arian churches until their extinction in the seventh century,"[82] spelled out the biblicist line of argument: "But as to the word "essence" (*ousia*), which was used by the Fathers in simplicity, but, being unknown to the people caused scandal, because the Scriptures do not contain it, it seems best that it should be taken away and no mention be made of it in the future, since the divine Scriptures nowhere made mention of the essence of Father and Son; nor, similarly, should the word *hypostasis* be used of Father and Son and Holy Spirit. But we say that Son is like the Father."[83] All this solved nothing, for relations of similarity no less than relations of identity presuppose some univocal notion of being by which they can be discriminated. Substantively what was in question was not the exegesis of this or that passage of Scripture, in any event, but the sense of Scripture as a whole. Is the Word of God to be taken as the living God Himself in His self-communication, or statically as only a secondary, derivative copy or replica of God, taken as utter transcendence? In Jesus, do we meet God or an inspired human being's representation of God? Is Jesus definitive for the understanding of God, or have we already an adequate notion of deity?

Biblicism failed because, as Gregory Nazianzus commented about the Arians, "their love for the letter [of Scripture] is but a cloak for their impiety [toward the deity of God the Son and God the Holy Spirit]."[84] Thus the Nicene theologians could declare with fervor equal to that of any Arian, "Let God-inspired Scripture decide between us; and on whichever side be found doctrines in harmony with the word of God, in favour of that side will be cast the vote of truth" (Letter 189). Basil could likewise charge that the intention of the Arians "is not to teach simple souls lessons drawn from Holy Scripture, but to mar the harmony of the truth by heathen philosophy." Thus the problem could not be solved on the level of mere biblicism. Rather Basil argued that the Arians "ought to confess that the Father is God, the Son God and the Holy Ghost God, as they have been taught by the divine words, *and by those who have understood them in their highest sense*" (Letter 8). Who are these? What is that?

Basil understands that there is no such thing as uninterpreted Scripture; that interpretation in turn stands knowingly or not in a definite tradition ("the Fathers," that is, the theology of the martyrs); and that accordingly the theological task is nothing but that of understanding Scripture in the highest sense, that is, the theological sense, *as kataphatic language about God* (duly qualified by the rule of divine simplicity). That is why one must confess the *homoousios*, even though the term itself is not biblical. What is manifestly biblical is the teaching that the Son and the Holy Spirit are the "source of sanctification," which only true God can be. Thus "in accordance with true doctrine [we] speak of the Son as neither like [that is, the Homoiousian position], nor unlike [that is, the Anomian position]. Each of these terms is equally impossible, for like and unlike are predicated in relation to quality, and the divine is free from quality. We on the contrary, confess identity of nature and accept the *homoousios* . . . God in substance, Who begat the Son, God in substance. From this the *homoousios* is proved" (Letter 8). For, as we have heard, divine is not a "quality" (like being immortal or impassible) that something can more or less possess or reflect. The adjective "divine" stands for the unique "nature" of the creator of the world, that which the real, singular, concrete God *is*, something describable in faith, even as it admittedly, indeed infinitely transcends our comprehension. The theological claim arising from the gospel's encounter with the antecedent metaphysics of Platonism is that Jesus, His Father, and their Spirit together as internally related *is* this one, unique, true God, the only creator of all that is other than God, a single transcendent "nature" to be manifest in His eternal reign over all things. *Homoousios* affirms that the three of the gospel narrative individually possess and together exercise this singular and exclusive set of capacities.

The Trinitarian Theology of the Cappadocians

Thus the solution of 381, mediated by the Cappadocians, involved a somewhat arbitrary semantical distinction between two Greek words that previously had been virtual synonyms: *ousia* and *hypostasis*. Both words in general loosely denoted something that is real. So these words could be used as synonyms in the anti-Arian anathema of the Council of Nicea in A.D. 325 that, recall, rejected those who teach that "the Son of God is of a different *hypostasis* or *ousia*" than His Father. The Cappadocians understood the one divine *ousia* of the Father, Son, and Spirit as the one, identical reign (*monarchia*) that is expressed in the creation, redemption, and sanctification of the world, with whatever capacities are requisite to eschatological creation: "How then, if one [is Father] and one [is Son], are there not two Gods? Because we speak of a king, and of the king's image, and not of two kings. The majesty is not cloven in two, nor the glory divided. The sovereignty and authority over us is one, and so the doxology ascribed by us is not plural but one" (HS 45). God's deity is not taken here as some "thing," not even a "spiritual" thing, a quality that various subjects might in varying degrees enjoy. Deity is *the event* of that One who comes to reign over all things, the Father, through the Son, in the Spirit, which must be conceived to have such and such capacities requisite to the Reign, preeminently power, wisdom, and love. To be God is to be this one Lord who lives and reigns over all, now and forever. So deity is one *ousia* as *event*, the divine capacities understood retrospectively from the event, as Karl Barth taught contemporary theology in his *Church Dogmatics*: "According to the Bible, God's being with us is the event of revelation."[85]

Each person of the Trinity is wholly agent in this event of divine life, though each in its distinct way, as determined by its relations to the other two. "Thus the way of the knowledge of God [in the economy, in revelation] lies from the One Spirit through the One Son to the One Father, and conversely [the gifts of God] extend from the Father through the Only-begotten to the Spirit" (HS 47). "Grace flows down in an unbroken stream from the Father, through the Son and the Spirit, on the persons worthy of it," as Nyssa says, echoing Basil.[86] This definite ranking or better sequence does not imply inequality in essence, since one may belong to "one only of two worlds. . . . No new attribute on the borderland of the Created and Uncreated can be thought of . . . anything . . . blended of the Created and the Uncreated."[87] Rather this sequence indicates difference in the personal exercise of the same essence. Thus Nyssa says that "the Holy Spirit is of the same rank as the Father and the Son, so that there is no difference between them in anything to be thought or named that devotion can ascribe to a Divine nature. We confess that, *save his being contemplated as with peculiar attributes in regard of Person*, the Holy Spirit is indeed from God, and of the Christ, according to Scripture, but that, while not to be confounded with the Father in being never originated, nor with the Son in being the Only-begotten, and *while to be regarded separately in certain distinctive properties*, He has in all else, as I have just said, an exact identity."[88] With this acknowledgment of the person of the Spirit, the church was brought to the formula of one *ousia* in three *hypostases*, though the internal relation of the hypostases, with the distinctive capacities assigned to each, does not get the proper attention it deserves in the abbreviated formula. Again, in Nyssa's words: "We are not to think of the Father as ever parted from the Son, nor to look for the Son as separate from the Holy Spirit. As it is impossible to mount to the Father, unless our thoughts are exalted thither through the Son, so it is impossible also to say that Jesus is Lord except by the Holy Spirit. Therefore Father, Son and Holy Spirit are to be known only in a perfect Trinity, in closest consequence and union with each other, before all creation, before all the ages, before anything whatever of which we can form an idea. The Father is always Father, and in Him the Son, and with the Son the Holy Spirit."[89]

Thus, as Grillmeier observes, "the Nicene triad is understood strictly within the Godhead,"[90] that is, not as a vertically descending hierarchy of being extending downward from the Unbegotten Father above through the Logos and so on down to the material world in the familiar Platonic scheme. By the same token, it was the discovery of the proper place of the Holy Spirit within the divine life that proved the key to understanding the "triad strictly within the Godhead." Not the world, but the Holy Spirit, completes God's deity, so that God may *freely* undertake the fulfillment of the non-necessary world in His own project of eschatological creation. For trinitarians, who are at the same time the truly radical monotheists, the world is understood as creation *ex nihilo, unfinished* creation, a history of salvation, an economy culminating in the Spirit's gift of life to the dead, the glory of God, and the eternal victory of His reign. The question during this fifty-year period, therefore, was not only how to find the right concepts logically to express the trinitarian view of God. Certainly "after Nicea there was necessarily a hard struggle to see how both the oneness of substance of the Son and the Father and the distinction between them could go together."[91] But that logical struggle was also, indeed chiefly, the soteriological struggle to see the Holy Spirit, Lord and Giver of life, rather than the static cosmos, as the final horizon within the eternal order of being, the divine life that is not some necessary part or aspect of the cosmos. As a consequence of conceiving the divine life, the living God, the Holy Trinity, then, the world could be freed up to become a history on the way to the best of all possible worlds. Or to say the same from the perspective of the cosmos: it was a soteriological struggle to understand how the resurrection of the body could be understood as the redemption and sanctification of this world, not flight from it. It is fitting therefore to conclude with a survey of the Cappadocian arguments for the divine personhood of the Holy Spirit.

Worshipped and Glorified, Together with the Father and the Son

To be God is to give—God. The Spirit cannot give the gift of eternal life unless He Himself possesses this gift as Lord and so gives it by right. It will not do to speak of the Spirit as an impersonal divine energy or an angelic ministering spirit, since the saving action attributed to the Spirit presupposes an agent: "If he is an Activity . . . He will cease to exist as soon as He has been effected, for this is the nature of an Activity." But the Holy Spirit is a personal agent, One who exists substantially as the one God and so acts personally in giving God: "He acts and says such and such things, and defines, and is grieved, and is angered, and has all the quality that belongs clearly to one that moves, and not to movement" (Nazianzus, OR V:6). So the Spirit must be regarded as a substantial agent, a personal reality or *hypostasis*, just like the Father and the Son. Of what rank is He in relation to these two? Is He creator or creature? Nazianzus asks, "If He is in the same rank with myself, how can He make me God, or join me with Godhead?" (OR V:6). "If He is not to be worshipped, how can He deify me by Baptism? But if He is to be worshipped, surely He is an Object of adoration, and if an Object of adoration He must be God; the one is linked to the other, a truly golden and saving chain. And from the Spirit comes our New Birth, and from the New Birth our new creation, and from the new creation our deeper knowledge of the dignity of Him from Whom it is derived" (OR V:28).

Nazianzus argues here from Christian experience and tradition, conceding that direct, explicit biblical testimony to the divine personhood of the Holy Spirit is sparse. The reason for this is the historical nature of revelation: "The Old Testament proclaimed the Father openly, the Son more obscurely. The New manifested the Son, and suggested the Deity of the Spirit. Now the Spirit Himself dwells among us, and supplies us with a clearer demonstration of Himself. . . . The Deity of the Spirit Himself [was one of the things] made clear later on when such knowledge should be seasonable and capable of being received" (OR V:26). The argument from soteriology convinces even one "who admits the silence of Scripture." Nevertheless, there is indeed a "swarm of testimony" in Scripture to the deity of the Holy Spirit for those with eyes to see. The testimony is chiefly christological: the Spirit is the Spirit of Jesus and His Father. "Look at these facts: Christ is born; the Spirit is His forerunner. He is baptized; the Spirit bears witness. He is tempted; the Spirit leads Him up. He works miracles; the Spirit accompanies them. He ascends; the Spirit takes His place. What great things are there in the idea of God that are not in His power? What titles that belong to God are not applied to Him, except only Unbegotten and Begotten?" (OR V:29). For Nazianzus, the scriptural testimony points in one direction only, but it is the soteriological argument that is conclusive, provided that soteriology is drawn from Christ and His death and resurrection. The Holy Spirit is the "creator Spirit, Who by Baptism and Resurrection creates anew" (OR V:29). If the Spirit is a person or agent, if the Spirit exists with the Father and Son and so does and can do the creating works that belong to God alone, then it follows that as the Son is *homoousios* with the Father, so likewise is the Spirit: "What then? Is the Spirit God? Most certainly. Well then, is He Consubstantial? Yes, if He is God" (OR V:10).

Basil was more reluctant than his friend explicitly to call the Holy Spirit God. He preferred the reserve of Scripture on this topic. Yet in a sense Basil's argument for the Spirit is even more impressive than that of Nazianzus, for he argues for the right of worshipping the Spirit together with the Father and the Son. The Arians had objected that the scriptural pattern of prayer and praise is to worship the Father, with the Son, in the Spirit, which economy they took in an ontologically subordinationist fashion. Basil agreed that this pattern is biblical and correct, as it expresses the economy of God: the Father loves the world by giving His Son in the Spirit, so that reborn by the Spirit, united with Christ, the world returns to the Father in the sacrifice of praise. But he points to the fact that in this economy, the Spirit is inseparably linked with the Father and the Son, sharing the same titles and operations and so the one divine being in its act. "Shall we not give Him glory?" That is, together with the Father and the Son? If we withhold worship from the Spirit, on the other hand, do we not "tear the Spirit asunder from the Father and the Son[?] Where then are we to take Him and rank Him? With the creature?" If not, we confess that the Spirit is to be worshipped and glorified together *with* the Father and the Son. The preposition "with" expresses the Spirit's "essential existence before the ages and His ceaseless abiding *with* the Son and the Father." This "fellowship"— "intimate, congenital, and inseparable"—cannot be "contemplated without requiring titles expressive of eternal conjunction." Thus "whenever we have in mind the Spirit's proper rank, we contemplate Him as being *with* the Father and the Son, but when we think of the grace that flows from Him operating on those who participate in it, we say that the Spirit is *in* us" (Basil, HS XXVI:63). This is to say, on reflection, that the Christian life of faith, so far as faith is rigorously understood as the Spirit's sovereign work "in us" by the proclamation of Jesus' resurrection as the Father's good news for the world—such faith is a personal participation in the tri-personal life of the Holy Trinity. While Basil shies from explicitly calling the Holy Spirit God, his argument nonetheless powerfully affirms the truth that the Holy Spirit completes the Trinity, even as it is the Trinity, inclusive of the Spirit, who is adored as true God.

True God! What can that be? What notion of divine nature is rendered by Trinitarianism? Gregory of Nyssa says: "It is the peculiar and exquisite privilege of Deity, and no other," to give blessings, while needing none from others.[92] *Esse Deum dare*—to be God is to give. This is the true Christian theology of divine *apatheia*, not mere immunity from change, not the false infinity of the unknowable Absolute, not the ambiguous formula of divine simplicity, but rather that freedom from self and freedom for others that the Spirit works in the Father's relation to the Son and the Son's to the Father. This is the divine *agape* as embodied in the gospel's mercy to the sinner, creative love that confers new life on those really dead, as also value to the scorned and new harmony for the estranged. This divine self-giving love—call it charity's divine complexity—becomes visible in the works on the earth of the Spirit of the Father of the Son. That divine gift of giving and being given is the best and greatest proof of the Spirit's co-equal divine personhood, when complexity of charity is the signature of deity. "If such, then, is the greatness of the Spirit, and whatever is morally beautiful, whatever is good, coming from God as it does through the Son, is completed by the instrumentality of the Spirit that 'works all in all,'" Gregory asks, why would we set ourselves against our own life, our own hope, against God the Holy Spirit?[93] The Father and the Son live in the Spirit, in whom their love irrepressibly reaches out to create, redeem, and perfect the world in ever new ways, in ever fresh initiatives. In the creator Spirit, the Father and the Son make all things new. In the Spirit, we see the being of God as love, infinitely beyond our grasping, yet truly expressed to us and for us. Therefore, to God the Holy Spirit, together with the Father and the Son, be all glory now and forever. Amen. Such doxology is the final and truest form of Christian theology.

We should not say, then, "God is triune," as if "God" were a personal name or denominated a simple intellectual substance that may also happen to be Father, Son, and Holy Spirit. We should say, "The Trinity is God," as Gregory of Nyssa daringly illustrates: Jesus, His Father, and their Spirit are three lamps focused into one beam and the beam is God. Father, Son, and Holy Spirit is the proper name. The Trinity is the subject of the predicates of the Creator such as omnipotence, omniscience, benevolence, and so on. The Father is the source of this divine life who rules, the Son is the gift of divine life and the revelation of the Father's reign who obeys, and the Spirit is the Great Exchanger who realizes the Father's reign in us by communicating the Son to us and us to the Son on the way to the Father's kingdom of eternal life. In this distinction, relation, and order, the Father through the Word in the Holy Spirit creates and renews all things. When we describe the reality of the God of the Bible, we discover these three irreducible but integrally related agencies of divine being that together constitute the one divine action of love bringing in the reign of God. The reality of God is thus realistically described in this trinitarian way as the coming of His reign among us, the project of eschatological creation. As a result, the true risk of faith in God is authentically and unmistakably identified and intensified. One speaks of God responsibly not only intellectually in the work of critical dogmatics, but also ethically with the martyrs of the Lord Jesus, whose prayer, like their Lord's in the Garden of Gethsemane, sounds out, "Thy kingdom come! Thy will be done!" In this theology, everything really depends on the resurrection of the dead.

The "Impassible Passibility" of the Trinity

With a characteristic display of logical precision, historical erudition, and theological insight, Bruce Marshall has recently shown the profound inconsequence of many "confused"[1] attempts in contemporary theology to abolish the distinction between natures that in classical Christian theology attends the Creator and the creature.[2] Suffering or passibility, which Marshall carefully defines as "real exposure to involuntary change,"[3] entails mutability and temporality; this bundle of vulnerabilities may coherently be ascribed to the creature that is not God, but not to the creator of everything other (unless you beg the question of true deity, in Luther's rejoinder, by positing another creator over Him!). If, however, the Christian claim is that the Trinity is this one true Creator, then it follows, Marshall argues, that by nature the Trinity is impassible, immutable, and (timelessly) eternal. The paradoxical Christian message of the impassible passiblity of God, in this light, speaks exclusively of the gracious miracle of the incarnate Word and refers to the communication of natural properties that occurs in His unique life, death, and resurrection by virtue of His personal assumption of human nature.[4] Jesus Christ, and He alone, is the impassible passibility of the creator God, the Holy Trinity. The assumption of human nature by the divine Word can and does help the sinful and perishing creature just because the divine Word is and remains impassibly, that is to say, immutably and eternally united with His Father even at the darkest depth of the Crucified's cry of dereliction on our behalf (*in persona nostra*—Thomas[5]). Otherwise, the "resurrection of the forsaken Son would . . . only serve to eternalize his godforsakenness,"[6] not to reveal that dying man as the beloved Son, freely and out of the Father's own love bearing away the sin of the world with all eternal woe. It should be evident that the christological tendency of the present study accords with Marshall's cogent defense of the "two natures" doctrine.

Yet the oneness of the Trinity, no less than the tri-personality, is and remains an article of faith seeking understanding, not of comprehending sight. Until faith gives way to sight, the knowledge of God as creator, and therewith of divine unity, remains not only in doubt for afflicted faith. It remains ferociously disputed, as we witnessed in Irenaeus's confrontation with the Gnostics. As such, the oneness of God cannot be taken for granted even in Christian theology as some kind of axiomatic first principle, a rational or philosophical insight upon which to build, as upon a foundation, the edifice of revealed theology. In this interim time, the construal of divine nature as one and so simple in being is something that critical reason can attain, as we saw in the Platonists, but even this construal is highly precarious, unstable, and ambiguous. We can reason about what God is not and could rightly conclude that if there is that unique One who would be creator of all others, in relation to us creatures, who exist as passible, mutable, and temporal, this One would have to be impassible, immutable, and eternal. But even to think of God as creator, radically as creator *ex nihilo*, is to borrow a proposition from revealed theology, which natural theology would not otherwise entertain. Even with this borrowing, moreover, the way of negation in Christian theology tells us nothing positive about God in and for God, only about what God cannot be so far as God is related to us as Creator to creature. Materially, then, even this modified natural theology cannot tell us of the Creator who is also the Redeemer and Fulfiller of the creation, who must be therefore thought of as the perfect harmony of power, wisdom, and love, not only as Alpha but also as Omega. It cannot tell us of the complexity of that divine One and Only, of its own dynamism or life as a harmony ever to be ventured and gained, not a simplicity never ventured nor risked. We can only affirm such beliefs about divine complexity from the gospel narrative's further construal of divine nature as capable of a folly wiser than men, that "severe mercy" (Augustine) that justifies the ungodly and gives life to the dead. Nor then is it an innocent mistake when and if we reify this otherwise reverent rule for speaking about the ineffable singularity that is our Creator (and Redeemer and Fulfiller, since we have actually borrowed the radical idea of creator *ex nihilo* from the gospel's *oikonomia*) into a metaphysical ghost of pure abstraction from all that we creatures know of life in the moving, material world.

So it has not sufficed to leave the matter with a defense, howsoever cogent, of the two natures' distinction and their unique and saving communion in the person of the incarnate Son. Nor, of course, would Marshall think it suffices. But our reasons for thinking of this insufficiency may diverge. According to the argument of this book, it does not suffice because the otherwise very useful language of "nature," along with its conceptual cognates of oneness and simplicity in respect to God, has a long tradition in natural theology of inclining us to think in a way subversive of a thoroughgoing Trinitarianism—one that goes "all the way down." It inclines us to think, not of a set of characteristic possibilities in the reach of a living person or persons, but of actualities, that is, things as things in a settled state of realization, perfected, and as such not vulnerable, not changeable, not in motion, going nowhere, pure, sheer existence, one may suppose, but just the same supremely dead. It is a very different matter when we think of the immaterial substance of God as a social event (not a disembodied mental operation) where "nature" is a range of possibilities for relationship, rather than static perfections of an identity. This is to think of "nature" in terms of what Jenson called a metaphysics of anticipation rather than of persistence, and what I have urged in this book as the gospel's revision of classical metaphysics.

Taken as the eternal event of a unique Life, the immutable and impassible Trinity (so I have argued in this book) came to recognition in the development of creedal Christianity as the (intra-divine[7]) condition for the possibility of the impassible passibility of the merciful Christ, crucified, risen, and coming to reign as victorious Lord over all. The logical status of the doctrine of the immanent Trinity is that of a second-order reflection on the economic Trinity, as presented to us in the primary theology of the gospel narrative. Its reflection allows us to see, as Irenaeus first realized, that the economy proceeds as a free and sovereign decision, a divine self-determination *ad extra* of the three who are one life *ad intra*. That is all. Anything else is undisciplined speculation, and such speculation becomes pernicious, as Karl Barth so rightly maintained, if it makes this self-determination of the Trinity to create, redeem, and fulfill the world subject to, or limited by, a supposedly simple nature that cannot be ventured or risked even in its own self-determination.

Just this notion of the divine decree, however, gives us a fittingly trinitarian way to think of divine passibility as that venture or risk that attends any forgoing of some possibilities in favor of others. To God all things are possible, but not all things are wise or good. In acting according to the harmony of power, wisdom, and love, God thereby suffers God both in the kenosis of creation and in the kenosis of the Incarnation. In the fullness of time, the Father does not heed the Son's cry for deliverance. The Son obeys the Father's uncanny will to ignominious death. There is thus a true moment of eternal death in the life of God. That the Spirit surpasses this contradiction with a new possibility, also for God, is the Easter conviction of Christian faith.

But this self-surpassing of the God who gives has its basis in the eternal Trinity. According to such reflected faith, there is movement or circulation in the life of the Trinity. "You see," writes Nyssa, "the revolving circle of the

glory moving from Like to Like. The Son is glorified by the Spirit; the Father
is glorified by the Son; again the Son has His glory from the Father; and the
Only-Begotten thus becomes the glory of the Spirit."[8] This life is antecedent,
superintending, and subsequent to the temporal span of our world, so that
"faith completes the circle, and glorifies the Son by means of the Spirit, and the
Father by means of the Son."[9] It is fitting in turn that in our time it is the Son,
begotten of the Father before all worlds, who should be born of Mary; that it
is the Spirit, breathing the Father's favor on the Son, who should unleash the
gospel of God's free favor upon the earth; and that it is the almighty Father
who should so commission. For the God and Father of our Lord Jesus Christ
is determined by His Son and Spirit to create, redeem, and fulfill this world;
as true God He dwells no longer in blissful beatitude, but lives and reigns in
this fitting self-determination, inclusive of the cross of Jesus and of His Spirit-
steeled martyrs and confessors. True and living faith cannot resort to a transcendental guarantee borrowed from natural theology to evade the decision
and the risk that the Trinity itself does not evade in setting out to make of us
perishing sinners fit subjects of that Beloved Community straining to be born.

Anything that lives ventures and risks. The Holy Trinity ventures and risks.
Living faith ventures and risks. The assurance of living faith lies in its conviction
of the triune God's self-determination to prevail in a battle for us all that is as
real as the earth upon which the cross of Jesus stood, where once and for all
God surpassed God in order to become eternally and immutably God for us.

Notes

Introduction

1. Paul R. Hinlicky, "Luther's Antidocetism in the *Disputatio de divinitate et humanitate Christi* (1540)," in *Creator est creatura: Luthers Christologie als Lehre von der Idiomenkommunikation*, ed. O. Bayer and Benjamin Gleede (Berlin: de Gruyter, 2007), 139–85.

2. Paul R. Hinlicky, *Paths Not Taken: Fates of Theology from Luther through Leibniz* (Grand Rapids: Eerdmans, 2009).

3. Thomas F. Torrance, *The Trinitarian Faith: The Evangelical Theology of the Ancient Catholic Church* (Edinburgh: T&T Clark, 1993).

4. J. N. D. Kelly, *Early Christian Doctrines*, rev. ed. (San Francisco: Harper, 1978).

5. Jarolslav Pelikan, *The Christian Tradition: A History of the Development of Doctrine*, vol. 1, *The Emergence of the Catholic Tradition (100–600)* (Chicago: University of Chicago Press, 1975).

6. Tarmo Toom, *Classical Trinitarian Theology: A Textbook* (New York: T&T Clark, 2007).

7. Robert W. Jenson, *The Triune Identity: God according to the Gospel* (Philadelphia: Fortress Press, 1982).

8. See especially chapter 3 below.

9. See especially chapters 1 and 2 below.

10. See especially chapter 5 below.

11. Lewis Ayres, *Nicea and Its Legacy: An Approach to Fourth-Century Trinitarian Theology* (Oxford: Oxford University Press, 2006), 296–301. It is, in my view, revealing that Ayres here appeals to Augustine, *De Trinitate*, book 15, to crown his case for divine simplicity. Here the Bishop of Hippo "insists that each divine person possesses memory, understanding and will. But again, this assertion is necessary lest anyone think of the persons as performing a partial function within the Godhead. Augustine's insistence draws us to the full consequences of the logic or grammar of divine simplicity" (296). It also effectively neutralizes the doctrine of the Trinity as a theological account of the gospel narrative, the "economic" Trinity, as I show in this book. Ayres's stance may be contrasted to Luther's commentary on the Sentences of Peter Lombard, which forms the epigraph to this book; Ayres, in any case, associates divine *complexity*, as I would have it, with the errors of modern Protestantism, systematic theology, and the social rather than mental Trinity (see the final chapter, "In Spite of Hegel, Fire, and Sword," 384–429). There are no doubt many such errors, but challenging the Platonic dogma of simplicity in the name of the crucified God is not one of them. See here Robert W. Jenson's retort to Thomas G. Weinandy and his nuanced counterproposal in *Divine Impassibility and the Mystery of Human Suffering*, ed. James F. Keating and Thomas Joseph White (Grand Rapids: Eerdmans, 2009), 117–26.

12. Wilhelm Maurer, *Historical Commentary on the Augsburg Confession*, trans. H. George Anderson (Philadelphia: Fortress Press, 1986), 246–56.

13. Alisdair MacIntyre, *Against the Self-Images of the Age: Essays on Ideology and Philosophy* (Notre Dame: University of Notre Dame Press, 1984), 12–26.

14. See especially chapter 4 below.

1. The Primacy of the Gospel

1. Philip Melanchthon, *On Christian Doctrine, Loci communes 1555*, trans. C. L. Manschreck (Grand Rapids: Baker, 1982), 3.

2. Ibid.

3. For a succinct statement of the so-called Regnon thesis by a contemporary Eastern theologian, see John Meyendorff, *Byzantine Theology: Historical Trends and Doctrinal Themes* (New York: Fordham University Press, 1979), 180–81.

4. See Dennis Bielfeldt, "Semantics, Ontology and the Trinity," chapter 2 in Dennis Bielfeldt, Mickey Mattox, and Paul Hinlicky, *The Substance of Faith: Luther's Doctrinal Theology for Today* (Minneapolis: Fortress Press, 2008), 59–130.

5. Think merely of the different kinds of arguments for divine unity that must follow from starting with the metaphysical postulate of divine simplicity or from the trinitarian idea of the Spirit as the bond of love between the Father and the Son. Augustine teaches both, even though they may not fully cohere with each other.

6. Alan Richardson, *Christian Apologetics* (New York: Harper, 1947), 108.

7. Ibid., 223.

8. Ibid., 242–44.

9. Ibid., 77, 99.

10. Ibid., 37.

11. Ibid., 75.

12. Ibid., 231.

13. Ibid., 135.

14. On the author's subtle disagreement with Barth's critique of natural theology, see Paul R. Hinlicky, *Paths Not Taken: Theology from Luther through Leibniz* (Grand Rapids: Eerdmans, 2009), 104–12.

15. Following Jaroslav Pelikan, I read the Cappadocians, treated in the culminating chapter of this book, in the same way: They "reserved their sharpest polemics for those who claimed to know the secret being of God well enough to use it as a basis for the knowledge of the creation, or who, starting from natural theology about that secret being, presumed to judge and to distort revealed theology in the light of it." Jaroslav Pelikan, *Christianity and Classical Culture: The Metamorphosis of Natural Theology in the Christian Encounter with Hellenism*, Gifford Lectures at Aberdeen, 1992–1993 (New Haven: Yale University Press, 1993), 71.

16. Martin Luther, *Commentary on Romans*, LW 25:344.

17. LW 25:360, 362. See also "The Gospel versus the Metaphysical Tradition," in Eric W. Gritsch and Robert W. Jenson, *Lutheranism: The Theological Movement and Its Confessional Writings* (Philadelphia: Fortress Press, 1978), 103–9.

18. Oswald Bayer, *Martin Luther's Theology: A Contemporary Interpretation*, trans. T. H. Trapp (Grand Rapids: Eerdmans, 2007), 215.

19. On the "primacy of the gospel" and its relation to dogma, see *Teaching Authority and Infallibility in the Church: Lutherans and Catholics in Dialogue VI*, ed. Paul C. Empie, T. Austin Murphy, and Joseph A. Burgess (Minneapolis: Augsburg, 1978).

20. *Explanations of the Ninety-five Theses* (1518), LW 31:77–252.

21. See Luther's account of the debacle in *The Leipzig Debate* (1519) in LW 31: 307-325.

22. Martin Luther, "The Freedom of the Christian," LW 31:346: "You may ask, 'What then is the Word of God, and how shall it be used, since there are so many words of God?' I answer: The Apostle explains this in Romans 1. The word is the gospel of God concerning his Son, who was made flesh, suffered, rose from the dead, and was glorified through the

Spirit who sanctifies. To preach Christ means to feed the soul, make it righteous, set it free, and save it, provided it believes the preaching. Faith alone is the saving and efficacious use of the word of God, according to Rom. 10[:9]: 'If you confess with your lips that Jesus is Lord and believe in your heart that God raised him from the dead, you will be saved.' Furthermore, 'Christ is the end of the law, that every one who has faith may be justified' [Rom. 10:4]. Again, in Rom. 1[:17], 'He who through faith is righteous shall live.' The word of God cannot be received and cherished by any works whatever but only by faith. Therefore it is clear that, as the soul needs only the word of God for its life and righteousness, so it is justified by faith alone and not any works; for if it could be justified by anything else, it would not need the word, and consequently it would not need faith" (LW 35:358).

23. Bruce D. Marshall, *Trinity and Truth* (Cambridge: Cambridge University Press, 2000). "Epistemic primacy" designates what belief is necessary to a community's survival, what is least dispensable, what one is least willing to give up (44). As a belief, it is a sentence held to be true, a truth claim (45), in relation to which other beliefs are logically subordinate, depending for their truth on their coherence with the primary one (46–47). Marshall notes that this analysis of epistemic primacy reverses the procedure of *Vermittlungstheologie* (liberal Protestant mediation theology), which stakes Christian belief on other foundations. This reversal, however, does little to justify—explain the right to hold—such a belief (48); hence the present endeavor.

24. See Paul R. Hinlicky, "The Lutheran Dilemma," *Pro Ecclesia* 8/4 (Fall 1999): 391–422.

25. "The little word 'gospel' is not used and understood in the same, single sense at all times, but in two different ways. Sometimes it is used in such a way to mean the entire teaching of Christ, our Lord, which in his own ministry on earth and in the New Testament he commanded to be carried out. In this sense the term includes the explanation of the law and the proclamation of the favor and grace of God, his heavenly Father. . . . When the word 'gospel' is used as a *generalis definitio* (that is, in its broader meaning apart from the proper distinction of law and gospel [i.e., promise]) it is correct to define the word as a proclamation of repentance and the forgiveness of sins." "Formula of Concord, Solid Declaration," in Robert Kolb and Timothy J. Wengert, *Book of Concord* (Minneapolis: Fortress Press, 2000), 582. The gospel as narrative issues in the performative distinction between law as that which reveals sin and promise as that which forgives sinners.

26. On Luther's "catholicism," see Luther's 1528 *Concerning Rebaptism*, LW 40:225–262.

27. Heiko A. Oberman, *The Harvest of Medieval Theology: Gabriel Biel and Late Medieval Nominalism* (Grand Rapids: Baker, 2000); Oberman, *The Dawn of the Reformation: Essays in Late Medieval and Early Reformation Thought* (Edinburgh: T&T Clark, 1986).

28. George A. Lindbeck, *The Nature of Doctrine: Religion and Theology in a Postliberal Age* (Philadelphia: Westminster, 1984), 79–84.

29. Robert W. Jenson, *Systematic Theology: The Works of God*, vol. 2 (New York, Oxford University Press, 1999), 292–93.

30. On the 1999 Lutheran–Roman Catholic *Joint Declaration on Justification*, see Paul R. Hinlicky, "Process, Convergence, Declaration: Reflections on Doctrinal Dialogue," *The Cresset* 64/6 (Pentecost 2001): 13–18.

31. Athanasius, "On the Incarnation of the Word," in *Christology of the Later Fathers*, ed. Edward R. Hardy (Philadelphia: Westminster, 1954), 88.

32. See Luther's commentary on Romans 3:28, LW 25:254.

33. As Hans Urs von Balthasar, *Theo-Drama: Theological Dramatic Theory, vol. 4, The Action*, trans. Graham Harrison (San Francisco: Ignatius, 1994) rightly understands. See the author's discussion in chapter 2 of *Luther and the Beloved Community: A Path for Christian Theology after Christendom* (Grand Rapids: Eerdmans, 2010).

34. Dietrich Bonhoeffer, *The Cost of Discipleship*, trans. R. H. Fuller (New York: Simon & Schuster, 1995), 43.

35. "God the Father and the human soul so ennobled that it can and does unite with him." Adolph Harnack, *What Is Christianity?* trans. T. B. Saunders (New York: Putnam, 1901), 63.

36. Hinlicky, "Lutheran Dilemma," 394–96.

37. "Formula of Concord, Solid Declaration," in Kolb and Wengert, *Book of Concord*, 526.

38. Ronald Thiemann, *Revelation and Theology: The Gospel as Narrated Promise* (South Bend: University of Notre Dame Press, 1987).

39. LW 35:357.

40. Robert Jenson, *God after God: The God of the Past and the God of the Future, Seen in the Work of Karl Barth* (1969; repr., Minneapolis: Fortress Press, 2010), 30–31.

41. I note that this preliminary exercise is meant only to prepare readers with the basic idea of gospel as promissory narrative in Christian theology as it is used in this book, so that they can engage facilely the ensuing chapters that take this primary, canonical theology as given. If it oversimplifies matters from the historical-critical perspective, as the purists will undoubtedly detect, that might be forgiven of a pedagogy that has to erect some temporary scaffolding. Naturally, as a debt to be paid in a future work, I acknowledge here that we today cannot take the canonical gospel narrative as simply "given," but the epistemic right to do so in an appropriately complex way will have to be warranted in terms of what historical-critical method can affirm about Jesus of Nazareth.

42. The word of God is a proclamation, a preaching, an announcement grounded in the divine speech-act designated narrowly as the "resurrection" and broadly as the "incarnation."

43. The God of the Fathers, the God of the Exodus, the God of Moses and the prophets, the God of King David and his heirs, the God of the sages and wise men, the priests and temple officials—the God of the Hebrew Scriptures, the Christian "Old Testament."

44. The historical person from Nazareth who was born during the reign of the Emperor Augustus and was "crucified under Pontius Pilate."

45. Thus relating Himself to God as son to father.

46. The title "Messiah" means the Lord's Anointed, not merely with the sign of oil but with the Spirit of the living God.

47. The reign of God or "kingdom of God" is the unifying theme of all Scripture.

48. From the Greek *para* and *doxia*, meaning "against common opinion," against "what seems to be the case." I take "paradox" not to imply a logical contradiction (which would assert something literally nonsensical or meaningless) but as a rhetorical device that aims to subvert usual ways of thinking by asserting something apparently absurd within a dominant discourse.

49. In obedience to God Jesus died forsaken by God in order to establish divine solidarity with the lost.

50. The saving incarnation extends to those helplessly estranged from God by the hostile powers of sin, death, and the devil and imprisoned by them. Sin and death are not merely moral and biological categories in Scripture but rebel powers that oppose the coming of the reign of God.

51. Not merely resuscitation or return to "normal life" that will someday die again, but elevation to union with God in His own immortal life.

52. Salvation as "eternal life" in the New Testament is above all participation in God's own life: the gift of the Spirit is a down payment on resurrection life, the Johannine spring of living water welling up to eternal life.

53. Faith is the ecstatic mode of human existence in which the gospel word of God (which is a promise of how the world will turn out) is apprehended and appropriated *for oneself*. Yet as the believer is body and so immediately also a social creature, love is the mode in which the gospel word of God is enacted *for others*. Faith alone justifies (makes right with God) the individual, but this very faith is immediately active in Christ's love for others since the individual before God is also socially

related. Both faith and love depend on *hope*, which is the mode of the believer's corporate existence in the community of those called out of the dying world as harbingers of God's new humanity. The ground of hope is Jesus Christ crucified and risen, and the object of hope is Jesus Christ ascended and returning to judge the living and the dead.

54. The literal meaning of the word "gospel."

55. The Eucharist is the sacrifice of praise to the Father, in unity with the Son by virtue of the gracious gift of the communion of His body and blood, in the power of the Spirit as opposed to expiatory rites of the religions. On this, see *Luther and the Beloved Community*, chapter 3.

56. The realm of the Spirit who proclaims Jesus as risen from the dead, hence the realm of the dawning new creation in the world, is the assembly of believers, the *ecclesia* (from the Greek *ek* and *klesia*, meaning "to call out"), badly rendered by the English word "church," connoting a chapel or religious building rather than a community.

57. By each believer's daily death to sin and resurrection to newness of life, with the result that the Lord Jesus becomes the real operative agent supervening the believer's life.

58. The free and joyful worship of the Father, with the Son, in the Spirit is the goal of all salvation history, which is already experienced now in the church's eucharistic worship. Notice how the trinitarian structure is integral to the gospel story as also eucharistic worship.

59. The reign of God is inaugurated manifestly wherever and whenever the proclamation of this gospel succeeds in creating faith and forming the church and latently wherever and whenever true love occurs, since true love is participation in the city of God. The reign of God is fulfilled when human history is finally judged and redeemed and God becomes all things to all people.

60. Robert W. Jenson, *Systematic Theology: The Triune God*, vol. 1 (New York: Oxford University Press, 1997), 16. A history of crucial interpretive decisions by the church about the gospel's meaning includes the doctrines of the Trinity, the doctrine of two natures of Christ in one person, and the doctrine of grace.

61. This is the inquiry involved in *Dogmengeschichte*, the history of doctrine, of which in part the present book is an exercise.

62. Christopher Morse, *The Logic of Promise in Moltmann's Theology* (Philadelphia: Fortress Press, 1979), 77.

63. Ibid., 89.

64. Ibid., 76–77.

65. Ibid., 77.

66. Reinhard Hütter, *Suffering Divine Things: Theology as Church Practice*, trans. D. Stott (Grand Rapids: Eerdmans, 2000), 85, in reference to Oswald Bayer's Luther interpretation.

67. Dietrich Bonhoeffer, *Christ the Center: A New Translation*, trans. E. H. Robertson (New York: Harper & Row, 1978).

68. On this, see *Luther and the Beloved Community*, chapter 2.

69. Adam Drozdek, *Greek Philosophers as Theologians: The Divine Arche* (Burlington: Ashgate, 2007), 128. Likewise with antecedents among the Pre-Socratics, 119. The apophatic doctrine of divine simplicity thus may be traced quite directly to Platonism.

70. Cicero, *On the Nature of the Gods*, trans. C. P. McGregor (New York: Penguin, 1972), 212.

71. Ibid., 218.

72. Ibid., 204.

73. Ibid., 205.

74. Ibid., 234.

75. Ibid., 230.

76. Robert W. Jenson has pioneered this "drastic rearrangement" in the organization of dogmatics: "I have adopted a plan that diverges from both the Catholic and Protestant standard outlines. The basic Scholastic division is taken up [i.e., of God and of His creatures],

but Christology and pneumatology, together with the discussions of the historical Jesus, of the doctrine of the atonement, and of the resurrection are drawn back into the doctrine of God" (*Systematic Theology*, vol. 1, x). See also in this connection his incisive exposé of the pretension of natural theology "to be a body of knowledge about God and his intentions not intrinsically dependent on historically particular divine dispositions, and therefore the common property of humanity. In fact, however, this body of theology was as historically particular as any other" (ibid., 7).

77. Dietrich Bonhoeffer, *Sanctorum Communio: A Theological Study of the Sociology of the Church*, trans. Reinhard Kraus and Nancy Lukens, ed. Joachim von Sooten and Clifford J. Green (Minneapolis: Fortress Press, 1998), 165.

78. Ernst Käsemann, *Commentary on Romans*, trans. and ed. G. Bromiley (Grand Rapids: Eerdmans, 1980), 41.

79. *City of God*, XIV:3–4.

80. LW 25:157.

81. Thus in the Heidelberg Disputation, Article 24, LW 31:55.

82. Käsemann, *Romans*, 41. For the Hellenistic background in "Stoic theology, in opposition to the national cults, their sacrifices, and their anthropomorphic ideas," see 39. Paul's gloss on this knowledge of God "since the creation of the world" sets the natural theology of Stoicism into the context of revealed theology. "The result of God's self-manifestation in His creation is not a natural knowledge of God on men's part independent of God's self-revelation in His word, a valid though limited knowledge, but simply the excuselessness of men in their ignorance. A real self-disclosure of God has indeed taken place and is always occurring, and men ought to have recognized, but in fact have not recognized, Him." C. E. B. Cranefield, *A Critical and Exegetical Commentary on the Epistle to the Romans*, vol. 1 (Edinburgh: T&T Clark, 1975), 116.

83. Adolph Schlatter, *Romans: The Righteousness of God*, trans. S. S. Schatzmann (Peabody: Hendrickson, 1995), 29.

84. See Bielfeldt on semantic realism in Bielfeldt, Mattox, and Hinklicky, *Substance of Faith*, 86.

2. From Resurrection Kerygma to Gospel Narrative

1. Christopher Morse, *Not Every Spirit: A Dogmatics of Christian Disbelief* (Philadelphia: Trinity Press International, 1994), 141. See also Leander E. Keck, *A Future for the Historical Jesus: The Place of Jesus in Preaching and Theology* (Philadelphia: Fortress Press, 1981), a neglected work that unmasked the tacit notion of private selfhood in liberal and neoliberal quests for the historical Jesus and the Kantian assumption of the "categorical inadequacy of historical fact as the basis of the absolute certitude of faith" (49): "Just as Jesus' career does not initiate belief in God, so his resurrection cannot generate it; rather, it serves to designate and clarify the God who is to be trusted and thereby intersects with our presumed understanding of God and of what is the last word on human life. The vindication of Jesus includes the vindication of his own unswerving dependence on God expressed in the cry of dereliction spoken *to* God. For God to ratify that life is to disclose that he had been implicated in Jesus all along" (238–39). See the discussion in *Luther and the Beloved Community*, chapter 2.

2. Rudolf Bultmann, *The History of the Synoptic Tradition*, rev. ed.,trans. J. Marsh (Oxford: Basil Blackwell, 1972).

3. Wolfhart Pannenberg, *Jesus: God and Man*, trans. Wilkins and Priebe (Philadelphia: Westminster, 1975), 47–49, with reservations regarding Pannenberg's too-rationalistic notion of objectivity.

4. Modest, sober historical study can give us, Keck rightly affirms, not the "essential" but the "characteristic" Jesus, by which to test the church's proclamation of "Jesus Christ" for truthfulness to the name of Jesus. But many today want history to replace theology; against

this abuse of history by "religious studies," Keck carefully writes, "Historiography is by no means invulnerable to distortion and subversion, but it remains our major defense against absorbing Jesus into modern secular piety" (*Future*, 217). To the contrary, he concludes: "Actually a systematic theology might well state afresh everything we have argued thus far, and do so from the standpoint of God's initiative—at least if one is prepared to think in a Trinitarian way" (ibid., 241), since "the central theme is the role of Jesus in our understanding of God" (ibid., 243). A *non-theological* Jesus is precisely a *historical* absurdity.

5. Morse, *Not Every Spirit*, 141.

6. Ibid.

7. Ibid., 142.

8. Ibid., 161.

9. "The emphases of normative Christianity were not the result of speculation on the nature of Christ but were intricately tied into a worldview and ethos that are larger than Christology alone. A Christology reflects one's worldview and also one's community values. It also, in turn, shapes these. If one looks upon the world and assigns to it an origin from, and care by, a benevolent God in whom trust can be placed, as the Scriptures of Israel would lead one to believe, christological reflection will stress the unity of that God and his Christ, endorsing the monotheism of the Scriptures and providing a place for Christ within the larger story of Israel—that is, redemptive history. Then too if a primary value is placed on human relationships in a world that is not rejected as hopeless, but is understood as loved and redeemed by the God who created it, christological reflection will stress the commonality between Christ and humanity as a whole. If, on the other hand, one views the world as a tragic mistake in which people are trapped, and if the greatest good is release from the entrapment that envelops the world and its masses, then the alternative Christologies presented by Marcion and the Gnostics may very well be more satisfying." Arland J. Hultgren, *The Rise of Normative Christianity* (Minneapolis: Fortress Press, 1994), 92.

10. "Thus we end up in a remarkable hermeneutical circle: Jesus' living and dying on earth suggested to Christians, in virtue of their experiences after Jesus' death, the idea of the resurrection or of the coming Parousia of Jesus, while on the basis of their faith in the risen or coming crucified One they relate the story of Jesus in the gospels." Edward Schillebeeckx, *Jesus: An Experiment in Christology*, trans. H. Hoskins (New York: Crossroads, 1979), 401. This is a sophisticated defense of Easter as an event in history, "partly undergirded by new experiences after his death. This is the crucial point. Yet the new experience is not 'empty tomb' or 'appearances' as such but the conversion and restitution of the disciples in an encounter of grace" (394).

11. Frederick W. Norris, "Ignatius, Polycarp, and I Clement: Walter Bauer Reconsidered," *Vigiliae Christianae* 30:23–44. Bauer is unable "to grasp the difference between the beginning of a process and its fullest development" (34); he demands "such characteristics of monepiscopacy that it would be difficult to find many such bishops in any period of history. The imposition of an 'ideal' definition kept Bauer from reading the evidence correctly" (35). Bauer "has a tendency to use peculiar definitions to important terms, employing them with these meanings in such fashion as to apparently strengthen his argumentation" (35–36). Any "number of his arguments are conjecture based on silence. . . . Bauer's major methodological errors, however, are not confined merely to the treatment of silence. A large proportion occur in his treatment of texts" (42). "The basic error is in reading history backwards. . . . Frankly, he misreads the texts" (43).

12. Walter Bauer, *Orthodoxy and Heresy in Early Christianity*, ed. R. Kraft and G. Krodel (Philadelphia: Fortress Press, 1971; repr., Sigler, 1996). Hultgren's *The Rise* contains exquisite dissections of Bauer's circular reasoning, which fixes "a particular text within a trajectory" by "later developments of a genre as much as by earlier ones." Hultgren, *Rise*, 17.

13. Hultgren, *Rise*, 17.

14. The literature is vast. Aside from Bauer's seminal argument, I am informed by the recent and no doubt lucrative works of Bart D. Ehrman, *Lost Christianities: The Battles for Scripture and the Faiths We Never New* (Oxford: Oxford University Press, 2003), and, more seriously, Gregory J. Riley, *One Jesus, Many Christs: How Jesus Inspired Not One True Christianity but Many* (Minneapolis: Fortress Press, 2000). The argumentation of both of these authors descends from the school of Walter Bauer.

15. For the literature, see *The Nag Hammadi Library in English*, 3rd ed., ed. James M. Robinson (San Francisco: Harper, 1988); for a classical analysis of Gnosticism, see the penetrating study of Hans Jonas, *The Gnostic Religion: The Message of the Alien God and the Beginnings of Christianity*, 2nd ed. (Boston: Beacon, 1958), and, more broadly, E. R. Dodds, *Pagan and Christian in an Age of Anxiety* (New York: Norton, 1965). The formative role played by the conflict with Gnosticism will occupy us in detail in chapters 3 and 4 below.

16. For example, Surah 3:42-47.

17. Norris, "Walter Bauer Reconsidered," 42. This article carefully deconstructs Bauer's "positive reconstructions" of the Apostolic Fathers. Yet I can safely acknowledge that the general picture Bauer draws of the development of orthodox doctrine is one with which I concur, e.g., "The genuine successors of the original Paul and Cephas parties gradually drew closer to each other, so that finally they would merge to produce 'orthodoxy.' In opposition to the Gnosticizing Christianity in whom perhaps the spirit of the syncretistic Alexandrian Apollos continued to flourish." Bauer, *Orthodoxy and Heresy*, 101.

18. Hultgren, *Rise*, 17, emphasis added.

19. Ibid., 22.

20. N. T. Wright, *The Resurrection of the Son of God*, vol. 3 of *Christian Origins and the Question of God* (Minneapolis: Fortress Press, 2003), 7.

21. Ibid., 720.

22. Ibid.

23. Ibid., 597.

24. The public face, not the inner self-consciousness!

25. Wright, *Resurrection*, 712, emphasis original.

26. Bruce Marshall, *Christology in Conflict: The Identity of a Savior in Rahner and Barth* (Oxford: Basil Blackwell, 1987), 175.

27. J. Louis Martyn, *Galatians: A New Translation with Introduction and Commentary*, Anchor Bible 33A (New York: Doubleday, 1997), 325.

28. According to Martyn, it was "in the cross that Paul came to see a momentous fact about the Law: its cursing voice is not the voice of God," which is rather a voice of blessing and promise. Yet Paul "saw also that that voice was robbed of its power when, approved by God in his Law-cursed death, Christ embodied the Law's curse, for in that embodiment Christ vanquished the curse, freeing the whole of humanity from its power." (*Galatians*, 326). The real issue then "is not whether a human being observes the Law or fails to do so. The issue is whether the voice with which God pronounces his blessing has proved to be stronger than the voice with which the Law pronounces its curse" (ibid., 327). This is surely right so far as it goes, but one must also ask whether it is only a *matter of power*—power that in highly paradoxical way manifests in weakness and apparent defeat, as Martyn notes (*Galatians*, 326). Is there not also a question about the justice of this power by which blessing defeats the curse, by which God "approves" of Christ's accursed death and so justifies the ungodly?

29. See Paul R. Hinlicky, "A Lutheran Contribution to the Theology of Judaism," *Journal of Ecumenical Studies* 31/1–2 (Winter–Spring 1994): 123–52.

30. Eberhard Jüngel, *God as the Mystery of the World: On the Foundation of the Theology of the Crucified One in the Dispute between Theism and Atheism*, trans. D. L. Guder (Grand Rapids: Eerdmans, 1983), 361–65.

31. Karl Barth, CD IV:1, 157.

32. Paul Tillich, ST II:159.

33. Ibid., 165.

34. Ibid., 364.

35. Ibid.

36. Ernst Käsemann, *Commentary on Romans*, trans. and ed. G. Bromiley (Grand Rapids: Eerdmans, 1980),123.

37. Karl Barth, CD IV:1, 159.

38. Necessity becomes the God of such philosophers. See Adam Drozdek on Democritus, *Greek Philosophers as Theologians: The Divine Arche* (Burlington: Arhgate, 2007), 107.

39. Käsemann, *Romans*, 124.

40. Stephen Hawking with Leonard Mlodinow, *A Briefer History of Time* (New York: Bantam, 2005), 142.

41. Paul Hinlicky, *The Substance of Faith: Luther's Doctrinal Theology for Today* (Minneapolis: Fortress Press, 2008), 162–68.

42. Herbert Braun, *Jesus of Nazareth: The Man and His Time*, trans. E. Kalin (Philadelphia: Fortress Press, 1979), 122–23.

43. Braun, *Jesus*, 118.

44. Pannenberg, *Jesus: God and Man*, trans. L. L. Wilkins and D. A. Priebe (Philadelphia: Westminster, 1975), 67–73.

45. Ibid., 66.

46. Ibid., 398.

47. Albert Schweitzer, *The Quest of the Historical Jesus: A Critical Study of Its Progress from Reimarus to Wrede*, trans. W. Montgomery (New York: Macmillan, 1968), 391. See the extended discussion in *Luther and the Beloved Community*, chapter 1.

48. Hans Conzelmann, *Jesus*, trans. J. R. Lord (Philadelphia: Fortress Press, 1973), 94–95.

49. Ibid., 95.

50. Käsemann, *Romans*, 10.

51. Pannenberg, *Jesus*, 321. Jüngel draws attention to this passage and concurs with "the ontological possibility of an event having retroactive ontic effects" (*Mystery*, 363).

52. Pannenberg, *Jesus*, 321.

53. Marshall, *Christology*, 174.

54. Karl Barth and Rudolf Bultmann, *Letters 1922–1966*, trans. G. W. Bromiley (Grand Rapids: Eerdmans, 1981), 93.

55. Ibid., 97.

56. For Jesus, "God is present where he is active. Jesus then does not make known a new conception of God, or revelations of the nature of God; instead, he brings the message of the coming Kingdom of God and of the will of God. He speaks of God in speaking of man and showing him that he stands in the last hour of decision, that his will is claimed by God." Rudolf Bultmann, *Jesus and the Word*, trans. L. P. Smith and E. Huntress (New York: Scribner, 1934), 152.

57. "The decision which Jesus' disciples had once made to affirm and accept his sending by 'following' him, had to be made anew and radically in consequence of his crucifixion. *The cross*, so to say, raised the question of decision once more. Little as it could throw into question the content of his message, all the more it could and did render questionable his legitimation, his claim to be God's messenger bringing the last, decisive word. The Church had to surmount the scandal of the cross and did it in the Easter faith." Rudolf Bultmann, *Theology of the New Testament*, vol. 1, trans. K. Grobel (New York: Scribner, 1951), 44–45.

58. Gerhard Ebeling, "The Significance of the Critical Historical Method for Church and Theology in Protestantism," in *Word and Faith*, trans. J. W. Leitch (Philadelphia: Fortress Press, 1964), 36.

59. Rudolf Bultmann, "New Testament and Mythology," in *Kerygma and Myth: A Theological Debate*, ed. H. W. Bartsch (New York: Harper, 1961), 2.

60. Ibid., 3, emphasis original.

61. Hans W. Frei, *The Eclipse of Biblical Narrative: A Study in Eighteenth- and Nineteenth-Century Hermeneutics* (New Haven: Yale University Press, 1974).

62. James F. Kay, *Christus Praesens: A Reconsideration of Rudolf Bultmann's Christology* (Grand Rapids: Eerdmans, 1994), 14.

63. Bultmann, *Synoptic Tradition*, 370–71.

64. Kay, *Praesens*, 28–29.

65. Ibid., 26.

66. Ibid., 57.

67. Ibid., 139.

68. Ibid., 133.

69. Ibid., 140.

70. Ibid., 141.

71. Ibid., n. 54, taking up the argument here, not directly of Frei, but of Richard B. Hays that Bultmann's demythologizing effects denarrativizing.

72. Frei, *Eclipse*, 272–73.

73. Ibid., 130.

74. Ibid., 312–13.

75. Friedrich Schleiermacher, *Life of Jesus*, trans. S. M. Gilmour, ed. J. C. Verheyden (Philadelphia: Fortress Press, 1975), 415.

76. Frei, *Eclipse*, 313.

77. Ibid., 315.

78. Bultmann, op. cit., 10.

79. Robert W. Jenson, *The Triune Identity: God according to the Gospel* (Philadelphia: Fortress Press, 1982),16.

80. Dorothee Soelle, *Beyond Mere Obedience: Reflections on a Christian Ethic for the Future* (Minneapolis: Augsburg, 1970).

81. Rosemary Ruether, *Faith and Fratricide: The Theological Roots of Anti-Semitism* (New York: Seabury, 1979).

82. See Karl Barth's introduction in Ludwig Feuerbach, *The Essence of Christianity*, trans. G. Eliot (New York: Harper, 1957), x–xxxii.

83. George A. Lindbeck, *The Nature of Doctrine: Religion and Theology in a Postliberal Age* (Philadelphia: Westminster, 1984),66.

84. Ibid., 52.

85. Ibid., 59, 68.

86. Ibid., 49.

87. Ibid., 62.

88. Ibid., 55.

89. Ibid., 56.

90. Ibid., 59.

91. Ibid., 51.

92. Ibid., 60.

93. Ibid., 61.

94. Ibid., 66.

95. Paul R. Hinlicky, "Luther's Antidocetism in the *Disputatio de divinitate et humanitate Christi* (1540)," in *Creator est creatura: Luthers Christologie als Lehre von der Idiomenkommunikation*, ed. O. Bayer and Benjamin Gleede (Berlin: de Gruyter, 2007), 169–77.

96. Jenson, ST I:169.

97. Barth, CD IV/1:177.

98. On this, see the pioneering redaction criticism study of Willi Marxsen, *Mark the Evangelist: Studies on the Redaction History of the Gospel*, trans. R. Harrisville (Nashville: Abingdon, 1969), 135–38.

99. In the discussion of the Gospel of Mark that follows, I am drawing on my previously published article "The Petrine Witness to Jesus Christ, the Son of God," *Lutheran Forum* 30/2 (May 1996): 54–62, and the analysis of Marcan demonology in D. Beifeldt, M. Mattox, and P. Hinlicky, *The Substance of the Faith: Luther's Doctrinal Theology for Today* (Minneapolis: Fortress Press, 2008), 181–89.

100. We are much indebted to the studies of E. P. Sanders, who has exposed "the persistence of the view of Rabbinic religion as one of legalistic works-righteousness," tellingly, in the shift from Reformation theology to Neo-Protestantism. "Through the eighteenth-century Christian literature had primarily tried to show the agreement of Jewish views with Christian theology . . . [but w]ith F. Weber [writing in 1880] everything had changed. For him, Judaism was the antithesis of Christianity." E. P. Sanders, *Paul and Palestinian Judaism: A Comparison of Patterns of Religion* (Philadelphia: Fortress Press, 1983), 33. See the author's discussion of the "new" perspective on Paul in *Luther and the Beloved Community: A Path for Christian Theology after Christendom* (Grand Rapids: Eerdmans, 2010), chapter 6.

101. James M. Robinson, *The Problem of History in Mark* (Naperville: Allenson, 1957), 59.

102. Joel Marcus, *Mark 1–8: A New Translation with Introduction and Commentary*, Anchor Bible 27 (New Haven: Yale University Press, 2000), 33–39.

103. Jack Dean Kingsbury, *The Christology of Mark's Gospel* (Minneapolis: Fortress Press, 1983), 132.

104. Marxsen, *Mark*, 216.

105. Ibid.

106. Ibid., 212.

107. Werner H. Kelber, *Mark's Story of Jesus* (Philadelphia: Fortress Press, 1979).

108. Ernst Käsemann, "Sentences of Holy Law," in *New Testament Questions for Today*, trans. W. J. Montague (Philadelphia: Fortress Press, 1979), 66–81.

109. Ibid., 245.

110. Hinlicky, "Luther's Antidocetism," 147–80.

111. Keck, *Future*, 244.

112. For a fuller case, see Hinlicky, *Substance of Faith*, 180–90. For a structurally similar case on the relation of Paul to Jesus, see Eberhard Jüngel, *Paul und Jesus: Eine Untersuchung zur Praezisierung der Frage nach dem Ursprung der Christologie* (Tübingen: Mohr-Siebeck, 1979).

3. The Scriptures' Emergence as the Church's Canon

1. The argument made in this chapter had its now distant origin in a series of articles in the 1990s: "Resurrection and the Knowledge of God," *Pro Ecclesia* 4/2 (Spring 1995): 226–32; "St. John the Theologian: An Approach to the Fourth Gospel," *Lutheran Forum* 29/2 (May 1995): 58–62; "A Criticism of the Criticism of the Gospel of John," *Lutheran Forum* 29/3 (August 1995): 56–62; "The Anti-Docetic Theology of the Gospel of John," *Lutheran Forum* 29/4 (November 1995): 64–70; "Incarnation and the Knowledge of God," *Lutheran Forum* 30/1 (February 1996): 56–62.

2. Cited from Gerald H. Ettlinger, *Jesus, Christ and Savior*, Message of the Fathers of the Church 2 (Wilmington: Michael Glazier, 1987), 95–101.

3. See Exodus 33:7-10.

4. Gregory J. Riley, *Resurrection Reconsidered: Thomas and John in Controversy* (Minneapolis: Fortress Press, 1995).

5. John Ashton, *Understanding the Fourth Gospel* (Oxford: Clarendon, 1993), provides an excellent summation of the course of contemporary Johannine research. It tells the story of how contemporary research has overcome Bultmann's supposition of a Gnostic-Mandean signs source that has been redacted by the evangelist by grasping instead the thoroughly Jewish milieu in which the Johannine traditions developed in the first century.

This amounts, as we shall see, to a renewal of Edwyn Hoskyns's approach. The seminal contemporary work here is J. Louis Martyn's *History and Theology in the Fourth Gospel*, 3rd ed. (1968; repr., Louisville: Westminster John Knox, 2003), which uncovered the martyriological situation of Jewish Christians following the destruction of the temple. From another angle entirely, I have found Marianne Meye Thompson's *The Humanity of Jesus in the Fourth Gospel* (Philadelphia: Fortress Press, 1988); Udo Schnelle's *Antidocetic Christology in the Gospel of John: An Investigation of the Place of the Fourth Gospel in the Johannine School*, trans. Linda M. Maloney (Minneapolis: Fortress Press, 1992); and Gregory J. Riley, *Resurrection Reconsidered: Thomas and John in Controversy* (Minneapolis: Fortress, 1995), especially helpful in overcoming the stigma of docetism which Käsemann cast on John. The martyriological situation stands behind John's striking depiction of Christ's "passionless passion," which seems to follow Luke in this tendency. Ignorance of this has led so many modern commentators astray, beginning with Friedrich Schleiermacher in his *The Life of Jesus*, who took up the Johannine depiction of the passionless mind of Christ to ground historically his notion of a historical Jesus' perfect God-consciousness. David Friedrich Strauss in turn pilloried Schleiermacher's account in *The Christ of Faith and the Jesus of History*, trans. Leander E. Keck (Philadelphia: Fortress Press, 1977), by showing that the miraculous mind of the Johannine Jesus with its perfect "God-consciousness" was no less "docetic" than the orthodox Chalcedonian Christology which Schleiermacher thought he was overcoming. The root error in this entire development is Schleiermacher's equation of docetism with psychological implausibility, or, conversely, his location of Christology in the consciousness of a historical Jesus.

6. Peter Stuhlmacher, *Jesus of Nazareth, Christ of Faith*, trans. Siegfried Schatzmann (Peabody: Hendrickson, 1988), 13. Whatever the Gospel of John's prehistory might have been, in the Christian canon John functions as a "spiritual," or better, "theological" interpretation of the Synoptic Gospels, constituting, with Acts, a bridge to the Pauline corpus. Raymond Brown rightly remarked that "the ultimate check" on dangerous readings of the Gospel was the "church's hermeneutical decision to place it in the same canon as Mark, Matthew and Luke" (Raymond E. Brown, *The Community of the Beloved Disciple: The Life, Loves and Hates of an Individual Church in New Testament Times* [Mahwah: Paulist, 1979], 163). That is true, but it begs the critical question whether John's distinctive witness is thereby blunted, whether John is being illicitly harmonized at the cost of historical and theological precision—the question which Ernst Käsemann pressed relentlessly. We shall see, however, that the canonical function of John as the theological interpretation of the Synoptics is corroborated by better understandings of the Gospel's prehistory than those determined by the Bultmann school's hypothesis of Mandean, Gnostic sources or Brown's own hypothesis of a marginal Christian community representing a sui generis development in primitive Christianity.

7. James D. G. Dunn, "Let John Be John: A Gospel for Its Time," in *The Gospel and the Gospels*, ed. Peter Stuhlmacher (Grand Rapids: Eerdmans, 1991), 294. Aloys Grillmeier makes a similar claim at the outset of his massive and detailed study, *Christ in Christian Tradition*, vol. I (Louisville: John Knox, 1975): "It was not without reason that the christological formula of John 1:14 could increasingly become the most influential New Testament text in the history of dogma" (26).

8. The general thesis derives from Adolph von Harnack, although interestingly, he demurred from its categorical application to the Gospel of John: "Moreover, the origin of the Johannine writings is, from the stand-point of a history literature and dogma, the most marvelous enigma which the early history of Christianity presents: Here we have portrayed a Christ who clothes the indescribable with words, and proclaims as his own self-testimony what his disciples have experienced in him, a speaking, acting, Pauline Christ, walking on the earth, far more human than the Christ of Paul and yet far more divine, an abundance of allusions to the historical Jesus, and at the same time the most sovereign treatment of the

history. . . . The elements operative in the Johannine theology were not Greek Theologoumena—even the Logos has little more in common with that of Philo than the name, and its mention at the beginning of the book is a mystery, not the solution of one." *History of Dogma*, vol. 1, trans. N. Buchanan (New York: Dover, 1898), 96–97.

9. Edwyn Clement Hoskyns, *The Fourth Gospel*, ed. Francis Noel Davey (London, 1947), 91.

10. As J. L. Martyn predicted in his seminal monograph, "I believe studies in Jewish Christianity hold considerable promise for historians of the Johannine community and for Johannine interpreters in general" (*History and Theology*, 146).

11. Whatever use or abuse Gnostics and Docetists might have made of the Gospel of John, it seems incontrovertible that it was also a significant inspiration to the second-century Fathers, culminating in Irenaeus, as we shall see. Irenaeus does not merely protect the Fourth Gospel from a supposedly predominant Gnostic interpretation of it. Irenaeus himself is decisively determined by his knowledge of the Fourth Gospel. The Johannine theology of the Word of God, which Irenaeus correctly understands in light of the Old Testament background, is *the* link which binds together creation and redemption: "Through the same Word through whom God made this world order he also bestowed salvation on the men who belong to this order." Irenaeus, "Against the Heretics," in *Early Christian Fathers*, ed. Cyril Richardson (New York: Macmillan, 1975), 378.

12. Raymond Brown, *The Gospel according to John*, 2 vols., Anchor Bible (New York: Doubleday, 1966), 1:23–24.

13. Ibid., 31.

14. Ibid., 33; cf. John 4:23-26.

15. Paul LaMarche, "The Prologue of John," in Ashton, *Understanding the Fourth Gospel*, 39. LaMarche draws important parallels with the theology of Romans and Ephesians: the concern is with "the apparent incoherence of the history of salvation, and with grasping the unity of the divine plan." LarMarche concludes from this that it is today more than "ever necessary to rediscover in the holy Scripture the great fundamental truths concerning the unity of the divine plan, creation in and through Christ, the role of the Logos in history, the universality of salvation" (ibid., 47).

16. Craig R. Koester, *The Word of Life: A Theology of John's Gospel* (Grand Rapids: Eerdmans, 2008), 214.

17. Ibid.

18. Schnelle, *Antidocetic Christology*, 226.

19. Ibid., emphasis added.

20. "The decision which Jesus' disciples had once made to affirm and accept his sending by 'following' him, had to be made anew and radically in consequence of his crucifixion. *The cross*, so to say, raised the question of decision once more. Little as it could throw into question the content of his message, all the more it could and did render questionable his legitimation, his claim to be God's messenger bringing the last, decisive word. The Church had to surmount the scandal of the cross and did it in the Easter faith." Rudolf Bultmann, *Theology of the New Testament*, vol. 1, trans. K. Grobel (New York: Scribner, 1951), 3:91.

21. Rudolf Bultmann, *Faith and Understanding*, ed. Robert W. Funk, trans. Louise Pettibone Smith (Fortress Press, 1987), 165–83. I draw the following summary from this exceptionally lucid essay, even though already here Bultmann is ruling out texts like 5:25 and 6:54 as "suspected to be the result of redaction." Bultmann in a footnote defers the problem to further study.

22. Bultmann, *Theology*, 3:33.

23. Rudolf Bultmann, *The Gospel of John: A Commentary*, trans. G. R. Beasley-Murray (Louisville: Westminster, 1976), 201, commenting on John 4:39-42.

24. Ibid., 390–91.

25. Ibid., 81.

26. See further chapter 5 below.

27. Bultmann, *Gospel of John*, 296.

28. Modernized Platonism, that is, Kant, who made this very argument crucial in his brief "On the Conflict of the Faculties" against revealed theology at the end of his life: "For if God should really speak to a human being, the latter could still never know that it was God speaking. It is quite impossible for a human being to apprehend the infinite by his senses, distinguish it from sensible beings, and be acquainted with it as such." *Religion and Rational Theology*, Cambridge Edition of the Works of Immanuel Kant, trans. A. W. Wood and G. Di Giovanni (Cambridge: Cambridge University Press, 2001), 283.

29. Ibid., 355. It is not my intention to blunt the prophetic aspect of Bultmann's interpretation expressed in this citation. Rather I think it belongs in a much different context.

30. Ibid., 279.

31. Ibid., 62.

32. Ibid., 445.

33. Ibid., 63.

34. Ibid., 251.

35. Ibid., 145.

36. "The Structure and Purpose of the Prologue to John's Gospel," in *New Testament Questions of Today*, trans. W. J. Montague (Minneapolis: Fortress Press, 1979), 158–60. I will add to Käsemann's criticism: the postulation of a primitive "miracles Gospel" or "Signs Gospel," supposedly with a "divine man" Christology, which supposedly the evangelist is correcting, does not help. Commenting on 1:35-51, for example, Bultmann wrote, "*The source* showed Jesus as the *theos anthropos*, whose miraculous knowledge overwhelms those who meet him. . . . It is easy to see how the *Evangelist* could use this narrative . . . as an illustration of the paradox of the *doxa* of the Incarnate. . . . Faith in him is grounded in the fact that in the encounter with him the believer's own existence is uncovered." Typically in Bultmann's interpretation, the existential interpretation obscures the biblical-narrative dimension of the text. Completely ignored is the central fact that in this initial encounter Jesus *renames* the disciples in view of their mission. In any event, not only is it impossible to reconstruct such a source with any safety; it also implausibly assumes that the evangelist takes up a source toward which he is basically unfriendly and yet allows exactly the theology about miracles toward which he is hostile to survive his otherwise thorough and critical editing.

37. Käsemann, *New Testament Questions*, 156.

38. Ibid., 161.

39. Ernst Käsemann, *The Testament of Jesus* (London: SCM, 1968).

40. Käsemann, *New Testament Questions*, 159.

41. G. Bornkamm, "Toward the Interpretation of John's Gospel," in *The Interpretation of John*, ed. J. Ashton (Minneapolis: Fortress Press, 1986), 92.

42. Ibid.

43. Ibid., 93.

44. Ibid., 94.

45. Bultmann, *Gospel of John*, 250–55.

46. Nils A. Dahl, "Johannine Church and History," in Ashton, *Understanding the Fourth Gospel*, 134.

47. Ibid., 134–36.

48. The situation is complex. Raymond Brown finds evidence of "the Jews" as a term not only for normative Judaism evolving from the Pharisee movement after 70, but also for "crypto-Christians," like Nicodemus who will not openly confess Jesus, from "Jewish Christian Churches of Inadequate Faith." The worst (mutual) vilification in John is reserved for these latter Jewish Christians, whom Brown detects behind the exchange in 8:31-59. See Brown, *Community*, 73–81.

49. Jacob Neusner, *Judaism in the Beginning of Christianity* (Minneapolis: Fortress Press, 1984).

50. Dunn, "Let John be John," 294.

51. Ibid., 321.

52. Ibid., 296.

53. Ibid., 295.

54. Hoskyns, *Fourth Gospel*, 48.

55. Ibid., 68.

56. Ibid., 82.

57. Quoted in conclusion by D. Moody Smith, *John among the Gospels: The Relationship in Twentieth-Century Research* (Minneapolis: Fortress Press, 1992), 188. Hoskyns's approach to John is finding new support, according to Moody, although Hoskyns receives surprisingly little consideration in this otherwise excellent study (184).

58. Hoskyns, *Fourth Gospel*, 68, 84.

59. Ibid., 69.

60. Ibid., 45.

61. Ibid., 46.

62. The following summary is drawn from "The Historical Tension of the Fourth Gospel," chapter 4 in Hoskyns, *Fourth Gospel*, 58–85.

63. C. H. Dodd in his rich and still instructive *The Interpretation of the Fourth Gospel* (Cambridge: Cambridge University Press, 1995) repeatedly pointed to the Fourth Gospel's theological reworking of the Synoptic Christology in *Interpretation*, 227–29, 238, 316, 320, 334, 343, 354, 361–62, 369, 373, 390, 408, 429, although like Hoskyns, he denied that this reworking occurred as a literary redaction; instead he envisions a common oral tradition to account for John's reworking (449).

64. Udo Schnelle, who in many respects revives and modernizes Hoskyns's approach, comes to the same conclusion: "The historical and theological standpoint of the fourth evangelist is to be sought in the discussions and conflicts within the Johannine school . . . located at the center of the theological history of earliest Christianity, at a point where important currents in developing Christian theology converged" (*Antidocetic Christology*, 236).

65. Hoskyns, *Fourth Gospel*, 130.

66. Ibid., 49.

67. Dunn, "Let John Be John," 295.

68. We "have always to ask," wrote C. H. Dodd at the end of *Interpretation*, "how far it appears that the specifically Johannine concepts (often indicated by the use of a quasi-technical vocabulary) have worked to produce the form of story or saying. That is why a detailed examination of Johannine thought such as we have here essayed is an indispensable preliminary to any estimate of the historical element in the gospel" (452).

69. Hoskyns, *Fourth Gospel*, 65.

70. Karl Barth, *The Epistle to the Romans*, trans. E. C. Hoskyns (Oxford: Oxford University Press, 1972), 8.

71. Bruce McCormack, *Karl Barth's Critically Realistic Dialectical Theology: Its Genesis and Development 1909–1936* (Oxford: Clarendon, 1995).

72. Hoskyns, *Fourth Gospel*, 148.

73. Ibid., 85.

74. Dodd, *Interpretation*, 186.

75. Ibid., 90.

76. Hoskyns, *Fourth Gospel*, 101.

77. Brown, *Community*, 113.

78. Hoskyns, *Fourth Gospel*, 55.

79. Brown, *Community*, 147.

80. Ibid., 156–58. If we reckon with several early editions or redactions of the Gospel of John, as many suggest, the question of its relation to the First Epistle becomes even more complex.

81. Ibid., 56.

82. Ibid., 57.

83. Schnelle, *Antidocetic Christology*, 61. I do not find any reference to Hoskyns in Schnelle's book, though the convergence of their viewpoints seems to me remarkable. Stuhlmacher likewise, *Jesus*, 95.

84. Schnelle, *Antidocetic Christology*, 204. The passage continues: "It is not a symbolic 'eating' of the bread of heaven or a spirit-filled 'eating' of the Son of man that gives eternal life, but only the real eating and drinking of the flesh and blood of Jesus Christ in the Eucharist."

85. All citations from Ignatius's authentic letters (the so-called Middle Recension dated around 115). Polycarp and the *Martyrdom of Polycarp* are taken from *The Apostolic Fathers: Revised Greek Texts with Introductions and English Translations*, ed. J. B. Lightfoot and J. R. Harner (Grand Rapids: Baker, 1984). I have taken over the translations of Lightfoot or W. R. Schoedel (in the Hermeneia Commentary; see n. 277 below), or modified them slightly in light of the Greek text as seemed best for my purposes. References to the patristic literature will be provided in parentheses following the citation with standard chapter and paragraph enumeration. While I am sympathetic to the early dating of the Long Recension, and the case made in Jack W. Hannah, "The Setting of the Ignatian Long Recension," *Journal of Biblical Literature* 79/3 (September 1960): 221–38, for placing it within the anti-Gnostic trajectory I am arguing, it is not essential to the argument I am making about anti-docetism. Hannah claims that the "letters of Ignatius can hardly be said to have been used popularly by the early Christian writers. Prior to the third century his works are alluded to only by Polycarp, the Martyrdom of Polycarp, Irenaeus and Origen" (230). Arguing that the Long Recension is attributable to Polycarp between 135 and 155, Hannah concludes that it "becomes the earliest truly anti-Gnostic writing. The remarks of Ignatius were changed and directed against specific Gnostic systems. Perhaps as part of this anti-Gnostic polemic, there is extensive quotation of texts from the Gospels and Paul which also indicate an objective of formulating an orthodox dogma for the church" (234).

86. Bultmann, *Theology of the New Testament*, 2:195.

87. Ibid., 197.

88. See Talal Asad, *Formations of the Secular: Christianity, Islam, Modernity* (Stanford: Stanford University Press, 2003).

89. Ignatius "invites fellow Christians to see beyond appearances and to grasp the hidden meaning of his wretched condition. It seems obvious that Christians who had been nurtured on the story of the crucified Lord and who had experienced rejection by society in their own lives would be prepared to welcome such a figure." William R. Schoedel, *Ignatius of Antioch: A Commentary on the Letters of Ignatius of Antioch*, Hermeneia (Minneapolis: Fortress Press, 1985), 12.

90. William R. Farmer, *The Formation of the New Testament Canon: An Ecumenical Approach* (Mahwah: Paulist, 1983), 42.

91. It is significant confirmation of Farmer's analysis that the careful literary and text critical study of David Trobisch, *The First Edition of the New Testament* (Oxford: Oxford University Press, 2000), comes substantively to the same conclusion. Trobisch identifies the "conflict with the Marcionite movement," along with the attempt to overcome the tension between Asia Minor and Rome over the dating of Easter, as "characteristic features of the implied readership of the Canonical Edition." His commentary on this conclusion is further refutation of the Bauer thesis: "The success of this publication did not depend on an authoritative decision of the church; rather, readers found their convictions better expressed in the Canonical Edition than in competing literary works. During hard times of persecution, this book was capable of defining or reinforcing the identity and unity of its readers" (106).

92. Daniel Boyarin's case for the affinity of Christian martyrdom with its Jewish antecedents is a powerful correction of the anti-Judaism of liberal Protestant historiography. Boyarin rightly sees in the passionate desire of Ignatius "the idea of martyrdom as a positive and eroticized religious fulfillment"; that is, the refusal of idolatry as a kind of adultery correlates

with "the gift of death" (Derrida) one makes to the supreme object of one's love. "To put this in more classic Jewish terminology, in the past, martyrs refused to violate a negative commandment—to worship idols. Now [in early Catholicism] we find martyrs fulfilling through their deaths a positive one—to love God." Daniel Boyarin, *Dying for God: Martyrdom and the Making of Christianity and Judaism* (Stanford: Stanford University Press, 1999), 114.

93. Schoedel, *Ignatius*, 14.

94. Similarly, the *Martyrdom of Perpetua and Felicitas*.

95. Schoedel, *Ignatius*, 64.

96. E. R. Dodds, *Pagan and Christian in an Age of Anxiety* (New York: Norton, 1965), for example, "To identify oneself with such [a decaying society, as depicted by the church father Cyprian], to take it seriously as a place to live and labour in, must have demanded more courage than the average man possessed: better treat it as an illusion or a bad joke, and avoid heartbreak" (12).

97. The debate about the sources and origins of Gnosticism (and its relation to the docetism which Ignatius was battling) continues, but certainly among Jews and Christians early Gnosticism is associated with the failure of apocalyptic hopes. This is the truth correctly grasped by Jean Danielou, in his dated but still very interesting "The Origins to the End of the Third Century," part 1 of *The Christian Centuries*, vol. 1 (Darton, Longman & Todd, 1964): "The basic element was the opposition between the hidden God, who became manifest in Christ, and the angels who create the world, to whom Yahweh belongs. . . . After the year 70 a certain number of Jews and Judeo-Christians adopted it as the expression of their revolt against the God who had disappointed them in their eschatological hopes and against the creation which was his work" (65). This historical context provides the backdrop for Danielou to affirm the second-century development of the theology of the history of salvation as the faithful alternative which could simultaneously preserve and transcend the failed hopes of early Christian apocalypticism. This interpretation derives from Robert M. Grant, *Gnosticism and Early Christianity* (New York: Columbia University Press, 1966). See also William R. Farmer, *New Testament Canon*, 92 n. 66. Ernst Käsemann states the thesis crisply and accurately: "It becomes apparent that nascent catholicism was the historically necessary outcome of an original Christianity whose apocalyptic expectation had not been fulfilled. It may likewise become clear that— expressed or not—the mark of nascent catholicism is the message about the world-pervading Church as the reality of the kingdom of Christ on earth. . . . The Pauline concept of the Church [as the Body of Christ] paved the way for the early Catholic view [which] inseparably linked ecclesiology and christology together and thus made the Church an integral factor in the salvation event" ("Paul and Early Catholicism" in *New Testament Questions*, 245–46). Kasemann is, to be sure, less than enthused at this turn of events.

98. Rudolf Bultmann, *Theology*, 199.

99. Schoedel, *Ignatius*, 55.

100. Paul Wesche, "Saint Ignatius of Antioch: The Criterion of Orthodoxy and the Marks of Catholicity," *Pro Ecclesia* 3/1:97–98.

101. "The Eucharistic function of the ministry becomes central in the vision of the local Church presented by Ignatius of Antioch. It is not accident that those who ascribe to Eucharistic ecclesiology find their inspiration in Ignatius and the typical expression, truly normative of the nature of the Church." J.-M. R. Tillard, *Church of Churches: The Ecclesiology of Communion*, trans. R.C. De Peaux and O. Praem (Collegeville: Liturgical, 1987), 185. Tillard has in mind positions like that of John D. Zizioulas, *Being as Communion: Studies in Personhood and the Church*, with a foreword by John Meyendorff (Crestwood: St. Vladimir's, 1993), 78. Tillard has it that "the one who presides at [the Eucharist normally will] be that same person who presides daily over [the community's] unity and its charity. Ignatius proceeds from the 'unitive' function of the bishop to his 'Eucharistic' presidency, and not vice versa" (ibid.). But this judgment is surely arbitrary.

102. Schoedel prefers here a reference to the oral Gospel, not allusions to the written Gospels. Indeed, Schoedel finds certain citations in all of Ignatius's letters only from Matthew and 1 Corinthians. But the prisoner bound in chains is not carrying his library with him from Antioch! He cites from memory. The allusions and references to Petrine (Synoptic), Pauline, and Johannine literature are indisputable and pervasive. One needs only to think of the role which Jesus' birth from the virgin Mary (unique of course to the Gospels of Matthew and Luke) played in Ignatius's antidocetic polemic.

103. Farmer, *Formation*, 85.

104. 11. Frederick W. Norris, "Ignatius, Polycarp, and I Clement: Walter Bauer Reconsidered," *Vigiliae Christianae* 31–32.

105. Walter Bauer, *Orthodoxy and Heresy in Early Christianity*, ed. R. Kraft and G. Krodel (Philadelphia: Fortress Press, 1971; repr., Sigler, 1996). Bauer sets up his treatment of the same material considered in this section with the psychological speculation that Ignatius, representing a minority position in predominantly and increasingly heterodox Christianity, "easily arrives at the conclusion that his legitimate claims are being neglected by the circle of leaders and then the desire stirs in him for a dictatorship that would establish the supremacy of his own party" (*Orthodoxy and Heresy*, 62). In a representative council, Ignatius would have to sit alongside "representatives of the Gnostics and of acknowledged Jewish Christians. . . . If, however, the leadership of the community responds to the command of the one bishop, then orthodoxy can hope to take the helm even where it is only a minority" (ibid., 62–63). This Protestant nightmare has no bearing whatsoever on the real history in question here.

106. Ibid., 33.

107. Schnelle, *Antidocetic Christology*, 64.

108. Gregory, Bishop of Nyssa, "Against Eunomius," II:4, in NPNF V:105.

109. Ibid., 108.

110. Otto Weber, *Foundations of Dogmatics*, vol. 2, trans. D. L. Guder (Grand Rapids: Eerdmanns, 1983), 163.

4. The Trinitarian Rule of Faith

1. See above, chapter 1.

2. "Whatever other uses they may have been put to in the course of history, the true and original use of creeds, their primary raison d'etre, was to serve as solemn affirmations of faith in the context of baptismal initiation." J. N. D. Kelly, *Early Christian Creeds*, 3rd ed. (New York: McCay, 1972), 31.

3. Recall the discussion above of John 6 in relation to Ignatius's teaching on the Eucharist. "Wherever Jesus Christ is, there is the Catholic church" (*Smyrn.* 8) means wherever the Eucharist is kept in faith: "I want the bread of God, which is the flesh of Christ who is of the seed of David; and for drink I want his blood, which is incorruptible love" (*Rom.* 7).

4. Käsemann, *Romans*, 123. And again: "Human beings do not precede God; God does not bypass mankind. The relation between justification and faith dialectically combines these two statements" (ibid., 125).

5. Victor Paul Furnish, "On Putting Paul in His Place," *Journal of Biblical Literature* 113/1 (1994): 4–7. Furnish thinks that the churchly Paul is too much a "confiscation" of the historical Paul: "Paul's place in the church was won at the cost of his place in history" (7). But, as with study of the so-called historical Jesus, this severe judgment severs Paul from his own destiny. It is through the early catholic theology of the martyrs that Paul speaks, if he speaks at all. Furnish actually acknowledges this; see below.

6. Krister Stendahl, "Paul and the Introspective Consciousness of the West," in *Paul among Jews and Gentiles* (Philadelphia: Fortress, 1976), 78–96. See my sustained appreciation and critique of the so-called New Perspective on Paul in chapter 6 of *Luther and the Beloved*

Community: A Path for Christian Theology after Christendom (Grand Rapids: Eerdmans, 2010).

7. J. Christian Beker, *Paul the Apostle: The Triumph of God in Life and Thought* (Philadelphia: Fortress Press, 1984).

8. Furnish, "Paul in His Place," 12.

9. Ibid., 14.

10. Ibid., 17.

11. Jonathan Z. Smith, *Drudgery Divine: On the Comparison of Early Christianities and the Religions of Late Antiquity* (Chicago: University of Chicago Press, 1990), 142–43.

12. Ibid.

13. Ibid., 141.

14. Peter Stuhlmacher, *Reconciliation, Law, Righteousness: Essays in Biblical Theology*, trans. Everett R. Kalin (Minneapolis: Fortress Press, 1986), 172. This approach to Paul's theology was also Bultmann's: "The question thrust upon [Paul] by this kerygma was whether he was willing to regard the crucified Jesus of Nazareth, whom the kerygma asserted to have risen from the dead, as the expected Messiah." Rudolf Bultman, *Theology of the New Testament*, Complete in one volume, trans. K. Grobel (New York: Scribner, 1955), 187. Bultmann, however, regards this change in perspective as Paul's decision in response to the kerygma, not the risen Christ's decision to enlist Saul in His cause. Stuhlmacher, taking the latter approach, will not, like Bultmann, reduce theology to anthropology.

15. LW 27:141–42.

16. "The church as the body of Christ is the earthly body of the risen and exalted Lord—that is, it is not the crucified body, which was Jesus' alone and in which no one can be incorporated." Ernst Käsemann, *Perspectives on Paul*, trans. M. Kohl (Philadelphia: Fortress Press, 1978), 111–12. Käsemann continued: "By incorporating our earthly bodies in his kingdom, Christ at the same time shows that the sphere of his earthly kingdom is a body. Christ communicates with his people—and beyond them with the world as well—through sacrament, Word and faith. As the sphere of this communication the church is the earthly body of the risen Lord. Paul was not particularly fortunate in his attempts to organize the communities he had gathered, which detracted from his work considerably. Consequently it was not without reason that the Pastoral Epistles saw in this their most important task" (115).

17. Benjamin D. Crowe, *Heidegger's Religious Origins: Destruction and Authenticity* (Bloomington: Indiana University Press, 2006). See the author's review essay, "Luther and Heidegger," *Lutheran Quarterly* 22/1 (Spring 2008): 78–86.

18. Hans Conzelmann, *1 Corinthians: A Commentary on the First Epistle to the Corinthians*, trans. J. W. Leitch (Philadelphia: Fortress Press, 1975), 15.

19. Nils Alstrup Dahl, *Studies in Paul: Theology for the Early Christian Mission* (Minneapolis: Augsburg, 1977), 40–61.

20. I am indebted to Dr. Christian von Dehsen, Carthage College, for this insight.

21. My own woodenly literal translation.

22. Stuhlmacher, *Reconciliation*, 174.

23. Ibid., 175.

24. Citing *Mein Kampf*, the European Jewish refugee Maurice Samuel wrote in 1940 to Americans, that is, prior to the onset of the Holocaust: "Very clearly then, what Hitler hates, in common with Nietzsche, whose hand lies heavy on the quoted passage, is fundamental Christianity. . . . It does not matter that moral opposition to the Nazi-Fascist view of the human being is often without the specific Christian stamp. The unmistakable relationship is there. Nazism-Fascism says that man exists in and by virtue of the machine; Judaeo-Christianity says that a machine must exist for man, or must not exist at all. And everyone who takes this point of view allies himself ultimately with Judaeo-Christianity." Maurice Samuel, *The Great Hatred* (1940; repr., New York: Knopf, 1948), 108–9. "Christ and Christianity are not attacked by name; but their significance must be destroyed from the earth, and the values they stand for

must be discredited by the indirect method. And so the Jews are hated as the givers of Christ, but denounced as the killers of Christ" (ibid., 139). Samuel's indictment—that the German Christians' ranks were filled with liberal theologians—has been justified by recent historical research; see Doris L. Bergen, *Twisted Cross: The German Christian Movement in the Third Reich* (Chapel Hill: University of North Carolina, 1996). See also Richard Steigmann-Gall, *The Holy Reich: Nazi Conceptions of Christianity, 1919–1945* (Cambridge: Cambridge University Press, 2003). The reader is also referred to Susannah Heschel, *The Aryan Jesus: Christian Theologians and the Bible in Nazi Germany* (Princeton: Princeton University Press, 2008).

25. *Luther, Lutheranism, and the Jews*, ed. J. Halperin and A. Sovik (Geneva: Lutheran World Federation, 1984). "'First,' [Luther] wrote, 'their synagogues should be set on fire.' Jewish homes, he said, should likewise be 'broken down or destroyed.' Jews should then be put under one roof, or in a stable, like Gypsies, in order that they may realize that they are not masters in our land." Martin Gilbert, *The Holocaust: A History of the Jews in Europe during the Second World War* (New York: Holt, Rinehart, and Winston, 1986), 19. The excerpts are drawn from Luther's late tract "On the Jews and Their Lies" (1543). See above all in this connection Heiko Obermann, *The Roots of Anti-Semitism in the Age of Renaissance and Reformation*, trans. J. I. Porter (Philadelphia: Fortress Press, 1984), which demonstrates in the manner of *Sachkritik* the material, theological contradiction between Luther's venomous statements of 1543 and his own gospel: "Our heinous crime and weighty sin nailed Jesus to the cross, God's true Son. Therefore, we should not in bitterness scold you, poor Judas, or the Jewish host. The guilt is our own" (ibid., 124).

26. The destruction of the temple in Jerusalem by the Romans in 70 was the event that gave birth to rabbinic Judaism no less than to normative Christianity, as Neusner explains: "The entire history of Christianity and Judaism alike flowed across the abyss of that catastrophe. Each religious tradition had to make sense of what it meant to worship God in ways lacking all precedent in the history of Israel, of which each religious tradition claimed to be the natural outcome and fulfillment." Jacob Neusner, *Judaism in the Beginning of Christianity* (Minneapolis: Fortress Press, 1984), 89. This event was a "theological challenge," which required both interpretation and reconstruction of religious life that in effect would transfer the atonement and sanctification that the temple worship had provided to the now scattered community's life in the world. The old temple built with hands would now be rebuilt in the sacred community. I am paraphrasing Neusner's account of the rabbis, but what he says here applies no less to the post-apostolic Christian community.

27. "The first believers were Jews, for whom conversation with the Sacred Scriptures was the primary mode of theological reflection. Exegesis was fundamental to Christian reflection; it was in the language of the Scriptures that Jesus' followers spoke about the 'gospel.'" Donald Juel, *Messianic Exegesis: Christological Interpretation of the Old Testament in Early Christianity* (Philadelphia: Fortress Press, 1988), 8.

28. Pinchas Lapide and Peter Stuhlmacher, *Paul: Rabbi and Apostle* (Minneapolis: Augsburg, 1984), 68.

29. David Trobisch, *Paul's Letter Collection: Tracing the Origins* (Minneapolis: Fortress Press, 1994), 55.

30. Ibid., 97–98.

31. The cosmic dimension of Paul's legacy is especially developed in these letters. This brings the insight, so important in extracting the Pauline legacy from Kantianism and existentialism: "Every doctrine of salvation must involve a metaphysic of some kind, if not a cosmology; and every metaphysic or cosmology has soteriological implications." Rev. S. Barbour, "Salvation and Cosmology: The Setting of the Epistle to the Colossians," *Scottish Journal of Theology* 20 (1967): 257–71.

32. A version of the following material first appeared as "Proclaiming Paul Today," *Pro Ecclesia* 7/3 (Summer 1998). For the theological implications of the critical discussion of the Pastorals since F. C. Baur, see the incisive and still unsurpassed essay of Ernst Käsemann, "Paul

and Early Catholicism," in "The Structure and Purpose of the Prologue to John's Gospel," in *New Testament Questions of Today*, trans. W. J. Montague (Minneapolis: Fortress Press, 1979), 158–60. The best modern case for the Apostle's authorship of the Pastoral Epistles may be found in J. N. D. Kelly, *A Commentary on the Pastoral Epistles* (London: Adam & Charles Black, 1963). For the critical consensus that the Pastoral Epistles are the work of an inferior imitator who misunderstood Paul and distorted the understanding of him for years to come, see J. L. Houlden, *The Pastoral Epistles: I and II Timothy, Titus* (Philadelphia: Trinity Press International, 1989). A persuasive argument locating the Pastorals historically in the second Christian generation and in theological continuity with the historical Paul is made by Jerome D. Quinn, "Timothy and Titus, Epistles to," in *The Anchor Bible Dictionary*, ed. David Noel Friedman (New York: Doubleday, 1992), 6:560–71. Quinn also ventures the illuminating hypothesis with some supporting evidence that in the original order Titus preceded the two letters to Timothy, serving as an overture to the themes developed in the two letters to Timothy, which in turn concluded with the dramatic "last will and testament" of the imprisoned apostle in 2 Timothy.

33. Dahl, *Studies in Paul*, 59.

34. Citing 1 Timothy 6:10 and 6:7 at Philippians 4; perhaps 2 Timothy 2:12 at Philippians 5, with a number of other possible allusions.

35. *The Ecclesiastical History of Eusebius Pamphilus* IV:8, trans. C. F. Cruse (Grand Rapids: Baker, 1993), 135.

36. *Apostolic Fathers*, 233–37.

37. See the discussion of the Girard thesis in *Luther and the Beloved Community*, chapter 2.

38. Daniel J. Sheerin, *The Eucharist*, Message of the Fathers of the Church 7 (Wilmington: Glazier, 1986), 23–24.

39. Paul Wesche, "Saint Ignatius of Antioch: The Criterion of Orthodoxy and the Marks of Catholicity," *Pro Ecclesia* 3/1: 89–109: "The dictum 'Scripture interprets itself' would make little sense to the early Church, for in the experience of the early Church, Scripture does not interpret itself: something else does, namely the context in which the Scriptures themselves were judged for their canonicity. To uphold Scripture as the supreme authority therefore closes one off to the ethos and experience of the early Church that provided the context for understanding the Scripture. . . . The terms 'old' and 'new testament' could *not* refer to a closed set of divinely inspired books; they had to refer to something or some*one* else. And in fact, in the writings of the New Testament itself, the term 'new covenant' or 'new testament' refers to the Eucharist, more specifically, to Jesus himself."

40. *Apostolic Fathers*, 235.

41. W. H. C. Frend, *The Rise of Christianity* (Philadelphia: Fortress Press, 1984), 174.

42. "Dialogue with Trypho, a Jew," ANF I:194–270; citations also drawn from Message of the Fathers of the Church (Wilmington: Glazier, 1987).

43. W. H. C. Frend, "The Old Testament in the Age of the Greek Apologists," *Scottish Journal of Theology* 26/2 (1973): 140.

44. Ibid., 138–39.

45. Ibid., 149.

46. Charles Nahm, "The Debate on the 'Platonism' of Justin Martyr," *The Second Century: A Journal of Early Christian Studies* 9/3 (1992): 151. This article provides an excellent bibliographical survey along with an overview of the debate in recent scholarship.

47. Ibid., 150.

48. Ibid., 141.

49. Ibid., 135.

50. "The Second Apology of Justin," ANF I:188–193; citations also drawn from Message of the Fathers of the Church (Wilmington: Glazier, 1987).

51. L. W. Barnard, "Justin Martyr in Recent Study," *Scottish Journal of Theology* 22/2 (1969): 160.

52. Ibid., 161.

53. "The First Apology of Justin," ANF I:163–187; citations also drawn from Message of the Fathers of the Church.

54. Christopher Morse, *Not Every Spirit: A Dogmatics of Christian Disbelief* (Philadelphia: Trinity Press International, 1994), 18.

55. "The coming Arian struggles are no more than the consequences of the error which was introduced at the time of the Apologists." Aloys Grillmeier, *Christ in Christian Tradition*, vol. 1, *From the Apostolic Age to Chalcedon (451)*, 2nd ed., trans. J. Bowden (Atlanta: John Knox, 1975), 109–10.

56. Barnard, "Justin," 163.

57. Cf. Aloys Grillmeier, S.J., *Christ in Christian Tradition*, vol. 1 (Louisville: John Knox, 1975), 90.

58. Barnard, "Justin," 157.

59. Ibid., 90–91.

60. See Talal Asad, *Formations of the Secular: Christianity, Islam, Modernity* (Stanford: Stanford University Press, 2003), chapter 2, 67–99.

61. Origin's foe, Celsus, for whom Plato teaches "true theology," exemplifies the anti-Gnostic stance (but he equates Catholic Christianity with Gnosticism). See the reconstruction of his critique of Christianity: Celsus, *On the True Doctrine: A Discourse against the Christians*, trans. R. J. Hoffmann (Oxford: Oxford University Press, 1987). Valentinian Gnosticism is a borderline case; see John Dillon, *The Middle Platonists, 80 B.C. to A.D. 220*, rev. ed. (Ithaca: Cornell University Press, 1996), 384–98.

62. Frend, *Rise of Christianity*, chapter 6, 193–228, inteprets Gnosticism as "acute Hellenization."

63. Kurt Randolph, "Gnosticism," in *The Anchor Bible Dictionary* (New York: Doubleday, 1992), 2:1035.

64. Pelikan, TCT I:83.

65. Hans Jonas, *The Gnostic Religion: The Message of the Alien God and the Beginnings of Christianity*, 2nd ed. (Boston: Beacon, 1963).

66. For the highly simplified picture that follows, I draw on Dillon's account of the old Plato, and his immediate disciples' reading: "The process described in the *Timaeus* was timeless and eternal" (ibid., 7).

67. Pelikan, TCT I:87.

68. Ibid.

69. Ibid., 89, citing from *Gospel of Truth* and *Gospel of Thomas*.

70. Irenaeus, "Against Heresies," I:26:1, hereafter AH, in ANF I:352. See also Robert M. Grant, *Irenaeus of Lyons*, Early Church Fathers (London: Routledge, 2005).

71. Pelikan, TCT I:89.

72. Pelikan, TCT I:90.

73. I am frequently utilizing the felicitous translations of Peter C. Phan in *Grace and the Human Condition*, Message of the Fathers of the Church 4 (Wilmington: Glazier, 1988).

74. John Lawson, *The Biblical Theology of Saint Irenaeus* (London: Epworth, 1948), 117.

75. Thus Bauer can acknowledge in passing, "Roman Christianity, so far as we know, was from the beginning under the heaviest pressure from external enemies," as a result of which "there grew up here the one church of dependable orthodoxy" (*Orthodoxy and Heresy*, 128).

76. Lawson, *Irenaeus*, 97ff.

77. Richard A. Norris Jr., "Theology and Language in Irenaeus of Lyon," *Anglican Theological Review* 76/3: 289.

78. Ibid., 290.

79. Ibid., 292.

80. Ibid., 294.

81. Ibid., 295.

82. Pelikan, TCT I:97.

83. Pelikan states: "The early Christian picture of God was controlled by the self-evident axiom, accepted by all, of the absoluteness and the impassibility of divine nature" (TCT I:229).

84. Ignatius: "the Eternal, the Invisible, who for our sake became visible; the Intangible, the Unsuffering, who for our sake suffered," from "To Polycarp" in *Apostolic Fathers*, 3.

85. Among the older research, John Lawson, *Biblical Theology of Saint Irenaeus*, rightly emphasizes that Irenaeus never calls "for submission to the Church on the ground that loyalty to that body is a salutary moral exercise. Always it is that men should accept the Apostolic doctrine from the Church because this, and this alone, is God's saving truth" (255, 278).

86. Irenaeus, "Against the Heretics," in *Early Christian Fathers*, ed. Cyril Richardson (New York: Macmillan, 1975), 344.

87. The problem, however, was that this criticism could have applied equally to loose orthodox exegetical methods then current, especially the allegorical method which was developing in circles under the influence of Philo and Platonism. See the comparison of Valentinian, Alexandrian and Asiatic exegesis of the Parable of the Good Samaritan current in Irenaeus's time in Mary Ann Donovan, "Irenaeus in Recent Scholarship," *Second Century* 4/4 (1984): 229.

88. Dillon, *Middle Platonists*, 116 n. 6, following Wingren, Lawson, and the consensus of modern scholarship.

89. Donovan, "Recent Scholarship," 225. The reference is to William R. Schoedel, "Theological Method in Irenaeus," *Journal of Theological Studies* 35 (1984): 31–49.

90. Thomas F. Torrance, *The Trinitarian Faith: The Evangelical Theology of the Ancient Catholic Church* (Edinburgh: T&T Clark, 1993), 34.

91. Grillmeier, *Christ in Christian Tradition*, 101.

92. Frend, *Rise of Christianity*, 245.

93. Richardson, *Early Christian Fathers*, 351.

94. Donovan, "Recent Scholarship," 230.

95. Ibid. "Irenaeus never loses from view that the human as loved, as called, as free, as saved, is *flesh*" (236).

96. Phan, *Grace*, 49.

97. Frend, *Rise of Christianity*, 245.

98. Ibid.

99. Jenson correctly writes that Irenaeus "launched so principled a polemic against the gnostic systems that it became a polemic against myth in general, against the very notion of a mid-realm between God and creatures. He attacks the whole conception of reality as a descending set of levels emanating from the next above and especially of the origin of the Son as such an emanation" (Jenson, *Triune Identity*, 69).

5. The Confrontation of Biblical and Philosophical Monotheism

1. See here Philip Melanchthon's remarkable and little-known defense of Homer against Plato, "who, condemning Homer as for a capital crime, excludes him from his Republic, and thrusts him out and dispatches him into exile." *Philip Melanchthon: Orations on Philosophy and Education*, ed. Sachiko Kusukawa, trans. C. F. Salazar (Cambridge: Cambridge University Press, 1999), 49. Melanchthon agrees with Plato that Homer "related some ridiculous and absurd things about the immortal gods and about religion," yet defends Homer's depiction of the gods as showing that God "loves, protects and helps the good, hates the impious and the wicked and afflicts them with punishment, and attends to and rules human affairs" (50). He also defends Homer against the criticism of Stoics: "It seems praiseworthy to me that he did not think idly of the stupid and imaginary Stoic freedom from passions (apatheia), but presented such images of affairs and men as they are in the nature of things and in life" (51).

2. But, writes Jenson, upon citing St. Thomas on the immediacy of God's operation, "for God there are only two places: the place that he is and the place he makes for creatures, immediately and inwardly adjacent to him. Thus the creation is for God just one place. And the one creation is heaven and earth together, however otherwise they differ" (ST II:254).

3. Jenson, ST I:234–36.

4. Jenson, *Triune Identity*, 67–68.

5. John Dillon, *The Middle Platonists, 80 B.C. to A.D. 220*, rev. ed. (Ithaca: Cornell University Press, 1996). Dillon's analysis of the philosophical positions of Justin's near contemporary, Plutarch of Chaeroneia, is particularly instructive (*The Middle Platonists*, 192—230) in respect to the clear rejection of creation out of nothing (207) in place of the Logos as noetic-erotic intermediary both imposing order on chaos and leading the finite mind up by intellectual love to the reality of pure ideas (200–201). Intriguing also is the revealing analysis of the apparent origins of negative theology in Philo of Alexandria (155–56) which makes for a "totally transcendent God" and "straightway" the "acute" problem "of his relations with the universe" (157). Philo solves this by having the Logos sow seeds of reason, the *logoi spermatikoi* borrowed from Stoicism (159)—the notion that Justin also appropriated.

6. See here the sophisticated discussion of this neuralgic question in C. J. De Vogel, "Platonism and Christianity: A Mere Antagonism or a Profound Common Groud?" *Vigiliae Christianae* 39 (1985): 1–62. Taking an Athanasian position, Vogel argues that "Plato's metaphysics of transcendent and perfect being on which all things visible depend has actually become an essential and even a fundamental part of Christian thinking from the second century onward. And this was not a thing to be lost" (36). He took the human flesh on Him, "so that we might take part in Divine nature. That is the gospel of Christ, and it can only be explained in terms of being." By contrast, "how fatal it was to introduce terms of time into our speaking of God, could be seen from the case of Arius" (54). In order to appreciate the true nature of the "tension and struggle" over the Incarnation (29) between Platonism and Christianity, then, one has to appreciate the "common ground": "Not every form of Greek philosophy was acceptable to Christians" (27). De Vogel is wrong about Luther in this connection, who also, indeed notoriously, holds that the immutability of God is the basis for confidence in His promises. De Vogel attributes Luther's criticism of Aristotle to Plato as well (1), when in fact Luther philosophically thinks of himself as a renewer of Platonism, via Augustine to be sure, against the Latin appropriation of Aristotle in nominalism (LW 31:41–42). De Vogel, however, is not wrong about modern interpreters of Luther, like von Harnack (55).

7. Eric Osborn, "Clement of Alexandria: A Review of Research, 1958–1982," *Second Century* 3/4 (1983): 228, referring to *Timaeus* 28C, *Epist.* 2:312, and *Laws* 4:715–16 respectively.

8. De Vogel, "Platonism and Christianity," 54–55.

9. On the summons to deplatonization, see inter alia Robert W. Jenson, *Unbaptized God: The Basic Flaw in Ecumenical Theology* (Minneapolis: Augsburg Fortress, 1992), 107–47, and Eberhard Jüngel, *Death: The Riddle and the Mystery*, trans. I. and U. Nicol (Philadelphia: Westminster, 1974), 41.

10. Pelikan, TCT I:152.

11. Osborn, "Clement," 240.

12. Joseph M. Hallman, "Divine Suffering and Change in Origen and Ad Theopompum," *Second Century* 7/2 (1990): 87. He cites Prestige again: "It is clear that impassibility means not that God is inactive or uninterested, not that He surveys existence with Epicurean impassibity from the shelter of a metaphysical insulation, but that His will is determined from within instead of being swayed from without" (88).

13. Pelikan, TCT I:176.

14. Ibid., 178–82.

15. CD IV/1, 65, cited by McCormack.

16. John Meyendorff, *Byzantine Theology: Historical Trends and Doctrinal Themes* (Bronx, N.Y.: Fordham University Press, 1979), 180–81.

17. It may be Barth who misunderstands the Western tradition in a one-sidedly mentalist fashion that makes the two approaches seem mutually exclusive. See Dennis Bielfeldt, *The Substance of Faith: Luther's Doctrinal Theology for Today* (Minneapolis: Fortress Press, 2008), 121–26, who argues that in Luther both approaches are found in mutually complementary ways.

18. Vladimir Lossky, *In the Image and Likeness of God*, ed. J. H. Erickson and T. E. Bird (Crestwood: St. Vladimir's, 1985).

19. Cornelius Plantinga Jr., "Gregory of Nyssa and the Social Analogy of the Trinity," *The Thomist* 50/3 (1986): 325.

20. Perichoresis, that is, "the mutual indwelling of the divine hypostases," as seen in John 17, "has great theological significance because it indicates that they give themselves to each other in love. . . . This relationship among the persons is an eternal rest in each other but also an eternal movement of love, though without change or process . . . a dynamism which need not in any way compromise the eternity and impassibility of God." Verna Harrison, "Perichoresis in the Greek Fathers," *St. Vladimir's Theological Quarterly* 35 (1991): 64. Harrison sees it as a second cause of divine unity, alongside that of common essence (60). I am arguing that we not assume as axiomatic a Platonic essence of God by the way of negation and then use it positively as a source of divine unity. Rather the divine nature is to be approached by way of the perichoresis.

21. Clement of Alexandria, "Exhortation to the Heathen," hereafter EX in ANF II:171–206.

22. *Paganism and Christianity, 100–425 C.E.: A Sourcebook*, ed. Ramsay McMullen and Eugene N. Lane (Minneapolis: Augsburg Fortress, 1992), 167.

23. Augustine, *Confessions*, trans. R. S. Pine-Coffin (New York: Dorset, 1986), VII:9; 144.

24. Ibid., VII:10; 146–47.

25. Ibid., VII:14; 150.

26. It is disputable whether Augustine's reflection at this point remains within the possibilities of Platonism. In the intervening VII:12 he has argued his interpretation of the goodness of the being of the creature, including its matter. This reflects the biblical teaching of creation *ex nihilo* and this reading is confirmed by the catena of biblical allusions in VII:13.

27. Ibid., VII:15; 150.

28. Ibid., VII:20; 154.

29. Arthur Norris Cochrane, *Christianity and Classical Culture: A Study of Thought and Action from Augustus to Augustine* (New York: Oxford University Press, 1957), 396–97.

30. Ibid., 394.

31. Ibid., 397.

32. *Confessions*, VII: 20; 154.

33. Torrance, *Trinitarian Faith*, 97. Bernard W. Anderson, "The Kingdom, the Power, and the Glory: The Sovereignty of God in the Bible," *Theology Today* 53/1 (1996): 7, has argued impressively for this view of creation in Israel's recension of the Babylonian creation myth.

34. Frances Young, "'Creatio ex nihilo': A Context for the Emergence of the Christian Doctrine of Creation," *Scottish Journal of Theology* 44 (1999): 150–51.

35. H. Richard Niebuhr, *Radical Monotheism and Western Culture* (New York: Harper, 1970), 32.

36. Gerd Theissen, *Biblical Faith: An Evolutionary Approach* (Philadelphia: Fortress Press, 1984), 71.

37. Gerhard von Rad, *Genesis: A Commentary*, rev. ed. (Philadelphia: Fortress Press, 1973), 45–46.

38. Theissen, *Biblical Faith*, 69.

39. Athenagoras, "A Plea for the Christians [Apology]," x, in ANF II:133.

40. Dillon, *Middle Platonists*.

41. Adam Drozdek, *Greek Philosophers as Theologians: The Divine Arche* (Burlington: Ashgate, 2007), 128. Likewise with antecedents among the Pre-Socratics. Drozdek insightfully gives to his chapter on Plato as theologian the title "Plato and the Demiurge," pointing to the mythological—if you will, kataphatic—return of the elder Plato in *Timaeus* and *The Laws*. Plato's divine Craftsman is both wise and good, and thus deliberate in the act of cosmic formation: "The Demiurge considers an infinity of possible worlds and chooses the best, which requires that the Demiurge's understanding be infinite" (163). In this way, "Plato prepared the ground for Christianity, and it is not surprising that Christian theologians, beginning with the Church Fathers, valued Plato very highly although none of them identified Plato's God with the Christian God" (164). The increasingly apophatic direction of subsequent Platonism is traced by Drozdek already to the "transcendence" of Aristotle's "Unmoved Mover" (170–72) and Speusippus, Plato's successor at the Academy, whose "God is a super-principle that is elevated above everything: being, what is beyond being, nonbeing, and what is beyond nonbeing" (191).

42. Margaret R. Miles, *Plotinus on Body and Beauty: Society, Philosophy, and Religion in Third-Century Rome* (Oxford: Blackwell, 1999).

43. The ritual invocation of "a plurality of personal beings who are understood by analogy with man and imagined in human form; the notion of the 'gods,' anthropomorphism and polytheism are found everywhere as a matter of course." Walter Burkert, *Greek Religion*, trans. J. Raffan (Cambridge: Harvard University Press, 1994), 119.

44. Deirdre Carabine, *The Unknown God: Negative Theology in the Platonic Tradition: Plato to Eriugena*, Louvain Theological and Pastoral Monographs 19 (Louvain: Peeters and Eerdmanns, n.d.), 17.

45. Ibid., 306.

46. Hans Lietzman, *A History of the Early Church* (New York: World, 1961), 3:298.

47. Ibid., 319.

48. Russel P. Moroziuk, "Heathen Philosophers and Christian Theologians: Apophaticism and Nicene Orthodoxy at Nicea," *Patristic and Byzantine Review* 12/1–3 (1993): 59.

49. Drozdek, *Philosophers as Theologians*, 27–41.

50. Plato, *The Republic*, trans. G. M. A. Grube, revised C. D. C. Reeve (Indianapolis: Hackett, 1992), X, 613a, 284.

51. Thus still Maximus of Tyre (fl. A.D. 152), Carabine, *Unknown God*, 61, when his contemporary, Origen's nemesis Celsus, is already seeking "God beyond being" (63).

52. Moroziuk, "Heathen Philosophers," 60.

53. Carabine, *Unknown God*, 3.

54. "The Arian controversy brought the implications of these two competing and at time contradictory worldviews into direct confrontation" (Moroziuk, "Heathen Philosophers," 61). There occurred "a confrontation between fundamental and irreconcilable metaphysical principles. The biblical idea of creation was opposed to the Platonic notion of God's changelessness and to the affirmation that any true existence is eternal." John Meyendorff, "Creation in the History of Orthodox Theology," *St. Vladimir's Theological Quarterly* 27/1 (1983): 7–8. More sharply, "the patristic doctrine of creation is inseparable from eschatology—the goal of created history, of time itself, is oneness in God" (29–30), precisely not a pantheistic abolition of real, temporally created existences in purely Platonic ascent of the mind to God: "The ultimate eschatological union will not be a confusion of natures" (30).

55. Lietzman, *A History*, 3:322.

56. Ibid., 325.

57. Ibid., 328.

58. Ibid., 331.

59. Plantinga saves Nyssa's doctrine of divine simplicity as a "modest and plausible" account of divine transcendence in being which does not preclude ontological distinction in

God. Indeed, Gregory clearly does think of a "simplicity" that "is compatible with multiple exhibitions of it in personal hypostases" ("Social Analogy," 343).

60. John Peter Kenny, "The Critical Value of Negative Theology," *Harvard Theological Review* 86/4 (1993): 451.

61. William E. Mann, "Immutability and Predication: What Aristotle taught Philo and Augustine," *Philosophy of Religion* 22 (1987): 32. This article makes a strong defense of God's immutable creative act, cogently pointing out that "since God is a metaphysically simple being and ordinary substances are not, Aristotle's theory of predication does not apply to God in the ways it does to ordinary substances" (33). God is His perfections, nothing in God is accidental, God's action is essentially creative so that "a closer approximation to the divine perspective would be to say that there is one vast, single, non-successive activity of God which has as part of its content" the sequences of temporal history (34). "To be God is just to be (not: to instantiate) the essence that is immutable, great, good, wise, blessed, true, and creatively active" (35). But this is to make God essentially creative, rather than essentially the Father of the Son and Breather of the Spirit. With justice, Hegel then infers that essential creativity requires God to distinguish Himself from nothingness.

62. Philo of Alexandria, "Who Is the Heir of Divine Things," in *The Works of Philo*, trans. C. D. Yonge, foreword by David M. Scholer (Peabody: Hendrickson, 1993), 293.

63. Claus Westermann, *Roots of Wisdom: The Oldest Proverbs of Israel and Other Peoples*, trans. J. D. Charles (Louisville: Westminster John Knox, 1995), 132.

64. "The Appropriation of the Philosophical Concept of God as a Dogmatic Problem of Early Christian Theology," in *Basic Questions in Theology*, vol. 2, trans. G. H. Kehm (Philadelphia: Fortress Press, 1971), 119–83.

65. Origen, *On First Principles*, trans. G. W. Butterworth (Gloucester: Peter Smith, 1973).

66. Joseph W. Trigg, *Origen* (London: Routledge, 2002), 21–22.

67. Trigg, *Origen*, 136, cited from Commentary on John, Book 1, XXIX, 204.

68. Ibid., 145, citing from Commentary on John, Book 1, XXXVI, 266.

69. Ibid., 172, citing from Commentary on John, Book 13, XXV, 151.

70. "Origen against Celsus," hereafter CC in ANF IV:395–669. See also the instructive reconstruction of Celsus's brief against the Christians in Celsus, *On the True Doctrine: A Discourse against the Christians*, trans. R. Joseph Hoffmann (Oxford: Oxford University Press, 1987).

71. Friedrich Schleiermacher, *The Christian Faith*, 2 vols., ed. H. R. Macintosh and J. S. Steward (New York: Harper, 1963), 2:747.

72. Ibid.

73. Ibid.

74. Ibid., 750.

75. Ibid.

76. Ibid., 739.

77. Ibid., 741.

78. Trigg, *Origen*, 129, cited from Commentary on John, Book 1, XXIV, 152.

79. Killian McDonnell, "Does Origen Have a Trinitarian Doctrine of the Holy Spirit?" *Gregorianum* 75/1 (1994): 28. McDonnell acutely diagnoses the privatization of the Holy Spirit in "interiority, inwardness and the spiritual life," by virtue of the effective removal of agency from the Spirit in the creative act of God in Origen (32–33).

80. Origen, *Prayer and Exhortation to Martyrdom*, trans. J. J. O'Meara, Ancient Christian Writers 19 (New York: Newman, 1954), 172.

81. Ibid., 177.

82. Albert C. Outler, "Origen and the Regulae Fidei," *Second Century* 4/3 (1984): 133–41.

83. W. H. C. Frend, *The Rise of Christianity* (Philadelphia: Fortress Press, 1984), 368–83.

84. Gerald Watson, "Celsus and the Philosophical Opposition to Christianity," *Irish Theological Quarterly* 58/3 (1992): 166–67.

85. Ibid., 165.

86. Ibid., 168.

87. Ibid., 176, citing from Trigg, reference not supplied.

88. Hallman, "Divine Suffering," finds statements attributing compassion, happiness, joy, and jealousy to God in the exegetical works, though he acknowledges Origen's "lack of consistency regarding divine impassibility" (92–93).

89. Trigg, *Origen*, 135, cited from Commentary on John, Book 1, 196.

90. "Against the Heavenly Prophets," in LW 40:79–91.

91. Eberhard Jüngel, *The Doctrine of the Trinity: God's Being Is in Becoming* (Grand Rapids: Eerdmans, 1976), 94.

92. Tillich, ST I:236–37.

93. Ibid., 238–39.

94. Ibid., 245.

95. Ibid., 252.

96. Charles Wesley, "Love Divine, All Loves Excelling," *Lutheran Book of Worship* (Minneapolis: Augsburg, 1985), #315.

97. Wolfhart Pannenberg, *Basic Questions in Theology* (Louisville: Westminster, 1969), 2:138. The passage continues: "Because this freedom of God in relation to the world necessarily remains inaccessible to the inferential procedure that is fundamental to philosophical theology, neither could it grasp the fact that a special gift of God to men was necessary for the knowledge of God." Thus the crisis in epistemology and the programmatic revision of the antecedent metaphysics follow: "Christian theology can link up with the philosophical idea of God only by breaking through it at the same time. . . . Clearly, every mere combination here must remain superficial. Theology must push on to the basic elements of the philosophical idea of God and transform these elements in the light of the biblical idea of God" (ibid., 138–39). Whether Pannenberg has adhered to this assignment in his *Systematic Theology* is a question for another occasion.

98. Torrance, *Trinitarian Faith*, 88.

99. Josiah Royce, *The Problem of Christianity* (Washington: CUA Press, 2001), 162.

100. It is no accident incidentally that Augustine follows his important critique of the devaluation of creation (taken as irrevocable history) in Origen and his followers with a discussion of Trinitarianism, especially the problem of the Holy Spirit as the third in the divine triad. As we have hinted, this is the crucial move which both de-divinizes the world and at the same time affirms it as good creature (*City of God*, XI:23–24) and confers upon it decisive ethical significance. In answering the question about creatures, "Who made it? How? and Why?" Augustine concludes against Origen, "The answers are: 'God,' 'by His Word,' and 'because it is good.' These answers, he immediately suggests, mystically intimate "the Trinity itself—Father, Son and Holy Spirit," the creative harmony of power, wisdom, and love. Augustine, *City of God*, XI:23, 456.

101. This is surely more relevant an interpretation theologically than De Vogel's argument that Platonism was sufficiently mutable to have developed in equally Arian, Athanasian, and Eusebian ways, "Platonism and Christianity," 32, which is a merely historicist observation. More nuanced, it seems to me, even if somewhat dated now is G. C. Stead, "The Platonism of Arius," *Journal of Theological Studies* 15 (1964): "Arius draws upon a Platonic tradition evolving within the Church, rather than representing a violent incursion of an alien philosophy. . . . Arius no doubt conceived himself to be reasserting traditional Christian positions which Origen and his followers had obscured: the absolute primacy of the Father," which was compromised by the doctrine of eternal generation and eternal world. Arius was able "to strike against both with one blow, when he made the Son a creature in time" (30). To bring the point up to date: it is instructive to compare Stead's 1964 position with Charles Kannengiesser, S.J., "Arius and the Arians," *Theological Studies* 44 (1983): 456–75. This study was a plea for objective historical criticism of Arius against any "prejudiced dogmatistic attitude," which continues to use Arius as a cipher for whatever errors the theological critic

wants to discover in the light of their own notions of true orthodoxy (462), that instead "wonder[s] what Arius' proper doctrine actually meant for his contemporaries." The same criticism applies to revisionist studies of Arius (for example, Gregg and Groh) trying to turn the hersiarch into a hero (470–71). Kannengiesser concluded with praise for R. D. Williams, "The Logic of Arianism," *Journal of Theological Studies* 34/1 (1983), as satisfying his desire finally to encounter "the real Arius" (474). We will take up this brilliant contribution below. Stead responds to the criticisms of Kannengiesser in "Arius in Modern Research," *Journal of Theological Studies* 45/1 (1994): 24–36, sustaining with some qualifications his position that "the traditional estimate of Arius"—that is, the Athanasian one—"is the right one. His main concern was to uphold the unique dignity of God the Father in the face of attempts to glorify the Logos, as he thought, unduly" (36). Athanasius has only "slightly, but persistently, exaggerated the extent of Arius' unorthodoxy" (28). While there is some evidence for the view of Gregg and Groh that Arius thought of salvation in exemplarist terms, it can hardly be the exclusive motive they claim, and in any case it is the soul of Jesus, adhering to the Logos in love, which provides an example for us to follow (30–31). In short, ontological subordinationism unmediated by the notion of eternal generation, that is to say, Middle Platonism, controls Arius's theological agenda. In further support of Stead's thesis that "Arius drew on a Platonic tradition existing within the Alexandrian Church," see L. W. Barnard, "The Antecedents of Arius," *Vigiliae Christianae* 24 (1970): 172–88.

102. Henri Crouzel, "The Literature on Origen 1970–1988," *Theological Studies* 49 (1988): 499–516, distinguishes "two opposed conceptions" in research, but argues that Origen's own "thought is more supple than the system," that it is "not possible to confound the late Origenism with the thought of Origen himself," and that we ought to read him as "the whole man . . . exegete, spiritual master and speculative theologian," so that even *On First Principles* is interpreted properly as offering "a theology in research, not a complete system" (499). Crouzel is undoubtedly justified in such defenses of the historical Origen, but in the doctrinal development of Christian theology, more is at stake than any individual's reputation. We now turn to the *Wirkungsgeschichte* of Origen's historical deposit.

103. Hans Lietzman, *A History of the Early Church*, trans. B. L. Woolf (Cleveland: Meridian, 1961), 3:95.

104. Ibid., 96.

105. Basil, "Letters," 9, hereafter Letter, in NPNF VIII:122–23; on Athanasius's defense of Dionysius, see NPNF IV:173f.

106. Lietzman, *A History*, 101.

107. Ibid., 102.

108. Ibid.

109. Athanasius, *De Synodis*, in NPNF IV:457–58, hereafter DS. On the reliability of the sources, given proper suspicion for Athanasius's selective and polemical citation of Arius, see Stead, "Modern Research," 24–25.

110. Francis M. Young, *From Nicea to Chalcedon: A Guide to the Literature and Its Background* (Philadelphia: Fortress Press, 1983), 62. R. D. Williams, drawing on a study of S. G. Hall, demolishes the claims of Gregg and Groh with a few deft strokes: "Much of their evidence is actually Alexander or Athanasius' version of what the Arians were saying"; that is, they take the polemic argument about what the Arian Christology implies as if this is what the Arians intended. "Logic," 74.

111. Jenson, *Triune Identity*, 81.

112. Williams, "Logic," 59.

113. Ibid., 61.

114. Ibid., 62.

115. Ibid., 63.

116. Ibid., 66.

117. Ibid., 67.

118. Ibid., 78. He is the mediator "between Being and Becoming—a 'becoming' creature, and in that sense ontologically unstable, yet perfectly in communion with the realm of Being, morally stable by the confluence of God's prior grace and his own unfaltering response" (ibid., 79).

119. Lietzman, *A History*, 109; Athanasius's criticism of biblicism, 471; also J. N. D. Kelly, *Early Christian Doctrine* (New York: Harper One, 1978), 230.

120. Lietzman, *A History*, 108.

121. In this connection, incidentally, Grillmeier has demonstrated that "Arius' Christ has no human soul. Its place is taken by the created higher spirit which is the seat of his freedom of choice." This means that Arius has "mythicized" the picture of Christ every bit as much as his Athanasian opponents are sometimes said to have done. "The ontological basis for this was that in Jesus of Nazareth a high angelic being became incarnate" (Grillmeier, *Christ in Christian Tradition*, vol. I [Louisville: John Knox, 1975], 242–43). It is hard to see how such a halfway being, neither truly human nor truly divine, could be a model to follow, even if Arius was seeking some such model to follow. It is true that Athanasius, as we shall see, follows the wording of John 1:18, "and the Word became flesh," and thinks in terms of a Logos-Sarx rather than a Logos-Anthropos incarnation. In this framework, it is likewise difficult at first glance to comprehend the role of Jesus' human soul, though Athanasius expressly affirms its reality in Jesus.

122. See here the highly instructive essay of Oyvind Nordeval, "The Emperor Constantine and Arius: Unity in the Church and Unity in the Empire," *Studia Theologica* 42 (1988): 113–50, which reading I am adopting in what follows.

123. Lietzman, *A History*, 189; Frend, *Rise of Christianity* 535, 542.

124. *Christology of the Later Fathers*, ed. Edward R. Hardy (Philadelphia: Westminster, 1954), 22.

125. Williams, "Logic," 80–81.

126. Ibid., 81.

6. The Holy Trinity as the Eternal Life

1. J. Louis Martyn, "Epistemology at the Turn of the Ages: 2 Cor 5:16," in *Christian History and Interpretation: Studies Presented to John Knox*, ed. W. R. Farmer et al. (Cambridge: Cambridge University Press, 1967), 269–87. This study is a critique of Bultmann's reduction of the Pauline text to the existentialist sense of a "private event . . . a radical change in self-understanding" in favor of the thesis "that there are two ways of knowing and that what separates the two is the turn of the ages, the eschatological event of Christ's death and resurrection" (274). Martyn takes "eschatology" in a realistic, not Gnostic sense (278–79), and therefore present "at the painful and glorious juncture where some are being saved and some are perishing," with the result that "until the parousia, the cross is and remains the epistemological crisis" (285). "For the riddle, 'How can the best of news be proclaimed in the midst of an unchanged world?' a riddle to which the super-apostles had a ready but false answer, is precisely the riddle, How can the resurrection be proclaimed in the midst of the cross? This is just the point. The cross is the epistemological crisis for the simple reason that while it is in one sense followed by the resurrection, it is not replaced by the resurrection" (286). In gospel narrative, as we have seen, the Risen One is recognized by His scars; the man Jesus remains the parable of God. I take Martryn's Pauline insight up in tandem with my own appropriation of the early Luther's *theologia crucis* and the mature Luther's summons to a "new and theological grammar" in distinction from the old philosophical language; see Paul R. Hinlicky, *The Substance of Faith* (Minneapolis: Fortress Press, 2008) 131–90.

2. Frend, 457–58.

3. Ibid., 937, 456.

4. Athanasius, "On the Incarnation of the Word," 56:2, hereafter IW in NPNF IV:66. I have also cited from the translation in *Christology of the Later Fathers*, ed. E. R. Hardy (Philadelphia: Westminster, 1954), 55–110.

5. The "classic picture" of his career as confessor is perhaps somewhat idealized, but in all essentials it remains true to the facts. See Young, 62–67; Kelly, *Creeds*, 283.

6. Kelly, *Creeds*, 31.

7. Robert W. Jenson, *Triune Identity* (Portland, Ore.: Wipf & Stock, 2002), 7, 5.

8. Kelly argues that doctrinally motivated insertions were already customary in the expansion from the earliest creedal forms in *Creeds*, 144.

9. Kelly, *Doctrines*, 235.

10. Thomas F. Torrance, *Trinitarian Faith: The Evangelical Thoelogy of the Ancient Catholic Faith* (London: Continuum, 1993), 145.

11. Kelly, *Creeds*, 216, emphasis added.

12. Kelly, *Doctrines*, characterizing Arius, 227.

13. Ibid., 233.

14. Ibid., 234.

15. Lietzman, 123–24.

16. Ibid., 135, 169–70.

17. Ibid., 124.

18. Ibid., 198.

19. "On the one hand are they who confound the Persons and are carried away into Judaism; on the other hand are they that, through the oppositions of the natures, pass into heathenism" (Basil, *On the Spirit*, XXX in NPNF VIII:49).

20. Kelly, *Doctrines*, 253.

21. Joseph T. Lienhard, "Basil of Caesarea, Marcellus of Ancyra, and 'Sabbelius,'" *Church History* 58/2 (1989): 166.

22. Kelly, *Doctrines*, 240–41.

23. Lietzman, *A History*, 190.

24. Torrance, *Trinitarian Faith*, 246. See his Athanasian critique of Cappadocian doctrine of the Father as "sole Principle or Cause or Source of Deity," which, he argues, "weakens the Athanasian axiom that whatever we say of the Father we say of the Son and the Spirit except for Father" (241). But Torrance's point may be more Augustinian than Athanasian. The issue here is the association of causality in God exclusively with the Father in order to secure the unity of God, which seemingly diminishes the agency of the Son and the Spirit. But the proper point of the primacy of the Father is to explicate the relations in which the varied agencies of the trinitarian persons are concretely exercised (238–39). I am not convinced that the vigorously "Athanasian" view Torrance advances is wholly adequate to the task, since it tends toward the modalistic view of divinity as fourth, as an unknown underlying substance. Thus R. D. Williams concluded his challenge to the heirs of Athanasius by requiring them to rethink the Platonic axiom of the incommunicability of divine essence. In any case, the concern to affirm that each hypostasis fully and equally possesses and exercises divinity as a causal agent cannot in the process overlook the personal distinctions of the three agencies as Giver, Given, and Giving, as Speaker, Spoken, and Hearing, as Lover, Loved, and Love, each fully God but each in its own way as defined by the Father as the font of the deity, the Son as His issue, the Spirit as His return. The solution lies, as Jenson has argued, in complementing the primacy of the Father with the finality of the Spirit.

25. Wolfhart Pannenberg, *Systematic Theology*, vol. 1, trans. G. W. Bromiley (Grand Rapids: Eerdmans, 1991), 264.

26. Ibid., 266.

27. J. Gerald Janzen, "On the Most Important Word in the Shema (Deuteronomy VI:4-5)," *Vetus Testamentum* 37/3 (July 1987): 300.

28. "God's eternal love in which Father, Son and Holy Spirit become eternally one would then be the ground (with respect to all that is not God) of his groundless mercy." Eberhard Jüngel, *The Doctrine of the Trinity: God's Being Is in Becoming* (Grand Rapids: Eerdmans, 1976), 101.

29. Ibid., 99.

30. Christopher Stead, *Divine Substance* (Oxford: Oxford University Press, 1977), 273.

31. Lietzman, *A History*, 249.

32. Athanasius, "Four Discourses against the Arians," 54:3, hereafter AA in NPNF IV:65.

33. The excellent study of Khaled Anatolios, *Athanasius: The Coherence of His Thought* (New York: Routledge, 2005), takes its point of departure from the pre-controversy *Contra Genetes—De Incarnatione* treatises to interpret the coherence of Athanasius's trinitarian and especially christological teaching from the perspective of soteriology in the tradition of Irenaeus (19–25). This enables a penetrating critique of the Harnack/Grillmeier approach of "analytic Christology" which theorizes a psychologically plausible account of the Incarnation and thus imposes a "Word/flesh" scheme on Athanasius that does not arise organically out of his study of the texts (70–71). With some reservations about Anatolios's comprehension of theology in the Reformation tradition—one wonders if he even knows of Luther's great admiration and profound appropriation of Athanasian theology or Cyrillian Christology—I am following the basic lines of his interpretation.

34. Jenson, *Triune Identity*, 89.

35. Torrance, *Trinitarian Faith*, 149.

36. Dietrich Bonhoeffer, *Letters and Papers from Prison*, ed. Eberhard Bethge (New York: Collier, 1972), 360.

37. Ibid., 393.

38. For all the danger when God's power is not grasped in trinitarian conjunction with wisdom and love, this was Luther's decisive point against Erasmus: "God is He for Whose will no cause or ground may be laid down as its rule and standard; for nothing is on a level with it or above it, but it is itself the rule for all things. If any rule or standard, or cause or ground, existed for it, it could no longer be the will of God. What God wills is not right because He ought, or was bound, so to will; on the contrary, what takes place must be right, because He so wills it. Causes and grounds are laid down for the will of the creature, but not for the will of the creator—unless you set another creator over him!" Martin Luther, *Bondage of the Will*, trans. J. I. Packer and O. R. Johnston (Grand Rapids: Revell, 2000), 209.

39. Christopher Morse, *Not Every Spirit: A Dogmatics of Christian Disbelief* (Harrisburg, Pa.: Trinity Press International, 1994), 136.

40. Anatolios, *Athanasius*, 152.

41. Paul R. Hinlicky, "Reclaiming the Theodicy of Faith: Luther by Way of Leibniz" (lecture, University of Aarhus, Denmark, August 2009, forthcoming).

42. Karl Barth, *Epistle to the Romans*, trans. E. Hoskyns (Oxford: Oxford University Press, 1972), 314.

43. Hallman, "Divine Suffering and Change," 94, cited from Homily on Ezekiel 6:6.

44. Ibid., 95. Hallmann explains: "It is blasphemy to place God under the restriction of necessity by opposing his nature to his will. . . . Almighty God can never be kept by his nature from doing what he wills, because God is superior to all things, able to do all things, and under no necessity. It is impious to take away the freedom of almighty God." I should prefer to analyze the possibility of divine suffering differently, in that divine power is never exercised in the Trinity except in perfect harmony with wisdom and love.

45. This is a thought experiment, which, as Rev. F. Stuart Clarke, "Lost and Found: Athanasius' Doctrine of Predestination," *Scottish Journal of Theology* 29, 435–50, has rightly seen, constitutes Athanasius's doctrine of the *oikonomia* of God, determined before the foundation of the world, to restore and fulfill the lost creature in Christ by the Spirit. Clarke also rightly notes the affinity of this doctrine with Karl Barth's christological doctrine of election in CD II/2.

46. Anatolios, *Athanasius*, 43.

47. Oswald Bayer, *Martin Luther's Theology: A Contemporary Interpretation* (Grand Rapids: Eerdmans, 2008), 215.

48. Athanasius, *"Ad Epictetum,"* 6, hereafter AE in NPNF IV:572.

49. Athanasius took up the tradition of antidocetic Christology this way. The Logos, he says, "took pity on our race, and had mercy on our infirmity, and condescended to our corruption, and unable to bear that death should have the mastery—lest the creature should perish, and His Father's handiwork in men be spent for naught—He takes unto Himself a body, and that of no different sort than ours. For he did not simply will to become embodied, or will merely to appear. For if He willed merely to appear, He was able to effect His divine appearance by some other and higher means as well. But he takes a body . . . as a temple unto himself, and makes it His very own as an instrument, in it manifested and in it dwelling. . . . He gave it over to death in the stead of all, and offered it to the Father—doing this, moreover, of His loving-kindness [first, to overcome divine judgment against sin, and second, to return humanity again to God]" (IW 8:2).

50. Anatolios, *Athanasius*, 39. Thus the key question of what is, or is not, "fitting" for God is framed by the Incarnation received in faith, and is not posed a priori from some perspective of natural theology. It is God's goodness as creator and redeemer of the creation which justifies the Incarnation as fitting the very God so identified. By contrast, Athanasius detects in the pious claims for radical divine volunteerism—"the inability to say anything about the subject of willing beyond the mere assertion that it wills"—a kind of divine omnipotence that can never be qualified by wisdom or love (95).

51. Christopher R. Smith, "The Life-of-Christ Structure of Athanasius' De Incarnatione Verbi," *Patristic and Byzantine Review* 10/1–2 (1991): 18. See in this connection the vigorous critique of Grillmeier's Logos-Sarx schematization by Richard J. Voyles, "The Fear of Death and a False Humanity as the Human Dilemma: The Argument of Influence in Athanasius' Christology," *Patristic and Byzantine Review* 8/2 (1989): 135–44. Voyles shows, convincingly in my view, that Athanasius takes body as inclusive of soul, and together as created mortal; that is, in his anthropology he has broken from the fundamental mind/matter dualism of Platonism in favor of the creator/creature distinction. Body is now understood as visible and Spirit as invisible, thus the martyrs make visible the Spirit.

52. "It is folly to argue much about God outside and before time, because this is an effort to understand the Godhead without a covering, or the uncovered divine essence. Because this is impossible, God envelops Himself in His works in certain forms, as today He wraps Himself in Baptism, in absolution, and so on. If you should depart from these, you will get into an area where there is no measure, no space, no time, and into the merest nothing, concerning which, according to the philosopher, there can be no knowledge." Luther, *Lectures on Genesis*, in LW 1:11.

53. Cf. Aloys Grillmeier, S.J., *Christ in Christian Tradition*, Vol. 1, *From the Apostolic Age to Chalcedon (451)*, revised ed., trans. J. Bowden (Atlanta: John Knox, 1975), 271.

54. Thus Athanasius too can speak in the "Cappodocian" way; pace Torrance, *Trinitarian Faith*, 238.

55. Kelly, *Doctrines*, 243–44, 247.

56. Jenson, *Triune Identity*, 89.

57. J. Patout Burns and Gerald M. Fagin, *The Holy Spirit*, Message of the Fathers of the Church 3 (Wilmington: Glazier, 1984), 104.

58. Cited from the Letter to Serapion in Michael A. G. Haykin, "'The Spirit of God': The Exegesis of 1 Cor 2:10–12 by Origen and Athanasius," *Scottish Journal of Theology* 35, 513–28.

59. Charles Kannengiesser, "Athanasius of Alexandria and the Holy Spirit between Nicea I and Constantinople I," *Irish Theological Quarterly* 48/3–4 (1981): 174.

60. Anthony Meredith, "The Pneumatology of the Cappodocian Fathers and the Creed of Constantinople," *Irish Theological Quarterly* 48/3–4 (1981): 196–211, rightly argues that Athanasius influenced the Cappadocians, overcoming Basil Origenist reticence to affirm the Spirit as creator God.

61. Jenson, *Identity*, 89.

62. J. N. D. Kelly, *Athanasian Creed* (New York: Harper, 1964).

63. Kelly, *Creeds*, 296. See also Adolph Martin Ritter, "The Dogma of Constantinople (381) and Its Reception within the Churches of the Reformation," *Irish Theological Quarterly* 48/3–4 (1981): 228–32, and Wolfgang A. Bienert, "The Significance of Athanasius of Alexandria for Nicene Orthodoxy," *Irish Theological Quarterly* 48/3–4 (1981): 181–95.

64. Kelly, *Creeds*, 302f., appendix for comparison.

65. Ibid., 331; cf. Pelikan, TCT I:211.

66. Kelly, *Creeds*, 261.

67. Lietzman, *A History*, 197.

68. "The Letter of Eusebius of Caesarea Describing the Council of Nicea," in Hardy, *Later Fathers*, 338–39; emphasis added.

69. Pelikan, HCT I:209.

70. Jenson, *Triune Identity*, 85.

71. Lietzman, *A History*, 220.

72. Ibid., 221.

73. Athanasius, *De decretis*, V:20 in NPNF IV:164.

74. Frend, *Rise of Christianity*, 597.

75. Lietzman, *A History*, 277.

76. "Letter on Nicea," in Hardy, *Later Fathers*, 339.

77. Frend, *Rise of Christianity*, 530, from the "Second Creed of Antioch . . . first of a dozen creeds that were compiled during Constantius' reign to rid the church of the *homoousios* formula." Pace his astonishing claim that if it had been accepted, "this formula could have had a profound and beneficial effect on the future history of the church, for it represented a meeting of Origenist and Antiochene ideas that could have led also to a rapprochement with the West."

78. Lietzman, *A History*, 219; on Constantius's declaration of 355.

79. Ibid., 221.

80. Ibid., 226.

81. Ibid., 230.

82. "The Creed of Ariminum," in Hardy, *Later Fathers*, 341.

83. Ibid., 342.

84. Gregory of Nazianzus, "Theological Orations," V:3, hereafter OR, in NPNF 7:318.

85. Barth, CD I:307.

86. Gregory of Nyssa, "On the Holy Spirit," in NPNF V:323. Since no enumeration is provided by the editor, I will note each citation according to the NPNF pagination.

87. Ibid., 322. Thus Nyssa, who certainly does affirm and utilize the principle of divine simplicity, as at the beginning of this treatise ("We can recognize no distinctions . . . that would divine the Divine and transcendent nature within itself by degrees of intensity and remission, so as to be altered from itself by being more or less. . . . We firmly believe that it is simple, uniform, incomposite," ibid., 316), thinks of simplicity as a correlate of the creator/creature distinction, thus as a function of kataphatic theology. See the comprehensive discussion of Pelikan, *Classical Culture*, 200–230.

88. Ibid., 315, emphasis added.

89. Ibid., 319.

90. Grillmeier, *Christ in Christian Tradition*, 271. He continues: "The subordinationist phase of theology, initiated by the so-called Christian Platonism of the ante-Nicenes, is concluded [by the new word *homoousios* as the Nicenes understood it], though its consequences have still by no means

been overcome. Athanasius defines the significance of the *homoousios* in contrast to the 'godless talk' of the Arians: (a) summing up what Scripture says about the Son, it is meant to express the fact that the Son is not only 'similar' to the Father but, as the one who has come forth from the Father, is quite equal to him, (b) it says that the Son is not separate from the substance of the Father" (ibid).

91. Ibid.

92. Nyssa, "On the Holy Spirit," in NPNF V:322.

93. Ibid., 324.

Postscript: The "Impassible Passibility" of the Trinity

1. Bruce D. Marshall, "The Dereliction of Christ and the Impassibility of God," in James F. Keating and Thomas Joseph White, eds., *Divine Impassibility and the Mystery of Human Suffering* (Grand Rapids: Eerdmans, 2009), 281–83.

2. Marshall especially subjects Moltmann's patripassionist account in *The Crucified God* to withering, indeed fatal criticism (ibid., 287–88). I would point to my dispute with Jörg Baur in "Luther's Antidocetism" as parallel to Marshall's critique of Moltmann. Paul R. Hinlicky, "Luther's Anti-Docetism in the Disputatio de divinitate et humanitate Christi (1540)" in *Creation est creatura: Luthers Christologie als Lehre von der Idiomenkommunikation*, ed. O. Bayer and Benjamin Gleede (Berlin/New York: Walter de Gruyter, 2007), 139–85.

3. Ibid., 295.

4. Ibid., 279.

5. Ibid., 260. Marshall calls attention to the intriguing "proximity" here between Thomas and "Luther's teaching that Christ is a "sinner" in our person rather than in his own person" (261 n. 31).

6. Ibid., 258.

7. Thus I assume, in terms of Marshall's analysis, the "undesirable" position he numbers "2" that holds that while "the identity of the divine persons and of the one God is not contingent . . . the identity of the triune God depends on temporal actions and events" (ibid., 288). I take this strained formulation to mean that in eternal bliss God's trinitarian self-relation is not in jeopardy, but in deciding to create, redeem, and fulfill a world, God's trinitarian self-relation is itself genuinely put at risk, supremely in the Son's sin-bearing endurance of the wrath of God His Father, a risk met and overcome not by the Father's immutable generating but by the Spirit's fresh mediating, if we take resurrection, as argued in chapter 1 of this book, as a causal event not merely a disclosure event. In an ensuing tour de force Marshall reduces this position 2 to absurdity. His critique deserves a far fuller response than I can give here. Suffice it to say that an eternal, intra-divine event requires an eternity that is time-like, and so capable of creaturely time. In such time, having freely determined to create, redeem, and fulfill this actual world as the best possible, it has become

necessary that the Father so sends and the Son so goes to the cross, such that counter-factually, if Jesus had not obeyed, He would not be the eternally determined Son of God and Savior of humanity. Marshall's own position falters in wanting both (rightly) to affirm the voluntary agencies of the trinitarian persons and (wrongly) to deny that this very tri-personhood introduces contingency in any sense to the divine life (294). The manifest contradiction here is only apparently resolved by appeal to Thomas's "radical understanding of God's difference from creatures, that is, of God's transcendence . . . God's supra-temporal eternity, which can be neither equated with created time nor its negation" (294 n. 91). While I am grateful for this refusal to think of eternity as the negation of time, it is not clear that it is warranted. It begs the question raised throughout this book of the ambiguity of the doctrine of divine simplicity.

8. Nyssa, "On the Holy Spirit," in NPNF V:324.

9. Ibid.

Index

alpha-privative, 18, 188, 210

Anatolios, Khaled, 215, 271–72

Anderson, Bernard W., 264

Anomians, anhomoios, 226, 229–30

anti-docetic Christology, 95, 97, 138–41, 157, 162, 182, 217, 251, 255, 257, 272

apocalyptic theology, viii, xi, 16, 39, 53, 112, 184–93, 242

apocalyptic, x, 20, 26, 46, 55, 67–8, 76, 78, 81, 83–84, 89, 100, 123, 134, 256–57

apokatastasis, 192

Apollinarius, 187

apophaticism, apophatic theology, 17, 22, 79, 140, 144, 156, 163, 174–76, 180, 188–89, 225, 245, 265

Aristotle, 175–76, 211, 263, 265–66

Arius, viii, 184, 193–201, 203–8, 220, 223–25, 228, 263, 267–70

Asad, Talal, 256, 261

aseity, 189

Ashton, John, 251–54

Athanasius, 10, 23, 70, 72, 170, 193, 195, 197, 199, 200, 202–3, 206–8, 212–13, 215–23, 226, 228–29, 243, 268–73

Athenagoras, xii, 173, 265

Augustine, vi, ix, 3–4, 6–7, 9, 168–70, 192, 238, 241–42, 263, 265–67

Ayres, Lewis, xi, 241

Balthasar, Hans Ur von, 243

Barbour, R. S., 260

Barnard, L. W., 130, 132, 261, 268

Barth, Karl, 6, 11, 35, 40, 50, 53–54, 79, 87, 90–91, 165, 188, 190, 215, 231, 239, 242, 244, 250, 255, 264, 271, 273

Basil, 193–96, 208, 222–23, 227–28, 230–31, 234, 246, 268, 270, 272

Baur, F. C., 260

Baur, Jorg, 274

Bayer, Oswald, 7, 241–42, 245, 272

Beker, J. Christian, 258

Bergen, Doris L., 259

biblicism, viii, 90, 198, 228–31, 269

Bielfeldt, Dennis, 23, 211, 242, 264

Bienert, Wolfgang A. 273

Bonhoeffer, Dietrich, 11, 16, 19, 63, 214, 243, 245–46, 271

Bornkamm, Gunther, 83–84, 254

Boyarin, Daniel, 256

Braun, Herbert, 249

Brown, Raymond E., 74, 93–94, 252–5

Bultmann, Rudolph, vii, x, 42, 44–45, 49–60, 65–66, 76–90, 97, 108, 134, 246, 249–58, 269

Burkert, Walter, 265

canon, canonical narrative, vii–iii, ix–x, 2, 12–3, 27–8, 54, 69–108, 109–119, 130, 140–43, 158, 171, 201, 203–4, 206, 244, 251–52, 256–57, 260

Carabine, Dierdre, 265

catechism, catechesis, 9, 110

catholicity, ix–xi, 2, 8, 9–11, 28, 30, 65, 76, 98–99, 106, 126–27, 138, 149, 185, 201, 205, 242–45, 258, 260–65, 269

Celsus, 181, 185–88, 261, 265–67

christological paradox, 148, 157, 221–22

christology, 16, 25, 30, 33, 43, 50, 58–60, 62–65, 69–72, 75–76, 79–84, 86, 98, 100, 108, 111, 117, 122–23, 151, 162, 181–82, 186–87, 195, 197–98, 213, 233, 238, 241, 243, 245, 247–49, 251–54, 257, 260, 268, 270–71

Christus praesens, 50, 54, 249

Cicero, 17–18, 245

Clarke, F. Stuart, 271

Clement of Alexandria, 1676–8, 263–64

Cochrane, Arthur Norris, 169–70, 264

communicatio idiomatum, 147

Conzelmann, Hans, 44–45, 115, 249, 259

Cranefield, C. E. B., 246

creation as finitude, 80, 128, 148, 151, 153, 179

creation as free decision, 161, 190–91, 232, 260
 out of love, 143–45

creation by the Word, 77, 109, 111, 131, 253

creation *ex nihilo*, 15, 36–37, 44, 170–71, 188, 196, 204, 232, 238, 263–64

Creator-creature, distinction and relation ix, xi, 3, 4, 7, 10, 14, 20–21, 23–24, 26, 37, 39–41, 69, 70, 73–74, 77–78, 82–83, 98, 110,

129, 131, 140, 144–48, 150, 152,
154–56, 158–59, 163, 165, 167,
169–70, 175–78, 183–86, 190,
192, 195–96, 198, 200, 209, 213–
14, 219–22, 230–31, 233, 235,
237–41, 245–46, 263, 265, 271–73

  gnostic revulsion at, 135, 142,
  154, 247, 256
  Incarnation, as affirmation of,
  145–46, 157–58, 216, 272
  recapitulation of, in New Adam,
  147, 150

Crouzel, Henri, 268

Crowe, Benjamin D., 259

Dahl, Nils A., 84–85, 254, 258–60

Danielou, Jean, 256

De Vogel, C. J., 161, 263, 267

Dehsen, Christian von, 259

Democritus, 249

demythologization, 51–52, 59, 76,
79–83, 88, 134, 170, 174–75, 250

Dillon, John, 261–63, 265

Dionysius of Alexandria, 193–94,
268

divine simplicity, vii–iii, x, xi, 3–4,
16–22, 35, 133, 144, 155–56, 173–
79, 180–81, 184, 188, 191, 198,
206, 218, 226, 229–30, 235, 238–
39, 241–42, 245, 266, 273–74

docetism, antidocetism, 29, 41,
50, 65, 69, 71, 74, 76, 78, 80,
83–84, 91–97, 102, 104–6, 110,
114–15, 125, 137–38, 140–41,

153, 157, 162, 182, 217, 241,
250–52, 255–57, 272, 274

Dodd, C. H., 92, 254–55

Dodds, E. R., 100, 248, 256

dogma, viii, 11, 15, 22–24, 28,
42, 53, 72, 75–76, 79–80, 86,
93, 114, 116, 119–24, 129, 131,
159, 176, 201, 241–42, 252,
256, 273

dogmatics, viii–ix, 1, 9, 11–12, 16,
22, 24, 55, 60, 69, 76–77, 79–80,
90, 96, 108, 110, 112, 119, 138–
46, 158, 228, 231, 236, 245–46,
257, 266

dogmatism, 39, 41, 78, 98, 138,
268

Donovan, Mary Ann, 144, 149,
262

Drozdek, Adam, 16, 245, 249, 265

Dunn, James D. G., 72, 86, 90,
252, 254–55

early Catholicism, 65, 69, 75, 103,
109, 111, 124, 126, 133, 143, 173,
241, 256–60

Ebeling, Eberhard, 51, 249

Ehrmann, Bart D., 247

enthusiasm, 120

Epicurus, Epicureanism, 17, 264

epistemic primacy, 8, 16, 24, 28,
103–4, 106, 110, 204, 243

epistemology, x, 8, 21, 244

Erasmus, 7, 138, 215, 271

Eriugena, 265

eschatological creation, 149, 151, 162, 167, 183, 190–92, 201, 215, 220, 229, 231–32, 236, 265

eschaton, eschatology, xi, 2–3, 15, 21–22, 24, 44, 59, 62–65, 77–78, 80, 87–88, 98, 123, 129, 134, 144, 146, 149, 151, 153, 159, 162, 199, 212, 256, 265, 269

eternity, viii, 1–2, 4, 8, 14–15, 20–21, 23–26, 35–36, 38, 46–49, 52, 59, 72–76, 91–97, 101, 106–7, 120–21, 127, 129, 133, 144, 147–50, 153, 155–57, 179–84, 188, 190–98, 200–1, 205–9, 211, 215, 218–23, 264–65, 267–69, 271, 274

Ettlinger, Gerald H., 251

Eucharist, 13, 15, 41, 49, 64, 71, 94–95, 99, 101–3, 105–6, 109, 114, 116, 125–26, 153–54, 245, 255, 257–58, 260–1

Eusebius of Caesarea, 125, 199, 200, 207, 224–28, 260, 273

faith as creature of the Word, 45, 64, 73, 82, 84, 201, 245

Farmer, William R., 98, 103–4, 256–57, 262

Feuerbach, Ludwig, 57–58, 250

Frei, Hans W., 51–57, 249–50

Frend, W. H. C., 129, 133, 145, 202, 261–62, 267–70, 273

Furnish, Victor Paul, 111–12, 258

Gilbert, Martin, 259

Girard, Rene, 260

gnosticism, viii, 27–28, 53, 65, 70, 74, 78, 80–84, 86, 94, 98, 100–2, 115, 124, 126–27, 129, 133–45, 147, 149–54, 156–58, 168, 171, 177, 179, 185, 206, 238, 247–48, 251–52, 255–57, 261–62, 269

Grant, Robert M., 257, 261

Gregory of Nazianzus, 228, 230, 233–34, 273

Gregory of Nyssa, 107, 228, 231–32, 235, 239, 257, 264, 266, 273, 274

Hallman, Joseph M., 163, 264, 267, 271

Halperin, J. 259

Hannah, Jack W., 255

Hardy, Edward R., 243, 269–70, 273

Harnack, Adolph von, 11, 133–34, 244, 252, 263, 271

Harrison, Verna, 264

Hawking, Stephen, 40, 249

Haykin, Michael A. G., 272

Hays, Richard B., 250

Hegel, G. F., 157, 241, 266

Heidegger, Martin, 115, 259

hellenization, 20, 53, 72, 129,

134, 161, 172, 178, 197, 225, 227, 242, 246, 261

hermeneutics, vii, x, 25–29, 55–56, 75, 87, 94, 103, 111, 124, 143, 228, 247, 249, 252

Heschel, Susannah, 259

Hitler, Adolph, Hitlerism, 6, 259

Homer, 79, 134, 139, 142, 159, 168, 173–74, 186, 263

homoios, 150, 229

homoiousios, 225–26, 229

homoousios, 23, 52, 70, 74, 165, 171, 173, 194–97, 205–9, 213, 223–31, 234, 273

Hoskyns, Sir Edwyn Clement, x, 73, 86–95, 143, 252, 254–55, 271

Houlden, J. L., 260

Hultgren, Arland, 247–48, 278

Hütter, Reinhard, 245

Hypostasis, 193, 195, 198, 205–6, 208–9, 211, 229, 231, 233, 270

Ignatius of Antioch, vii, 28, 69, 90, 92–106, 110, 114, 121, 123–26, 128, 138–39, 141, 148, 153, 157, 160, 187, 204–5, 212, 217, 221, 243, 247, 255–60, 262

imago dei, 101, 145, 157, 168

incarnation, 3, 9, 11, 15, 19, 24, 31, 47–50, 59, 70–71, 73–5, 78, 80–82, 85, 90, 93, 95, 99–101, 104–5, 107, 124, 126, 129, 132, 139, 141, 144–45, 147–49, 155–59, 162–63, 165, 168, 170, 182, 190, 197, 199,

202, 205, 208, 212–13, 215–18, 221, 225, 229, 238–39, 243–44, 251, 254, 263, 269–72

Irenaeus of Lyon, viii, 28, 98, 101, 110, 114, 124, 128–30, 137–58, 161, 191, 204, 212, 221, 228, 238–9, 252–3, 255, 261–2, 271

Janzen, T. Gerald, 270

Jenson, Robert W., x, xii, 10, 12, 59, 154, 176, 197, 201, 203, 213, 221–22, 225, 239, 241–45, 250, 262–63, 268, 270–73

Jonas, Hans, 134, 248, 261

joyful exchange, 10, 52, 113

Juel, Donald, 260

Jüngel, Eberhard, 36, 188, 191, 211, 248–49, 251, 263, 267, 271

justification, ix–xi, 9–10, 22, 30, 36–37, 61, 63, 75, 103, 110, 113, 117–18, 123–24, 127, 164, 215, 243, 258

Justin, viii, 110, 114, 124, 128–40, 145–46, 160–61, 178, 180, 185–86, 261, 263

Kannengiesser, Charles, S.J., 268, 272

Kant, Immanuel, Kantianism, x, 4–5, 12, 17–18, 25, 45, 51–52, 83, 108, 189, 246, 253, 260

Käsemann, Ernst, vii, 20, 47, 81–83, 87, 92–93, 246, 248–49, 251–54, 257–60 kataphaticism, kataphatic theology, vii, x, 1, 22–24, 109, 140, 144, 156, 163, 175–76, 180, 191, 197, 230, 265, 273

Kay, James F., 52–56, 60, 249

Keating, James F., 241, 274

Keck, Leander E., 246, 251–52

Kelber, Werner H., 251

Kelly, J. N. D., x, 206, 221, 223, 241, 258, 260, 269–70, 272–73

Kenny, John Peter, 266

kerygma, vii, 3, 25, 27, 29, 49–52, 54–55, 60, 65–66, 69, 204, 246, 249, 258

Kingsbury, Jack Dean, 251

knowledge of God, vii, 1–2, 5, 9, 17, 21, 77, 106–8, 121, 123, 143–44, 156–57, 176, 231, 238, 246, 251, 267

Koester, Craig R., 74, 253

Koester, Helmut, 28

LaMarche, Paul, 74, 253

Lane, Eugene N., 264

Lapide, Pinchas, 260

Lawson, John, 137, 262

Lienhard, Joseph T., 269

Lietzman, Hans, 173, 199, 207, 223, 227, 265–66, 268–73

Lindbeck, George, 23, 58–60, 243, 250

(The) Logos, 49, 52, 70–75, 81–82, 84, 91, 93, 104, 129–32, 135–37, 148–49, 151–52, 154–55, 157, 159–62, 165, 170, 177–78, 180, 182–83, 186–87, 189, 192–99, 205, 208–9, 212, 216–18, 220–21, 224–25, 227, 229, 232, 252–53, 263, 268–69, 272

Logos-sarx, Logos-anthropos christologies, 152

Lombard, Peter, 241

Luther, Martin, Lutheranism, vi, x, xii, 6–12, 20, 40, 52, 59–60, 68, 79, 113, 138, 188–89, 197, 215, 228, 237, 241–46, 249–51, 258–60, 263–64, 269, 271–74

MacIntyre, Alisdair, xi, 242

Mann, William E., 266

Marcus, Joel, 251

Marshall, Bruce D., 8, 103, 115, 204, 237–38, 243, 248–49, 274

Martyn, J. L., 75, 116, 248, 251–52, 269

martyr, martyrdom, theology of the martyrs, vii–viii, xi, 46, 49, 60, 65, 69, 76, 85, 92–106, 110, 113–14, 116, 120–21, 124–28, 132–32, 137–41, 152–54, 168, 184–85, 187, 193, 198–99, 202–3, 212, 214, 217–19, 227, 230, 236, 240, 251, 255–56, 258, 266, 272

Marxsen, Willi, 42, 65, 250–51

Maurer, Wilhelm, xi, 241

Maximus of Tyre, 265

McCormack, Bruce, 255, 264

McDonnell, Killian, 266

McMullen, Ramsey, 264

Melanchthon, Philip, 109, 242, 263

Meredith, Anthony, 272

Meyendorff, John, 165, 242, 257, 264–65

Miles, Margaret R., 265

modalism, 163–67, 181–82, 193–95, 198, 207–9, 228, 270

Moroziuk, Russell P., 265

Morse, Christopher, 16, 26–27, 130, 245–47, 261, 271

Nahm, Charles, 129, 131, 261

narrative, gospel-, canonical-, biblical-, promissory-, resurrection-, passion-, as theology, ix, 1–4, 9–15, 22–31, 33–34, 42–75, 80, 86–89, 91, 94, 97, 103–4, 109–10, 113, 138–41, 143–45, 151, 158–64, 167–68, 171, 182, 190–91, 199, 201, 203–4, 206, 209–10, 220, 231, 238–39, 241, 243–44, 246, 249–50, 253–54, 269

natural theology, vii, 6–7, 16–23, 68, 79, 159, 202, 238–40, 242, 246, 272

Neusner, Jacob, 254, 259–60

new creation, 9, 30–31, 38, 109, 111–14, 118, 126, 129, 150, 161–62, 169, 190–91, 201, 233, 245

Niebuhr, H. R., 170–71, 265

Nordeval, Oyvind, 269

Norris, Frederick W., 247–48, 257

Norris, Richard A., Jr., 139, 142, 262

Oberman, Heiko, 243, 259

Origen of Alexandria, Origenism, 98, 139, 160, 167, 179–88, 190, 192–96, 199–207, 215, 221, 223–25, 227–8, 264–68, 272–73

Osborn, Eric, 161, 163, 263–64

ousia, 194, 205–6, 209, 211–12, 221, 229, 231–32

Outler, Albert C., 267

Pannenberg, Wolfhart, 40–43, 48, 57, 90, 178, 191, 209, 246, 249, 267, 270

parousia, 66, 77, 132, 247, 269

passibility (impassibility), viii, xi, 18–19, 141, 162–63, 199, 212–13, 218–19, 237–39, 241, 262, 264, 267, 274

Pelikan, Jaroslav, x, xii, 134, 140, 162, 241–42, 261–62, 264, 273

perichoreisis, 166, 264

persona(ae), personal union, tri-personalism, 22–23, 29–31, 34–35, 47–49, 52, 56, 61–62, 99–101, 106–7, 109, 117, 140–41, 148, 156, 164–67, 180, 182, 187, 193–94, 197, 204–5, 207, 209,

219, 221–22, 226, 231, 233–35, 237–38, 266, 270

personality, 52–54, 56, 75, 152, 189, 208

perspectivalism, 25, 40, 48, 58, 68, 72, 91–92, 112, 203, 258

Phan, Peter C., 149, 262

Philo of Alexandria, 177–80, 252, 262–63, 266

Plantinga, Cornelius, Jr., 204, 264, 266

Plato, Platonism, viii, xi, 1, 4, 7, 16, 19, 35, 72, 79–80, 91, 128–31, 133–37, 141, 148, 151, 154, 157–63, 167–205, 210–12, 218–19, 222, 225–32, 238, 241, 245, 253, 261–73

polycarp, vii, 96–99, 103–5, 110, 124–28, 137–41, 247, 255, 262

primary theology, ix–x, 9–13, 23, 51, 58, 110, 239

Quinn, Jerome D., 260

Randolph, Kurt, 134, 261

recapitulation, 143–44, 146–47, 149–51, 153–54

redemption of creation, 83, 107, 123, 129, 134, 139, 144, 146, 149, 171, 178, 212, 252

Regnon, Theodore, 165, 242

regula fidei, rule of faith, viii, 2, 13, 69, 109–10, 112–13, 118–19, 130–31, 137, 152–58, 179, 184, 204, 206, 228, 258

revealed theology, x, 18, 21, 110, 176, 238, 242, 246, 253

Revelation, 5–6, 9, 14, 16, 19–20, 32, 25, 44, 59, 61–62, 65, 67–68, 75, 77–78, 80, 82–83, 91, 93, 112, 116, 129, 131–32, 136, 140, 143–44, 146, 152, 155–56, 164, 169, 176, 179, 184, 188, 190, 194, 198, 208–9, 231, 233, 235, 244, 246, 249

Richardson, Alan, 4–6, 39, 242

Richardson, Cyril, 140, 253, 262

Riley, Gregory J., 247, 251

Ritter, Adolph Martin, 273

Robinson, James M., 248, 250

Royce, Josiah, 192, 267

Ruether, Rosemary, 250

Samuel, Maurice, 259

Sanders, E. P., 250

Schlatter, Adolph, 246

Schnelle, Udo, x, 94–95, 106, 251, 253, 255, 257

Schoedel, William R., 100, 144, 255–57, 262

Schweitzer, Albert, 44, 249

Sheerin, Daniel J., 260

Smith, Christopher R., 272

Smith, D. Moody, 254

Smith, Jonathan Z., 112, 121, 258

Soelle, Dorothee, 250

Sovik, A., 259

Speussippus, 265

Spiritus creator, 115, 210, 221–22, 234–35, 267, 272

Stalinism, 6

Stead, G. C., 211–12, 267–68, 272

Steigmann-Gall, Richard, 259

Stendahl, Krister, 258

Stoicism, 17, 20, 130, 168–69, 173, 246, 263

Strauss, David Friedrich, 80, 251

Stuhlmacher, Peter, 72, 112, 116–17, 252, 255, 258–60

subordinationism, 163, 166–67, 173, 180–82, 186, 192–95, 199, 223, 227, 234, 243, 268, 273

Theissen, Gerd, 171–72, 203, 265

theodicy, 158

theosis, divinization, 158, 178, 187, 219–20

Thiemann, Ronald, 244

Thomas Aquinas, 84, 261

Thomson, Marianne Meyer, 251

Tillard, J.-M. R., 257

Tillich, Paul, 35, 189–91, 225, 248, 267

Toom, Tarmo, x, 241

Torrance, Thomas, x, 144, 170–71, 191, 205, 241, 262, 264, 267, 270–72

Trigg, Joseph W., 186, 266–67

tritheism, 163–67, 208

Trobisch, David, 119, 256, 260

voluntarism, 39

Von Rad, Gerhard, 265

Voyles, Richard J., 272

Watson, Gerald, 186, 267

Weber, Otto, 108, 257

Weinandy, Thomas G., 241

Wesche, Paul, 102, 257, 260

Wesley, Charles, 267

Westermann, Claus, 266

Williams, R. D., 197–98, 200, 210, 268–70

Wright, N. T., 29–30, 44, 248

Young, Frances M., 170, 264, 268, 270

Zizioulas, John D., 257

CPSIA information can be obtained
at www.ICGtesting.com
Printed in the USA
BVHW040227271120
594323BV00017B/563